To Mark

On the occasion
departure from Hertfordshire County
Council

11 March 1988

FARM TENANCIES

MICHELE SLATTER

BA, LLM, Lecturer in Law at the University of East Anglia,
Norwich; Visiting Lecturer at the University of Canterbury,
Christchurch, New Zealand

with

William Barr, LLB, Solicitor

BSP PROFESSIONAL BOOKS
OXFORD LONDON EDINBURGH
BOSTON PALO ALTO MELBOURNE

First published 1987

British Library
Cataloguing in Publication Data
Slatter, Michele
    Farm tenancies
    1. Farm tenancy—England
    I. Title II. Barr, William
    344.2064'348   KD907

ISBN 0-632-01957-3

BSP Professional Books
Editorial offices:
Osney Mead, Oxford OX2 0EL
  (*Orders*: Tel. 0865 240201)
8 John Street, London WC1N 2ES
23 Ainslie Place, Edinburgh EH3 6AJ
52 Beacon Street, Boston
  Massachusetts 02108, USA
667 Lytton Avenue, Palo Alto
  California 94301, USA
107 Barry Street, Carlton
  Victoria 3053, Australia

Typeset by DP Photosetting Ltd,
  Aylesbury, Bucks
Printed and bound in Great Britain by
  Billing and Sons Ltd

Contents

Preface   **ix**

Part I: The Definition of an Agricultural Holding

1   Land Used for Agriculture   **1**
Introductory – 'Land' – 'Used for agriculture' – Agriculture: considering the context – Agriculture: the predominant use – Agriculture: the 'legal' use – Change of use during the currency of a lease – Used for agriculture 'for purposes of a trade or business' – Ministerial designation – The Agricultural Holdings Act and other statutory codes.

2   The Agricultural Tenancy   **20**
Introductory – A single contract of tenancy – 'A term of years': fixed terms – Continuation automatically of fixed terms of two years or more: section 3 – Section 5: fixed terms without subsequent security of tenure – No contracting out of section 3 – 'Letting from year to year' – Section 2: lesser interests transformed into tenancies from year to year.

3   Arrangements Which Avoid Full Statutory Protection   **31**
Introductory – Grants to employees, office holders etc. – Section 2: 'insecure' grants approved by the Minister – When is approval for an 'insecure' grant appropriate? Sections 2 and 5 – Grazing and mowing agreements – Grantor's limited interest – *Gladstone* v. *Bower*: lettings for between one and two years – Gratuitous licences – Licences which do not grant exclusive occupation – Partnerships – Contractor or manager agreements – Share farming: joint ventures – Contracting out of the Act.

Part II: The Contents of the Contract

4   The Terms of the Tenancy   **53**
Introductory: the sources of tenancy terms – A written tenancy: section 6 and Schedule 1 – The tenancy: good agricultural practice: the rules of good estate management and good husbandry – The tenancy: fixed equipment – Cultivation of land and disposal of produce – Section 24: no penal rents for breach of covenant – Miscellaneous statutory terms.

5   Rent Reviews and Distress for Unpaid Rent   **74**
Introductory – Rent review by agreement – The statutory right to
demand arbitration – Demand 'by notice in writing' – Arbitration
determines rent 'as from the next termination date' – Demand
followed by appointment – The rent properly payable at the date of the
reference – Frequency of rent review – Increases in rent to reflect
landlord's improvements – Distress for unpaid rent – Which arrears
are enforceable by distress? – Property subject to distress – Compensation set off against arrears – Disputes concerning distress.

Part III: Security of Tenure

6   The Notice to Quit   **93**
Introductory – Who can give notice? – Tenant's notice or a surrender?
– The form of the notice – Clarity – Expiry of the notice – The period
of notice – Stating the period of notice – Waiver of the statutory period
of notice – Short notice – Mistakes in notices to quit – Second notices
– Notice to quit part – Effect of sale of the landlord's interest during
the currency of a notice to quit – Service of notice – Co-owners and
notices to quit – Subtenants and notice to quit – Notice to quit when
tenant is a member of the reserve or auxiliary forces – Notice to quit
when the landlord's 'uncertain' interest ends.

7   Counter-notices and Tribunal Consent   **118**
The counter-notice: introductory – Form and wording – Time limit –
Co-owners and counter-notices – Restricting counter-notices: contracting out – The landlord's application for Tribunal consent:
introductory – Form and wording – Time limit – The grounds for
consent: approved purposes, section 27(3) – Good husbandry – Sound
management – Agricultural research etc. and smallholdings – Allotments – Greater hardship – Non-agricultural user not within Case B
of Schedule 3 – Applying in the alternative – Section 27(2): the fair and
reasonable landlord test – Sweeteners – Separate issues – Imposition
of conditions on a consent by the Tribunal – Costs.

8   Incontestable Notices to Quit   **141**
Introductory – What are the 'incontestable' grounds? – Construction
of incontestable notices: landlord's watch points – The tenant's
challenges – Arbitration on Cases A, B, D and E – No relief in the
courts – Case A: retirement of smallholders at age 65 – Case B: non-
agricultural use – Case C: certificate of bad husbandry granted – Case
D(a): failure to pay rent due – Case D(b): failure to comply with a
notice to remedy – Case E: irremediable breach – Case F: insolvency
of the tenant – Case G: death of the tenant – Case H: Ministry
amalgamation.

9 Termination Otherwise Than By Notice To Quit 174

Introductory – Effluxion of time – Surrender of the tenancy – Forfeiture – Forfeiture for non-payment of rent – Forfeiture for breaches other than non-payment of rent – Waiver of breach – Forfeiture and compensation in agricultural leases.

Part IV: Succession Tenancies

10 Succession on Death 189

Introduction: when do succession rights apply? – When must applications be made? – Who may apply? – Who is a 'surviving close relative?' – The principal source of livelihood test – Person 'treated as eligible': section 41 – The commercial unit test – What is a commercial unit? – 'Occupation' of a commercial unit – Occupation: interests which may be disregarded – Deemed occupation: arrangements concerning connected persons – Deemed occupation: applicant's existing Tribunal direction – Occupation: joint occupiers – When must the applicant be eligible? Section 39(2) – Suitability – The Tribunal's duty – Procedure when there are several applicants – Multiple holdings – The landlord's notice to quit – Succession to part only of a holding and the Case G notice to quit – Effect of a direction for a tenancy: the new tenancy – Concurrent leases – Agreed succession on death.

11 Succession on Retirement 220

Introductory – Agreed succession during the lifetime of the tenant – The scheme of the statutory retirement provisions – The retirement notice – The eligible person/nominated successor – Situations where the right to apply to the Tribunal is excluded – Notice to quit and the retirement notice procedures – The application to the Tribunal – The unsuccessful nominated successor – Effect of the death of the retiring tenant – Effect of Tribunal direction – Tribunal direction: 'deemed occupation' – Terms of the succession tenancy.

Part V: Compensation Rights and the Resolution of Disputes

12 Compensation Entitlement at the Termination of a Tenancy 237

Introductory – The tenant's claims – Compensation for disturbance – The amount of compensation for disturbance – When is compensation for disturbance payable? – Compensation for disturbance in cases of early termination – Subtenancies and compensation for disturbance – Notice to quit part – Compensation for long-term improvements begun on or after 1st March 1948: Schedule 7 – Limited owners:

consents from landlords – Limited owners and Schedule 7 improvements – Subtenants and Schedule 7 – Hill farming – Short-term
improvements begun on or after 1st March 1948: Schedule 8, Part I –
'Old' improvements begun before 1st March 1948: Schedule 9 –
Compensation for tenant right matters – Improvements: successive
tenancies – Improvements: Crown compensation – Tenant's payment
on entry for improvements – 'High farming': section 70 – Termination
of tenancy of part of a holding and the severed reversion – Exclusion
of certain improvements – Market gardens – What is a 'market
garden'? – Improvements and compensation – Removal of tenants'
fixtures from market gardens – The 'Evesham custom' for market
gardens – Compensation for milk quotas – The landlord's claims:
introductory – Compensation for specific deterioration – Compensation for general deterioration – Landlord's claims during the tenancy
– Termination of tenancy of part only of the holding – Transfer of the
landlord's interest during the tenancy – Making the claim.

13 Jurisdiction Over Disputes Concerning Agricultural Holdings   263

Introductory – Arbitration – Seeking an arbitration: preliminary
notices – The appointment of the arbitrator – Initiating proceedings:
particulars of claim – The hearing and the view – The award and costs
– Review of the arbitration and award by the county court –
Agricultural land tribunals: Introductory – Constitution – Tribunal
procedure – Time limits – The tribunal's decision – Challenges to the
tribunal's decision – Costs – The courts.

Part VI: Agricultural Tied Cottages: An Overview

14 The Rent (Agriculture) Act 1976   283

The scheme of the Act – The 1976 Act: an exclusive jurisdiction – The
'protected occupancy' and the 'protected occupier' – The 'qualifying
worker' – A relevant licence or tenancy – Qualifying ownership –
When must the criteria be satisfied? – Protected occupier by transfer
– Protected occupiers by succession – Statutory intervention during
the contractual period – The statutory tenancy – Statutory tenants by
succession – The terms of the statutory tenancy – Transition terms –
Payment of rent during the statutory tenancy – Obtaining possession
from a protected occupier or statutory tenant – Subtenants' security –
The rehousing provisions – Power to obtain information.

Appendix I: Agriculture Act 1986, Schedule 1: Tenants' Compensation for Milk Quotas   305

Appendix II: Forms and Precedents   316

Appendix III: Tied Cottages Statutes   **337**

Table of Cases   **344**

Table of Statutes   **353**

Index   **358**

Preface

1986 marked two important points for the law relating to farm tenancies in England and Wales. Firstly, it saw the tenth anniversary of the Rent (Agriculture) Act. This statute, designed to provide security of tenure for farm workers in their tied cottages was heralded by some commentators as sounding the death knell for the tied cottage system. In fact, the Act has seemed so far to work reasonably well and tied cottages remain an important feature of agricultural life.

Secondly, 1986 saw the enactment of the Agricultural Holdings Act, a major work of consolidation which brings together in an orderly presentation the previously scattered provisions, including, of course, the important changes introduced by the 1984 Agricultural Holdings Act. Although the 1986 Act introduces no substantive changes in the law, the reorganisation and rearrangement of the earlier provisions prompt a review of the whole topic at least to accustom those affected to the new guises of familiar provisions.

It seems opportune, therefore, to draw together at this time the elements of the law concerning farm tenancies, whether tenancies of agricultural holdings or of tied cottages. I hope that the present book will be of help to those who find themselves tangling with these sometimes rather daunting areas of law.

The law is stated as at 1st April 1987. Unless the context requires otherwise, references in Chapters 1 – 13 to 'the Act' refer to the Agricultural Holdings Act 1986, and in Chapter 14 to the Rent (Agriculture) Act 1976. The book is meant to be used in conjunction with the Agricultural Holdings Act 1986.

Thanks

A number of very busy people have given me generously of their time and expertise during the preparation of this book. In particular, I am truly grateful to:

- William Barr, who not only prepared the precedents for Appendix II but also read each chapter in draft and offered his characteristically perceptive comments;
- My colleagues Robert Burgess at East Anglia and Andrew Alston at Canterbury, New Zealand who both read the manuscript in draft and have saved me from the worst of my excesses;

– Peter Smith, senior partner of Thos. Wm. Gaze, Surveyors of Diss, Norfolk, who scrutinised Chapters 4 and 5 from a valuer's viewpoint and very kindly contributed the illustrative costing in Chapter 5;
– Richard Miles, who has been everything a discreet editor should be;
– Julianne Higgins who completed the final typing;
– Helen Cummings of the Law School at East Anglia who typed the whole manuscript from my long-hand notes with great good humour (and accuracy). In addition, after I had left for my sabbatical in New Zealand, Helen acted as co-ordinator of all the various comments on drafts and, from this unenviable position, produced the final text. Thank you.

In the light of these thanks, it need hardly be stressed that the responsibility for such remaining errors as may be found rests fairly and squarely on my shoulders.

Michele Slatter
Christchurch, New Zealand.

Part I

The Definition of an Agricultural Holding

Introduction

Section 1 of the Agricultural Holdings Act 1986 defines an agricultural holding and thus delimits the area of operation of the Act. Although somewhat lengthy, it is of such fundamental importance to this Part in defining the elements of an agricultural holding that it is useful to quote it here in full:

'1. (1) In this Act "agricultural holding" means the aggregate of the land (whether agricultural land or not) comprised in a contract of tenancy which is a contract for an agricultural tenancy, not being a contract under which the land is let to the tenant during his continuance in any office, appointment or employment held under the landlord.
    (2) For the purposes of this section, a contract of tenancy relating to land is a contract for an agricultural tenancy if, having regard to

(a)   the terms of the tenancy,
(b)   the actual or contemplated use of the land at the time of the conclusion of the contract and subsequently, and
(c)   any other relevant circumstances,

the whole of the land comprised in the contract, subject to such exceptions only as do not substantially affect the character of the tenancy, is let for use as agricultural land.
    (3) A change in user of the land concerned subsequent to the conclusion of a contract of tenancy shall be disregarded for the purpose of determining whether a contract which was not originally a contract for an agricultural tenancy has subsequently become one unless it is effected with the landlord's permission, consent or acquiescence.
    (4) In this Act 'agricultural land' means

(a)   land used for agriculture which is so used for the purposes of a trade or business, and

(b)   any other land which, by virtue of a designation under section 109(1) of the Agriculture Act 1947, is agricultural land within the meaning of that Act.

(5)   In this Act 'contract of tenancy' means a letting of land, or agreement for letting land, for a term of years or from year to year; and for the purposes of this definition a letting of land, or an agreement for letting land, which, by virtue of subsection (6) of section 149 of the Law of Property Act 1925, takes effect as such a letting of land or agreement for letting land as is mentioned in that subsection shall be deemed to be a letting of land or, as the case may be, an agreement for letting land, for a number of years.'

The principal elements of the definition are, therefore:

(i)   land;
(ii)   used for agriculture;
(iii) for the purposes of a trade or business;
(iv)   comprised in a contract of tenancy.

In the following three chapters, this definition will be considered in the following ways:

(1)   Land used for agriculture for the purposes of a trade or business.
(2)   The agricultural tenancy: tenancies and licences.
(3)   Arrangements which avoid full statutory protection.

Chapter 1

Land Used for Agriculture

1.01. Introductory

In this first chapter we shall consider that part of the definition of an agricultural holding which defines

(i)   land
(ii) used for agriculture which is
(iii) so used for the purposes of a trade or business.

In addition, the chapter describes the relationship of the major statutory landlord and tenant codes governing lettings of agricultural holdings, of residential dwellings and of business premises respectively.

1.02 'Land'

As is clear from section 1 of the 1986 Act, 'land' is the essence of agricultural holdings: an agricultural holding is 'the aggregate of the land comprised in a... contract for an agricultural tenancy'.

There is *no* minimum size for an agricultural holding. An allotment of half an acre (*Stevens* v. *Sedgeman* (1951)) and a garden of one-third of an acre (*Look* v. *Davies* (1952)) which satisfied all the statutory criteria have been held to be protected holdings. Indeed 'land' includes all buildings on the land and will include buildings *alone* in appropriate cases. In *Blackmore* v. *Butler* (1954) and in the earlier case of *Godfrey* v. *Waite* (1951) it was assumed that a dwelling house without any land other than a small garden could in appropriate circumstances constitute an agricultural holding. Thus a building for battery hens or any other intensive livestock breeding could similarly constitute a holding.

1.03 'Used for agriculture'

It is essential that the land is used 'for agriculture' for the 1986 Act to
apply.

'Agriculture' defined

'Agriculture' is defined in section 96 of the Act, but this definition is, as
we shall see, not exhaustive. Section 96(1) defines 'agriculture' to include:

> 'horticulture, fruit growing, seed growing, dairy farming and livestock
> breeding and keeping, the use of land as grazing land, meadow land,
> osier land, market gardens and nursery grounds and the use of land for
> woodlands where that use is ancillary to the farming of land for other
> agricultural purposes.'

This omits, for example, any reference to 'the commonest form of
agriculture, namely the growing of corn' (Stamp LJ in *McClinton* v.
McFall (1984)). Such activities, which are clearly ordinary 'agricultural'
activities, would satisfy the Act. Section 96(1) does, however, invite some
further comment.

    'Horticulture' includes, for example, watercress beds in or near part of
a river. The growing of crops and weeds for the purpose of testing
weedkillers on them is not agriculture, however: *Dow Agrochemicals Ltd* v.
E.A. Lane (North Lynn) Ltd (1965)).

'Livestock' is further defined in section 96(1) as including

> 'any creature kept for the production of food, wool, skins or fur or for
> the purpose of its use in the farming of land or the carrying on in
> relation to land of any agricultural activity.'

'Creature' is a broad term. It would include fish, bringing fish farms
potentially within the Act. It could also include snails and frogs, whose
rearing for food is undertaken commercially in a small way in England and
Wales and raising deer for venison. Similarly, the keeping of bees for
honey production could also be 'agriculture'. Breeding foxes for fur
would be included. The commercial breeding of maggots or silkworms,
however, is not since they are not directly bred for 'the production of food,
wool, skins or fur'.

    Birds and fowl are certainly 'creatures' and their breeding and keeping
will constitute 'agriculture' if the object is the production of food. In *Earl
of Normanton* v. *Giles* (1980), the House of Lords considered whether the
raising of pheasant for shoots was 'agriculture' under the similarly worded

definition in the Rent (Agriculture) Act 1976. They decided it was not agriculture, but was essentially to provide sport and enjoyment (for the guns): a recreational rather than agricultural use. Lord Wilberforce said,

'It may be the case that unless people in general were willing to eat pheasants and pay for that pleasure, shooting would become uneconomic, but it does not follow from this that pheasants are produced for food. If they were to be so produced many easier ways of rearing and killing them could be found.'

Notice that the breeding, keeping and training of animals are not agricultural activities. Kennels, catteries, stud farms, riding schools and paddocks are therefore outside the scope of the Act, although a breeder who proved that he primarily bred and trained working sheep dogs for sale to farms might argue the point.

Horses, unless bred for meat or used as working farm animals (both are rare occurrences in England and Wales) will not be 'livestock'. Keeping horses and breeding horses are not therefore normally 'agriculture': *Belmont Farm Ltd* v. *Minister of Housing and Local Government* (1962). However, grazing of horses will be 'agricultural'.

'*The use of land as grazing land*' is 'agriculture' *regardless* of the type of animal grazing. This highlights the rather odd situation regarding horses. Although keeping and breeding horses will not be 'agriculture' unless for meat or use on the farm, the use of land to *graze* horses is an agricultural use and if used 'for the purposes of a trade or business', such as a riding school or a stud farm, the grazing land will be an agricultural holding. Lettings of land for other uses concerning horses, however, for example for jumping, training, breaking or showing (discussed in *Wetherall* v. *Smith* (1980) or for 'gallops' (as in *University of Reading* v. *Johnson-Houghton* (1986)) will not constitute agricultural holdings but in some circumstances the letting may fall within the Landlord and Tenant Act 1954 Part II as a business tenancy.

'*Market gardens*' are nowhere statutorily defined. In *Lowther* v. *Clifford* (1927) when considering whether a small orchard, underplanted with rhubarb and vegetables, was used as a market garden, Scrutton LJ said

'The produce of the trees and the crops of vegetables grown under them are sent regularly to Covent Garden market for sale and the land seems used substantially for no other purpose. The use of the land is to grow fruit and vegetables and flowers for market; it seems to be essentially a market garden.'

Incidental sales of produce from a private garden are not sufficient: *Bickerdike* v. *Lucy* (1920) and land used as a bulb farm was held not to be a market garden in *Walters* v. *Hunter* (1927). This could nevertheless be 'horticulture' and therefore 'agriculture' within the 1986 Act.

'*Woodlands*' must be *ancillary* to other agricultural purposes to be within the Act. Land used *primarily* for forestry or silviculture independent of other agriculture is therefore outside the Act.

1.04 Agriculture: considering the context

In determining whether the land is let as agricultural land, section 1(2) of the 1986 Act directs that attention be paid to

'(a)   the terms of the tenancy,

(b)   the actual or contemplated use of the land at the time of the conclusion of the contract and subsequently and

(c)   any other relevant considerations.'

In some cases the use will be obviously and inherently 'agricultural' as for example when land is used for cereal crops or one or more of the activities specified in section 96(1). In other cases, however, the *context* of the arrangement may imbue an inherently non-agricultural use with an agricultural character.

Two examples are the cases of *Godfrey* v. *Waite* (1957) and *Blackmore* v. *Butler* (1954) both of which concern the letting of a dwelling house for residence: not an inherently 'agricultural' use. In *Godfrey* v. *Waite*, the tenant of 32 acres of agricultural land subsequently took the lease of half a manor house adjacent to the land. The lettings of the land and the house were completely separate transactions between the same landlord and tenant. When the landlord served notice to quit the house, it was argued that it was an agricultural holding. Evershed M.R. said that the question was a matter of fact and degree in each case, and treated the purpose of the letting and the intention of the parties as crucial. In this case, no point having been made of any office use of the house in connection with the farmland, the parties' intention was construed as the letting of 'a more convenient dwelling house', *not* of a farmhouse for the 32 acres. Mere propinquity was not sufficient to imply an agricultural use.

The intention of the parties must normally be deduced from the agreement between them. Where that is expressed in a written tenancy, parole evidence is not easily introduced to contradict the document, but extrinsic evidence may be used to indicate the context of the agreement: for example 'the actual or contemplated use of the land' and 'any other relevant circumstances', as indicated in section 1(2)(b) and (c).

In *Blackmore* v. *Butler*, for example, Butler, the tenant of a farm had insisted that as a condition of renting the farm he should also be given the tenancy of an adjacent cottage, when it became available, to accommodate one of his agricultural workers. The cottage had apparently always been used as an agricultural worker's cottage. When the existing occupier moved out, Butler paid rent for the cottage and one of his workers moved in. In due course the new owner of the cottage who had bought it knowing of Butler's tenancy and use, served him with notice to quit. Butler argued that the cottage was an agricultural holding protected by the 1948 Act and the notice to quit was therefore ineffective. *Godfrey* v. *Waite* was considered. The mere fact that a house was occupied by someone who is engaged in agricultural pursuits will not of itself constitute that house an agricultural holding. However, in all the circumstances of this case, Butler's claim was upheld, Romer LJ commenting:

> 'set as it seems to be in the midst of pastures and farmlands it has, at all material times, been used for the purpose of housing agricultural workers... Taking then the history of this cottage into account, its situation and the purpose for which it was let ... it follows almost inevitably that it is agricultural land.'

1.05 Agriculture: the predominant use

Section 1(2) of the Act (originating in the 1984 Act) requires that

> 'the whole of the land comprised in the contract (of tenancy), subject to such exceptions only as do not substantially affect the character of the tenancy, is let for use as agricultural land.'

This incorporates into statutory form the 'predominant use test' which has been articulated with increasing confidence by the courts in their construction of the 1948 Act.

It is of course quite possible that some of the land included in the tenancy agreement will not be used 'for agriculture for the purposes of a trade or business'. Section 1(1) of the Act expressly defines an agricultural holding as

> 'the aggregate of land (*whether agricultural land or not*) comprised in a contract of tenancy.'

The use may in other words be mixed. Section 1(2) now makes it quite clear that it is the nature of the letting *as a whole* which must be determined. The *predominant* user, ignoring uses which 'do not substantially affect the character of the tenancy' must be ascertained. If it is substantially agricultural, *all* the land will be protected by the Act. If not, *none* of the land will be subject to the agricultural holdings code. Section 1 seems to make quite clear that there can be no severance of the land included in a single contract of tenancy into 'agricultural' and 'non-agricultural' land. Thus, for example, if the use is predominantly agricultural and the tenancy therefore within the Act, any notice to quit will affect all the land included in the contract and will be subject to the requirements of the 1986 Act. It will not be possible to seek possession of the 'non-agricultural' part separately or through different procedures.

One of the earliest cases to expound the predominant use test (although somewhat tentatively) was *Howkins* v. *Jardine* (1957). A tenancy containing provisions usual in the lease of an agricultural holding was granted for seven acres of land including three cottages on the land. At first the tenant lived in one of the cottages but he subsequently moved out and sublet all three to people not engaged in agriculture. Ultimately the landlords sought possession of the three cottages but not of the seven acres. The Court of Appeal, in holding that there could be no such severance, stated that

> 'one must look at the substance of the matter and see whether, as a matter of substance, the land comprised in the tenancy, taken as a whole, is an agricultural holding. If it is, then the whole of it is entitled to the protection of the Act. If it is not, then none of it is so entitled.'

Jenkins LJ continued:

> 'The cottages in question must, I think, be regarded as ancillary to the holding of the seven acres of undeniably agricultural land. The whole, including the cottages, was let under an agreement in terms clearly appropriate to an agricultural holding. The character of the demised premises as agricultural or non-agricultural land cannot, in my judgement, be made to depend on the occupation of the persons to whom the cottages may be let from time to time.'

A similar point was raised in *Monson* v. *Bound* (1954) where the tenant made a rather ingenious plea for the protection of the 1948 Act. He leased approximately one-third of an acre and was subject to a covenant in the lease to use the premises only for the purposes of an horticulturist. The premises comprised a shop in a row of shops in suburban Surrey with various outbuildings, greenhouses and a very small 'stock garden'. The tenant's business was the retail sale of horticultural products and sundries and it was calculated that only about one-tenth of the total turnover was attributable to horticultural processes effected on the premises. McNair J found that although 'undoubtedly horticultural processes were carried on in substantially the whole of the premises,... as a matter of substance the premises as a whole were at the material time being used for the purpose of a retail shop'

and the horticultural activities were merely ancillary to this predominant non-agricultural use. The tenant's case therefore failed: his shop was not an agricultural holding.

As a final example of the predominant use test, we might consider *McClinton* v. *McFall* (1974). The tenant owned a stud farm and leased 56 additional acres to use for this business. The agreement described the 56 acres as being let 'as an agricultural tenancy'. It included a permissive user clause whereby it was 'agreed that... the land may be used as a stud farm'. In fact the land was found to be used mainly for pasture, grazing and haymaking. From time to time it was also used for breaking in horses, schooling them, jumping them and showing them to customers. The horse-breeding and these associated activities were not 'agriculture'. However, Stamp LJ held that on the facts these activities were not inconsistent with a predominantly agricultural use of the land (pasture, grazing and haymaking):

'The area of the holding is relatively large. Provided the use of land otherwise than for agriculture does not substantially impede the use for agriculture, the former does not in my judgement, prevent the land being agricultural land within the meaning of the Act.'

On the facts therefore the Court of Appeal was satisfied that the predominant use of the 56 acres was agricultural, and the land constituted a holding within the Act.

Although many indications may be relevant in identifying the predominant use of land, these cases suggest that factors such as

(i)   the contribution to the income or profits of the tenant: *Monson* v. *Bound, Deith* v. *Brown* (1956);
(ii) the continuous as opposed to intermittent user: in *McClinton* v. *McFall* the example of allowing land to be used for point-to-point races was quoted as an example of insubstantial non-agricultural use;
(iii) the proportion of the land used for various purposes: *McClinton* v. *McFall*;
(iv) the paramount purpose of the letting: *Howkins* v. *Jardine*

are all likely to be useful guidelines.

1.06 Agriculture: the 'legal' use

The Agricultural Holdings Act will only apply to protect a holding where
the agricultural use of the land is a legal, or permitted, use in the context
of the particular lease. Problems here usually arise from the inclusion of
restrictive user covenants in the lease, and the interpretation of any
particular covenant will be all-important, the court's primary aim being to
give effect to the intention of the parties and then to consider the
lawfulness or otherwise of the particular land use.

In *Kempe* v. *Dillon Trenchard* (1951), for example, a lease of a house,
garden and 9½ acres of land included a restriction against the user
'otherwise than as a private dwelling house.' The land was used by the
tenant for agriculture without obtaining the landlord's permission. In the
local County Court it was held that the agricultural use was contrary to the
restriction. Therefore the property was not let as agricultural land and the
letting was not protected by the 1948 Act.

However, in construing such use covenants, their context must not be
ignored. In *Iredell* v. *Brocklehurst* (1950), the landlord brought an action
against his tenant for possession, damages for breaches of covenant and
mesne profits. The lease was of a house with twelve acres of pasture land.
The lease contained a covenant against use for any 'profession, trade or
business' and also a limitation that the property should not be used other
than as a private residence. The tenant used the property to accommodate
his employees working on his neighbouring farm. In the County Court,
the tenant's claim that the land was an agricultural holding succeeded on
the grounds that use for 'agricultural purposes' was not expressly
excluded. In the Court of Appeal the landlord's appeal was dismissed.
Their Lordships' reasoning differed from that in the County Court and is
illustrated by Somervell LJ:

'Where we find a cottage with 12 acres of land let, the conclusion was
almost inevitable that the premises were to be let for agricultural use.'

His Lordship found no difficulty in construing the words 'profession
trade or business' as meaning other than the business of agriculture since,
he held, it was clearly intended by the parties that the tenant should use
the premises for his business of farming. Here the all-important intention
of the parties was largely deduced from the circumstances of the letting
and the restriction interpreted accordingly.

Where the tenant's use of the land is in breach of a use covenant, it is
possible for the landlord to condone or waive the breach, thus 'legalising'
the use. If the newly 'legalised' use is agricultural, this could cause the
land to be classified as an agricultural holding in appropriate
circumstances. However, it must be stressed that the evidence to support

such a waiver must be clear and unambiguous and must demonstrate the landlord's knowledge of the breach and his acceptance of it. Reliance on the landlord's constructive knowledge of the breach can be especially precarious and the mere receipt and acceptance of rent after or during the breach is not necessarily conclusive of his acceptance of the breach.

Section 1(3) of the 1986 Act emphasis the need for any change of use relied on to bring a tenancy within the Act to be a 'legal' or permitted use [1.07(i)]

1.07 Change of use during the currency of a lease

It is clear that a change in the predominant use of land during a tenancy may take the tenancy outside the scope of the 1986 Act or, alternatively, may bring it within the Act's protection. Section 1(2) in requiring regard to be had to

'(b) the actual or contemplated use of the land at the time of the conclusion of the contract *and subsequently*'

recognises this. In recent years case law has considerably clarified the requirements necessary to demonstrate that by change of user an originally non-agricultural letting has come within the Agricultural Holdings Act or alternatively that an original agricultural use has been abandoned and the protection of the Act thereby lost.

(i) *Change to an agricultural use: acquiring the protection of the 1986 Act*

The principles applicable when a tenant seeks to show that by a change of use he has acquired the protection of a particular statutory code, such as the Agricultural Holdings Act, were articulated by the Court of Appeal in *Russell* v. *Booker* (1982). Although in the particular case the tenant was arguing that the change of use had taken the land out of the Agricultural Holdings Act and into Rent Act protection, the principles will apply whichever 'new' code is in question.

It is absolutely clear that in any such case a mere *unilateral* change of use by the tenant will *not suffice*: it must be possible to discern a new bilateral contract binding both landlord and tenant which recognises the new use.

In *Russell* v. *Booker* a dwelling house and three acres of land were originally let as an agricultural holding. Gradually the agricultural use declined until the land was merely serving as recreational land to accommodate the house. Ultimately the landlords served a notice to quit appropriate to an agricultural holding on the daughter of the original tenant (now deceased). Although she had earlier applied for a direction under the Agriculture (Miscellaneous Provisions) Act 1976 entitling her to a tenancy of the property *as an agricultural holding,* she ultimately contended that by reason of the change in use of the land which had occurred during her father's lifetime, the agricultural holdings legislation no longer applied to the tenancy but that, instead, she was a protected or statutory tenant of the house and land under the Rent Act 1977.

In the Court of Appeal the following principles were articulated:

(a)   Where the terms of the original tenancy agreement provide for or contemplate the use of the premises for some particular purpose, then normally that purpose is the essential factor in deciding whether or not the premises fall within the claimed code of protection (e.g. within the Agricultural Holdings Act or alternatively the Rent Act).

(b)   However, where the original tenancy agreement provided for or contemplated a particular use but, by the time possession proceedings were begun that agreement has been superseded by a subsequent contract providing for a different use, the subsequent contract may be looked at to determine the relevant code.

(c)   If a tenant changes the use of the premises and the fact of the change is known to and accepted by the landlord, it may be possible for the court to infer a subsequent contract appropriate to the 'new' code of protection, e.g. a contract for agricultural use which brings the tenancy within the Agricultural Holdings Act.

(d)   However, unless such a new contract can be spelled out, a mere unilateral change of use will not enable a tenant to claim the protection of the new code where the original stated purpose of the contract of tenancy is outside that code.

(e)   Where the original tenancy agreement does *not* provide for or contemplate any particular use of the premises, the actual subsequent use has to be considered in deciding whether the protection of the code sought by the tenant is available.

Of course, if the tenant does change his use of the land but no subsequent agreement can be identified concerning the change of use, he may find that he has slipped out of one scheme of protection without slipping into another, thus finding himself in a legal 'limbo' without any statutory protection at all. Such was the case in *Russell* v. *Booker* itself. The Court of Appeal could find no subsequent contract between landlord and tenant for the letting of the property 'as a separate dwelling' to bring it within the Rent Act. As Slade LJ said:

'We accept that unilateral abandonment by the tenant of agricultural user of land may cause it to cease to be an 'agricultural holding'. However, ... we cannot accept that a mere unilateral change or abandonment of user by a tenant which is not embodied in a new contract between landlord and tenant, express or implied, can operate to take a tenancy which did not begin by being protected by the Rent Acts into the protection of the Rent Acts.'

Such a decision could lose the tenant *all* statutory protection, Slade LJ said

'we do not find this conclusion unacceptable. In a case where the original tenancy agreement provides for or contemplates the user of the premises as an agricultural holding for agricultural purposes and the tenant subsequently contemplates a change of user, it is always open to him to attempt to negotiate a new contract with the landlord.'

The essence of *Russell* v. *Booker* is now found in section 1(3) of the 1986 Act which provides that

'a change in user of the land concerned subsequent to the conclusion of a contract of tenancy which involves any breach of the terms of the tenancy shall be disregarded for the purpose of determining whether a contract which was not originally a contract for an agricultural tenancy has subsequently become one unless it is effected with the landlord's permission, consent or acquiescence.'

(ii) Abandonment of agricultural use: losing the protection of the Act

It has been recognised in the Court of Appeal that in some situations the tenant will be found to have abandoned the agricultural use of the land and thereby to have lost the protection of the Act. However, clear evidence of abandonment over a substantial period is necessary before this seriously prejudicial result will be acknowledged. The criteria are deduced from the leading case of *Wetherall* v. *Smith* (1980) which discussed and confirmed the earlier decision of the Court of Appeal in *Hickson and Welch Ltd* v. *Cann* (1977).

In *Wetherall* v. *Smith* the tenant, Wetherall, had been granted a yearly tenancy of a field. At the outset this was an agricultural holding within the 1948 Act, the field being used for grazing. Ultimately, however, the landlords served him with a notice to quit, claiming that the field was being used only as a jumping paddock, therefore merely for recreation, and was thus no longer protected by the 1948 Act. The tenant denied this.

The landlords here did not base their argument on a breach of the tenancy conditions (which they indeed claimed by implication to have condoned) but were claiming more radically that the change of use was in effect an abandonment of the agricultural use by which the tenant had necessarily relinquished the protection of the Act. In his leading judgment, Sir David Cairns said:

'on principle it is in my judgment right that the protection of the statute should be lost if agricultural activity is wholly or substantially abandoned during the course of the tenancy even if without the consent of the landlord. At the same time... the tenancy is not to be regarded as alternating between being within and outside the Act as minor changes of user take place, and ... when the tenancy is clearly an agricultural one to start with, strong evidence is needed to show that the agricultural user has been abandoned.'

Thus,

(a) the tenant, by change of use, can *unilaterally lose* the protection of the Act;
(b) 'strong evidence' is needed to bring about such a result:

(1) there must be clear evidence that agricultural activity has been wholly or substantially abandoned; a change in the *predominant* (or substantial) use is required; for example as in *Wetherall* a change from grazing to recreation. The change of minor, ancillary or incidental users will not affect the status of the tenancy. For example, in a situation such as that in *Howkins v. Jardine* [1.05], letting the cottages, whether to agricultural workers or to tenants totally unconnected with agriculture, was merely ancillary to the predominant agricultural use of the holding, so that changes of tenants would not affect the nature of the tenancy of the whole, including the cottages.

(2) the duration of the new use must be considered. Attention must be directed to the period preceding the service of the notice to quit, or other such step as is taken to challenge the status of the tenancy. It is unlikely that

'the change can, in the absence of some very exceptional circumstances, be brough about in a matter of days or weeks': Sir David Cairns in *Wetherall* v. *Smith*.

In *Hickson and Welch Ltd* v. *Cann*, the period of two years prior to notice to quit was considered. In *Wetherall* v. *Smith* the period of two years was again used.

Temporary or transient changes of the substantial use may be breaches of covenant but will *not* be sufficient to take the tenancy outside the Act altogether – for example, where a field usually used as grazing land is used for a horse show or horse sale.

1.08 Used for agriculture 'for the purposes of a trade or business'

(i) What constitutes 'a business'?

The agricultural holdings legislation is intended to govern commercial concerns, not the private (non-trade) use of land. The agricultural use of land must be 'for the purposes of a trade or business' for the letting to be within the Act's protection. Land leased to graze pet ponies or for goats producing milk purely for their owner would not therefore constitute an agricultural holding, even though the use is 'agricultural', since these are not lettings for a trade or business purpose.

What amounts to a 'trade or business' is a question of fact and degree in each case. In *Hickson and Welch Ltd* v. *Cann* (1977), for example, the tenant relied on his activities of livestock breeding and keeping to bring him within the protection of the 1948 Act. In the Court of Appeal, Roskill LJ was

> 'perfectly willing to accept... that (Mr Cann) was doing what one might call some legitimate casual horse trading, buying and selling the odd horse, and perfectly ordinary pig dealing by breeding, fattening and reselling pigs. There were obviously more dealings in pigs than in horses. There is, however, all the difference in the world between what hundreds and hundreds of people all over this country do, that is, add a small amount to their earnings by buying or selling animals of one sort or another, and the carrying on a trade or business... by means of that type of transaction.'

(Only the pig breeding would have qualified as 'agricultural' because of the anomalous position of horses [1.03]). In *Russell* v. *Booker* (1982), on the other hand, the tenant had sold eggs, livestock and apples from his property and had run a bed and breakfast business there. His annual receipts from all these various sources were 'never more than very modest', rarely exceeding £30 p.a. from apples, £55 from eggs and latterly less than £100 p.a. from bed and breakfast guests, whilst the occasional sale of livestock did little more than cover the expenses of feeding and caring for the livestock. Nevertheless, despite these minimal returns the Court of Appeal (perhaps impressed by the continuity of effort and the punctilious bookkeeping of the tenant) recognised these activities as constituting apparently two businesses for the purpose of the Act: fruit and vegetable sales and a bed and breakfast business.

(ii) 'Agricultural' business not necessary

Russell v. Booker also illustrates the other important point to note: that although the *use* of the land must be agricultural, the business with which it is linked need *not* be: a bed and breakfast business, for example, is not an 'agricultural' business, but the production of fruit, vegetables and eggs for the use in that business was 'the use of land for agriculture for the purposes of trade or business' and satisfied the Act. Similarly in *Rutherford* v. *Maurer* (1962) the proprietor of a riding school took a lease of a five acre field as grazing land for the horses from her school. It was held that this arrangement was within the 1948 Act: grazing (by whatever animal) is an agricultural use, and it was here 'for the purpose of' the riding school, a trade or business. Ormrod L.J. gave it as his view

> 'that the words trade or business mean what they say and should not be qualified or narrowed in their application by the use of a term like agricultural.'

1.09 Ministerial designation

In addition to land which is shown to be used for agriculture for the purposes of a trade or business, section 1(4)(b) of the 1986 Act provides that 'agricultural land' will mean

> 'any other land which, by virtue of a designation under section 109(1) of the Agriculture Act 1947 is agricultural land within the meaning of that Act.'

1.10 The Agricultural Holdings Act and other statutory codes

It may be helpful at this point to consider briefly the relationship of the agricultural holdings legislation to the other major statutory codes governing landlord and tenant relationships.

It is intended that the codes should be mutually exclusive and complementary. In *Russell* v. *Booker* an example of their relationship was seen, the tenant there claiming, unsuccessfully, to have relinquished the protection of the 1948 Act for the protection of the Rent Act 1977. We have already quoted the section of the 1986 Act which essentially defines its scope: tenancies concerning land used for agriculture for the purposes of a trade or business. The following paragraphs indicate the provisions made in the other codes which respect the exclusive jurisdiction over such tenancies of the 1986 Act.

(i) The Rent Act 1977

The Rent Act is concerned with tenancies 'under which a dwelling-house... is let as a separate dwelling'. It is essentially concerned with residential dwellings, and thus has a quite different focus from the agricultural holdings legislation which is concerned with land used for agriculture for the purpose of a trade or business. However, where a residential dwelling house is let as agricultural land as defined in the 1986 Act it will be an agricultural holding, or part of an agricultural holding, as exemplified in *Blackmore* v. *Butler* [1.04] and *Howkins* v. *Jardine* [1.05]. The Rent Act 1977 excludes from its own jurisdiction any dwelling house

'comprised in an agricultural holding and... occupied by the person responsible for the control (whether as tenant, or as a servant or agent of the tenant) of the farming of the holding.'

The second ('occupation') condition here requires further comment. Firstly, there may be situations where the occupying tenant of the farmhouse falls outside both the Rent Act 1977 and the Agricultural Holdings Act 1986 because his tenancy is directly linked to his employment by his landlord. Section 1(1) of the 1986 Act excludes lettings to a tenant 'during his continuance in any office appointment or employment held under the landlord'. Such cases are likely to be rare: the tenant farmer is unlikely to be a manager for his landlord. The phrase in section 1(1) of the 1986 Act is intended to exclude from that Act the agricultural tied cottage (now protected by the Rent (Agriculture) Act 1976), whilst section 10 of the Rent Act 1977 aims to avoid overlap with either the 1986 Act or the Rent (Agriculture) Act.

Secondly, the Rent Act only excludes a dwelling house 'occupied by the person responsible' for farming the holding. If, therefore, the tenant sublets cottages or even the farmhouse of an agricultural holding, the situation must be carefully considered. If the subtenants are agricultural workers and the lettings are tied cottages, they should be protected by the Rent (Agriculture) Act 1976, as against their immediate landlord. If, however, the subtenants are not connected with agriculture, the Rent Act 1977 may apply, unless the lettings fall within one of the exceptions in that Act, such as holiday lettings.

A subtenant who is protected by either of these two codes has an additional protection in section 137(3) of the Rent Act 1977 and Schedule 8 para. 20 of the Rent (Agriculture) Act 1976, should his immediate landlord's own (agricultural) tenancy be terminated.

Section 137(3) provides that

'where a dwelling house

(a)   forms part of premises which have been let as a whole on a superior tenancy but do not constitute a dwelling house let on a statutorily protected tenancy

and

(b)   is itself subject to a protected or statutory tenancy [or one within the 1976 Act] then on the coming to an end of the superior tenancy, the Rent Acts shall apply in relation to the dwelling house as if, in lieu of the superior tenancy, there had been separate tenancies of the dwelling house and the remainder of the premises, at rents equal to the just proportion of the rent under the superior tenancy.'

The subtenant under a lawful subletting thus becomes the direct tenant of the head landlord at a *pro rata* rent, protected by the Rent Act 1977. This applies where the head lease is of an agricultural holding.

(ii) The Rent (Agriculture) Act 1976

Although this Act is considered in detail in the last chapter of this book it is useful to mention here that the Act applies to lettings on a low rent or no rent of premises provided by the tenant's employer in situations where the letting is inextricably linked with the tenant's contract of employment. The Act therefore seeks to protect the agricultural worker's occupation of a tied cottage and to provide security of tenure, irrespective of the tenant's employment, once the initial 'qualifying period' of work in agriculture has been served. The link with employment and the low rent levels distinguish tied cottages from lettings covered by the Rent Act or the Agricultural Holdings Act.

(iii) The Landlord and Tenant Act 1954 Part II

The potential overlap between this statute, governing business tenancies, and the Agricultural Holdings Act is avoided by section 43(1)(a), of the

1954 Act, as amended by the Agriculture Act 1958, which excludes from its scope all tenancies of agricultural holdings.

(iv) The Allotments Act 1925

There is authority that in the case of land used as allotments, two alternative codes of protection co-exist: the Allotments Act 1925 *and* the Agricultural Holdings Act and the tenant may apparently opt for whichever scheme of protection he prefers: *Stevens* v. *Sedgeman* (1951).

Chapter 2

The Agricultural Tenancy

2.01 Introductory

An agricultural holding is 'the aggregate of the agricultural land ... comprised in a contract of tenancy': section 1(1).

Section 1(5) defines a contract of tenancy as 'a letting of land, or an agreement for letting land, for a term of years or from year to year'. In this chapter we consider that definition and the related sections 2, 3, 4 and 5. Section 2 includes within the Act's protection lesser grants which 'take effect as' contracts of tenancy. Sections 3 and 4 extend and continue the fixed term tenant's interest after the expiry of the original term. Section 5 provides for the grant of fixed term leases of agricultural holdings without any subsequent security of tenure if certain prescribed conditions are satisfied by the parties both in their pre-grant preparations and in their preparation of the lease.

These sections, in defining the contract of tenancy also expressly or implicitly exclude certain arrangements from the scope of the Act. Such arrangements, which do not constitute agricultural holdings, are discussed in Chapter 3.

2.02 A single contract of tenancy

An agricultural holding is agricultural land comprised in a *single* contract of tenancy. As we have seen, there can be no severance of land comprised in a single contract into agricultural and non-agricultural holdings: the nature of the land *as a whole* is based on its primary or predominant use. Where there is more than one contract of tenancy, however, the circumstances of each must be considered individually to determine whether or not the 1986 Act will govern it.

In *Darby* v. *Williams* (1974), for example, the tenant was separately granted lettings of a cottage and the adjoining 12 acres of agricultural land, for different terms, at different rents and each subject to different covenants. Although he had been required to take both leases or neither, this was held not to alter the separate identity of the two contracts. The land was an agricultural holding but on the facts the cottage was not and the tenant could not therefore avail himself of the security provisions of the 1948 Act when his landlord sought possession of the cottage.

In some cases, however, it may be possible to show on the particular facts that one contract is merely ancillary or supplemental to another so that together they genuinely constitute *a single* contract of tenancy. This was acknowledged, *obiter*, in *Blackmore* v. *Butler* [1.04] when Birkett LJ recognised that

'cases may arise, of course, where after the original contract of tenancy, other agreements are entered into either adding to or subtracting from the land in the original tenancy and it will be a question for consideration in each case whether such agreements may be read together with the original contract of tenancy and form the contract of tenancy referred to in section 1(1).'

2.03 'A term of years': fixed terms

Section 1(5) first mentions as a contract of tenancy a 'letting of land ... for a term of years'. For the purposes of the 1986 Act the phrase 'term of years' is stated in section 1(5) to include lettings or agreements for lettings converted into terms of 90 years by section 149(6) of the Law of Property Act 1925. Apart from this single elaboration the phrase is not defined or qualified. There is, for example, no equivalent of section 205(1) (xxvii) of the Law of Property Act 1925 and so there is some uncertainty whether the phrase 'term of years' in the 1986 Act includes, as does the 1925 Act, 'a term for less than a year or for a year or years and a fraction of a year', or whether the phrase is only intended to include grants of complete or integral years. Would a lease for six months constitute a 'term of years' for the purposes of the Act? The point was discussed in *Re Land and Premises at Liss, Hants* (1971) and *Esso Petroleum Co. Ltd* v. *Secretary of State for the Environment* (1971). It has not been conclusively decided. Fortunately in practice it is of little significance, but it may be technically important in just two situations:

(a) Lettings for less than a year

As we shall see [2.08] most leases granted for a fixed term of a year or less are converted automatically by section 2 of the Act into tenancies from year to year to become indubitably agricultural tenancies within the Act.

However, under the same section the Minister has power to approve such lettings taking effect exceptionally without being so converted. If a letting for such a fraction of a year is 'a term of years' for the purposes of the Act, then such 'approved' short term lettings will constitute agricultural holdings for their duration, although they certainly confer no security of tenure on the tenant but terminate naturally by effluxion of time. Thus, if approved by the Minister under section 2, a grant of six months would take effect as just that, without any subsequent statutory continuation.

Since this interpretation of the phrase would necessarily result in a distinction being drawn between short *leases* approved under section 2 and *licences* approved under the same section (which as 'mere' unconverted licences cannot of course constitute agricultural tenancies), and since it relies on an 'artificial' interpretation which had to be expressly enacted into the Law of Property Act, it seems most unlikely to prevail. The whole tenor of section 2 is that grants which fall within its scope should be treated similarly: as *not* constituting agricultural holdings for their limited duration.

(b) Lettings of between one and two years

As we have seen, fixed terms of one year or less (unless approved in advance by the Minister) are converted automatically into tenancies from year to year by section 2. Lettings for fixed terms of two years or more are continued automatically after their natural expiry date as tenancies from year to year by virtue of section 3 [2.04]. However, *Gladstone* v. *Bower* (1960) made it clear that nothing in the legislation affects the natural expiry date of a grant between one and two years and such a grant, say for eighteen months, will thus terminate at its due date as agreed by the parties. The case, however, did not consider whether the grant constituted an agricultural tenancy albeit an unusual one which enjoyed no security of tenure or whether the grant was entirely outside the Act. If a 'term of years' for the purposes of the Act includes terms of 'a year and fractions of a year' then for its duration a *Gladstone* v. *Bower* lease will constitute an agricultural tenancy. If, on the other hand, a 'term of years' for the purposes of the Act is restricted to integral years then such a grant would take effect *entirely* outside the Act, but possibly within Part II of the Landlord and Tenant Act 1954 as a business tenancy not being the tenancy of an agricultural holding. Whilst neither of these results is entirely satisfactory, again the second, more natural interpretation seems preferable.

This theoretical difficulty, however, has little practical importance. Compensation claims in the absence of a notice to quit are minimal and it is difficult to imagine any tenant in such circumstances availing himself of any substantial advantage even if such grants were to be 'agricultural holdings' for their duration.

2.04 Continuation automatically of fixed terms of two years or more: section 3

Section 3 of the 1986 Act severely modifies the operation of fixed terms of years of two years or more of agricultural holdings. Instead of terminating at their agreed term date so that the landlord could repossess at that time the section provides that such leases will continue automatically after their term date as tenancies from year to year which can only be terminated by notice to quit in accordance with the provisions of the Act. Section 3 is designed to give considerable security of tenure to tenants. An ostensibly finite grant becomes an indefinite grant under which it is impossible to predict when the land may again be available for reletting or taking in hand, particularly in the case of leases to which the statutory succession rights apply. Section 3 does *not* apply to:

(i) terms of less than two years: section 3(1);
(ii) cases where written notice of termination has been given by one party to the other 'not less than one year nor more than two years' before the contractual term date: section 3(1);
(iii) terms granted *on or after* 12th September 1984 if the tenant, or the survivor of joint tenants, dies before the term date. If the 'last' death is a year or more before the term date, the lease will expire on the term date. If the 'last' death was at any other time, (i.e. less than one year before the contractual expiry date) then the tenancy will continue for one year after its original term date and then expire 'on the first anniversary' of its term date: section 4;
(iv) tenancies converted by section 149(6) of the Law of Property Act 1925 into terms of 90 years: section 3(3). These tenancies terminate in accordance with the provisions of section 149(6).
(v) tenancies of between two and five years where the parties have satisfied the requirements of section 5. Section 5 is a provision introduced by the 1984 Act to enable short term 'insecure' fixed tenancies to be granted over agricultural land in circumstances which are felt by M.A.F.F. and W.O.A.D. to justify the curtailment of the tenant's normal statutory right to a 'lifetime' security of tenure. It is worth stressing at this point that in every other respect a 'Section 5 lease' constitutes an agricultural holding which enjoys the full protection of the Act. The tenant, for example, may be entitled to rights to compensation on quitting and the lease may be subject to

rent reviews. The only, but crucially important, difference is that when the fixed term expires the tenant *must* leave.

(vi) tenancies granted or agreed to be granted before 1st January 1921: para 2, Schedule 12.

In these six specified cases, since section 3 does not apply, the fixed term tenancy will terminate either by effluxion of time in the normal way or as indicated above.

2.05 Section 5: fixed terms without subsequent security of tenure

Section 5 was introduced in 1984. It provides a new alternative type of grant available in some circumstances where there is a genuine agricultural need for a short fixed term tenancy which *will* terminate as agreed between the parties and will *not* give the tenant any further security of tenure. During its course, such a lease is in every other respect a full agricultural tenancy within the Act.

If a prospective landlord and tenant want to take advantage of section 5, then *before* the tenancy is formally granted they must themselves agree that section 3 will not apply to the lease and thus that no tenancy from year to year will arise at the expiry of the original term: section 5(2)(a). They must then jointly apply in writing to 'the Minister' for his approval of their agreement to exclude section 3 from their arrangement: section 5(2)(b) and they must have been notified by him of his approval: section 5(2)(c). *All* of these steps must have been taken *before* the tenancy is granted.

The tenancy itself must then be expressed in a *written* contract of tenancy which must include, or have endorsed upon it, a statement that section 3 does not apply to the tenancy: section 5(3). There is no prescribed wording for this statement.

The procedure in section 5 is a refinement of the 'minister's approval' mechanism for vetting intended 'insecure' grants which first appeared in section 2 of the 1948 Act and is retained in section 2(1) of the 1986 Act [3.03]. Sections 5 and 2 recognise that situations do arise when it is genuinely in the wider interests of agriculture that the occupier of agricultural land should not enjoy the full complement of statutory rights normally provided by the agricultural holdings code. At the same time, however, it is felt necessary to maintain a regular check on such claims and to do this they are submitted to the scrutiny of 'the Minister', for his approval (a function usually exercised on his behalf by the local Divisional Executive Officers of the Ministry).

It is clear that section 5 envisages an openness between the parties during their early negotiations of the grant and it is to be hoped that the *joint* action which is required *before* the grant is made and the final *written* contract with its explicit endorsement excluding section 3 will minimise doubt and litigation on section 5 grants. The section contains no indication of criteria to be applied by the Minister when considering agreements submitted to him under the section. However, a policy statement issued by M.A.F.F. and W.O.A.D. shortly after the 1984 Act was passed gives a clear description of various circumstances considered by them to justify the approval of an 'insecure' grant and also gives helpful indications of the maximum duration of any such grant which is likely to meet with approval in the various cases. This document is substantially reproduced later [3.04].

It is clear that in practice the Ministry has largely aggregated the powers under section 2(1) and 5 to provide the greatest flexibility of response to any application. This apparent 'simplification' may, however, be somewhat misleading. The scope of *section 2(1)* is considered in the following chapter because grants approved under that power do not constitute 'contracts of tenancy of an agricultural holding' and therefore are *in no way protected* by the Act. This must be contrasted with grants under section 5 which are clearly tenancies of agricultural holdings which, exceptionally, enjoy no security of tenure once the original term has expired although in every other respect they *are* subject to the Act. The situations where section 5 was originally intended to be of help were 'trial tenancies' for new entrants to agriculture and 'interim tenancies' for a purely limited period where there is a definite intention that the landlord's son or daughter will take over a vacant holding within five years. It seems clear that in such cases an application under section 5 would be sympathetically considered. Although, in theory, licences approved under section 2 could accommodate such situations, the difficulties of drafting an unassailable *licence* for the occupation of land are now so great that it was felt that an express provision for fixed-term 'insecure' *leases* would inspire more confidence and thus be of more value. For a detailed discussion of the exercise of the Minister's discretion, under sections 5 and 2, see the comment on the Ministry guidelines [3.04].

2.06 No contracting out of section 3

Notice that apart from the closely defined and monitored situation of section 5 it is expressly provided that section 3 'shall have effect notwithstanding any agreement to the contrary'. Therefore all fixed term leases of two years or more will automatically be followed by a statutory tenancy from year to year and if such a grant has been made no attempt by the parties to contract out of this result will be countenanced.

2.07 'Letting from year to year'

The second meaning given to 'contract of tenancy' by section 1(5) is 'a
letting of land ... from year to year'. The annual periodic tenancy was the
traditional agricultural lease. The 1986 Act, like its predecessors, employs
the tenancy from year to year to achieve a new statutory balance between
the landlord and tenant. As we have seen, a statutory tenancy from year
to year is imposed at the expiry of fixed terms granted for two years or
more. The Act also used the device of the tenancy from year to year in
section 2 whereby lesser interests will, in certain circumstances 'take effect
as' tenancies from year to year and will thus become effectively fully
protected tenancies of agricultural holdings within the Act.

2.08 Section 2: lesser interests transformed into tenancies from year to year

Section 2(1) provides that, with the necessary modifications, agreements
for the following grants will take effect as tenancies from year to year:

(a)   agreements under which any land is let to a person for use as
      agricultural land for an interest less than a tenancy from year to
      year; and
(b)   agreements under which a person is granted a licence to occupy land
      for use as agricultural land.

In each case, it must be clear that

> 'if the circumstances (were) such that if his interest were a tenancy from
> year to year he would in respect of that land be the tenant of an
> agricultural holding'.

What, then, is the scope of the 'statutory magic' of section 2 which affects
these transformations?

(i) The 'necessary modifications'

Any 'transformed' arrangement will take effect as a tenancy from year to
year 'with the necessary modifications': section 2(1). In *Goldsack* v. *Shore*
(1950) Evershed MR said that the transaction in question

> 'must be capable of being so modified (and that must mean modified

consistently with its own terms) as to become enlarged into a tenancy from year to year'.

The same point was addressed by Pearson LJ in *Harrison-Broadley* v. *Smith* (1964) in a helpful and frequently quoted passage:

'That which is to take effect is the original agreement with the necessary modifications. It is not permissible to substitute for the original agreement a radically different agreement and make that take effect instead of the original agreement ...

Of course, it must be recognised that any modification of an agreement must be in a sense inconsistent with its own terms. But I understand that passage to mean that the agreement must remain, so to speak, recognisably the same agreement after the necessary modifications have been made. The section is not applicable to an agreement which is not capable of taking effect, with the necessary modifications, as an agreement for the letting of the land for a tenancy from year to year. The necessary modifications have to be distinguished from a transformation of the agreement into something radically different.'

For example, in *Walters and others* v. *Roberts* (1980) a prospective purchaser of sheep farming land, allowed into possession pending completion as a licensee under the then current National Conditions of Sale (19th ed.) argued that his licence was transformed by section 2(1) of the 1948 Act into a tenancy from year to year with full security of tenure. The argument was rejected by Nourse J who had no hesitation in concluding that the defendant vendor had a very clear right to possession as against the licensee-purchaser:

'broadly speaking, the object of (the 1948) Act is to extend the rights of a person who is contractually entitled to no more than the right to occupy land for agricultural purposes. It is not its object to extend the rights of a person who has contracted to purchase the land, who is let into occupation pursuant only to that contract and whose occupation was never intended to survive its extinction.'

(ii) Lettings for interest 'less than a tenancy from year to year'

In *Bernays* v. *Prosser* (1963) it was held that a fixed term tenancy for one year exactly was 'an interest less than a tenancy from year to year' and was therefore to take effect as a tenancy from year to year for the purposes of the Act.

Also in *Bernays* v. *Prosser*, although *obiter*, Lord Denning MR stated

that it was 'quite clear' that a fixed term of six months, nine months or
even 364 days would also take effect as a tenancy from year to year for the
purposes of the Act, being interests 'less than a tenancy from year to year'.

Although not entirely unproblematical [2.03], it seems always to be
assumed in decisions and to be implicit in section 2 (1) that a short fixed
term of this kind will *only* take effect as a tenancy of an agricultural
holding when 'transformed' by section 2 into a tenancy from year to year.

(iii) Licences to occupy agricultural land

There is no limit to the length of a licence which can be transformed into
a tenancy from year to year. However, the need for the grant to undergo
the 'necessary modifications' consistently with its own nature has
produced various requirements which any licensee must show are
satisfied if he is to achieve the status of tenant under the Act.

(a)   The licence must grant the right to *occupy* land and not simply the
      right to take produce from it: *Wyatt* v. *King* (1951).
(b)   The licence must grant the licensee *exclusive occupation* of the land,
      at least for agricultural purposes, so that he can exclude any other
      person including his grantor during the period of his licence:
      Bahamas International Trust Co. Ltd v. *Threadgold* (1974). A licence
      which does not grant exclusive occupation cannot take effect as a
      tenancy, since exclusive occupation is an essential characteristic of a
      lease. The point was first decided in the well-known case of
      Harrison-Broadley v. *Smith* (1964), which has subsequently proved
      to be the inspiration of numerous arrangements designed to avoid
      granting protection under the legislation. In that case, a working
      farmer was taken into partnership by a landowner. The Court of
      Appeal decided that the farmer's right to enter and occupy the
      farmed land was a licence granted to him necessarily for the
      purposes of the partnership and that as such it was not an exclusive
      licence which allowed him to exclude his grantor-partner. As a mere
      licence, it did not constitute 'a contract of tenancy' and, being non-
      exclusive, it was not converted into a tenancy by section 2. There
      was, therefore, no agricultural holding and the farmer was not
      protected by the 1948 Act. Farming partnerships have consequently
      been promoted as structures which fall outside the Acts and have
      enjoyed much popularity for this reason. They are discussed further
      in the following chapter.
(c)   The licence must be supported by *consideration* if it is to be
      transformed by section 2. *Goldsack* v. *Shore* (1950) decided that the
      'agreements' to be transformed by the section are contracts

'enforceable at law, that is to say (contracts) supported by valuable consideration flowing to the grantor from the grantee'.

If the consideration is monetary, it need not be the full market value of the holding: *Collier* v. *Hollinshead* (1984). Non-monetary consideration may also suffice: in *Verrall* v. *Farnes* (1966) the work of a 'trial' tenant was treated as valuable consideration. In *Mitton* v. *Farrow* (1980), a more unusual case, an occupier who was let onto the land before any tenancy had been agreed but who anticipated such a tenancy, and who thus undertook substantial work in clearing the land, was seen to have given consideration. He

'was let into possession as a licensee and the grant of the licence was supported by consideration moving from him; that is to say, his undertaking to clean the land ... Mr Farrow could not have abandoned the work of reclaiming the land without becoming liable for at least nominal damages for breach of contract.'

There being an enforceable agreement between the parties, the licence was converted by section 2 and Mr Farrow as deemed to have a fully protected tenancy of the land. Finally, as an example of valuable but non-monetary consideration, in *Epps* v. *Ledger* (1973) a licensee who took possession of agricultural land prior to a grant of a lease and who had, at the grantor's insistence, dissolved his pre-existing agricultural partnership with a third party was held to have given value in these acts of part-performance so that section 2 operated to convert his licence into a tenancy from year to year. Alternatively, it was also held that the acts of part-performance avoided the need for a memorandum in writing of the contract, and that the oral agreement was a binding and enforceable contract for a lease.

A *truly gratuitous* licence will, of course, *escape* transformation by section 2 and will remain revocable at the will of the grantor, subject to reasonable notice being given to the occupier. As the cases quoted above indicate, however, the courts are astute to recognise consideration so that any allegedly gratuitous arrangement must be very carefully considered.

Where the courts identify '*consideration*', the exchange of value, they will tend to assume that it indicates the existence of a legally-binding contract. This is not to say, however, that any exchange at all between the occupier and grantor will necessarily be seen as consideration and will thus lead to the conclusion that a legally binding contract existed. In any particular case the courts will take notice of the context of the agreement and where there are indications that no legally binding agreement was intended these will be given full effect. If, for example, the 'consideration' is ill-defined, or payment is voluntary, or is left entirely to the convenience of the occupier it is most unlikely that a legally enforceable contract between the parties can be deduced. In *Personal Representatives of Gibbs deceased, Russell* v. *Fellows* (1986), for example, a dispute arose over an informal and originally friendly arrangement between neighbours. Miss Gibbs, an elderly lady, owned a field which she allowed Mr Fellows to use to graze his cattle. They were moved out from July-November each year. In return for these limited grazing rights, Miss Gibbs was originally provided with unspecified quantities of milk and manure and subsequently manure and wood. When, ultimately, Miss Gibbs' executors wished to obtain possession of the field, it was argued on behalf of Mr Fellows that there was a tenancy protected by section 2 of the 1948 Act.

The Court of Appeal unanimously found that in these circumstances there was no binding legal relationship between the parties. This was 'one of those arrangements that are so often made between neighbours'. The lack of definition of what Miss Gibbs was to receive 'militates most strongly against there being any legal binding agreement'. Although the 'small return' offered by Mr Russell could arguably have constitued consideration, the whole context of the agreement, as partly evidenced by the informality of the duty to 'pay' suggested that there was not an enforceable right in the occupier. The court in this case also took the opportunity of counselling against the too-ready presumption of a contract from the chimera of consideration.

If this case is contrasted with *James* v. *Lock* (1978), the importance of the 'context' of the agreement is highlighted. *James* v. *Lock* is frequently cited as a 'hard' case where the rigour of the 1948 Act transformed a purely friendly agreement into a full agricultural tenancy. Admittedly, in *James* v. *Lock* the agreement was apparently reached in an informal chat 'over the farm gate'. However, very specific (and not negligible) amounts of money were stipulated to be payable by the occupier for the use of the land, and the use itself was far from intermittent. There is no doubt that an enforceable agreement was intended and the precision with which the consideration was defined merely underlines that. However, the terms of the agreement, and in particular whether the occupier's use was contractually limited to grazing and/or mowing for a specified period of the year were much more difficult to prove, and it was ultimately the problem of detail rather than the more fundamental question of whether a contract had been brought into being, which was the grantor's downfall in the case.

Situations where section 2 does *not* operate are clearly *advantageous* to the *landowner*, since he retains there a high degree of control over the land use, and is able to revoke the licence as he wishes. These and other cases where no agricultural tenancy is created are examined in further detail in the next chapter.

Chapter 3

Arrangements Which Avoid Full Statutory Protection

3.01 Introductory

Many prospective landlords of agricultural land, anxious about the effect of the security of tenure provisions of the legislation (and between 1976 and 1984, even more anxious about the statutory succession rights) have carefully scrutinised the various Agricultural Holdings Acts to discover express or implied exceptions and lacunae in the codes of protection. Like tax statutes, the Agricultural Holdings and related Acts have inspired their fair share of schemes for avoidance and even, on occasion, evasion.

The legislation in fact recognises that there are situations where the imposition of a fully-protected agricultural tenancy is inappropriate, and thus specifies various 'exempted' grants from the general scheme. In addition, litigation has demonstrated the precise limitations of sections 1, 2 and 3 of the 1986 Act, and has thus identified implied exceptions to the Act. In this chapter we consider arrangements which do not enjoy the full protection of the Agricultural Holdings Act, either because they do not constitute negotiated or imposed tenancies of agricultural holdings, or because they are merely 'insecure' agricultural tenancies.

EXPRESSLY EXEMPTED ARRANGEMENTS

3.02 Grants to employees, office holders etc.

Section 1(1) of the Act states that agricultural land granted by 'a contract under which the land is let to the tenant during his continuance in any office, appointment or employment held under the landlord' is not an agricultural holding.

The provision originated in the 1948 Act. It clearly applies to agricultural land let to an agricultural worker or to a manager employed by the farmer-landowner. In any such case it is the *substance* of the relationship which is all-important and not, for example, the label given by the parties to their arrangement. For example, where in fact the 'manager' effectively operates as an independent businessman, paying a fixed amount for the holding in rent but taking the risks associated with the enterprise and keeping the profits, the reality of a tenancy rather than a contract of employment is likely to be recognised.

Section 1(1) also dovetails together the provisions of the agricultural holdings legislation and the Rent (Agriculture) Act 1976. An agricultural worker who leases a house provided by or on behalf of his employer at a low rent will be protected the 1976 Act if he is a 'qualifying worker' for the purposes of that statute [14.05].

3.03 Section 2: 'insecure' grants approved by the Minister

It is possible to grant a short-term lease or a licence of agricultural land without conferring on the occupier any statutory rights *if* the grant is approved by the Minister before it takes effect. Section 2(1) expressly provides there where the Minister's approval of the arrangement has been obtained in advance, the section's 'statutory magic' [2.08] is not effective to transform the short term lease, or the licence, into a tenancy from year to year. Thus, the imposition on the parties of a full agricultural lease is avoided and no agricultural holding is constituted. Section 2 does not apply to agreements made before 1st March 1948: para 1, Schedule 12.

In this provision the legislation expressly recognises that, although its aim of promoting the interests of agriculture is usually best served by giving tenants security and compensation rights (regardless of the intention of grantor and occupier during their negotiations), nevertheless there will be situations where a genuine agricultural advantage is achieved by permitting a finite grant to take effect exactly as proposed by the grantor and thus denying the tenant subsequent security. In making such 'insecure' grants dependent on the Minister's scrutiny and approval, however, the intention seems clearly to limit the opportunities for 'giving the go by' to the Act to those occasions where a genuine agricultural reason can be shown for denying the occupier his 'normal' statutory rights.

The practice under section 2 has traditionally been for the intending grantor to apply unilaterally for Ministry approval, often before any particular tenant or licensee has been approached or even identified. In this way the grantor can be confident that he may make an 'insecure' grant of the land in question for the desired period before entering into any negotiations. It is, of course, crucial that he observes the requirements of the section if he is to obtain an effective approval which preserves the merely transient character of the occupier's rights.

(i) Section 2: relevant types of grant

The Minister's power under section 2 is limited to approving 'insecure' *lettings* 'for an interest less than a tenancy from year to year', which include lettings for one year exactly: *Bernays* v. *Prosser* (1963) and *licences* of any duration for the occupation of agricultural land. In other words, his power is limited to approving interests which would otherwise be 'transformed' by the section into tenancies from year to year. Although the statute imposes no maximum period for a licence to be eligible for approval, in practice it is most unlikely that approval would be granted to a licence for more than three years in the first instance. In practice, therefore, the section is used to validate insecure *short* lettings and licences. Arrangements limited to grazing and/or mowing for a specified period of the year only do not require Ministry approval. They are expressly stated to take effect outside the protection of the Act by section 2(3)(a) [3.05].

It should perhaps be stressed here that merely restricting the occupier's interest to 364 days will not *of itself* prevent the constitution of a fully protected agricultural holding. 364 day lettings and licences will normally be converted into tenancies from year to year by section 2, *unless* they have received prior ministerial approval, *or* are only for grazing and/or mowing *or* are purely gratuitous. Thus, for example, the very common 364 day grants for say, carrot growing, unless approved under section 2, give the occupier *full statutory rights*: whilst extra-legal considerations encourage him to move on, he is not under any legal obligation to do so.

(ii) Section 2: what is approved?

Under the 1948 Act, section 2 required that 'the letting or grant' was the subject of the Minister's approval, and it was held in *Epsom and Ewell Borough Council* v. *C. Bell (Tadworth) Ltd* (1983) that therefore

> 'the Minister was not concerned with the particular terms of the agreement to be entered into. There is nothing which requires the Minister to approve the terms of the agreement which, *ex hypothesi*, has not then been entered into and, indeed, may not by then have been finally settled ... [The Minister] was not concerned with ... the rent or anything else of that nature ... He was not concerned with the terms of the particular agreement.'

Thus, as previously mentioned, the practice with section 2 applications has been for the intending landlord/grantor to approach the local Ministry office and ask for approval for an intended grant, specifying only the land concerned, the length of the proposed grant, the nature of the proposed grant (lease or licence) and the circumstances which he felt made a full agricultural tenancy inappropriate. It has not been necessary even to have identified a prospective occupier and the availability of details of the grant such as rent etc. has not been thought necessary to enable the Minister to reach a decision. Thus, section 2 has usually been the subject of unilateral applications solely by grantors looking, in effect, for 'outline' approval of a future arrangement.

In the 1986 consolidation, however, section 2 refers to 'the agreement' being approved by the Minister before it takes effect. This suggests very clearly that a different requirement from the earlier Act, as interpreted in *Bell*, is imposed, a requirement that the basic elements of a bilateral arrangement should now be the subject of scrutiny. Whilst such a change would align the procedures of section 2 more closely to those of section 5 for the grant of insecure fixed term agricultural leases [2.05] [3.09] there is of course the strongest possible presumption that a consolidation Act does *not* make any substantive changes in the law. The effect of this change in wording in the legislation is therefore in doubt. In practice, local ministry offices seem at present to continue as before, requiring for section 2 approvals only a unilateral application by the grantor with sufficient information merely to assess the purpose and extent of the proposed grant. Even under this relatively informal regime, however, it now seems most unlikely that a 'blanket' approval of all grants by a named grantor/applicant would be given as was done in the peculiar case of *Finbow* v. *Air Ministry* (1963). In that case, approval had been granted for

'every licence to occupy and use as agricultural land any land which belongs to [the Secretary for Air] ... for any estate or interest and which is at the time of such licence being managed on behalf of [him].'

The Minister, in granting this approval, had only 'scrutinised' the identity of the grantor, and had presumably inferred from this a justification of 'national security' for *any* grant which might be made. Although the case may well be correct, especially in view of its particular facts and its date, there is no doubt that other items of information regarding intended 'insecure' grants will now be required from any applicant, and individual grants, identified by commencement date and duration, are always likely to be specified. Indeed, as indicated above, there is at least an argument based on the wording of the present section 2 that application procedures should become even more precise and demanding.

(iii) Section 2: the timing of the approval

Section 2 requires that the agreement was approved by the Minister 'before it was entered into'. It is of paramount importance that this requirement is observed: approvals cannot be backdated and a grant which takes effect before an approval is given will be transformed by the remaining provision of section 2 into an agricultural tenancy and the grantor's advantage will have been lost. It is *always* therefore advisable to apply for approvals in good time.

Where grantors are inefficient in this regard, very small time margins may make all the difference to the status of their grant. The Minister's approval is effective from the moment it is signed by or on behalf of the Minister. In *Bedfordshire County Council* v. *Clarke* (1974) the council, as grantor, sought to rely on a ministerial approval signed on the same day as their licence to Clarke took effect. They were unable to show that the approval was signed earlier in the day than Clarke signed (and thus made effective) his licence agreement and the council were thus unable to rely on the approval. Clarke therefore was found to have a full agricultural tenancy of the land with security of tenure and all statutory rights, rather than the 'insecure' licence intended by the council. Such a difficult problem will only arise where the grantor has failed to take appropriate care over his (or their) paperwork: the case is a very salutary tale. The burden of proof in such a case is always on the party who seeks to rely on the approval (usually the grantor). That party must be able to show that the approval *preceded* the grant.

Where a series of successive grants is made, each successive grant must be approved: the approval of the original grant will not endure nor will it automatically renew itself to cover later grants: *Secretary of State for Social Services* v. *Beavington* (1982)

(iv) Section 2: the effect of approval

It seems to be generally agreed that where a letting or licence is granted with Ministerial approval under section 2, no agricultural holding is constituted, even where a short lease is given [2.03]. Thus the occupier under such a grant has neither security of tenure nor any of the other statutory rights (or duties), since the remainder of the 1986 Act is inapplicable.

(v) Section 2: no appeal

There is no appeal against the Minister's decision whether or not to grant approval to a proposed insecure grant. His exercise of discretion would, of course, be subject to judicial review but this procedure will not lead to a re-examination of the *merits* of the application.

3.04 When is approval for an 'insecure' grant appropriate? Sections 2 and 5

As has already been mentioned in detail in Chapter 2, the·1984 Act introduced a new type of agricultural tenancy: the fixed-term 'insecure' tenancy of an agricultural holding granted in accordance with what is now section 5 of the 1986 Act. It will be recalled that the procedures of section 5 require a *joint* application from both landlord and tenant for the Minister's approval of their *joint* decision to exclude the effect of section 3 of the Act from the fixed term lease for between one and five years which they intend to conclude. If approval is given, there must be a written lease which must include a declaration that section 3 does not apply to it. Such an arrangement will constitute an agricultural holding with all statutory rights and duties for its duration *except* that the tenant will not have security of tenure. Instead, the lease will end by effluxion of time when the contractually agreed period is over.

Section 2 and section 5 arrangements are therefore quite different in procedure and substance. However, in both sections, the effective operation of an 'insecure' grant is dependent on the Minister's prior approval. Neither section gives any indication how the Minister might exercise his discretion in considering approvals. However, the Ministry and the Welsh Office Agriculture Department have clear guidelines on the use of both sections and in 1984 these guidelines were given broad publicity for the first time.

The applicant(s) must decide whether their case is best accommodated by

(a) an insecure lease of one year or less: section 2;
(b) an insecure licence: section 2; or
(c) a fixed-term tenancy with no additional security of tenure: section 5.

The Ministry cannot make that decision for the parties, nor will it advise on this point in individual cases. The decision is for the applicant(s) in the light of their independent adviser's opinions.

However, the 1984 Ministry document helps grantors and their advisers by indicating situations when approval may be justified, and by indicating the maximum duration of grant likely to be approved.

The Ministry document stresses that the policy is to restrict approvals to cases where it would be unreasonable to expect the landlord to let his land on a full agricultural tenancy. Normally such cases will be temporary situations, although in some cases where the overriding use of the land is non-agricultural, a longer term arrangement may be permitted.

It is clear from the document that approval will not normally be given to any grant longer than five years. A series of successive short lettings may be permitted if the landlord can justify them. It is perhaps worth pointing out that although under the Act the Minister's power to approve licences is *not* subject to *any* maximum period, nevertheless the Ministry's 'informal extra-statutory guidelines' seem quite explicit on the application of the five year upper limit in practice.

The 'usual' circumstances for approval, with the maximum period usually approved are as follows:

(1) Specialist cropping: grants to specialist growers requiring 'clean land' (for example, carrots or brassicas): 1 year.
(2) Amalgamation or regrouping of the holding by the landlord: a transitional 'insecure' grant may be approved: 3 years.
(3) Allowing a prospective purchaser to work the land before the completion of a sale: 3 years.
(4) A temporary arrangement pending the sale or letting of the land or, for example, on the death of a tenant before reletting or selling: 3 years.
(5) A trial tenancy for an inexperienced tenant: 5 years.
(6) An interim arrangement where there is a definite intention that the landlord's son or daughter will take over the holding: 5 years.
(7) Where non-agricultural development is intended in the near future. In such a case a normal agricultural tenancy would be expected. If it could be demonstrated that if such a tenancy were granted the tenant's claim for statutory compensation might exceed the rent paid, then an insecure grant may be approved: 5-7 years.
(8) Allotment land temporarily surplus to requirements: 5 years.
(9) Overriding operational or training requirements affecting government (especially Ministry of Defence) land: 5 years.

Finally, the document stresses that these categories are *not* definitive, and that if a landlord has land, 'usually a small area', which he would like to let subject to an insecure grant he should seek advice from the local Divisional Office of the Ministry or Agriculture Department. It is in any event always advisable to approach the local Divisional Office informally before making any such grant since some local offices use particular, and very precise, 'informal guidelines': for example, refusing to authorise a limited let of the same field in two consecutive years. Such guidelines, although not based on any statutory authority, are in practice very difficult to challenge.

Table 3.1 summarises and compares the sections 2 and 5.

Table 3.1 Insecure grants: sections 2 and 5 compared

	Section 2	Section 5
Type of grant:	Lease: 1 year or less. Licence: any period. s.2(2)(a),(b).	lease: 2-5 years: s.5(2).
What is 'approved'?	Agreement for the grant: s.2(1).	Agreement between parties that s.3 will not apply to lease: s.5 (2)(a).
Who applies?	Not clear. In practice, grantor.	Landlord and tenant jointly: s.5 (2)(b).
Form of application:	No statutory form. Letter to Divisional Office.	Must be 'in writing': s.5(2)(b). Apply to Divisional Office.
When is approval effective?	When signed by/for Minister: *Beds. C.C.* v. *Clarke* (1974).	When notified by Minister to applicants: s.5(2)(c).
When must approval be obtained?	'Before the agreement was entered into': s.2(1).	'Before the grant of (the) tenancy': s.5(2).
Formal grant required?	No. Oral grant would suffice.	Yes. Contract of tenancy must be 'in writing' *and* must include statement that s.3 does not apply: s.5(3).
Consequences of approval:	No agricultural holding constituted [2.03].	Agricultural holding without security of tenure.

Despite their apparent similarities, the chart highlights the differences especially in procedure and effect between these two sections. It cannot be sufficiently stressed that an applicant *must* satisfy *all* the requirements appropriate to the section he is relying on. Advice should be sought from the local Divisional Office when *any* such grant is in prospect. Local officers are most helpful and informative as to the appropriate procedures.

3.05 Grazing and mowing agreements

Section 2(3)(a) provides that an agreement for a lease or licence to occupy land

> 'made (whether or not it expressly so provides) in contemplation of the use of the land only for grazing or mowing (or both) during some specified period of the year'

will not be transformed into a tenancy from year to year and thus into an agricultural tenancy. A grant made in accordance with section 2(3)(a) therefore confers no security of tenure nor any other statutory right on the occupier. Where the section is satisfied, the grantor can be confident that he will be entitled to vacant possession when the termination date arrives. It is *essential* that the various requirements of the section are observed if this is to be achieved and in particular that the grant must be restricted both as to use *and* duration: *Scene Estate Ltd* v. *Amos* (1957). The burden of proving that a grant satisfies section 2(3) and therefore gives no security to the occupier lies on the grantor: *Scene Estate Ltd* v. *Amos, Lory* v. *Brent London Borough Council* (1971).

The grant of grazing rights under section 2(3) is not a 'device' to avoid the protection of the Act. It is a transaction designated by the Act as one which does not create an agricultural holding. If it were otherwise there would be widespread reluctance to let areas of good grazing land: per Oliver LJ in *South West Water Authority* v. *Palmer* (1983).

Nevertheless, some grantors have been energetic in their attempts to exploit the section and its predecessor, the so-called proviso to section 2(1) of the 1948 Act, and have had some degree of success. Remember that section 2 does *not* apply to agreements made *before* 1st March 1948: para 1, Schedule 12.

(i) Use

It is the actual permitted use expressed and contemplated in the agreement of the land which is conclusive. In *Lory* v. *Brent London Borough Council* a detailed written lease for a year less one day included a limited right to plough 'in the interests of good husbandry and crop rotation basis' for the purpose of maintaining grassland in good condition for grazing. It was held that this grant took effect as a tenancy from year to year since it contemplated uses other than grazing and/or mowing, and the fact that the 'other uses' were intended to promote the primary, grazing use was irrelevant.

(ii) Duration

'Some specified period of the year' includes lettings up to and including 364 days: *Reid* v. *Dawson* (1955). The words 'specified period' have not been interpreted strictly by the courts as meaning a period necessarily fixed by dates but will include 'any period which is so named or described as to be identifiable by persons versed in agricultural matters': Lord Macintosh in *Mackenzie* v. *Laird* (1959) adopted in *Watts* v. *Yeend* (1987). Seasonal grants are therefore within the section.

(iii) 'Contemplation'

According to Denning LJ (as he was then) in *Scene Estate Ltd* v. *Amos* the word, 'contemplation' was present in the section 'to protect a landlord who has not expressly inserted a provision that the grant is for grazing only ... or that it is for a specified part of the year but, nevertheless, both parties know that that is what is contemplated'. The word has certainly given some difficulties of construction to the courts. From their various decisions the following points should be noted:

(a) It is the 'contemplation' of both parties which is to be sought, not that of the grantor alone: *Scene Estate Ltd* v. *Amos*.

(b) In the same case, it was made clear that it was the parties' contemplation at the *inception* of the grant, or each of a series of grants, which was relevant.

(c) 'Contemplation' seems to approximate to 'intention'. It is stronger than a mere 'expectation', and it must be sufficiently certain to be capable of being given effect in law: *Short Bros (Plant) Ltd* v. *Edwards* (1979).

(d) The contemplation of the parties is normally to be deduced solely from the terms of their agreement. Extrinsic evidence is only permissible in two situations: (i) where the agreement is silent, containing no express limitations on user and/or time; (ii) where the agreement is thought to be a sham, and not a genuine record of the understanding between the parties. However, if an agreement contains *express* provisions concerning user and duration, it will in all other circumstances be *conclusive* and the courts may not go behind it: Parker J in *Scene Estate Ltd*. Two contrasting cases may be quoted to show the application of this approach.

In *Scene Estate Ltd* v. *Amos* land was let to Amos for grazing for three months under a written grant which clearly satisfied what is now section 2(3). Subsequently, 21 identical 3-monthly grants were made until, five years after his original entry, the landlords gave Amos notice of termination. He argued that, at the outset, it was 'contemplated' by both parties that the original grant would be renewed for at least one year's occupation and therefore their agreement was not within the section but instead took effect under section 2(1) as a tenancy from year to year. The Court of Appeal found for the landlords, holding that the written agreements were genuine and therefore decisive. Although the Court found that both parties 'expected' the original arrangement to be renewed, this 'expectation' had not been communicated. There was no binding agreement between them as to such renewal and nothing sufficiently definite to amount to their 'contemplation' was proved.

> 'Each party had it at the back of his mind that the agreement would be renewed ... every three months but each kept it to himself and did not actually make a stipulation about it.'

In the absence of any such express stipulation, the court found no justification for looking behind the document. They fully recognised the reason for adopting this form of grant: the landlords did not want to let Amos have the land on a tenancy which, under the Act, would become indefinite, indeed almost permanent, whilst Amos was ready to agree to any legal arrangement, knowing that unless he entered into an agreement which enabled the landlords to get possession when they desired he would not get the grazing at all. For the landlords, surely, a case of silence being golden, especially when compared with *Short Bros (Plant) Ltd* v. *Edwards*.

In *Short Bros*, the prospective landlords stated to the tenant during the preliminary negotiations that he would be allowed to use the land only for grazing, that he would be granted a succession of written agreements each for six months' limited use of the land and that there was no reason why such an arrangement should not continue 'for several years'.

The tenant signed the first of these agreements in 1963, relying on the assurance of renewals and subsequently further agreements were forthcoming which left him in untroubled occupation of the land until 1977, when the owners sought possession. Edwards then argued as Amos had done that he was protected by the 1948 Act. The Court of Appeal supported the decision in *Amos* on its own facts and repeated that there is nothing intrinsically objectionable for the purposes of section 2(3) in a series of written agreements stretching well over a year. However, on the facts of *Short Bros* they found that the written agreements were not accurate representations of the understanding between the parties, since there was an agreement between them that renewals would give the tenant 'several years' security and the tenant had relied on this assurance. The true 'contemplation of the parties' was not, therefore, limited to occupation for 'some specified period of the year' and consequently the grant constituted an agricultural tenancy within the 1948 Act. Any such collateral contract relied on by the tenant to disturb the evidence of a written grant must, however, be clear and unequivocal: *South West Water Authority* v. *Palmer* (1983).

(iv) An agreement

Where section 2(3)(a) is in issue it is particularly important to show that there was *consensus* between landlord and tenant on the *two* limitations of user and duration.

In some situations the difficulty will be merely evidential. In *Midgley* v. *Stott* (1977) both parties to the original, oral, agreement were dead and the court was obliged to infer the terms of their agreement from the way in which they had behaved.

In other cases where a party pleads 'no consensus', the matter may be resolved by considering the parties' acts *objectively*. This 'rule' from *Smith* v. *Hughes* (1871) was stated by Blackburn LJ in that case in the well-known dictum:

'if whatever a man's real intention may be, he so conducts himself that a reasonable man would believe that he was assenting to the terms proposed by the other party, and that other party upon that belief, enters into the contract with him, the man thus conducting himself would be equally bound as if he had intended to agree the other party's terms.'

In *Chaloner* v. *Bower* (1983), for example, the occupier had negotiated a series of annual grants with the plaintiff's husband and latterly with the plaintiff herself. There was no doubt that the earlier grants had been merely grasskeep agreements. However, the occupier had in fact used the land for a number of agricultural purposes other than grazing and mowing and it seemed that for a number of years the subjective intention of the occupier had been to obtain an unlimited grant whereas the subjective intention of the plaintiff had been to continue the established pattern of grasskeep arrangements. On this level, therefore, there was no consensus. However, the Court of Appeal, using the approach indicated in *Smith* v. *Hughes* held that on the facts the defendant.

'did so conduct himself that he must be taken to be asking for, and entering into an agreement for, a licence for grazing purposes for a limited period ... even though there is a finding that the defendant did not actually contemplate letting for grazing for a specified period only, he nonetheless will be taken to have contemplated such a licence.'

In *James* v. *Lock* (1978), on the other hand, the Court of Appeal considered that an informal conversation 'over the farm gate' between two neighbours was to be construed as the grant of a licence which was transformed into a tenancy from year to year by section 2(1), and not 'merely' a grazing licence, since no appropriate use limitation could objectively be identified in their agreement.

3.06 Grantor's limited interest

Section 2(3)(b) provides that any agreement made by a person whose interest is less than a tenancy from year to year which has not been transformed into such a tenancy by section 2(1) will not grant the occupier an interest which will be converted by that section. This is a little used provision.

IMPLIED EXCEPTIONS TO THE ACT

3.07 *Gladstone* v. *Bower*: lettings for between one and two years

A tenancy for a fixed term of between one and two years will attract no statutory security of tenure for the tenant: *Gladstone* v. *Bower* (1960). The case concerned a fixed term tenancy of agricultural land for a term of eighteen months.

Section 2 treats tenancies of one year exactly, or any lesser term, as tenancies from year to year: section 2(1), 2(2)(a). Section 3 causes a statutory tenancy from year to year to arise at the expiry of a fixed term tenancy of two years or more: section 3(1). Terms such as eighteen months, however, fall into a lacuna between these two provisions and thus enjoy no security of tenure but terminate on their contractual term date, when the landlord will be entitled to vacant possession.

Gladstone v. *Bower* exposed this particular omission for the 1948 Act. The lacuna remains to the advantage of the prospective landlords and indeed the refinements of the statutory succession scheme introduced in 1984 confirm the correctness of the decision: see now Schedule 6 para. 6(b). A series of such leases could, of course, also be granted so long as no allegation of sham could be supported: a collateral stipulation on renewal would destroy the effectiveness of the grants since the agreement then would be subject to section 3, being in substance an agreement for two years or more.

Although it is clear that a '*Gladstone* v. *Bower*' tenancy does not confer security of tenure under the Agricultural Holdings Act, it has not been decided whether such a grant is for its duration a lease of an agricultural holding. This point is discussed at length above [2.03].

3.08 Gratuitous licences

Goldsack v. *Shore* (1950) held that a purely gratuitous licence quite unsupported by valuable consideration remained revocable at the will of the licensor subject only, as appropriate, to reasonable notice. Many informal neighbourly agreements may fall within this heading, although the courts are often astute to find valuable consideration, whether monetary or not.

However, where the amount of consideration is unspecified, the implication may be that the arrangement was not intended to be an 'agreement' enforceable at law, but merely a gesture of goodwill: *Russell* v. *Fellows* [2.08(iii)(c)].

3.09 Licences which do not grant exclusive occupation

It has been clear since *Harrison- Broadley* v. *Smith* [2.08(iii)(b)] affirmed in *Bahamas International Trust Co. Ltd* v. *Threadgold* (1974) that licences which do not grant the occupier exclusive occupation of land as against the grantor and all third parties, at least for agricultural purposes, cannot be and will not be transformed into tenancies from year to year by section 2. When granting such a licence the grantor may therefore be confident that the licensee will not enjoy any security of tenure: the licence will remain revocable with reasonable notice.

Merely reserving a right of access over the land granted away will not suffice to interfere with the licensee's exclusive occupation: *Lampard* v. *Barker* (1984). Similarly, it was said *obiter* in *Secretary of State for Social Services* v. *Beavington* (1982) that a licensee farming land which was subject to (i) a right of way, (ii) an easement for drains, (iii) access by tree surgeons to a tree on the land, (iv) occasional entry by cross-country runners and (v) even more occasional entries by confused patients from an adjacent hospital *did* enjoy exclusive possession of that land. The various intrusions were all at most intermittent, and none was inconsistent with the exclusive nature of the grant to the licensee. In practice, although 'non-exclusive occupation' is often pleaded by grantors seeking to recover possession, it is most frequently successful where there is a partnership arrangement: *Harrison-Broadley* was of course just such a case.

3.10 Partnerships

According to the Partnership Act 1890, a partnership is 'a common venture with a view to profit'. Partners suffer the disadvantages of full personal liability for partnership debts and they are also under a duty to participate actively in the partnership enterprise. However, partly at least because they can be used as a device to avoid conferring security of tenure under the Agricultural Holdings Act, farming partnerships of various types flourish and may provide a convenient structure for an effective farming business.

It is, of course, essential that any partnership relied on to avoid the Act is a true partnership in substance and not merely a sham arrangement disguising a simple tenancy. The name given to the arrangement by the parties is not conclusive, and for example a 'management partnership' between a landowner and a working farmer in which the landowner's sole participation was the periodic receipt of a fixed sum of money would be, to say the least, open to the suggestion that it was in fact a straightforward, and protected, tenancy. Shams here, as elsewhere, are vulnerable to the scrutiny of litigation, although the burden on a party seeking to controvert a written partnership agreement to show that it is merely a sham is very heavy.

Apart from landowner–working farmer partnerships in the *Harrison–Broadley* mould, two common arrangements in agriculture are the family farming partnership and the 'institutional subsidiary' partnership.

In family farming partnerships, it is common for a landowner to lease agricultural land to a partnership of himself and other family members. Although the doubt raised in *Rye* v. *Rye* (1962) now seems to have receded, so that the possibility of granting a lease to oneself and others seems assured, nevertheless participation as a partner in such an arrangement may pose problems if on the landowner's death one of his relatives lays claim to a succession tenancy under Part IV of the 1986 Act: *Brooks* v. *Brown* (1985). This is discussed further below in Chapter 10. At this point it is sufficient to say that in any partnership where a succession claim is foreseeable great care must be taken with the partnership agreement which will effectively govern the partners' title to the land used for their business.

Many institutional landowners have adopted the practice of leasing agricultural land to a partnership comprised of a wholly owned subsidiary company and working farmers, with a provision to be included in the partnership deed that the tenancy will terminate if the partnership is dissolved. Apart from denying the working farmers exclusive occupation of the land, such an arrangement was until recently believed to offer a second attraction to the landlords, as it was thought that in practice the existence of the 'company' partner would render impossible effective service of the various counter notices which trigger much of the statutory protection. Such notices must be served by *all* joint tenants and it was foreseeable that a captive company would not participate in an action against the interests of its owner. However, it is now clear from *Sykes* v. *Land* (1984) that one joint tenant can oblige another to join in such service.

It is also of interest that in *Featherstone* v. *Staples* (1986) Slade LJ gave as his opinion, *obiter*, that where the landlord himself is also one of the joint tenants his concurrence will be waived.

3.11 Contractor or manager agreements

Where a farmer or a farming partnership is employed as a contractor to work agricultural land there will be no tenancy protected by the Act as the contractors will merely enjoy a non-exclusive licence to enter to perform their contract.

Where a manager is employed to farm the land, the same argument would apply. If he were in fact able to show a lease, it would remain outside the Act by reason of section 1(1), excluding office holders' tenancies from the protection of the Act.

3.12 Share farming: joint ventures

In recent years occupiers of agricultural land and their advisers have expended much energy in formulating structures for collaborative farming enterprises which avoid the traditional forms of either agricultural tenancies or partnerships. Two principal considerations have led towards this effort. Firstly, the landowner's desire to farm his land efficiently whilst yet avoiding the 'burden' of creating protected agricultural tenancies which drastically reduce his control over it (particularly through the provisions relating to security, succession and rent review). Secondly, the ever-present desire to obtain the optimum benefit from the tax laws: merely receiving rent attracts few tax advantages and partnership taxation may also be disadvantageous.

The arrangements devised to overcome these difficulties are now increasingly widespread and are popularly known as 'share farming' arrangements or 'joint ventures'. Neither term is a legal term of art, however, and, in legal analysis, these arrangements are a species of 'simple' *farming contract* which does not constitute the parties' landlord and tenant, partners or employer and employee but merely equal contracting parties whose liabilities remain entirely separate, whose contributions are defined by the agreement between them, whose responsibility for planning and managing the farming enterprise is *joint* and whose rewards are an agreed share of the revenue, (not profit) of that enterprise.

The contractual form is almost infinitely flexible but an example of such a share farming arrangement is one whereby the occupier or owner of the land contributes the right to farm the land, the buildings and the fixed equipment (essentially the capital costs) and the farmer contributes essentially labour and working machinery whilst both *together* participate (albeit in varying degrees) in the management and planning of the exercise throughout the farming calender. To avoid the creation of a tenancy it is essential that the landowner retains possession of the land and does *not* grant exclusive possession to the farmer; crops remain the property of the landowner until severed, all livestock where jointly owned are each shared in an agreed proportion. To avoid the implication of a partnership, there should be *no* element of joint and several liability for the debts and liabilities of the farming enterprise: both parties must be separately responsible for the liability each incurs.

Such an arrangement has obvious attractions for both parties. The landowner participates in the effective farming of his land without necessarily being involved in the day to day management of the farm or the cost of providing labour and equipment. He does not run the risk of losing the right to vacant possession. The farmer exploits his own skills in both agriculture and management without needing to involve himself in large capital outlay. It may thus provide an opportunity for a younger farmer to set a foot on the farming ladder or for a more established farmer to build up a very substantial business contract farming in collaboration with a number of landowners. In several areas the indications are that contract farming/share farming/joint ventures will eclipse the traditional agricultural tenancies.

3.13 Contracting out of the Act

All the arrangements described in this chapter are arrangements which fall outside the scope of the 1986 Act, by reason of express or implied exemptions. They are not therefore true examples of 'contracting out', although it is clear that where possible grantors will arrange their affairs in the most advantageous manner and will exploit such loopholes as exist wherever possible. As with the tax laws, in the analogy drawn at the beginning of the chapter, there is nothing legally wrong with *avoiding* the Act.

Contracting out in its true sense ('evading' the Act), however, where parties purport to agree between themselves that the Act will not apply, will not be upheld and the offending clause, conditions or agreement will be struck down and void.

This was first discussed in *Johnson* v. *Moreton* (1980) where the House of Lords held that for reasons of public policy a tenant could not bargain away his rights (in that case to security of tenure) in advance. Any part of the landlord/tenant agreement which purported to restrict or deny the tenant his statutory rights would be void as offending against public policy.

In *Keen* v. *Holland* (1984) the court was again required to consider the protective strength of the Act. In that case, the Court of Appeal held that once an arrangement *in fact* fell within the scope of the 1948 Act, it would automatically and necessarily attract the protection of the Act, regardless of the intention, aims or beliefs of either or both of the parties.

This approach was echoed to some extent in respect of the Rent Act 1977 in the leading House of Lords case of *Street* v. *Mountford* (1985) where the House of Lords similarly held that if an agreement *in substance* creates a lease which falls within the scope of Rent Act protection it will be protected irrespective of the title given to the arrangement by the parties and any express agreement between them purporting to avoid that result.

As Lord Templeman said:

'if the agreement satisfied all the requirements of a tenancy, then the agreement produced a tenancy ... The manufacture of a five-pronged implement for manual digging results in a fork even if the manufacturer, unfamiliar with the English language, insists that he intended to make and has made a spade.'

Finally, in *Featherstone* v. *Staples*, to date the most recent 'avoidance' case to be litigated under the agricultural holdings legislation, the Court of Appeal again stressed the strength of the public policy argument where agricultural holdings are concerned and in striking down an arrangement designed to deny scrutiny to the tenant, Slade LJ commented:

'any contrary decision of this court would be likely to open the door to widespread evasion of the ... Act to the detriment of the security of tenure which Parliament clearly intended to confer on agricultural tenants'

(*Johnson* v. *Moreton* and *Featherstone* v. *Staples* are both discussed in detail below in Chapters 6 and 7.)

Thus, whilst the parties are free, where possible, to arrange their affairs so as to fall outside the Act, any arrangements which fall within the Act will attract its protection, regardless of the aims or intentions of the parties or either of them.

Part II

The Contents of the Contract

Introduction

Two characteristics of the Agricultural Holdings legislation have always been its attempt to standardise the contract of tenancy and its attempt to provide a rent formula which will give the landlord a reasonable return and the tenant a degree of protection. The 1986 Act includes both features.

There is no provision which prescribes in detail a 'standard form' of tenancy. However, the Act does include various sections which give uniformity to tenancies of agricultural holdings. It also gives both parties, landlord and tenant, the right to request that a written tenancy is prepared which conforms with the various requirements of the Act. In this rather indirect way, the parties' freedom of contract is to some extent curtailed and a very basic 'pattern' of tenancy is established. Chapter 4 considers in more details the statutory requirements.

Chapter 5 considers the statutory provisions for rent reviews. The C.L.A./N.F.U. 'package' which formed the basis of the 1984 Agricultural Holdings Act included an agreed rent 'formula' to replace that used since 1948. Although the 'package formula' was somewhat modified in Parliament, the 1984 Act and now the 1986 Act include the new formula. It was believed to represent the 'price' of tenants giving up their succession rights. It was expected, therefore, that the new formula would favour tenants. However, even after two years it is difficult to state exactly what effect, if any, the change has had on rent levels. The details of the new 'formula' and its departure from the older calculation are both discussed in Chapter 5 which also includes a note on distress for rent.

Chapter 4

The Terms of the Tenancy

4.01 Introductory: the sources of tenancy terms

Just as no two holdings are identical, no two tenancy agreements are likely to resemble each other down to every last detail. Several 'standard form' basic contracts exist, but in as far as the *express*, or *contractual*, terms of the tenancy result from negotiations between the particular prospective landlord and tenant, they will necessarily reflect the parties' interests, strengths and weaknesses as well as local conditions and the needs of the time. In these respects each tenancy is unique. A degree of uniformity is imposed, however, by the effect of custom and statute on the parties' agreement.

Custom now plays only an incidental role in modifying agricultural tenancies. It may be expressly incorporated into a tenancy to govern, for example, aspects of valuation for compensation and it may be relevant, where the agreement is silent, in determining local cropping practices or pasture seasons or precise seasonal dates such as Michaelmas. However, customary terms can always be excluded by the parties' express agreement.

Statute in contrast now plays a decisive role in determining the terms of agricultural tenancies. Part II of the Agricultural Holdings Act 1986, and the related statutory instruments, modify the contractual agreement between the parties in several respects, with varying degrees of compulsion.

Firstly, Part II contains *directive* or *fundamental* provisions which aim to make uniform and certain the form and basic content of all agricultural tenancies. Section 6 encourages the preparation of written tenancies which make provision for a number of basic matters specified in Schedule 1 of the Act. If the agreement concluded by the parties does not conform to these statutory requirements, (because it is oral, for example, or because it fails to provide for one or more of the Schedule 1 matters) then either party, landlord or tenant, has the right to request the preparation of an agreement which does satisfy the Act.

If necessary he may procure this by referring the terms of the tenancy to arbitration. It is then for the arbitrator to draft an award in which he aligns the parties' agreement with the statutory requirements.

Whilst there is *no duty* on either party to avail himself of this statutory right to a written tenancy which conforms to the statute, the tendency of the Act towards encouraging, if not enforcing, uniformity is clear.

Similarly, sections 7, 8 and 9 of the Act provide for the preparation in statutory instrument of 'model clauses' to regulate the maintenance, repair and insurance of fixed equipment on the holding. These clauses are to have effect by implication in *every* tenancy. Where a written agreement expressly and directly contradicts them, arbitration is again available to align the agreement with the statutory requirements (and to allocate compensation if appropriate).

The aim of sections 6 to 9, therefore, is to direct or determine the form and basic content of all agricultural tenancies, and to provide a mechanism (arbitration) whereby agreements which diverge from the statutory pattern can be made to conform.

Secondly, the Act contains *overriding* terms which will be implied into all contracts and *cannot be excluded* by agreement between the parties. Most but not all of these strengthen the tenant's hand. All are intended to promote agricultural efficiency.

Thirdly, Part II includes various provisions which *supplement* all contractual agreements *unless expressly excluded*. Where the agreement concluded by the parties is silent, these supplementary provisions will therefore apply.

Table 4.1 illustrates at a glance how the provisions of Part II may modify the parties' negotiated agreement. The provisions concerning rent and distress deserve separate consideration and will be discussed in Chapter 5. This chapter discusses the remaining provisions. They may be grouped or classified in several ways: according to subject matter, 'force' or party benefiting, for example. The draftsman of the 1986 consolidation has arranged Part II in subject matter groups and this chapter follows his example.

4.02 A written tenancy: section 6 and Schedule 1

Oral tenancies of agricultural holdings are perfectly valid. Chapters 2 and 3 gave examples of informal, even 'accidental' tenancies of agricultural holdings which are fully protected under the Act. The Agricultural Holdings Act does not 'outlaw' such oral agreements. However, in the interests of certainty it encourages the preparation of written agreements and it stipulates certain basic matters which all written agreements should

Table 4.1 How the provisions of Part II may modify the parties' negotiated agreement.

Subject matter	Section	Strength	Who benefits	Provision
Written tenancy	6 (Schedule 1)	Directive: fundamental	Both/either	Provision of written comprehensive tenancy agreements, including Sch. 1 matters and model clauses
Fixed equipment	7	Directive: fundamental excluded only by specific allocation of responsibility in written tenancy	Either/neither	Maintenance repair and insurance of fixed equipment
	8	Directive: draws agreement into line with 7.		Arbitration in terms where at variance with M.C.
	9	Contingent on 6, 7, 8		Compensation
	10	May be excluded or modified	Tenant	Removal of fixtures and buildings
	11		Tenant	Provision of fixed equipment but uncertain limited circumstances
Cultivation of land and disposal of produce	14	Overrides where applicable	Either	Reduction of pasture land
	15	Overrides	Tenant	Freedom of cropping
	15 (3)	May be excluded	Landlord	Restriction removal of crops
Miscellaneous	20	Overrides	Tenant	Damage by game
	22	Supplemental	Both/either	Right to require records of condition to be made
	23	Supplemental	Landlord	Power of entry
	24	Overriding	Tenant	No penal rents

deal with.

Section 6 of the act gives either landlord or tenant the right to request a written agreement if

(i)   no written agreement embodying all the terms of their agreement exists; *or*

(ii) an existing written agreement fails to make provision for one or more of the stipulated essential matters listed in Schedule 1.

There is no obligation on either party to avail himself of this right to a written tenancy and therefore the responsibility for eliminating oral agreements rests ultimately with both parties. However, the policy of the Act is clear: to promote writing and thereby certainty and a degree of uniformity. It is always advisable that any request for a written tenancy agreement should itself be made in writing and proof of service on the other party should be obtained.

Section 6 does not specify any formalities for the request for a written tenancy which may therefore be oral or in writing. If the request is refused, the requesting party may refer the terms of the tenancy to arbitration. If the parties cannot agree on the appointment of an arbitrator (i.e. cannot agree on the arbitrator to be appointed) the requesting party may apply to the President of the Royal Institution of Chartered Surveyors (sending the appropriate fee, at present £70) and the President will make an appointment (Schedule 11).

The arbitrator, after a hearing, must make an 'award'. In effect, he is to draft a tenancy agreement for the parties. In doing so he is not given a free hand but is constrained by the express agreements between the parties and the requirements of Schedule 1. Section 6(2) provides that the award must specify the terms of the agreement already existing between landlord and tenant, subject to any variations which they have mutually agreed and, where that original agreement failed to provide for some or any Schedule 1 matter(s), the award must make provision for them either by including 'new' terms agreed between landlord and tenant prompted by the arbitration or, in default of their agreement, by including terms 'having such effect ... as appears to the arbitrator to be reasonable and just between them'. In certain circumstances this may permit the arbitrator to continue to omit provision for some or any Schedule 1 matters but in most cases terms will be included in the award which ensure that all nine matters in the Schedule are provided for in some way. Finally, the award may include any other terms expressly agreed between landlord and tenant which relate to the tenancy (these being over and above their original terms and the Schedule 1 additions).

The arbitrator is given power to vary the rent of the holding if this course of action appears 'equitable' to him as a result of any term which he is required to include in his award. The only 'required' terms are those of the original agreement (as expressly varied where relevant: section 6(2)(a)) and omitted Schedule 1 matters (section 6(2)(b)). If in drafting an award which aligns the original agreement with the statutory requirements the arbitrator is of the opinion that the value of the agreement to one party or the other has changed appreciably, he may take advantage of this power and alter the rent payable. For example, a rental adjustment would be appropriate if the arbitrator's award stipulated that drainage rates previously paid by the tenant in total should be borne by both landlord and tenant on the basis of an assessment by the drainage board. Similarly an agreed clause varying the repairing burden between the parties may also result in an adjustment of the rent.

Once completed, the arbitrator's award will have effect from the date it is made or from a later date if one is specified within its terms. Section 6(4) expressly provides that the award is to have effect

'by way of variation of the agreement previously in force in respect of the tenancy'.

These words, which originated in the 1984 Act, overcome the inconvenient decision in *Hollings* v. *Swindle* (1950) where it was held that a notice to quit given before an arbitrator's award was made thereby rendered ineffective because his award was held to take effect as a *new* contract of tenancy (which of course required a *new* notice to quit). Now, thanks to section 6(4), the award operates merely as a variation of the pre-existing contract and the original notice to quit would therefore remain effective in circumstances such as those in *Hollings*.

Where a *landlord* sets in motion the machinery of section 6 to obtain a written tenancy agreement, the tenant might try to escape the consequences by assigning his interest to a third party before the final agreement or award was effective if such a transaction was permitted. Where the parties' original agreement was in writing it may well contain a provision forbidding any such transaction without the landlord's consent. Sections 6(5) and 6(6) provide that where the parties' original agreement is silent on this matter, any assignment, sub-letting or parting with possession by the tenant must have the landlord's consent *in writing* or the purported transaction will be void if it is attempted by the tenant between the date the landlord requests him to enter into a written tenancy agreement and the date that such an agreement is concluded or an award is effective, as appropriate. Sections 6(5) and 6(6) originated in the 1984 Act. (Once a tenancy or award encompassing the statutory matters is in effect, it will contain such a prohibition on assignment without consent, since this is included as paragraph 9 of Schedule 1 (below) unless the parties have expressly agreed that assignment etc. shall be allowed – a rare occurrence.)

Schedule 1 of the 1986 Act, which is fundamental to the provisions of section 6, lists the following nine 'matters for which provision is to be made in the written tenancy agreements':

(1)   The names of the parties.
(2)   The particulars of the holding.
(3)   The term for which the holding is agreed to be let.

(4)   The rent reserved and the dates on which it is payable.
(5)   The incidence of liability for rates.
(6)   A covenant by the tenant to return to the land the full equivalent manurial value of any harvested crops grown on the holding and destroyed by fire, in so far as such return would be necessary to satisfy the rules of good husbandry.
(7)   A covenant by the tenant to insure all deadstock and harvested crops against damage by fire.
(8)   A power in the landlord of re-entry (of forfeiture) for breach of covenant by the tenant.
(9)   A covenant by the tenant not to assign, sublet or part with possession of the holding without the landlord's consent in writing.

Notice that Schedule 1 operates as a list of 'heads of agreement'; it does not prescribe detailed terms for wholesale incorporation into tenancies, it is merely be checklist of matters with which every tenancy should deal. So long as the parties have turned their minds to those matters and made some provision for each the Act will be satisfied, regardless of the precise agreement actually concluded. For example, as one term of their express agreement, landlord and tenant might agree that the tenant was *not* to insure deadstock against fire damage. If for some reason (perhaps because it was oral) this agreement was referred to arbitration under section 6, the arbitrator would find no fault with the parties' provision for the matter specified in paragraph 7 of Schedule 1: they have included a provision for fire insurance of deadstock and that is all that the Act requires. The *substance* of their provision on this matter, as on the others, is for the parties to determine, with or without the intervention of an arbitrator as appropriate.

Finally it is important to remember that the prohibition on assignment in paragraph 9 of Schedule 1 is an absolute prohibition unless the landlord's *written* consent has been obtained, and his consent may be refused for any reason or for no reason without challenge: there is *no* implied condition in paragraph 9 that consent will not be unreasonably withheld.

4.03 The tenancy: good agricultural practice – the rules of good estate management and good husbandry

Having made provision for the form and basic scope of the tenancy, the remainder of Part II of the 1986 Act includes provisions concerned with the rights, duties and liabilities of the parties. Part II is permeated by reference to the 'rules of good estate management' and 'rules of good husbandry': indeed these latter have already made an appearance since paragraph 6 of Schedule 1 requires that the tenant's liability under the paragraph shall be measured by what

'is required for the fulfilment of his responsibilities to farm in accordance with the rules of good husbandry.'

It is therefore convenient at this point to consider these two sets of rules and their status in contemporary law before looking in more detail at the remaining statutory modifications of the contract of tenancy.

(i) Common law

The common law implies into all tenancies which are otherwise silent on the matter a duty on the *tenant* to

'manage and cultivate the land in a good and husbandlike manner according to the custom of the country'.

This duty has been articulated since at least 1793: *Powley* v. *Walker* (1793). The 'custom of the country' need not date from time immemorial but must have subsisted for a reasonable length of time and be adequately proved: *Tucker* v. *Linger* (1882). It will be evidenced by observable practice on farms of a similar type to the holding in question. The standard of agriculture required of the tenant by this duty is related, therefore, to common local practice. It does not vary with the state of his holding: there is no requirement from the common law for example, that he put good heart into land that he finds in poor condition, nor that he should maintain land which he finds in particularly good condition because of previous high farming. (In fact such situations would normally prompt some express provision to be agreed in the tenancy, thus ousting the implied common law duty.) However, the proper observance over a period of years of the common law requirement to manage and cultivate the land in a good and husbandlike manner will itself create fertility and bring into good heart and condition previously impoverished land. In addition to good and husbandlike farming, the common law also implies a duty on the tenant to keep the premises 'wind and watertight': *Auworth* v. *Johnson* (1832) – again, not a particularly onerous standard to satisfy.

If the tenant is in breach of these common law duties, the landlord (or his assignee) may sue for damages to recover from the tenant the value of the injury to the reversion caused by his bad husbandry. The implied common law covenants are now of very secondary importance as they have been largely overtaken by the more explicit standards of care described and enforced by the Agricultural Holdings legislation. However, an action against the tenant for breach of the common law covenant remains a useful adjunct to the statutory remedies for the landlord in extreme cases. Where, for example, by bad husbandry a tenant has allowed land to deteriorate to such an extent that on re-letting the landlord finds it necessary to allow a rent-free or reduced rent period to the new tenant whilst he restores the land to good condition, the landlord may recover the rent lost from the former tenant at fault.

In contrast to the tenant's position, the common law implied *no* duties on the *landlord*, nor did it imply any rights or benefits into the tenancy in the tenant's favour against the landlord, except for a closely circumscribed right to emblements, which in certain circumstances entitled the tenant to harvest crops planted during the currency of his tenancy. This right was so closely qualified that it was of little value in practice to the tenant.

(ii) The statutory standards

The statutory descriptions of the rules of good estate management and good husbandry are found in sections 10 and 11 respectively of the Agriculture Act 1947 which are now incorporated into the 1986 Act by the definition section, section 96(3). The remainder of the 1947 Act has been repealed and the rules of good estate management and good husbandry which in that Act formed part of an effective code of good practice which could be enforced on owners and occupiers directly by the Ministry now have a less obvious role to play. They are referred to as standards of practice in various sections of the 1986 Act and the rules of good husbandry can be enforced, indirectly but effectively, against the tenant since a certificate obtained from the Agricultural Land Tribunal that he is not fulfilling his responsibilities to farm in accordance with these rules can be the basis of an 'incontestable' notice to quit leading to his possible eviction from the holding. Alternatively, since obtaining a Certificate of Bad Husbandry tends to be a last resort, the tenant's failure may result in his being served with a notice to remedy which itself may ultimately found an incontestable notice to quit if it is not complied with. The rules of good estate management cannot be enforced under the 1986 Act, directly or indirectly, against the landlord, although aspects of those rules, such as for example the provision and maintenance of fixed equipment will be relevant when rent reviews are undertaken and failure by the landlord to observe the appropriate standards may be thereby indirectly penalised.

Good estate management
In section 10, the essence of good estate management is that the landowner's management of his land should be

'reasonably adequate ... to enable an occupier of the land reasonably skilled in husbandry to maintain efficient production'

in both kind and quality of produce. The situation and character of the land and all other 'relevant circumstances' will be taken into account and specific attention will also be given to the extent to which the owner is providing, improving, maintaining and repairing fixed equipment on the land. However, these rules will not cast any responsibility onto the landowner in respect of the fixed equipment which any agreement imposes on another person. This aspect of the rules of good estate management must therefore be considered in the context of the parties' tenancy agreement as modified where appropriate by sections 7, 8 and 9 of the 1986 Act (below).

Good husbandry
From section 11, the essence of the standard imposed on the tenant is that in all the circumstances of the holding he should maintain

'a reasonable standard of efficient production ... while keeping the unit in a condition to enable such a standard to be maintained in the future'.

Whilst the standard will be judged in the context of the holding, nevertheless attention will be paid to specified operations such as the maintenance of pasture land; arable land; stocking, keeping and breeding of livestock; protecting crops and livestock from disease and infestation; protecting harvested crops and works of maintenance and repair.

4.04 The tenancy: fixed equipment

(i) The scheme of the Act

It is quite usual for a written contract of tenancy to contain express terms concerning the provision and upkeep of fixed equipment on the holding and specifying the allocation of liability for it between the parties. This is not surprising since the importance of adequate and appropriate fixed equipment for efficient agriculture is obvious. Part II of the 1986 Act includes three provisions on the matter.

Firstly, under powers contained in *section 7*, the Minister may prepare 'model clauses' prescribing terms governing the *maintenance, repair and insurance* of fixed equipment which are deemed to be incorporated in *every* tenancy agreement. Where a written tenancy agreement conflicts with the model clauses, *section 8* provides for arbitration to bring it into conformity with them and *section 9* establishes procedures for dealing with issues of compensation and liability where liability is transferred from party to party by reason of the model clauses. Their role is, therefore, comparable with Schedule 1 in that all contracts of tenancy are to be aligned with their provisions, by arbitration if necessary, unless the arbitrator considers that in the circumstances of the particular case the parties' own divergent provision is 'justifiable'. Section 7 is therefore directive or fundamental in nature, and imposes a degree of uniformity where it applies directly or is invoked to modify an existing contradictory agreement.

Secondly, *section 11* provides a closely defined right for the tenant to obtain an order from the Agricultural Land Tribunal obliging his landlord to *provide, alter* or *repair* fixed equipment on the holding to enable the tenant to comply with some statutory duty.

Thirdly, *section 10* gives the tenant rights in certain circumstances to remove on quitting fixtures and buildings which he has provided.

(ii) The definition of 'fixed equipment'

'Fixed equipment' is defined in section 96(2) of the 1986 Act to include

'any building or structure affixed to land and any works on, in, over or under land and also includes anything grown on land for a purpose other than use after severance from the land, consumption of the thing grown or of its produce or amenity'.

The definition therefore would include in addition to the obvious barns and buildings (including the farmhouse and any cottages), works such as the provision of drains, slurry pits, and possibly the maintenance of hedges planted for the prevention of erosion or wind blow.

(iii) The 'model clauses'

Section 7 of the 1986 Act provides that, after consultation with bodies representing the interests of landlords and tenants, the Minister is empowered to make regulations prescribing terms as to the maintenance, repair and insurance of fixed equipment. These regulations, known as the 'model clauses' are by section 7(3)

'deemed to be incorporated in every contract of tenancy of an agricultural holding except in so far as they would impose on one of the parties to an agreement in writing a liability which under the agreement is imposed on the other.'

The model clauses will not, therefore, automatically override a written tenancy agreement which directly contradicts their allocation of responsibility (such a tenancy can be referred to arbitration for ultimate alignment with the model clauses under section 8). The exception to section 7(3) has, however, been given wider effect than might be apparent by the decision in *Burden* v. *Hannaford* (1956) which has not been affected by subsequent legislation and must therefore be seen as continuing to express the law. In that case an express term of the parties' written agreement *removed* from the tenant any liability to repair hedges but failed to impose that liability on the landlords. The Court of Appeal held that in such a case the model clauses would *not* operate to cover the omission, with the result that *neither* party was under any obligation to maintain the hedges. Whilst the result may be surprising and inconvenient, it has remained despite opportunities for legislative reform and it highlights a problem to which those drafting any express maintenance clause must be alert.

Section 8 provides that where an agreement *in writing* relating to an agricultural tenancy effects 'substantial modifications' to the model clauses, then either party may request the other to vary the agreement to make it conform to the model clauses and if the request does not produce an agreed variation, the requesting party may refer those terms of the tenancy to arbitration. Proceedings under the section are rare in practice. Clearly the machinery is similar to that established in section 6. On arbitration, the arbitrator is to consider whether the parties' express deviations from the model clauses are, in all the circumstances of the holding 'justifiable'. If they are not, then he may make an award varying the parties' agreement 'in such manner as seems to him reasonable and just' between the parties. For example, one sometimes finds express arrangements made whereby the tenant is responsible for all labour costs and the landlord for the provision of materials. In practice this is a difficult and unworkable arrangement which may well be subject to variation by the arbitrator. Section 8(3) requires that the arbitrator shall disregard the rent payable when considering the variant clauses. Section 8(4) provides that he may vary the rent if the provisions of his award make such a step appear 'equitable' to him. The award once made shall have effect (as do the awards under section 6) as a variation of the pre-existing agreement which comes into effect on the date it is made or at such later date as may be specified in it. Arbitrations under section 8 may not be initiated before the expiry of three years from the award of any previous section 8 arbitration.

If an arbitration (or an agreement) under section 8 shifts liability for aspects of maintenance and repair from one party to the other there may be difficulties where the party originally liable under the express contract had failed to fulfil his responsibilities. Section 9 provides that any claims for such failure under the original contract are to be settled by arbitration. Any compensation then due shall be payable as if the tenant had quit the holding on the date the arbitrator's award came into effect. It thereby ensures that disputes concerning breaches of the original contract can be disposed of during the currency of the varied contract stemming from the arbitrator's award and that they are not held over until the tenant actually quits the holding, as would be the normal course of events.

Finally, section 9(4) is a section of intermittent application. It provides that on occasions when new model clauses are issued under section 7 which vary the terms of existing tenancies, an arbitrator who is required to settle the terms of a tenancy under the section 6 machinery may ignore the new model clauses in the period immediately after their issue and may instead give effect to the parties' contractual term. *Burden* v. *Hannaford* seems to pose another problem here since it suggests that even an oral term may exclude the regulations entirely.

(iv) *Section 11: provision, alteration and repair of fixed equipment*

Section 11 provides a remedy for the tenant who is already, or is in danger of being, in breach of his statutory duty by reason of the absence of or the state of fixed equipment which it is the landlord's duty to provide or maintain. The remedy is, however, little used by tenants because it is so closely defined that it is relatively rare that all its requirements can be satisfied. If successful, the tenant obtains a direction from the Agricultural Land Tribunal to his landlord that the equipment in issue be provided, altered or repaired within a stated time so that the tenant can satisfy the statutory requirements in respect of his farming. Notice that section 11 does not apply to crown or government land: section 95(1).

The first hurdle is that the tenant may only apply to Tribunal for a direction when the state or absence of the fixed equipment will cause the tenant to contravene some statutory requirement. There are relatively few such requirements, and this first condition therefore considerably reduces the scope of section 11. However, it may be of assistance to the tenant in satisfying the Public Health Acts for example, or the Dairy Industry Act in the provision of septic tanks or cesspool drainage systems or a supply of wholesome water.

Secondly, section 11 only operates when the landlord is not under a duty from any other source, contractual or statutory, to undertake the work in question.

Thirdly, the tenant must show that the equipment is required, or the work is necessary, for him to continue lawfully an 'agricultural activity' which he has been carrying out for at least three years prior to his application. If he cannot demonstrate this, he must satisfy the Tribunal that starting the activity specified has not constituted (or if prospective, will not constitute) a 'substantial alteration' of the type of farming on the holding.

Fourthly, the Tribunal must be satisfied that it is reasonable, having regard to the tenant's duties from the rules of good husbandry, that he should carry on the agricultural activity which he has specified to the extent and in the manner so specified.

Fifthly, they must also be satisfied that it would be reasonable to make the direction sought by the tenant *and* they must be satisfied that the landlord has already been requested by the tenant to do the requisite work and he has refused. Whether the direction is reasonable or not will reflect the standard of practice imposed by the rules of good estate management and must also have regard to the holding's likely continued independent existence in the future. A direction to provide or substantially alter or repair a major item of fixed equipment might be eminently unreasonable if plans for merger or reorganisation of the holding were far advanced.

If the tenant does clear these numerous hurdles, the Tribunal will order that the work be done within a specified period. The landlord may apply for one or several extensions of time which will be granted if he can show that the original limitation was inadequate to allow for the intitial arrangements for the work, including any relevant grant applications for government funds to be made, and for work to be done.

Should the landlord ultimately fail to comply with the Tribunal's direction, the tenant's remedies are the same as those for breach of covenant by the landlord: he is entitled to bring an action for damages (or possibly for an injunction). Section 11(b) makes clear that the tenant also has the right, if the landlord defaults, to carry out the work himself and recover the reasonable cost from the landlord. In such circumstances the amount of any grant which the tenant has received must be deducted from his claim. This latter is probably the more effective remedy. There is no provision for arbitration as to the 'reasonable cost'.

Section 11 in practice is of only marginal use to tenants, although the right to require *provision* of fixed equipment where no duty already exists on the landlord to do so may help in the very limited circumstances to which the section applies. If a tenant wishes to use his rights under the section, he should apply to the Tribunal.

(v) Section 10: the tenant's rights to remove fixtures

The last statutory modification of the parties' agreement concerning the fixed equipment on the farm is effected by section 10, which gives the tenant a statutory right, in addition to any similar rights from other sources, to remove fixtures on quitting, subject to the landlord's right to purchase, as detailed below.

At common law, the tenant of an agricultural holding originally had no right to remove fixtures which he had erected on the holding during his tenancy. As 'fixtures' they were treated as part of the land and thus became the landlord's property. Gradually, rights to remove a tenant's 'trade' and 'ornamental' fixtures evolved but 'agricultural' fixtures continued to be irremovable until a statutory right to remove them was introduced in 1923.

This right, slightly redefined, is now contained in section 10 of the 1986 Act. Given that many modern framed structures are fairly readily removable it is often better for the tenant now to erect a building as a fixture, with the right to remove, than to claim it as an improvement. Unless the building is of a specialist nature it is likely to be taken by the landlord at fair value to an incomer, to the tenant's advantage.

Fixtures are broadly defined for the purposes of section 10 to include

'any engine, machinery, fencing or other fixture (of whatever description) affixed whether or not for the purposes of agriculture, to an agricultural holding by the tenant' and 'any building erected by him'.

These are broad words indeed: the phrase in brackets qualifying 'other fixture' indicates that section 10 is *not* to be limited to agricultural fixtures: it is not limited only to a construction *eiusdem generis* with the preceding words and additional scope is thus given by extending the right of removal to fixtures whether for agriculture or not. Buildings or fixtures acquired by the tenant rather than fixed or erected by him are also included.

The statutory right does *not* include fixtures or buildings in place as a result of some obligation on the tenant to provide them, nor those which replace a fixture or building provided by the landlord, nor buildings in respect of which the tenant is entitled to compensation. Such fixtures and buildings remain the property of the landlord. A last minor exception includes buildings or fixtures placed on the holding before 1st January 1884, clearly a diminishing class.

Where a fixture may be removed by the tenant under the section, it remains his property so long as the right to remove exists. Section 10(1) states that fixtures are removable during the tenancy or within two months of its termination. To exercise the right, however, the tenant must satisfy two preconditions. *The two preconditions* are *firstly* that he has satisfied *all* his tenancy obligations in respect of the holding. The rent must be paid up to date and all other conditions must be met. If strictly enforced against the tenant this could be an almost insuperable burden but in practice does not pose substantial difficulties. *Secondly*, a tenant intending to remove a fixture must give his landlord at least one month's *notice in writing* of his intention. The notice must be served at least one month before *both* the exercise of the right and the termination of the tenancy. If removal is planned in the two months after quitting (as permitted by section 10(1)) the landlord will therefore have up to three months' notice by reason of this condition in section 10(3). The landlord, on receipt of the written notice, may elect to *purchase* the items specified, or some of them, at a price reflecting

'the fair value of that fixture or building to an incoming tenant of the holding'.

The landlord must serve a counter-notice in writing to this effect before the tenant's notice of removal expires. If the landlord does elect to purchase, the tenant is bound by this decision and cannot remove the item. If there is any dispute between them as to the 'fair value' it shall be determined by arbitration.

In removing fixtures, the section requires that the tenant shall make good any damage which does occur because of the removal 'immediately' after removing the item(s) concerned.

Section 10(8) makes it clear that the rights given by section 10

'shall not be taken as prejudicing any right to remove a fixture that subsists otherwise than by virtue of this section.'

Where the tenant seeks to remove a 'trade' or 'ornamental' fixture therefore, he may do so under his common law rights. This course avoids the need to notify the landlord and risk the obligation of selling such items to him. Obviously the definition of 'fixtures' in section 10(1) is broad enough to include various non-agricultural fixtures giving the tenant in respect of such terms an additional rather than a superior right.

Section 10 may be excluded or modified by the parties' contract of tenancy. It is not an overriding statutory term. In any event, section 10 will *not* apply to entitle a tenant to remove a fixture or building acquired by him *before* 1st January 1901: para 3, Schedule 12.

4.05 Cultivation of land and disposal of produce

(i) *The scheme of the Act*

As we have seen, the common law imposes only a minimum standard of care on the tenant to farm according to the rules of good husbandry and the common custom of the country. Although the 1986 Act indirectly enforces the statutory rules of good husbandry, these too are very generally described (in section 11 of the 1947 Act) and in many cases therefore it is desirable to take from the tenant express covenants on the tenancy agreement which regulate his farming practices. (This is, of course, particularly necessary where land is either in bad heart at the beginning of the tenancy and allowance is being made for the tenant to improve it or where, by reason of previous high farming, it is in especially good condition which he is expected to maintain.) In addition, covenants are regularly included to govern the maintenance of pasture land, the disposal of hay and/or manure, systems of arable cropping and systems of husbandry appropriate to the neighbourhood.

These provisions are clearly of central importance to the tenant and the efficiency of his farming. Because of their importance they are subject to statutory modification by sections 14 and 15 of the 1986 Act which originated in the 1948 Act and were designed to promote efficiency. Section 14 gives an overriding right to either party to seek a *reduction* of the area of land to be kept as permanent pasture. Section 15 gives the tenant an overriding right to freedom of cropping and disposal of produce. Section 15(3) prohibits the tenant from selling or removing from the holding manure, compost, hay, straw or roots during the last year of his tenancy, although this statutory prohibition may be expressly modified or excluded by an agreement in writing between the parties. Finally, amongst the 'miscellaneous' provision of Part II, the landlord's remedies for breach of covenant are restricted by section 24 which prohibits the imposition of so-called penal rents.

(ii) *Section 14: reduction of permanent pasture*

Where the tenancy expressly provides that specified land, or alternatively, a specified proportion of the land, in the holding shall be kept as permanent pasture, section 14 gives a right to both landlord and tenant (individually) to seek a *reduction* of the permanent pasture. The section is limited to reducing the pasture on the tenancy. There is no requirement in section 14 that the contract of tenancy be in writing: the section will apply whether the pasture provision is oral or in writing.

The procedure adopted by the section is to submit the 'pasture provision' to arbitration by giving each party the right to serve on the other a written notice demanding that the question

'whether it is expedient in order to secure full and efficient farming of the holding that the area of land ... maintained as permanent pasture should be reduced' should be submitted to arbitration. This makes clear the criterion which is to guide the arbitrator: the full and efficient farming of the holding.

If the arbitrator finds that a reduction is justified, his award will direct appropriate modifications to the contract of tenancy. Any reduction awarded will apply for the duration of the tenancy. However, the arbitrator may provide that *on quitting*, the tenant should leave a further area as permanent or temporary pasture, in addition to the reduced pastureland: section 14(4). However, such a requirement is limited by section 14(5) which provides that any additional area to be left as pasture on quitting may not exceed the area by which the original pasture land was reduced in the arbitration. The original area of permanent pasture therefore remains the maximum. Notice that section 76(1) expressly provides that no compensation shall be payable to the tenant in respect of anything done in pursuance of an order made under section 14(4).

Section 14 overrides the parties' agreement and cannot be excluded.

(iii) Section 15: disposal of produce and freedom of cropping

Section 15 gives the tenant a statutory freedom to dispose of the produce of the holding (except for manure) and to practise any system of arable cropping

'without incurring any penalty, forfeiture or liability'.

The statutory right is overriding: it enures to the tenant

'notwithstanding any custom of the country or the provisions of the contract of tenancy or any agreement'.

Section 15(4), however, provides that when the tenant exercises his statutory right to dispose of produce he shall make 'suitable and adequate' provision to return the full manurial value of any crops disposed of contrary to the custom or contract or any agreement between the parties. Similarly, if he exercises his right to freedom of cropping he must make provision to protect the holding from 'injury or deterioration' which would include, amongst others, deterioration of the soil structure, the failure to eradicate soil-borne pests and deficiences of soil nutrients or trace elements. Any falling away from the appropriate standard might well be indicated in the course of a rent review. Any such protective steps must be taken 'before or as soon as possible after' the exercise of the relevant right.

It may be mentioned that an increasingly common feature of agricultural leases, the 'quota clause', although an important method of obliging diversification of cropping, may be criticised as restricting the statutory freedom of cropping encapsulated in section 15. In some cases quotas are seen as the key to an adequate margin of return. Whether *loss* of quota would constitute 'injury or deterioration' for the purposes of section 15(5) is another novel point which still awaits determination.

If the tenant exercises his statutory rights without protecting the holding, so that his agriculture injures or deteriorates the holding, or is likely to do so, the landlord is restricted to the remedies specified in section 15(5), namely an injunction if the case requires it, and, in any case, the right to recover damages for deterioration of the holding from the tenant when he quits the holding. Whether or not the tenant's practices have deteriorated the holding, or have been likely to do so, is an issue to be resolved conclusively by arbitration under section 15(6).

The statutory freedoms under section 15 endure throughout the tenancy until its final phase. Section 15(2) provides that the freedoms are *not* available to the tenant of a tenancy from year to year during the last year before he quits the holding or any period after he has given or received notice to quit which results in his quitting the holding. Since notice to quit will normally be between one and two years' duration, this provision may exclude the tenant's statutory rights for up to 23 months. On the other hand, if he is given the so-called 'short' notice to quit, the rights will be excluded for the last year before he quits. During such period, the tenant will be subject to any restrictions which are expressly or impliedly incorporated into the tenancy whether from the custom of the country or from an agreement between the parties. If the tenancy is not from year to year, but is for example a fixed term tenancy without security (such as tenancies granted under section 5 of the 1986 Act) the statutory freedoms will not apply during the year before it terminates.

Like section 14, the rights in section 15(1) are overriding and cannot be excluded by the parties. The only exception to section 15(1) is that the section does not apply to small holdings approved by the Minister as cooperative farming ventures under section 82 of the Act.

(iv) Section 15(3): disposal of manure

Section 15(3) provides that after giving or receiving notice to quit the tenant shall not sell or dispose of

'any manure, or compost or any hay or straw or roots grown in the last year of the tenancy'

unless he has the landlord's prior consent in writing. This provision, however, is subject to any agreement between the parties to the contrary and may therefore be expressly excluded from the tenancy agreement. The usual course, in practice, is for the amount of hay, straw and roots left upon termination to be agreed between outgoing and incoming tenants.

Where the tenant abides by section 15(3), he is entitled to claim compensation on quitting through the machinery of arbitration provided by the Act for anything left on the holding. In *Thomas* v. *National Farmers' Union Mutual Insurance Society Ltd* (1961) it was held that this being so, section 15(3)'s predecessor, section 12(1) of the 1948 Act, effectively transferred the ownership of crops left on the holding on quitting to the landlord who would normally therefore insure them after such date. The tenant, who had no property in them after quitting, had no insurable interest and therefore no right to insure such crops against damage once he had quit.

Where the tenant fails to observe the provisions of section 15(3) the landlord's remedy will be to seek compensation for delapidation.

4.06 Section 24: no penal rents for breach of covenant

Where a tenant is in breach of any covenant in the tenancy agreement (whether it is our express, statutory or common law covenant) the landlord is limited by section 24 to recovering only compensation for the damage actually suffered by him as a consequence of the tenant's breach. Any provision in the tenancy which purports to impose on the tenant any additional penalty such as a higher rent or liquidated damages in any other form will be ineffective. Traditionally it was common for 'penal rents' for breach of covenant to be contractually imposed, the most common situation being the imposition of a penal rent for the ploughing out of pasture. Section 24 overrides any such provision and cannot be excluded by the parties.

4.07 Miscellaneous statutory terms

(i) Section 20: tenant's compensation for damage by game

This section provides that where the tenant suffers damage to his crops caused by game which he is not entitled to shoot, he will have a claim for compensation against his landlord who, if appropriate, will be entitled to be indemnified by his 'shooting tenant' against such claims: section 20(5). (In many cases the agricultural tenant will be subject to a covenant in the lease obliging him to preserve such game – and thus contribute towards the resulting damage for which he will claim compensation.)

Agricultural tenancies regularly contain provisions which reserve the right to shoot game to the landlord. A general incidence, or likelihood, of game damage is usually recognised in rent reviews in such cases. This does not, of course, affect the tenant's right to claim under section 20. The landlord may exercise the right himself or may let out such rights to a third party ('the shooting tenant'). Where the agricultural tenant suffers damage to his crops by 'wild animals or birds' which he does not have written permission to kill he will be entitled to compensation from his landlord if he observes the requirements of section 20(2). In referring to 'wild animals or birds' the 1986 Act incorporates the wording introduced in 1984 to replace the more specific list of 'game' in the 1948 Act.

Section 20(2) requires that the tenant *firstly* gives the landlord notice *in writing* within a month of becoming aware of the occurrence of damage, or within a month of the date when he might reasonably have become aware of the damage. This notice will indicate the damage and alert the landlord to the likelihood of a claim for compensation being made by the tenant. The tenant must *secondly* give his landlord a reasonable opportunity to inspect the damage: if the crop is growing, inspection should take place before steps are taken to reap, raise or consume it; if the crop has already been harvested, then before operations begin to remove it from the land. Seed which has been sown will be treated as a growing crop whether or not it has germinated.

Lastly, the tenant must serve a *written* notice of the claim, including particulars of it, on his landlord within a month from the end of the year for which the claim is made. 'Year' in this context will mean the twelve months ending on 29th September in any year unless the landlord and tenant agree a twelve month period ending on another date. They may, for example, agree that 'compensation years' for section 20 shall end on 1st February, when the pheasant and partridge season closes. Where the tenant has satisfied all the statutory requirements, compensation shall be as agreed between the parties, or, in default of agreement, as determined by arbitration. The rights to compensation given by section 20 are exclusive and overriding.

(ii) Section 22: rights to have a record of condition made

This section gives both landlord and tenant the right at any time during the tenancy to require that a record be made of the condition of fixed equipment on the holding and of the general condition of the holding. In addition, section 22(1)(b) gives the tenant the specific right to require that a record be made of any fixtures which section 10 of the Act entitles him to remove, and of any improvements which he has effected on the holding or for which he paid compensation to an outgoing tenant with the landlord's written consent. If the parties cannot agree on appointing a surveyor or other person to make the record, then they may apply to the

President of the R.I.C.S. to appoint someone, sending a requisite fee with their application. All the costs of the record are to be borne by the landlord and tenant in equal shares, unless they agree otherwise. The person ultimately appointed is given in section 22(2) a statutory right to enter the holding at all reasonable times for the purpose of making the record, subject to his producing evidence of his appointment.

A record made in accordance with section 22 is largely only of use as evidence of the state of the holding and the improvements etc. at the date of the record. (It may be invoked for or against the tenant in claims that he has not satisfied the standard of husbandry imposed by the 'model clauses', for example.) A common reason for a tenant to require a record of condition to be made is to protect his interest where the holding has been taken in poor condition and he is concerned that, should he quit after only a short period he might be unjustly penalised for the still deficient state of the farm.

The only exceptional limitation is where a tenant makes a claim for compensation for 'high farming' under section 70 of the Act, where section 70(2)(b) states that a prerequisite to such a claim is the making of a record of the condition of the fixed equipment and the general state of the holding.

The right in section 22 is supplemental to the express agreement between the parties.

(iii) Section 23: the landlord's right to enter

It is usual for a tenancy agreement to reserve a right of entry at reasonable times to the landlord to enable him to inspect the holding and to fulfil his own management duties in respect of it.

Where the tenancy is silent, section 23 gives the landlord or his authorised representative the right to enter for three specified purposes:

(i)   to view the state of the holding;
(ii) to fulfil his responsibilities under the rules of good estate management; and
(iii) to provide or improve fixed equipment otherwise than is required by the rules of good estate management.

Section 23 does not grant the landlord an unrestricted right of entry. It is merely supplementary to the contract between the parties. It is, of course, in addition to the right implied into tenancies by the 'model clauses'.

Chapter 5

Rent Reviews and Distress for Unpaid Rent

5.01 Introductory

Statutory provision for rent review in the case of agricultural holdings is a necessary provision to take care of those (few) cases where the parties to the tenancy do not resolve the point by agreement between themselves.

The 1984 Act was hailed as introducing a major revision of the rent review formula, at the instigation of the N.F.U. who had attached great importance to a reform in this area as their 'benefit' in return for agreeing to the loss of succession rights as sought by the C.L.A. In the event, the statutory changes are probably of less importance to the level of rents than are the introduction of production limiting mechanisms (such as quotas) and the widespread decline in farm product profitability. The details of the present provisions are discussed below.

(A) AGREEMENT BETWEEN THE PARTIES

5.02 Rent review by agreement

In many cases, rent review will be achieved amicably by the parties who, according to the express terms of the tenancy, agree the timing and the appointment of an informal arbitrator and abide by their joint decision. The statutory provisions discussed below are to provide for situations where such cooperation proves impossible or unsatisfactory for whatever reason.

(B) NO AGREEMENT: A RIGHT TO REVIEW BY ARBITRATION

5.03 The statutory right to demand arbitration

Where no rent review can be achieved by agreement, section 12 and

Schedule 2 of the 1986 Act confer a right on either party to demand that the rent be referred to arbitration so that the arbitrator may effect a review.

Section 12(1) provides that

'the landlord or tenant of an agricultural holding may by notice in writing served on the other demand that the rent to be payable in respect of the holding as from the rent termination date shall be referred to arbitration.'

An arbitration may produce an increased rent or a decreased rent or may confirm the current rent as appropriate. Obviously a demand for arbitration will reflect the optimism of the demandant. The phrase 'new rent' is used in the following paragraphs to indicate the rent assessed by the arbitrator. It is recognised that the amount payable may remain the same even after arbitration.

5.04 Demand 'by notice in writing'

There is no prescribed form for a demand for arbitration on the rent. The only statutory requirement is that the demand must be *in writing*. It must, of course, be clear and unambiguous and must be effectively served on the other party to the lease. In practice, a section 12 notice is invariably served as a prelude to any discussion on revision of the rent, whether or not arbitration is ultimately envisaged.

5.05 Arbitration determines rent 'as from the next termination date'

The rent assessed by the arbitrator will be payable from 'the next termination date'. 'The next termination date' is defined in section 12(4) as

'the next day following the date of the demand on which the tenancy of the holding could have been determined by notice to quit given at the date of the demand.'

This definition implicitly identifies both the *types of agricultural tenancy* to which the right to arbitration applies and also the *timing* of the demand for arbitration.

(i) Tenancies subject to statutory arbitration

The reference to a notice to quit necessarily implies that the right to demand arbitration on the rent is limited in the first instance to *periodic* tenancies, the agricultural tenancy from year to year. Notices to quit are only relevant to periodic tenancies (apart from rare situations when the lease contains an express right to terminate a fixed term lease in this way). Arbitration will therefore be available under section 12 for

(a)   Express annual periodic tenancies.
(b)   Grants treated as tenancies from year to year by virtue of section 2 [2.06].
(c)   Statutory tenancies from year to year arising on the expiry of fixed-term tenancies by virtue of section 3 [2.04].
(d)   In addition, an extension of the right to arbitration to *some fixed-term tenancies* is effected by the rule from *Edell* v. *Dulieu* (1924). This provides that where a fixed-term tenancy includes a 'break clause', alllowing either party to terminate the tenancy at specified premature dates within the full term, such break-dates may be treated as 'termination dates' and thus rent reviews may be arranged by reference to them and thus, where a fixed-term tenancy includes a break-clause the statutory right to arbitration will apply. The net result, therefore, is that despite the reference to a notice to quit, the *only* tenancies in which the parties will *not* have the right under section 12 to demand arbitration are fixed-term tenancies *without* a break clause.

(ii) Timing the demand for arbitration

The effect of section 12 is that the new rent awarded by the arbitrator is payable from the anniversary of the lease which falls between one and two years after the service of the demand for arbitration. This is the implication of the definition of the termination date: the normal period of notice required in respect of an agricultural tenancy from year to year is twelve months (section 25). The period is required by the common law to expire on the term date of the period [6.06]. The effect of para. 4 of Schedule 2 is, broadly, to prohibit statutory arbitrations on rent more frequently than once in three years. If a demand for arbitration is effectively served and pursued, therefore, the rent agreed between the parties at the outset of the tenancy could be revised with effect from the first day of the 4th, 7th, 10th and 13th years and so on, thus retaining the maximum control allowed by the Act. To achieve this result, bearing in mind the statutory delay between the demand and the imposition of the new rent, a demand for arbitration would have to be served during the 2nd, 5th, 8th, 11th years and so on as appropriate.

Where a fixed-term tenancy includes a break clause, the 'next termination dates' on which a new rent might become payable for the purposes of section 12(4) are the commencement dates of each new stage within the fixed term. It is not unusual, for example, for a 21-year lease to include a break clause permitting termination after the 7th or 14th years of the tenancy thus creating three equal seven-year stages for the purposes of rent arbitrations. The period between the demand and the new rent becoming payable remains a period of between one and two years ending on the term date of the particular stage of the lease. If, therefore, it is intended to use the statutory machinery to its utmost, the following pattern should be followed:

```
R .........D ...| R ...........D ... | R ..............
                |                    |
R         ↓     | R           ↓      | R
_____|_____|_____
1 2 3 4 5 6 7  | 8 9 10 11 12 13 14 | 15 16 17 18 19 20
```

R = new rent payable from first day of tenancy year
D = demand for arbitration to be served during tenancy year

5.06 Demand followed by appointment

A demand for arbitration will 'die', and cease to be effective unless steps have been taken to appoint an arbitrator '*before* the next termination date', i.e. before the date on which the new rent could become payable. Section 12(3) provides that either

(a) an arbitrator must have been appointed by agreement between the parties or, in default of their agreement,

(b) an application must have been made to the President of the R.I.C.S. for the appointment by him of an arbitrator

by the next termination date following the demand. Schedule 11 of the 1986 Act governs arbitrations. Para. 1 of the Schedule provides that where the parties cannot agree on the appointment of an arbitrator, either of them may apply to the President for him to make an appointment. To comply with section 12(3)(b) there only needs to have been an *application* to the President: his appointee does not need to be named or appointed by the next termination date to keep the demand alive. This alters the previous law which required the appointment to have been perfected by the relevant date: *Sclater* v. *Horton* (1954). Any such application must be accompanied by the appropriate fee (para. 2) which is presently £70. Only one fee is payable in respect of any one arbitration, even if in fact the President is further involved after the initial appointment, for example in the appointment of a second arbitrator in place of the first (para. 2). Para. 3 of the Schedule further provides that when appointing an arbitrator for a rent arbitration under section 12, the President shall *not* make an appointment earlier than four months 'before the next termination date following the date of demand'.

5.07 The rent properly payable at the date of the reference

(i) 'At the date of the reference'

As under the previous legislation the arbitrator is to assess the rent properly payable 'as at the date of the reference', that is, as at the date of his appointment: *Sclater* v. *Horton* (1954) (not affected by the 1984/1986 Acts on this point). As mentioned above, para. 3 of Schedule 2 provides that the President of the R.I.C.S. shall not appoint an arbitrator for a section 12 rent review earlier than four months before the 'next termination date following the date of the demand'. The assessment of rent should therefore be at a level appropriate, more or less, to the beginning of the new three year rental period. It is not unusual for the date of the reference to be a considerable period *after* the next termination date.

(ii) 'The rent properly payable'

The new formula introduced by the 1984 Act is largely contained in para. 1(1) of Schedule 2 which defines the 'rent properly payable' as

> 'the rent at which the holding might reasonably be expected to be let by a prudent and willing landlord to a prudent and willing tenant, taking into account ... all relevant factors, including (in every case) the terms of the tenancy (including those relating to rent), the character and situation of the holding (including the locality in which it is situated), the productive capacity of the holding and its related earning capacity and the current level of rents for comparable lettings.'

This paragraph lies at the heart of the new formula and is further defined and elaborated by paragraphs 1, 2 and 3 of the Schedule. The formula is much more detailed and explicit than its predecessor, section 8 of the 1948

Act, in its listing and defining of particular relevant factors and specific disregards to be applied by the arbitrator. Whilst many of these are clearly considerations which any competent valuer would necessarily have applied before 1984 without the need for legislative prompting, there are some apparently fairly major changes, at least in emphasis, and it may be helpful here to mention the more significant details of the formula. The effect of the change on the level of rents and, indeed, on the practice of arbitrators is still not entirely clear even after two years' experience. In any event it is difficult to distinguish the results of that particular change from the effects on rental values of lower profitability stemming largely from the reduction in farm product prices and the imposition of production quotas during the same period.

(a) No 'open market' reference

The first and most obvious change to notice is that this rent formula, unlike its predecessor, makes no direct or express reference to the open market when setting the level of the rent. However, as numerous commentators have remarked, the change may be more apparent than real since several of the 'relevant considerations' mentioned in para. 1 imply the existence of an open market context. For example, a 'willing' party to a lease cannot be assumed to be uncritically 'willing' to offer or accept a level of rent unrelated to current conditions; the reference to rents of 'comparable lettings' also suggests a market context and the direction in para. 3(a) of the Schedule (discussed below) to disregard any element of scarcity value in such 'comparable' rents also inevitably involves the projection of an open and undistorted market level of rent deduced from the actual level of rents for such comparable lettings as may be identified. This is so even though *in fact* the market for agricultural land may be extremely restricted.

(b) 'Prudent and willing' parties

Neither of these adjectives was present in the original draft of the formula. 'Willing' was introduced as an echo of the old section 8 formula after intensive lobbying in the House of Lords. 'Prudent' was added later, having been commended to some extent by the Northfield Committee in its 1979 Report. Since it is unlikely that a 'willing' party would be necessarily 'imprudent' either in accepting unrealistically high rent offers, or making such an offer based on unrealistic, speculative or irresponsible forecasts the consensus of opinion is that 'prudent' adds little or nothing to this consideration.

(c) 'All relevant factors'

The list of specific considerations following these words is indicative, not exhaustive, and it is difficult to believe that any competent professional would consciously reach a decision which was *not*, in his opinion, based on 'all relevant factors' and certainly there seems to be general agreement that even before 1984, arbitrators would inevitably have considered the terms of the tenancy, and the character, situation and locality of the holding. There is a clear statutory change in requiring attention to be paid to the terms concerning rent which were previously expressly excluded from the 1948 formula, although it was a usual practice for the existing rent level to be disclosed in cases stated in rent arbitrations. At the very least, however, its express inclusion may now remove any theoretical or academic doubt about the propriety of such practice. Similarly, the productive capacity of the holding and the level of comparable rents have always been clearly relevant to rent reviews. Because of their more detailed treatment in Schedule 2, however, they are considered separately here.

(d) 'The productive capacity of the holding and its related earning capacity'
Both of these concepts are expressly identified for the first time as relevant considerations to a rent review but it is generally felt in the valuation profession that they have traditionally been referants. Each is now not only identified but also defined in some detail by para. 1(2) of Schedule 2.
　　Para. 1(2) defines the '*productive capacity*' as

　　'the productive capacity of the holding (taking into account fixed equipment and any other available facilities on the holding) on the assumption that it is in the occupation of a competent tenant practising a system of farming suitable to the holding'.

Thus the criterion is an amalgam of the real holding and the hypothetical 'competent tenant'. What standard is to be assumed as the standard of 'competence' is not clear, but with such an ostensibly objective criterion it must be presumed to be a level of expertise neither extraordinarily high nor merely of subsistence level. In discussions preparatory to the drafting of the final 1984 Bill, there is some evidence that the Ministry and subsequently Parliament envisaged a slightly better than average standard being applied.
　　Para. 1(2)(b) defines the '*related earning capacity*' of the holding as

　　'the extent to which, in the light of (the) productive capacity, a competent tenant practising (a suitable) system of farming could reasonably be expected to profit from farming the holding'.

This concept introduces the consideration of the profitability of the holding, but only in relation to the system of farming which should be deployed, affected if appropriate by such factors as subsidies, quotas and other external controls on the system or profitability of farming. Profits from non-agricultural activities such as camping and recreational uses of the land are not elements of the productive capacity as defined, but would naturally be considered as 'relevant factors' when rent reviews are in progress. It will of course be for the parties to make the case as to how the profits from the holding (once ascertained) should be shared between landlord and tenant and thus the effect of the holding's profitability on the ultimate rent. Having found the gross margin of profitability before rent/finance it would seem appropriate then to allow a fair return to the tenant for capital employed including the 'locked-in' value of improvements, and for his entrepreneurial and management skills. The remainder is rent. The Act, of course, does not dictate this detailed approach, which is rather derived from valuers' practice. The simplified example of a farm costing given in Figure 5.1 illustrates this approach.

(e) Comparable rents

The final factor expressly specified in para. 1(1) as a factor to be taken into account is 'the current level of rents for comparable lettings' to be ascertained in the light of the conditions stated in para. 1(3). Here the arbitrator is directed to take into account any evidence of rents which are or are likely to become payable for comparable holdings where the terms of the tenancies in question (apart from the rent provisions) are similar to that under consideration. The paragraph thus encourages the arbitrator, again indirectly, to consider the market context and current market trends when he is reviewing rents under section 12. At the same time, para. 1(3) continues by specifying three aspects of the rent of comparable holdings which must be *disregarded* in every case, viz.

(i)   any appreciable scarcity element in the rents;
(ii) any 'marriage value' element of the rent of a comparable letting, whereby the current tenant or tendering prospective tenant is willing to pay an enhanced rent because he occupies other land in the vicinity of the 'comparable' and the occupation of both holdings together would be convenient and advantageous to him;
(iii) any effect on those rents of the charging of premiums.

The '*scarcity*' disregard resembles the provision in section 70(2) of the Rent Act 1977 that an assumption be made that demand and supply of 'similar' dwelling houses are in balance. Although this may be an unrealistic assumption it seems likely that in being required to ignore the effect of any 'appreciable' scarcity value, the arbitrators are in effect being required to disregard *any* 'scarcity' element whatsoever but will not be at fault if some vestigial scarcity effect does, in fact, remain.

Chestnut Hall

Little Milling

Gross margins – 1987 cropping

	Acres	/acre yield	total (tonnes)	unit price (£)	Gross return	v.c's acre	total v.c's	gross margin	g.m. acre
Wheat	243	2.8T	692	100	68,000	89	21,983	47,017	190
W. Barley	36.5	2.5T	90	100	9,000	75	2,737	6,263	171
Oil Seed Rape	44	1.25T	55	275	15,000	100	4,400	10,600	241
Sugar Beet	40	16T	640	29	18,500	160	6,400	12,100	302
Winter Beans	28.5	1.5T	42	178	7,500	44.50	1,270	6,230	218
Grass (Grazing Licence)	30				1,200	12	360	840	28
Total	426				£120,200		£37,150	83,050	195

Cattle enterprise   5,200
Bull beef contract rearing   £88,250

Projected 3 year cropping variation 1987/90
Substitute pulse crops for OSR. GM differential marginal £88,000, say

	Fixed costs	Total G.M.	£88,000

Labour

1 Man	8,000	
Casual/Pt. Time	3,500	11,500 (27/acre)

Machinery

Depreciation	11,250
Fuel & Power	5,000
Machinery Expenses Incl.	
Contract work	11,500
Misc. Expenses	3,000
Insurance	1,500
Property Repairs	1,500

33,750 (£79.22/Acre) £45,250 (£106.22/Acre)
N.F.I.   42,700
Less farmer's
manual labour   5,200
Income before rent
and finance   £37,550

Probable allocation to rent

Return on T's Capital 150,000 @ 8.5%	12,750	
Tenants Management Remuneration	10,000	
		22,750

Rental, say,   £15,000 – 35/acre

Note
The costing above illustrates one approach in conformity with the provisions of the Act. There is no definitive or conclusive method. Thorough appraisal of the holding and its potential is vital.

Fig. 5.1

Notice that it is only in contemplating the rents of comparable lettings that '*marriage value*' is to be disregarded: the arbitrator should not, and is not required by the Act to, eliminate any relevant 'marriage value' from the rent of the subject holding itself.

'*Premium*' in para. 1(3)(c) is to be given its narrow meaning of some financial consideration payable in addition to the rent.

Where evidence is presented of rents of comparable holdings, and especially of rents for comparables 'currently being tendered', great care must be taken to avoid mere hearsay evidence and to substantiate appropriately the figures put forward: *English Exporters Ltd* v. *Eldonwall Ltd* (1973). It will also be for the professional expertise of valuers and arbitrators to assess the weight to be given to *tender* rents as opposed to those fixed by 'the higgling of the market'. However, as with many other aspects of the new rent formula, all these factors have traditionally informed valuers' and arbitrators' assessments of rent and their decisions in rent reviews and it seems unlikely that their articulation in the Act will make any substantial difference to established practice but may, indeed, be seen rather as a vindication of it.

(f) Further disregards: tenant's and landlord's improvements

Para. 2 of Schedule 2 requires the arbitrator to disregard any increase in the rental value from an improvement effected by the tenant at his own expense (even if he may ultimately be reimbursed by grant aid) apart from those improvements effected on items of fixed equipment provided under an obligation in the tenancy. 'Improvements' are to include any voluntary and continuous adoption of a system of high farming by the tenant: para. 2(4) and also any improvements effected (or fixed equipment provided) by the tenant during a previous tenancy of the holding unless he has already been compensated for it on the termination of the previous or any other tenancy. Para. 2 also requires the arbitrator to ignore any increase in the rental value of the holding which is due to improvements effected by the landlord where he has received or will receive grants from central or local government funds in respect of those improvements. The difference in treatment between landlord and tenant as regards grant-aided improvements is conspicuous. The rationale underlying it is that the tenant should never be penalised for his improvements and the landlord should on the other hand reap the benefits of his improvements but should not be compensated twice over (by an increased rent *and* reimbursement from grant-aid services). There is no provision now to disregard relief from the payment of rates in the current legislation. Notice that 'improvement' here is not limited to those 'relevant improvements' listed in Schedules 7 and 8 but is apparently given its normal meaning of work which improves the holding

(g) Milk quotas and rent reviews

Notice that the Agriculture Act 1986 makes specific provision for the effect of milk quotas in rent reviews under section 12 of the Agricultural Holdings Act. Section 15 of the Agriculture Act provides that where there is a milk quota registered in respect of the holding, or a part of it, and the quota was transferred to the tenant by virtue of a transaction which he paid for, wholly or partly, then the arbitrator is required in assessing the rent to *disregard* any increase in rental value which may be attributed to the quota. The landlord and tenant may, however, agree that the quota shall be relevant to the new rent. Where there is such an agreement, the arbitrator must respect it.

(h) Final disregards: tenant's occupation and dilapidation
Para. 3 provides for two final disregards to be given effect by the arbitrator.

Firstly, para. 3(a) requires him to disregard any effect on the rent of the fact that the tenant who is a party to the arbitration is in occupation of the holding. Thus the sitting tenant should be neither prejudiced nor privileged by his position.

Secondly, para. 3(b) provides that the arbitrator should not fix the rent at a lower level than would otherwise be the case simply by reason of 'any dilapidation or deterioration of, or damage to, buildings or land caused by the tenant'. Thus the 'culpable' tenant will not be permitted to benefit in the long (rental) term from his own neglect of the holding.

As mentioned earlier, the explicit form now adopted for the rental formula in section 12 and Schedule 2 may simply validate established and existing practices and indeed may be treated by professionals as a somewhat unnecessary exercise akin to teaching grandmothers the elements of egg-sucking. It was anticipated that, as the principal item sought by the N.F.U. from the joint 'package', in exchange for which tenants were seen to relinquish the statutory succession rights granted by the 1976 Act, the new formula would produce lower rents. As mentioned above, however, lower rents may result from lower profitability, rather than from the new rental formula.

5.08 Frequency of rent review

Paragraphs 4, 5 and 6 of Schedule 2 are concerned with the frequency of rent reviews. The general rule expressed in *para. 4(1)* is that rent reviews should be no more frequent than once every three years. The three years will run from

(a) the commencement of the tenancy or
(b) the date of the previous rent review taking effect, whether the direction of the arbitrator was for an increase, decrease or no change on the rent payable.

Variation of the rent directed by an arbitrator under section 6(3) or section 8(4) (preparation of a written tenancy and accommodation of the 'model clauses') will *not* trigger a new three-year cycle, nor will a reassessment of the rent payable after the operation of the notice to quit part in accordance with section 33.

Although the general three-year scheme is very clear, two situations which may cause confusion are expressly provided for in paragraphs 5 and 6.

Para. 5 provides that where the landlord's interest is severed and sold to separate 'new' landlords and the tenant consequently enters into new proportionate tenancy agreements with each new landlord, the sale, severance, and renegotiation will *not* trigger a new rent cycle but instead the three-year period will continue to be calculated from the original (unsevered) tenancy. However, this situation is not common in practice, except where the severed parts each constitute balanced holdings. Apart from rental considerations, the succession consequences of such a situation would need serious consideration by the tenant.

Para. 6 provides for the situation where the parties to the tenancy make provision to adjust the boundaries of the holding or to vary any other term(s) of the tenancy, and to increase or reduce the rent accordingly. The paragraph provides that such an agreement or alteration in rent (where the alteration is solely attributable to the re-negotiation) will *not* trigger the rent periods.

5.09 Increases in rent to reflect landlord's improvements

Apart from making provision for periodic rent reviews, the 1986 Act in section 13 also authorises the landlord in certain specified cases to increase the rent of the holding to reflect improvements which he has undertaken and completed. The rent increase in these cases is limited to 'an amount equal to the increase in rental value' which can be attributed to the improvement, and section 13(4) provides that any such increase must be reduced proportionately where any part of the cost was met by central or local government grants. Any increase sought under section 13 must be notified in writing to the tenant within six months of the relevant improvement(s) being completed.

The improvements which may justify an increase in rent under section 13 are as follows:

(a) an improvement carried out at the request of, or in agreement with the tenant;

(b) an improvement carried out to comply with a Tribunal direction given under section 11 of the Act, requiring the landlord to provide fixed equipment to comply with existing statutory requirements. If, in any case, the *tenant* carries out such an improvement because the landlord fails to comply with the direction, a rent increase may still be effected under section 13 but it can only take effect after the tenant has recovered the expense of the improvement (minus the amount of any grant which he received from the landlord): section 13(5),(6);

(c)   a long-term improvement carried out by the landlord under section 67(5);

(d)   an improvement effected to comply with any statutorily authorised Ministerial direction;

(e)   works carried out to provide sanitary conveniences and washing facilities in compliance with a notice under section 3 of the Agriculture (Safety, Health and Welfare Provisions) Act 1956;

(f)   an improvement carried out in compliance with Part VII of the Housing Act 1985 or Part VIII of the Housing Act 1974.

Notice, however, that if an improvement falling within (a) (b) or (f) above is effected, and the tenant and landlord *agree* on 'an increase in rent or other benefit to the landlord' in respect of that work, then *no* increase in rent under section 13 may be made; section 13(3).

Any dispute which arises in respect of section 13 is to be determined by the statutory arbitration scheme: section 13(7).

DISTRESS: THE STATUTORY PROVISIONS

5.10 Distress for unpaid rent

If the tenant falls into arrears in his payment of rent the landlord has a choice of remedy to enforce payment. He may serve a notice to pay rent within two months which, if not complied with, will give grounds for the service of an 'incontestable' notice to quit under Case D [8.10]. Alternatively, he may forfeit the lease for breach of covenant [9.6]. A third possible remedy is the ancient remedy of levying distress or distraining against goods on the holding to recovery the unpaid rent. Whilst the details relating to distress in general are outside the scope of this book, it should be noted that sections 16-19 of the 1986 Act restrict the landlord's right to levy distress for the rent of an agricultural holding by limiting the arrears for which distress is available, by regulating the types of goods which may be seized and by providing for the resolution of disputes about rent.

5.11 Which arrears are enforceable by distress?

Section 16(1) provides that the landlord shall not be entitled to distrain in respect of rent which became due more than one year before the making of the distress. This is only modified in the single case of rent being regularly paid a quarter or half a year *after* it was due. Where the ordinary course of dealings between the parties indicates that such deferred payment has been the normal practice, section 16(2) provides that for the purposes of section 16(1) the rent shall be deemed to have become due at the expiry of that quarter or half year as the case may be. Thus normally only one year's rent for an agricultural holding will be recoverable by distress. Where arrears of more than one year are owing the additional debt may be recovered in proceedings at law subject to the six year limitation period.

5.12 Property subject to distress

Section 18 makes provision for excluding or protecting from distress various specified types of property which may be found on an agricultural holding.

Section 18(1) excludes two categories of property belonging to a third party. Machinery subject to an agreement 'for its hire or use in the conduct of (the tenant's) business' and livestock on the holding solely for breeding purposes may not be distrained upon. The machinery exception seems wide enough to include not only straightforwardly hired machinery but also goods subject to hire purchase agreements whilst the property in the machinery is in the seller or lender.

Section 18 also regulates the levying of distress on agisted livestock, that is, livestock taken on to the holding to be fed by the tenant of the holding at a fair price. 'Livestock' for this purpose is widely defined as 'any animal capable of being distrained': section 18(5). This is a broader definition of 'livestock' than that applicable elsewhere in the Act and would include, for example, horses. Section 18(2) provides that agisted livestock shall *not* be distrained for rent where there is other sufficient distress to be found on the holding. If, in appropriate circumstances, such livestock is distrained, the amount of rent recoverable is limited by the same subsection to the price agreed to be paid for the feeding of the stock, or any part of that price which remains unpaid. Section 18(3) gives the owner of the agisted stock the right to redeem his livestock from the distrainer by paying to him (i.e. to the landlord) a sum equal to the amount agreed to be paid for feeding the animals, or any outstanding part of that amount. Such payment must, of course, be made before the livestock are sold by the distrainer if it is to be effective to redeem the animals.

5.13 Compensation set off against arrears

If the tenant is entitled to compensation, whether by virtue of the 1986 Act or by virtue of custom or agreement, and the amount of such compensation has been ascertained before the landlord distrains for rent, the amount of the compensation may be set off against the arrears or rent owing and the landlord will only be entitled to distrain for the balance: section 17.

5.14 Disputes concerning distress

Section 19 provides that any dispute concerning the levying of distress on an agricultural holding may be determined by the county court or, on complaint, by the magistrates' courts and the relevant court may make any 'order that justice requires' including an order for the restoration of any livestock or things unlawfully distrained or an order declaring the price to be paid for feeding. If the magistrates' court is used, 'any person aggrieved' by its decision may appeal to the Crown Court: section 19(2).

Part III

Security of Tenure

Introduction

Substantial security of tenure was not introduced for tenants of agricultural holdings until the Agriculture Act 1947. Earlier legislation had given tenant farmers hardly more security than the common law. However, in the light of wartime experience, national policy favoured the development of an ever more efficient farming sector and the Agriculture Act 1947 sought to promote this. It was anticipated that tenants who were not liable to peremptory eviction would be more confident in making long-term farming plans and would be more willing to invest energy and money in 'their' land. As Lord Salmon said in *Johnson* v. *Moreton* (1980):

> 'The security of tenure which farmers were accorded ... was not only for their protection as an important section of the public, nor only for the protection of the weak against the strong; it was for the protection of the nation itself.'

The basic scheme of security designed in the 1947 Act is currently continued by the 1986 Act. There are three basic 'planks' of the scheme:

(1)   the automatic continuation of fixed term tenancies as tenancies from year to year on the expiry of the contractual fixed terms (section 3);
(2)   the requirement in most cases that 12 months notice be given (rather than the common law period of six months in an annual periodic tenancy): section 25;
(3)   the imposition of substantial restrictions on the operation of landlords' notices to quit: section 27 and Schedule 3.

Nine 'Cases' are defined in Schedule 3 when a so-called 'incontestable' notice to quit may be served on the tenant. Such notices are relatively free from challenge by the tenant. So long as the notice itself is valid, the only burden on the landlord may be to show that the reasons alleged in his incontestable notice apply to the circumstances of the particular case. If he can do this he will obtain possession from the tenant. The nine Cases of Schedule 3 are, however, very closely defined.

In all other circumstances, when an 'incontestable' notice is not appropriate, the landlord's notice to quit may be challenged by the issue of a *counter-notice* by the tenant. This will have the effect of:

(a)   suspending the operation of the notice to quit until
(b)   the landlord has applied for and obtained the consent of the Agricultural Land Tribunal. Their consent will only be granted if the landlord is able to satisfy them that

   (i)   one or more of only six grounds in section 27(3) applies *and*
   (ii) the circumstances of the case satisfy the 'fair and reasonable landlord test' of section 27(2).

Thus, apart from the very limited number of situations where an incontestable notice to quit is appropriate, the tenant's counter-notice is a formidable device, imposing a significant double hurdle between the landlord and his repossession of the holding. Its importance has not been lost on prospective landlords who have sought ways of sabotaging the counter-notice machinery, to date unsuccessfully in *Johnson* v. *Moreton* and *Featherstone* v. *Staples*. It remains the lynchpin of the tenant's security of tenure when a tenancy of an agricultural holding is granted.

All the notices and their dependent procedures prescribed by the Act are subject to strict statutory time limits which are inflexible and rigid. It is especially important, therefore, that such procedural points receive punctilious attention if the parties are not to lose substantive rights as a result of 'merely' procedural mistakes.

The following chapters consider in detail

•   the notice to quit;
•   the tenant's counter-notice and Tribunal consent;
•   'incontestable' notices to quit;
•   other methods of terminating agricultural tenancies.

The table summarises the Cases, grounds and statutory provisions relevant to notices to quit.

Landlord's grounds for notice to quit

Grounds for possession	Authority	Tenant's challenges				Court?	Comments
		Counter notice?	Tribunal?	Fair and reasonable landlord?	Arbitration?		
1. Good husbandry	s.27(3)(a)	✓	✓	✓	✗	✓	
2. Sound estate management	s.27(3)(b)	✓	✓	✓	✗	✓	
3. Agricultural research etc. or smallholdings	s.27(3)(c)	✓	✓	✓	✗	✓	
4. Allotments	s.27(3)(d)	✓	✓	✓	✗	✓	
5. 'Greater hardship' caused by withholding consent to notice than by consenting to its operation	s.27(3)(e)	✓	✓	✓	✗	✓	
6. Non-agricultural use authorised by planning legislation	s.27(3)(f)	✓	✓	✓	✗		Check also case B
7. Smallholdings tenant retiring at 65	Case A Sch.3	✗	✗	✗	✓	✓	Arbitration on (1) case (2) 'suitable accommodation'
8. Non-agricultural use needing planning permission or authorised other than by planning legislation	Case B	✗	✗	✗	✓	✓	
9. Certificate of bad husbandry obtained not more than 6 months before notice to quit served	Case C	✗	✗	✗	✗	✓	
10. Rent owing	Case D(a)	✗	✗	✗	✓	✓	1. Notice to pay must be served before notice to quit 2. Arbitration on notice to pay *and* notice to quit
11. Failure to remedy: work required	Case D(b)	✓	✓	✓	✓	✓	1. Arbitration also on notice to do work 2. Counter-notice where notice to do work
12. Failure to remedy: no work required	Case D(b)	✗	✗	✗	✓	✓	
13. Irremediable breach of tenancy condition	Case E	✗	✗	✗	✓	✓	
14. Tenant insolvent	Case F	✗	✗	✗	✗	✓	
15. Tenant dead (1) No succession rights (tenancy granted after 12.7.84) or (2) No application for succession tenancy or (3) No successful applicant	Case G	✗	✗	✗	✗	✓	N.B. (1) Only applies to death of sole or surviving tenant
(4) Succession application lodged	Case G	✗	✗	✓	✗	✓	(2) Where tenancy granted before 12.7.84 succession applications may be made and if successful, the landlord may apply to Tribunal for consent to notice to quit
16. Ministry notice for amalgamation or reshaping of units	Case H	✗	✗	✗	✗	✓	

N.B. 1. Where an effective counter-notice is served by the tenant, the *landlord* must (i) apply for Tribunal consent and in doing so (ii) show that the alleged grounds apply and (iii) satisfy the Tribunal on the 'fair and reasonable landlord' point.

2. Where arbitration is sought by the tenant the burden is on the *tenant* to demonstrate why the notice is inappropriate.

Chapter 6

The Notice to Quit

6.01 Introductory

A notice to quit an agricultural holding must satisfy the common law requirements for notices to quit which terminate periodic tenancies, and must accommodate the modifications introduced by the agricultural holdings legislation. The importance of an effective, valid notice to quit is obvious and cannot be over-emphasised: without one the procedure for terminating the tenancy has not even begun. The requirements, common law or statutory, must therefore be carefully observed to avoid, 'false starts'. As Denning LJ (as he then was) said in *Budge* v. *Hicks* (1951):

'If the landlord of an agricultural holding wishes to give his tenant notice to quit, he should get some good advice on the matter, because there are now many legal requirements that he has to fulfill before his notice will be good.'

6.02 Who can give notice?

The quotation from the younger days of Lord Denning should not be allowed to mislead. A notice to quit may be given by or on behalf of either the landlord *or* the tenant, although landlords' notices are much more frequently encountered in practice. It is an inherent characteristic of a periodic tenancy (such as the agricultural tenancy from year to year) that is is terminable by valid notice from either party: *Lower* v. *Sorrell* (1963). Any contractual provision which seeks to deprive a party wholly and permanently of this right will be void at common law as being repugnant to the tenancy and may be disregarded: *Centaploy Ltd* v. *Matlodge Ltd* (1974).

'Anticipatory' notices, served before the commencement of the lease will not be valid:

'A notice to quit is a notice given by an existing landlord to an existing tenant and ... it follows that a person cannot give a valid notice to quit before he has become a landlord and the recipient of the notice his tenant.' (Donovan LJ in *Lower* v. *Sorrell*.)

This common law position is reinforced by section 25 of the Agricultural Holdings Act 1986 which clearly proceeds, as did its predecessor in the 1948 Act

'on the assumption that a notice to quit is a notice which is given by an existing landlord to an existing tenant'.

Thus a prospective landlord cannot give a valid notice to quit before granting the lease, nor can a prospective purchaser of a landlord's interest give a valid notice to an existing tenant: he must wait until his purchase is completed.

Where there is uncertainty, for whatever reason, as to who *is* the tenant (or landlord) Robert Goff LJ suggested that

'it is very difficult to see what a landlord can do but to serve a notice to quit, in proper form, on each of the alternative tenants at the same time making it plain that such service is without prejudice to their contention as to who in fact is the tenant': *Re Cushing's Will Trusts: Cushing* v. *Bailey* (1984)

6.03 Tenant's notice or a surrender?

It may be useful at this point to contrast a *tenant's notice* to quit with a *surrender* by the tenant of his lease. A valid notice to quit will determine a periodic tenancy at the *end* of a period (for example, an annual periodic tenancy at the end of a tenancy year, considered in detail below). The tenant, like the landlord, has a *right* to give such notice if he desires and the *unilateral* notice will, unless restricted in operation by some extrinsic statutory mechanism, be effective to terminate the tenancy. In contrast, the tenant has *no right* to surrender his lease but if the surrender is accepted by the landlord, the lease will merge with the reversion and will be extinguished. Surrender necessarily implies the *premature* termination of a lease and requires a *bilateral* act of both landlord and tenant to be effective. The landlord has the right to refuse a surrender and may choose to do so if for some reason he wishes the tenant's liability under the lease to continue. If accepted, however, a surrender brings the tenancy to an immediate end, whereas a notice to quit, of course, merely introduces the period of notice at the end of which the contractual tenancy will end unless statutorily 'protected'.

6.04 The form of the notice

There is no required form for a notice to quit an agricultural holding. In theory, it may even be given orally: the common law will recognise an oral notice to quit as effective, at least where the tenancy is orally created: *Timmins* v. *Rowlinson* (1765) and there is no express statutory requirement that the notice be in writing. However, in practice it is most desirable that written notice be given. There are two major reasons.

Firstly, a written notice should minimise uncertainty and therefore will hopefully restrict the scope for dispute.

Secondly, landlords' notices to quit agricultural holdings need to contain precise information as to the grounds on which they are given. This is particularly true when a notice is given for one or more of the so-called 'incontestable' grounds in Schedule 3 of the 1986 Act, but in any case it must be clear to the tenant whether the notice is 'contestable' by counter-notice or is 'incontestable' or is given in both forms in the alternative. The likelihood of an oral notice satisfying this requirement is remote.

6.05 Clarity

A valid notice to quit, whatever its form, must leave its recipient in no doubt as to its nature and its terms.

(i) Clear as to its character

The often-quoted words of Coleridge CJ in *Gardner* v. *Ingram* (1889) encapsulate the first requirement of clarity:

'although no particular form need be followed, there must be plain unambiguous words claiming to determine the existing tenancy at a certain time.'

The standard is an *objective* standard, described by Lopes J in *Bury* v. *Thompson* (1885) thus:

'a notice to quit is a good notice if it be so expressed that a person of ordinary capacity receiving the notice cannot well mistake its nature: it must be clear and unambiguous.'

A notice to quit must be absolute in its terms, and not optional. If it appears to offer the tenant an alternative it will be invalid for uncertainty: 'you must improve your standard of farming or quit the holding', for example, leaves the tenant unsure of the step the landlord is trying to take: is this merely an admonition or is it a notice to quit? On the other hand, a valid notice to quit may be accompanied by an offer of a new tenancy on different terms and *will* remain effective. In such a case, if the new terms were accepted, the notice would terminate the existing lease so that the new terms could commence: *Ahearn* v. *Bellman* (1879).

(ii) Clear as to its terms

The notice must be drafted so that

'any reasonable agricultural tenant receiving it and reading it in the light of the Act (with which he is, perhaps, deemed to be acquainted)'

is in no doubt as to whether it is based on one or more of the 'incontestable' grounds of Schedule 3 or the grounds of Section 27. The rights and obligations of the tenant are quite different according to the provision relied on, and if the notice is ambiguous in this respect then

'like any other ambiguous notice to quit it is wholly invalid and can be treated as so much waste paper': Salmon LJ in *Mills* v. *Edwards* (1971)

No express reference to the Schedule or section is needed nor is there any prescribed form of words to indicate the Case(s) of Schedule 3 relied on but it must be reasonably clear from the words used whether the appropriate procedure for the tenant is that of a counter-notice under section 26, or the more limited methods of challenge available for Schedule 3 cases which also, of course, deny him compensation for disturbance if they succeed.

Section 27 grounds

It is *not* necessary for a landlord who serves a notice on Section 27 grounds (sometimes referred to as a 'general', 'simple' or 'common law' notice) to state any reasons at all in the notice to quit. Indeed, there are clear judicial dicta indicating that in such a case the landlord 'will, if he is wise, refrain from giving any reasons': Cross LJ in *Mills* v. *Edwards*, p. 395; (see also Salmon LJ p. 388: 'undesirable' to give reasons.) The danger is that if reasons *are* stated, the notice to quit may be ambiguous and therefore *void*. However, a notice without reasons will render the landlord liable to pay 'additional' compensation under Section 60 of the 1986 Act and careful drafting may therefore be preferred to the perfect but expensive safety of silence in this context.

Incontestable grounds

If a notice is given for one or more of the Cases of Schedule 3 it must be clear and certain *which* Case(s) are relied on: *Budge* v. *Hicks* (1951). Ambiguity on this point will render the notice invalid.

If a notice fails on an 'incontestable' ground, it cannot automatically be converted into and take effect as a 'general' notice: *Cowan* v. *Wrayford* (1953). If the landlord wishes to reserve an alternative basis for his claim he must do so expressly by serving a notice drafted 'in the alternative' or by serving two separate notices to quit.

Alternative grounds

It is, of course, always possible for the landlord to base his claim on 'incontestable' grounds *and, in the alternative,* on the general grounds subject to section 27. In such a case he should either serve separate notices to quit, each ambiguous, or he may rely on the 'combined invoking of the two (provisions) in one appropriately worded notice': Edmund Davies LJ in *Mills* v. *Edwards*. Separate notices are considerably safer but the danger of ambiguity in a 'combined' notice is not inevitable and it can be avoided by careful drafting.

6.06 Expiry of the notice

The common law requires that a valid notice to quit must terminate a periodic tenancy at the end of a periodic term and that the notice to quit must therefore expire either on the anniversary of the grant or on the preceding day: *Sidebottom* v. *Holland* (1895). For example, an annual periodic tenancy granted 'on and from April 1st' must be ended by a notice expiring either on a subsequent April 1st or on a subsequent March 31st. Each annual period will strictly end at midnight on each March 31st but a notice expiring instead on the anniversary date will be acceptable. The validity of a notice to quit 'ought not to turn on the splitting of a straw', said Lindley LJ in *Sidebottom* v. *Holland* and in this context at least the requisite latitude is extended.

Clearly, if this requirement is to be satisfied, the commencement date of the tenancy must be correctly identified *or* a form of words must be used in the notice which is both certain (to avoid ambiguity) and flexible (to avoid invalidating the notice by dogmatically tying it to an erroneous date). The 'running notice' satisfies both these criteria and is frequently used in practice for that reason [6.08].

6.07 The period of notice

To ascertain whether in any particular case notice has been (or will be) served in time to be effective it is necessary to know (i) when the notice must expire and (ii) what period of notice must be given, so that an appropriately early date for service may be identified.

Section 25(1) of the 1986 Act provides that

'a notice to quit an agricultural holding or part of an agricultural holding shall (nothwithstanding any provision to the contrary in the contract of tenancy of the holding) be invalid if it purports to terminate the tenancy before the expiry of twelve months from the end of the then current year of tenancy.'

This effectively imposes a requirement of a *minimum* twelve months' notice on all agricultural tenancies (apart from a very small number of closely defined exceptions discussed below). This statutory requirement expressly overrides any contractual stipulation providing for a shorter period of notice. It also overrides the common law period of six months' notice implied in the case of other annual periodic tenancies.

Imagine an agricultural tenancy beginning on 29th September 1985. By 1987 the landlord has decided to try to terminate the tenancy as quickly as possible. The landlord's notice must expire on either 28th or 29th September to be valid at common law: *Sidebottom* v. *Holland*. It must also be of at least twelve months' duration from the end of the current year of tenancy. The landlord cannot, therefore, hope to terminate the tenancy on 28th September 1987: the notice would not be long enough to satisfy Section 25. The earliest he can aim for is 28th September 1988. To accommodate the statutory period he must serve notice *before* the end of the current (1986/7) term of the tenancy, i.e. he must serve on or before 28th September 1987 a notice to quit expiring on 28th or 29th September 1988 if he is to move as quickly as the law allows him. If he delays and serves the notice after 28th September, the next expiry date which satisfies both statute and common law would be 28th September 1989. Keeping the notice dates and periods clearly in mind is essential if a year is not to be lost simply by a slip. It should be stressed, however, that in practice it is rare for such a specific notice to quit to be given. It is far preferable, and safer, to use the standard form of 'running notice' discussed in the following paragraphs, which by its very wording ensures that the minimum statutory period will always be satisfied.

6.08 Stating the period of notice

'A notice to quit, though it need not actually name the day must indicate with reasonable clearness when possession will be demanded or given, so that the other party may know what is required of him, and the time must be the proper time'

said Lush J in his first instance judgment in *Phipps (P) & Co. (Northampton and Towcester Breweries) Ltd* v. *Rogers* (1924). The period must be expressed with sufficient clarity to enable the recipient to tell whether adequate notice has been given and to challenge or ignore a notice to quit which is invalid for insufficient notice.

Where a *landlord* gives notice to quit a holding 'on or before' or 'by' a specified date this will be sufficiently certain. Such a notice serves a double purpose. Firstly, it indicates unambiguously to the tenant the last date by which he must quit, and therefore clearly defines the period of notice given. Secondly, it indicates that the landlord will accept an earlier surrender of the tenancy if the tenant so chooses: *Dagger* v. *Shepherd* (1946). Such a notice from the tenant, however, would be open to challenge since the landlord is not certain when he will regain possession. In any event, notices expressed in this way tend to raise the spectre of litigation and therefore although technically correct are in practice far less attractive than the 'running notice'.

The so-called 'running notice' is a standard form of words which is frequently used and is designed to overcome any uncertainty as to the precise tenancy dates whilst still ensuring a proper period of notice. This states that possession should be delivered up, or will be delivered up, on a specified date (thought to be the anniversary or term date of this period)

'or at the expiration of twelve months from the end of the now current year of tenancy'.

The form of words is

'intended to cast the duty on the (addressee) to satisfy himself ... what is the correct date. The fact that he is involved in that problem is no objection in itself to the form of words which have (*sic*) been used ... Assuming the (addressee) can read and write he needs two things only, namely a modern calendar and his document of tenancy'

said Evershed LJ in *Addis* v. *Burrows* (1948) upholding the validity of the well-established common form running notice.

The 'reasonable tenant' will be deemed to know the commencement date of his tenancy and thus be able to render certain a 'running notice'.

However, there are limits to the burdens which can be imposed on the tenant and to the knowledge which is reasonably to be imputed to him. These limitations have caused some of the most concise terms of notice to be held 'short, simple and wrong' (Bankes LJ in *Phipps* v. *Rodgers*, speaking of the notice in *May* v. *Borup* (1915) which required the tenant to leave 'at the earliest possible moment'). A case in point is *Phipps* v. *Rodgers* itself, where notice was given to the tenant of an hotel to quit

'on the earliest day your tenancy can be legally terminated by valid notice to quit given to you at the date of the service hereof.'

On the facts of the particular case this involved the tenant in deciding several issues of fact and law and resolving an accumulation of difficulties provided by the joint effect of the language of the tenancy agreement and the very unusual form of notice to quit. The Court of Appeal held that the notice was invalid for uncertainty, Atkin LJ saying:

'that the law should impute to every person knowledge of its provisions is one thing but that a notice between landlord and tenant which presumes such knowledge is certain and unambiguous seems to me to be a quite different proposition.'

In a more recent case, *Aslam & Co. Ltd* v. *Europa Poster Services* (1968), Buckley J suggested that the 'running notice' case, *Addis* v. *Burrows*

'clearly establishes that where a formula is used in a notice of this kind which involves reference to some other document in order to ascertain the date at which the notice is intended to operate and some question of law arises upon the interpretation of that document ... that fact is not of itself necessarily fatal to the validity of the notice.'

A notice terminating numerous licences 'so soon as may be legally possible' was here upheld.

It can be said with confidence that a 'running notice' will be valid. Beyond that, however, lies uncertainty and a division of judicial opinion. The attractions of apparently short and simple wordings which leave all clarification to the addressee should be eschewed: there is no virtue (or profit) in providing the material for further litigation.

6.09 Waiver of the statutory period of notice

The effect of Section 25 is that neither party in a tenancy agreement can be obliged to accept a notice to quit which is for a shorter period than the statutory twelve months. If either party serves such a 'short notice' (which is not validated by one of the exceptional statutory provisions discussed below) then the other party, the addressee, is entitled to ignore it as invalid, and as just so much waste paper. Similarly, the section expressly invalidates any agreement between the parties whereby they undertake *in advance* to accept any lesser period of notice.

However, if *during the currency of the tenancy* one party serves a 'short' notice to quit on the other, who agrees to accept it and thus to *waive* his statutory right to full twelve months, such a waiver may be binding and the notice, if otherwise valid, will be effective to terminate the tenancy.

Thus, in *Elsden* v. *Pick* (1980) the tenant of two holdings held of the same landlord found himself in difficult circumstances and notified the landlord's agent that he was likely to give notice in respect of at least one holding. The agent, sympathetically, suggested that he take a few days to consider his position further, and that if he decided to give notice he should give a pre-dated notice to quit which in the circumstances would be three days short of the statutory period, and it would nevertheless be accepted. The tenant followed this course of action but, subsequently, his circumstances having somewhat improved, argued that the notice to quit was invalid since it failed to give the statutory period of notice, and thus it was not effective to terminate his tenancy. The Court of Appeal, rejecting his argument, upheld the notice and the parties' right to waive the statutory period of notice if they choose to, Brightman LJ saying that the parties

'are entitled to agree that the notice shall be treated in all respects as if it were a notice of the statutory length. If the parties agree, the tenancy will come to an end on the agreed date by virtue of the defective notice to quit which it is agreed shall be treated as valid. Such an agreement could not effectively be made before a notice to quit is served, because the parties cannot agree that the tenancy shall be capable of being terminated by a short notice. Neither the landlord nor the tenant can bind himself in advance to accept a short notice from the other ... That would be 'a provision to the contrary' in, or supplemental to, the contract of tenancy and would not be effective. But once an invalid notice has been served, which the recipient is entitled to ignore, I see nothing in [section 25] to prohibit an agreement between landlord and tenant that the notice shall be followed by the same consequences as if it were valid.'

In *Elsden* v. *Pick* the Court was apparently willing to accept that the parties' mutual promises (presumably to decide and to accept) supported a binding contract between them which was legally enforceable. Whilst perhaps rather generous, the decision has the attraction of achieving a practical (and equitable) result. This is not to say that it should *encourage* the waiver of the statutory period of notice.

6.10 Short notice

In several closely defined situations, the normal requirement of the 12 months' minimum period of notice does not apply. These exceptional cases are now set out in section 25(2)(3) and (4) of the 1986 Act. They are as follows:

(1) Where the tenant is insolvent: section 25(2)(a).

(2) Where the notice to quit is given in pursuance of a provision in the tenancy which authorises the resumption of possession of the holding or part of it for a specified non-agricultural purpose: section 25(2)(b). This includes *any* non-agricultural purpose so long as it is expressly provided for in the tenancy: *Paddock Investments Ltd* v. *Lory* (1975). There is no specified minimum period of notice in the Act for such cases. *Re Disraeli's Agreement* (1939) and *Coates* v. *Diment* (1951), however, indicate that the period of notice must be sufficient to enable the tenant to make any appropriate claims for compensation: one month for 'high farming' compensation under section 70(2), for example. Failure to give the tenant adequate notice in such a case would render the notice invalid.

(3) Where notice is given by a tenant to a sub-tenant: section 25(2)(c) [6.17].

(4) Where the tenancy has been converted by section 149(6) of the Law of Property Act 1925 into a tenancy for 90 years: section 25(2)(d). The relevant period of notice in such a case, prescribed by the 1925 Act, is at least one month, terminating on a relevant quarter day.

(5) Where a tenant gives notice to quit after the rent has been increased in an arbitration under section 12 of the 1986 Act: section 25(3). This provision was introduced in 1984 as an incidental aspect of the reform of the rent formula. It was felt undesirable and unreasonable to oblige a tenant to suffer a full year's increased rental if he preferred to quit the holding after the rent had been increased. Section 25(3) therefore provides that a minimum of six months' notice expiring at the end of the first tenancy year after the increase will be sufficient. If the tenant does not leave during that first year, however, the normal twelve month period will apply to any later notice which he gives, whether his departure is attributable to the increased rent or to any other factor.

(6) Where the landlord applies for, and is granted, a Certificate of Bad Husbandry, the Agricultural Land Tribunal may specify in the

certificate that a shorter period of notice than the normal twelve months shall apply to a notice: section 25(4). The *minimum* period which they may specify as an alternative is *two months*.

(7) In addition, para. 4 of Schedule 12 provides that the normal statutory minimum period of notice will not apply when possession of the land in question is required for naval, military or air force purposes.

6.11 Mistakes in notices to quit

(i) 'Incontestable notices'

When a notice to quit is served in reliance on one or more of the 'incontestable' cases of Schedule 3, the courts' attitude towards any mistake in the notice, whether a 'mere' clerical slip or a more substantial error, has traditionally been unforgiving. The 'incontestable' grounds in effect allow the landlord to forfeit the tenant's interest, and forfeiture clauses have always been construed strictly against the landlord especially when, as under the agricultural holdings legislation, there is no provision for relief against forfeiture. In *Pickard* v. *Bishop and Another* (1975) a notice quoting what is now Case D(a) (failure to pay rent) was served which misnamed the landlord. A majority of the Court of Appeal held that the error rendered the notice invalid; as Lord Denning said, 'in order to be good, these notices must get the landlord right'.

Similarly in *Dickinson* v. *Boucher* (1983), a mistake in the amount of rent alleged to be owing (£650 stated rather than £665) was similarly fatal to a notice which relied on Case D (a).

However, some relaxation of this rigorous approach seems to be apparent, in *Official Solicitor to the Supreme Court* v. *Thomas* (1986), where Nicholls LJ refused to hold that a reference in a notice to remedy (subject to the same rigours of construction as incontestable notices to quit) to 'supplemental agreement' rather than 'supplemental agreements' was a sufficient inaccuracy to invalidate the notice. To find otherwise

'would be to carry the need for strict compliance with the statutory requirements to an absurd length and for no apparent purpose.'

On the facts, it had been admitted for the tenant that the misdescription (or 'terseness') could not reasonably have misled him and in the context of the case the criteria to be used were the sufficiency and accuracy of the description of the term of the tenancy which had been broken – criteria satisfied by the words used. Nicholls LJ held in effect that the statutory requirements were satisfied by the notice. His Lordship's judgment does not give precise indications of the limits of this new and more tolerant approach. Whether this case actually heralds a more forgiving approach or is merely aberrant is, as yet, not clear. If the courts are to relax their traditional rigour, his Lordship's judgment does not clearly indicate the new limits of tolerance which landlords and tenants may assume.

(ii) General notices

Where a 'general' notice to quit under section 2 is issued, however, the courts' attitude is less rigorous, at least in respect of clerical errors. The modern approach, exemplified in *Carradine Properties Ltd* v. *Aslam* (1976) and *Gemax Securities Ltd* v. *Spiegal* (1978) is to ask whether the notice 'is clear to a reasonable tenant reading it? Is it also plain that he cannot be mislead?'

In *Carradine* where a mistake in the expiry date had been made by clerical error and an impossible date quoted, the judge felt able to adopt a

'benevolent approach ... because reasonably read by a reasonable tenant the mistake is obvious and there is no doubt what the mistake was'

(nor, apparently, how it might be corrected). This approach appears at variance with older decisions such as *Hankey* v. *Clavering* (1942) and *Frankland* v. *Capstick* (1959) where notices to quit containing clear unambiguous errors were held invalid because of those mistakes. It is difficult to predict from *Carradine* and *Gemax* which errors a 'reasonable tenant' may be assumed capable of correcting, and how far the courts' discretion in these matters will extend. Where there is a genuine ambiguity the courts have always leaned in favour of an interpretation which will render the notice valid. Where, on the other hand, there is no ambiguity but instead a statement in the notice which is 'clear and specific but inaccurate' it now seems that unless the notice refers to an 'incontestable' ground, the courts will also strain in favour of validity if they can find that the error would not substantially prejudice a 'reasonable' addressee and even, from *Thomas*, in cases of 'incontestable' notices the approach may be changing somewhat.

6.12 Second notices

If the landlord is in any doubt as to the accuracy of a notice to quit in any respect, he will not be prejudiced by serving a second 'corrected' notice.

If the first notice is in fact valid, its effectiveness will not be impaired: *Lowenthal* v. *Vanhoute* (1947).

6.13 Notice to quit part

At common law a notice to quit part only of the premises included in a lease is invalid: notice can only be given for the whole: *Re Bebington's Tenancy* (1921). However, if permitted either by an express term of the contract or by statutory provision, such a partial notice will be valid. In the context of agricultural holdings there are three situations to be borne in mind:

(1)   cases covered by section 31 of the 1986 Act
(2)   cases covered by section 140 of the Law of Property Act 1925 (severance of the reversion); and
(3)   cases where express provision is made in the contract of tenancy for notice to quit part to be given.

In addition, the effect of sections 32 and 33 of the 1986 Act must be noted. *Section 32* gives the tenant the right to treat a notice to quit part validated either by section 31 of the 1986 Act or by section 140 of the 1925 Act as notice to quit the entire holding (the so-called right of 'enlargement'). *Section 33* provides that where the landlord resumes possession of part of a holding, either by reason of section 31 of the 1986 Act or by reason of a provision in the contract of tenancy, then the tenant will be entitled to a proportionately reduced rent which should also reflect any depreciation in the value of his retained land caused by the severance which the landlord has achieved or by the use intended for the severed land.

(1) Section 31 of the 1986 Act

This provides that a notice to quit part of an agricultural holding given by the landlord will not be invalid if it is for one of the purposes specified in the section and *it states this fact*. The approved purposes are

(1)   adjusting the boundaries between agricultural units or amalgamating units: section 31(1)(a)

and the 'public interest' purposes of the following subsection, *viz.*

(2)   (a)   the erection of cottages or other homes for farm labourers, with or without gardens;

(b)   the provision of gardens for cottages or other houses for farm
      labourers;
(c)   the provision of allotments;
(d)   the letting of land as a smallholding;
(e)   the planting of trees;
(f)   the opening or working of a deposit of coal, ironstone,
      limestone, brick earth or other mineral or a stone quarry or a
      clay, sand or gravel pit;
(g)   the making of a watercourse or reservoir;
(h)   the making of a road, railway, tramroad, siding, canal or basin
      or connected works.

To be validated by section 31, the landlord's notice must *state* that it is
for one of these purposes. The list is exhaustive – notice to quit part only
of the holding for *any other purpose* will be *invalid* under the normal
common law rule *unless* it is within section 140 of the Law of Property Act
1925 or is a notice given pursuant to a provision in the contract of tenancy.

(2) Section 140 of the Law of Property Act 1925

Section 140 provides that where the reversion is severed, the landlord of
any severed part may give an independent notice to quit that part. Thus
if the original landlord of the entire holding sells or gives his interest in a
defined part of the land to a third party, that person will be entitled to
serve on the tenant notice to quit the severed part which he now owns.

Any severance which is relied on as validating a notice to quit part must
be a genuine transfer of a part of the reversion, and not simply a device
designed to enable such a notice to be given. As with other attempts to
circumvent or 'avoid' the agricultural holdings legislation, the courts will
look at the *substance* of the transaction rather than its mere form. This was
made clear in *Persey* v. *Bazley* (1983) in which a transfer of part of the
reversionary estate to bare trustees was seen in substance to be merely a
transfer to agents for the purpose of serving notice to quit part. The
transaction was not, therefore, a true 'severance' and the notice to quit was
invalid.

Severance of the freehold reversion does not of itself create two
tenancies. The tenant continues to hold under one single lease, whether or
not there has been any apportionment of the rent: *Jelly* v. *Buckman* (1974);
Stiles v. *Farrow* (1977).

Section 140(2) of the 1925 Act gives the tenant who is served with
notice to quit part the right to serve a counter-notice on the owner of the
remainder of the reversionary estate which terminates the tenancy of the
entire holding. Such a counter-notice must be served within one month of

the notice to quit and must expire at the same time as that notice. The counter-notice operates as a notice to quit by the tenant and section 140(2) thus effectively gives the tenant the right to enlarge notice to quit part into notice to quit the whole. In the context of an agricultural holding it is advantageous for the tenant to exercise his right to enlarge under section 32 of the 1986 Act rather than section 140(2), however, since compensation for disturbance is not payable if the tenant quits pursuant to his *own* notice (as under section 140(2)). This problem does not arise with section 32.

(3) Contractual provision

There may be an express contractual provision in the tenancy itself which will validate a notice to quit part.

The same period of notice and other common law and statutory requirements apply to notices to quit part of the holding as apply to notices to quit the whole. Twelve months' minimum notice will be required unless the situation is one of the specified exceptions. Perhaps the most predictable exception is where the tenancy expressly provides for the landlord to resume possession of part of the holding for a specified non-agricultural purpose: section 25(2)(b).

Enlargement

Where a notice to quit part is given by the landlord under section 31 or by the owner of a severed part of the reversion under section 140 of the Law of Property Act 1925, the tenant is given the right, by section 32 of the 1986 Act, to treat the notice as notice to quit the entire holding. To exercise this right, the tenant must give the landlord(s) a counter-notice in writing. There is no prescribed form of words but it must be clear that the tenant is accepting the notice as notice to quit the entire holding. The counter-notice must be given within twenty-eight days of the notice to quit being given or within twenty-eight days of the notice being given effect by Tribunal arbitration proceedings under the Act.

Having 'enlarged' the notice to quit part by this means, the tenant is eligible for compensation for disturbance in respect of the entire holding. The only exception is found in section 63(3) of the 1986 Act which provides that if the part affected by the original notice to quit was less than 'one fourth' of the original entire holding, and the unaffected part of the holding was 'reasonably capable of being farmed as a separate holding' then compensation for disturbance will be paid *only* in respect of that part of the holding to which the original landlord's notice to quit related.

The tenant is *not* able to enlarge a notice to quit part given in pursuance of a contractual provision.

Rent reduction

If the landlord resumes possession of a part of the original holding either under section 31 or by reason of a contractual provision, then by virtue of section 33 the tenant is entitled to proportionate reduction in rent. The reduction should reflect the proportion of the original holding now lost to him and also any depreciation to his remaining land caused either by the severance itself or by the use made or to be made of the re-possessed part: section 33(1). If the parties cannot agree on a reduction, it may be determined by arbitration: section 33(2). If the holding has been severed by virtue of a contractual provision, the arbitrator must take into account

'any benefit or relief allowed to the tenant under the contract of tenancy'

in respect of the severed part.

If there is a variation of the rent under section 33, this will *not* trigger a new three year rent cycle: Schedule 2, para 4(2).

Notice that section 33 does *not* provide for any reduction in rent if the tenant *surrenders* part of the holding and the landlord accepts the surrender. The contract of tenancy may, of course, provide expressly for such a case. If in such circumstances the parties agree a reduction in rent, this *will* trigger a new three year rent cycle as the agreement falls squarely within Section 2, para. 4(1)(b).

6.14 Effect of sale of the landlord's interest during the currency of a notice to quit

Until 1984 the agricultural holdings legislation included a provision (latterly section 7 of the Agricultural Holdings (Notices to Quit) Act 1977) to the effect that a contract to sell or part with the landlord's interest concluded during the currency of a notice to quit the holding would render the notice of no effect. The provision was tiresome and increasingly difficult to justify. It was repealed by Schedule 4 of the 1984 Act.

Any sale of the landlord's interest can now go ahead without prejudicing any current notice to quit. Notices remain valid and effective regardless of transactions affecting the reversion.

6.15 Service of notice

The requirements as to service of notices to quit stem partly from common law and partly from section 93 of the 1986 Act which relates to the service of all notices (including for example counter-notices) under the Act.

Parties

It has been explained [6.02] that the right to give notice is an inherent right of both parties to a periodic tenancy and is characteristic of such a tenancy. The right is enjoyed only by *existing* landlords and *existing* tenants: notice cannot be given before the lease begins: *Lower* v. *Sorrell*.

Agents: (1) service by agents

Notices may effectively be served by an agent, and many notices concerning agricultural holdings of course are so served. The agent must have sufficient authority from his principal if the service is to be effective. Where the agent is concerned with the general letting and management of the property he will have sufficient inherent authority and may service notices in his own name: *Jones* v. *Phipps* (1968). Where the agent has less apparent connection with the property, however, he will require specific authority to serve notices and should do so in the name of his principal, whether the landlord or tenant: *Harmond Properties* v. *Gajdzis* (1968).

Signatures

There is no requirement at common law or in the agricultural holdings legislation that a written notice to quit must be signed. However, a notice needs to be authenticated so that the recipient is able to accept it with confidence and safely act on it and the clearest method of authentication is by signature. If the document is signed by an agent on behalf of his principal, this constitutes a signature by procuration and should be indicated by the letters 'p.p.', followed by the agent's initials or name after the signature. If this form is omitted it will not invalidate the signature so long as the agent signing had authority to sign.

Agents: (2) service on agents

At common law, service on the addressee's wife or employees at the premises is effective: *Mason* v. *Bibby* (1864).

Section 93(3) provides that a notice which is to be served on a landlord or tenant will be duly given or served to that party if it is given to or served on an agent or servant who is responsible for the management or farming of the holding in question. Delivery to a farm manager therefore would be effective service on the tenant.

Deceased parties

If the addressee has died leaving a will, service on the executors will be effective: once obtained, the grant of probate dates back to the death.

If the addressee has died leaving no will, and therefore intestate, the service should be effective on the President of the Family Division of the High Court, c/o The Treasury Solicitor, Queen Anne's Chambers, 28 Broadway, London SW1H 9JS. Where the tenant has died intestate but leaves someone in possession of and running the holding that person will be deemed to be the agent of the Probate Judge and service on him will be good service in that capacity. In *Egerton* v. *Rutter* (1951), for example, the tenant died intestate but his son continued in possession of the holding, farming and managing it. Service on the son was held effective on the President.

Where the landlord is uncertain whether the tenant died testate or intestate his safest course of action will be the service of multiple notices to the personal representatives, the President, the person in control of the management or farming of the holding and any solicitors, agents or relevant advisers believed to be acting for the deceased or his estate. If an explanatory note is attached indicating the reason for such multiple service the position will be clear to the recipients. A proliferation of notices will not of itself serve to invalidate the procedure: *Re Cushing* (1984) [6.02].

Transfer of landlord's interest

Section 93(5) provides that unless and until the tenant of an agricultural holding has been notified that the original landlord has ceased to be entitled to the rents and profits of the holding *and* has been notified of the name and address of his successor in interest, any documents served by him on the *original* landlord will be deemed to be served on 'the landlord of the holding' for the purposes of the 1986 Act.

Companies

If the recipient is an incorporated company or body, section 93(2) provides that service will be duly effected if notice is served on the secretary or clerk to the company or body. Section 93(4) provides that for the purposes of that section the proper address for service shall be the registered office of a company or body on the last known address of a person.

Methods of service

Section 93(1) provides that

> 'any notice, request, demand or other instrument under this Act shall be duly given to or served on the person to or on whom it is to be given or served if it is delivered to him or left at his proper address or sent by post in a registered letter or by the recorded delivery service.'

Personal delivery is perhaps the most precarious of these because of the difficulties of proof which may be encountered. *Newborough* v. *Jones* (1975) indicated that if the notice is served in such a way as would reasonably bring it to the addressee's attention, then the document will have been effectively served even if in fact the addressee does not find or receive it. In that case, although the notice was pushed through the letterbox at the addressee's premises, it fell under the linoleum and lay there undetected for six weeks. It was held to have been effectively served. *Delivery*, not receipt, was the crucial factor. (A result of this requirement in this case was that no counter-notice could be served in time.) *Datnow* v. *Jones* (1985) is a salutary example of the difficulties of proof which may be encountered in cases of personal delivery. An agent of the landlords gave evidence that he had delivered the notice and other documentation to a remote Welsh farm. He was unaccompanied. No-one was in when he posted the envelope of documents through the letterbox on the back of the porch. Twelve hours later, when one of the tenants returned, there was no envelope to be seen and none subsequently appeared. In such a case the service of the notice will depend on the credibility of the agent's uncorroborated evidence at trial.

If delivery is effected by post the following points should be noted:

(a)   Where the notice is sent by registered post or recorded delivery there is a rebuttable presumption that delivery and due service have been effected if the document was correctly addressed, pre-paid and posted.

This presumption can be rebutted by the addressee proving that the notice did not arrive at all or did not arrive 'in the ordinary course of the post' (i.e. the day after posting if sent by first class post: section 7, Interpretation Act 1978). The burden of denying service is on the *addressee*. In *Hallinan* v. *Jones* (1984) a recorded delivery notice was proved never to have been delivered, and thus not to have been served.

(b)   If the ordinary post is used, the notice is duly served if it can be shown to have been delivered. The burden here is thus on the *sender* to *prove* service – a less attractive option. The person giving notice to quit (usually the landlord) is therefore strongly advised to use the registered post or recorded delivery procedures.

6.16 Co-owners and notices to quit

Co-owners: joint tenant landlords and tenants

Where there are co-owning landlords or tenants they will be joint tenants in law. As such, they *together* enjoy the character of a single owner: together they are *the* tenant or *the* landlord. Consequently, with one apparent exception, they must act *unanimously* if they are to act effectively in respect of their interest in the holding. The apparent exception to this in respect of notices to quit is discussed below.

In relation to notices to quit, the following points relating to co-owners should be noted.

Co-owners as recipients of notices to quit
A notice to quit served on co-owners must be addressed to *all* of them or it will be invalid: *Jones* v. *Lewis* (1973). The notice, properly addressed, may be served on one co-owner on behalf of all. Thus, if a tenant holds of joint landlords (say, husband and wife) his notice to quit must be addressed to both but may be delivered or given to one and will be validly served. This applies similarly where there are co-owning tenants.

Co-owners serving notice to quit
A periodic tenancy such as the agricultural lease from year to year is said to 'renew itself unless either side bring it to an end': Somervell LJ in *Leek and Moorlands Building Society* v. *Clark* (1952). In such a case the co-owners are understood to act unanimously, as joint tenancy requires, when they (often tacitly) agree to continue the grant or lease into another period on the eve of each anniversary. In the words of one of the oldest and most quoted analyses:

'upon a joint demise by the joint tenants upon a tenancy from year to year the true character of the tenancy is this, not that the tenant holds of each the share of each so long as he and each should please but that he holds the whole of all so long as he and all shall please.'

Thus, if *one* co-owner 'breaks ranks' by refusing the renewal of the tenancy, his act, by destroying the unanimity of the joint tenancy, will be effective to prevent a renewal:

> 'as soon as any *one* of the joint tenants gives a notice to quit he effectively puts an end to that tenancy.'

(Both these quotations are taken from a continuous passage in the judgement of Lord Tenterden in *Doe d. Aslin* v. *Summerset* (1830) (emphasis added)). *Thus a single co-owning landlord can serve a valid and effective notice to quit, as can a single co-owning tenant.* This is the *only* situation where the requirement of unanimity operates to allow a *unilateral* action to bind the co-owners. *Greenwich L.B.C.* v. *McGrady* (1982) is a modern example of the rule. Compare, for example, the situation with regard to counter-notices which must be served jointly [7.05].

6.17 Subtenants and notice to quit

(i) Notice to quit given by head landlord to tenant

Where the head landlord serves notice to quit on his tenant and it is effective to terminate that tenancy, any dependent subtenancy will simultaneously terminate automatically, by operation of law. It is not necessary for any notice to be served on the subtenant for this result to occur. In such a situation, compensation for disturbance is payable by the tenant to the subtenant: section 63. If, on service of a notice to quit, the tenant fails to serve a counter-notice when he could do so under section 26, the subtenant has no remedy by which he might oblige the tenant to serve a valid counter-notice and thus protect both their interests (at least temporarily). In such a situation the subtenant has no right to serve a counter-notice (himself) on the landlord because, of course, he is not within section 26 as regards a notice to quit served by the head landlord on the tenant. Thus, in such a situation the subtenant's position is especially precarious. Where the tenant does serve a valid counter-notice, the subtenant is entitled to be heard in any tribunal proceedings which ultimately result: Agricultural Land Tribunals (Rules) Order 1978, r.13.

(ii) Notice to quit given by tenant to subtenant

(a) 'Consequential notice': where the tenant has himself been given notice to quit by the head landlord and he then serves notice to quit on the subtenant stating that fact, the subtenant is not able to serve a counter-notice on the tenant: Agricultural Holdings (Arbitration on Notices) Order 1978, art. 15.

If, in such a situation, the tenant's notice to quit does *not* state that it is given in consequence of the landlord's notice, then the subtenant may challenge it by serving a counter-notice, and the tenant would need to obtain Tribunal consent to the notice in the normal way under section 26. His justification must then be one or more grounds of section 27: he *cannot* use the head landlord's notice; his *failure* to refer to it in his notice causes him to '*lose*' its help.

Where the tenant has been given notice to quit and he consequently serves notice on the subtenant, he will have to pay compensation for disturbance to the subtenant, as he does (since 1984) if the subtenancy is terminated automatically by operation of law.

(b)   '*Independent notices*': where the tenant simply serves notice to quit on the subtenant in situations where he himself is not being proceeded against by the head landlord, then the tenant-subtenant action is the same as any landlord-tenant action under the agricultural holdings legislation *subject to* Section 25(2)(c), which provides that the statutory period of twelve months notice will not apply to such a notice to quit. No alternative minimum period is stipulated by the Act and the parties will thus be governed either by an express contractual term or by the common law period of six months' notice expiring on the term date or anniversary for an annual periodic tenancy in the absence of express provision. In any event it is submitted that at least one month's notice is necessary under the principle in *Re Disraeli* [6.10].

(iii) Forfeiture of the tenant's interest by head landlord

If the tenant's interest is forfeited, the subtenancy *will* be destroyed as it will fall with the tenancy from which it was carved. However, the subtenant has a right under section 146(4) of the Law of Property Act to apply to the court for relief from forfeiture in such a situation and the court has the power, on such an application, to vest the tenancy or any lesser term in the subtenant.

(iv) Tenant's notice to quit served on head landlord: surrender

If the tenant serves notice to quit on the head landlord, or if he voluntarily surrenders his tenancy before its proper termination date, then in either case the subtenant's interest will *not* be destroyed but he will instead hold directly of the head landlord: *Mellor* v. *Watkins* (1874) and section 139 of the Law of Property Act 1925. The tenant, in other words, is not permitted to destroy voluntarily an interest which he himself has created.

(v) Sham subtenancies

Although not as yet the subject of litigation, the potential of 'sham' subtenancies as a device to avoid granting security of tenure to tenant farmers is obvious. If the landlord can grant an agricultural tenancy to a 'trusted' tenant who may be relied on not to challenge any notice to quit, then any subtenant holding from that tenant is in a precarious position indeed. If, for example, a landowner grants a tenancy to a 'captive company' which then sublets to a farming subtenant, the farmer's security is in practice reduced to vanishing point. However, given the reaffirmation in *Featherstone* v. *Staples* (1986) of the need for the courts to look in such situations at the *substance* rather than the *form* of such arrangements, two possible weaknesses are exposed. Firstly, if evidence will support the contention that the intermediate tenancy is a mere sham, it may be struck down as such, and the farming tenant treated as the direct tenant of the landowner. Even if it is not a true 'sham' it may be vulnerable as an 'artificial transaction' and disregarded accordingly: *Furniss* v. *Dawson* (1984). Alternatively, the courts may analyse such an arrangement as one of agency whereby the company-tenant is essentially the landowner's agent in granting the tenancy to the farmer, who, again, is deemed to hold directly (and with protection) from the landowner.

If the tenant has some substantial function, of course, such imputations may be avoided.

6.18 Notice to quit when Tenant is a member of the reserve or auxiliary forces

Tenants who are members of the reserve or auxiliary forces and whose holding comprises a dwelling-house occupied by the person responsible for farming the holding are in a specially privileged position with regard to notices to quit their holding or the part of it comprising the dwelling house. The statutory scheme which defines their particular position is contained in Schedule 5 of the 1986 Act.

Where such a tenant performs a 'period of relevant service' (as defined in the Reserve and Auxiliary Forces (Protection of Civil Interests) Act 1951) and notice to quit the whole or the relevant part of the holding is served in time *during* the 'period of residence protection', then regardless of whether the notice to quit is based on grounds from section 27(3) or on one or more of Cases B to G of Schedule 3, the tenant may challenge the notice to quit by serving a valid counter-notice. Thus, any notice to quit served on such a tenant during the 'period of residence protection' becomes subject to Tribunal consent, and Schedule 5 para. (3) specifies particular considerations which are relevant to the Tribunal's decision in such a case. The 'period of residence protection' is the period of service plus the four months immediately after it.

In deciding whether to give or withhold their consent to the notice, the Tribunal are required to

(a) be satisfied that the landlord has made out the grounds of section 27(3) or Case B to G on which his application purports to be based;
(b) consider to what extent (if at all) these circumstances are directly or indirectly attributable to the tenant's having performed his period of service and
(c) consider whether (if at all) their consenting to the notice to quit during the 'period of protection' would cause the tenant

> 'special hardship in view of circumstances directly or indirectly attributable to his having performed the period of service.'

Similarly, Schedule 5 para. 4 provides that the Tribunal are to proceed in the same manner where a notice to quit was served on the tenant *before* the beginning of his period of residence protection, and a counter-notice has been duly served in response but the Tribunal's decision or consent has not been given before the period of residence protection begins.

Thus, in effect, the overriding public interest in volunteers performing their duties in the reserve and auxiliary forces is protected by attempting to ensure that any tenancy 'faults' attributable to the tenant's absence on such service will be seen in context and attempts to regain possession from him during or immediately after such a period of service will be viewed with particular caution by the Tribunal.

6.19 Notice to quit when the landlord's 'uncertain' interest ends

When the landlord of an agricultural holding has himself only an 'uncertain' interest, such as a life interest or a conditional or determinable interest then if that interest comes to an end any tenancy which he had granted from it would also normally terminate automatically. The tenant would therefore be in a precarious position which the common law mitigated only to the extent of giving him in such cases a right to emblements, that is, a right to enter the land again after he had quit simply so that he could 'reap what he had sown' and thus could gather such crops as normally mature within a year: *Graves* v. *Weld* (1883).

The 1986 Act, like its predecessor, makes provision to ensure that a tenant enjoys the normal statutory degree of security of tenure in this situation. Thus, section 21(1) provides that where the tenancy determines because the landlord's 'uncertain' interest comes to an end the tenant 'shall continue to hold and occupy the holding' until his occupation is brought to an end by the service and expiry of the normal statutory twelve months' notice to quit expiring at the end of a tenancy year. Section 21(2) entitles the 'successor' landlord to a proportionate rent for the period by which the tenant's occupation is thereby extended and section 21(3) preserves the parties' normal rights on quitting. Notice, however, that this degree of security of tenure *replaces* the tenant's right to emblements: section 21(1) clearly states that the security is given 'instead of' claims to emblements.

Chapter 7

Counter-notices and Tribunal Consent

7.01 The counter-notice: introductory

The tenant's right to serve a counter-notice in response to a notice to quit is the primary source of his security of tenure under the agricultural holdings legislation. An effective counter-notice suspends the operation of the notice to quit, which can then only become operative if the landlord applies for and obtains the consent of the Agricultural Land Tribunal. To succeed in such an application the landlord must satisfy the Tribunal on two counts: that the *purpose* for which he seeks repossession is a purpose within section 27(3) of the 1986 Act and that the *merits* of the situation satisfy the 'fair and reasonable landlord' test of section 27(2). Precisely the same considerations apply in respect of a notice to quit part, rather than the whole, of a holding where such notice is possible [6.13].

The only situations when the tenant has no right to serve a counter-notice are when the landlord's notice to quit is based on one or more of the 'incontestable' Cases in Schedule 3, and this is unambiguously apparent from the wording of the notice.

Where a *combined* notice to quit is served, based firstly on 'incontestable' grounds *and*, in the alternative, on section 27(3) grounds, the tenant should first pursue any right to arbitration he may have to challenge the 'incontestable' grounds and if he is unsuccessful in this challenge, he may then serve a counter-notice within one month of the conclusion of the arbitration: Rule 10 of the Agricultural Holdings (Tribunal) Rules 1978.

7.02 Form and wording

The only statutory requirements concerning the form and wording of counter-notices are in section 26(1)(b) of the 1986 Act which refers to 'a counter-notice in writing requiring that this sub-section shall apply to the notice to quit'.

Any document will therefore suffice so long as it makes clear that the procedures of the statute are to apply to the notice to quit. A letter, for example, will be perfectly adequate.

There is no need to refer in terms to 'section 26(1)(b) of the 1986 Act' although such precision obviously helps to ensure that the counter-notice is clear and unambiguous. A mistaken reference to the equivalent provision of earlier and now repealed legislation will not, apparently, invalidate the notice: *Ward* v. *Scott* (1956) (given a new currency by the 1986 comprehensive consolidation).

However, if the effect of the wording chosen is substantially ambiguous it will not satisfy the requirements of section 26(1)(b) and the document will not constitute a valid and effective counter-notice. In *Mountford* v. *Hodkinson* (1956), for example, a somewhat intemperate letter written by the tenant to the landlord after notice to quit had been served stated: 'I don't intend to go. I shall appeal against it, and take the matter up with the committee' (the predecessors of the Agricultural Land Tribunal). It was held that this wording was not sufficiently clear, even after making 'some allowance for the kind of language (tenant farmers) may happen to employ' (Birkett LJ). Nevertheless, as Romer LJ said in the same case:

'the court is indulgent in respect of a notice of this kind and does not, in effect, care for merely technical points, and if the meaning is so plain that the landlords cannot reasonably mistake what is meant, then effect should be given to the notice.'

7.03 Time limit

The counter-notice must be served on the landlord

'not later than one month from the giving of the notice to quit': section 26(1)(b).

'One month' is a calendar month (section 61 of the Law of Property Act 1925).

The time limit is absolute: there is no provision for any extension. It 'has to be given within a month, and if it goes beyond the month, the remedy has gone': Birkett LJ in *Mountford* v. *Hodkinson* (see also *Parrish* v. *Kinsey* (1983)).

7.04 Co-owners and counter-notices

(i) Co-owning tenants

In *Featherstone* v. *Staples* (1986) the Court of Appeal held that

> 'in the context of (section 26(1)(b)) the phrase "the tenant" in the case
> of any joint tenancy must mean "the joint tenants" and not "the joint
> tenants or any one or more of them".'

Thus, to be effective, a counter-notice must be served by *all* the joint
tenants or by one or more of them acting with express or implied authority
to bind the others. (For implied authority in a similar situation see
Chaloner v. *Bower* (1983).) If no such authority exists then the counter-
notice will be ineffective and the landlord's notice to quit will take effect
unhindered.

However, in cases where a co-owner refuses to concur in the service of
a counter-notice, and this threatens the security of tenure of the joint
tenants, his fellow co-owners may apply to the court for a mandatory
injunction directing him to participate. The jurisdiction stems from the
co-owners' status as trustees for sale of the lease under sections 34 and 36
of the Law of Property Act 1925, holding the lease on the statutory trusts
of section 35 of that Act, in most cases for themselves as beneficiaries. As
trustees they are under a *prima facie* duty to preserve the trust property.
In *Harris* v. *Black* (1983), a case concerning a parallel situation arising
under Part II of the Landlord and Tenant Act 1954, Slade LJ accepted
'that there is jurisdiction in the court at the suit of one trustee to make an
order compelling his co-trustee to join him.'

The jurisdiction is *discretionary*. Slade LJ continued his judgment in
Harris v. *Black* by saying:

> 'Nevertheless, I do not accept that there is any principle that, in *every*
> case where a lease of business premises exists, it is the duty of one
> trustee to co-operate with his co-trustee in the matter ... The matter is,
> I think, one for the discretion of the court in the exercise of its equitable
> jurisdiction. Everything must depend on the particular circumstances
> of the particular case.'

Where the lease is being held for third party beneficiaries the likelihood
of the court granting a mandatory injunction to compel co-operation and
preserve the lease is enhanced: *Re Biss* (1903).

Where the court refuses to grant an injunction compelling participation
in serving the counter-notice, the non-participant tenant-trustee may
nevertheless be liable for a breach of trust in refusing to co-operate and

thus preserve (at least temporarily) the trust property. Such liability would result in his paying pecuniary compensation to his now evicted former fellow tenants. The measure of damages in such a case would be the lost value of the tenancy including an amount for future profits where the counter-notice, if served, would probably have secured the continuation of the tenancy.

Where the reluctant co-owning tenant is the *landlord himself*, special considerations may apply. In *Sykes* v. *Land* (1984) an agricultural tenancy was held by a partnership of Sykes and the landlord. The partnership deed provided that when and if the partnership was dissolved, Sykes would be entitled to purchase the landlord's share of the partnership assets, principal amongst which was the tenancy itself. In the ultimate arrangements for the dissolution of the partnership, the landlord (as landlord) served notice to quit. Sykes gave notice of his intention to purchase the landlord's share of the assets, and the landlord (as tenant) refused to concur in the service of a counter-notice on himself (as landlord). Sykes' application for an injunction compelling the landlord's concurrence was granted. The court held that the duty imposed on trustees for sale by section 26(3) of the Law of Property Act

'to consult those beneficially entitled to the trust property and, so far as practicable, to give effect to their wishes where to do so is consistent with the interests of the trust'

was effective to oblige the landlord/trustee/tenant to act to preserve the trust property (the tenancy) as his co-trustee and beneficiary desired.

In *Featherstone* v. *Staples* (1986) which is considered in detail below [7.05], dicta of Slade LJ suggest a simpler remedy for co-owning tenants whose landlord/co-tenant declines to concur in serving a counter-notice on himself in an attempt to defeat the others' security of tenure. His Lordship there said, *obiter*, that there were in his opinion

'quite strong grounds for saying that in the particular context, where the landlord himself is one of the tenants, the word 'tenant' in (section 26(1)) would be capable of bearing more than one meaning, namely (1) all the joint tenants or (2) all the joint tenants other than the landlord himself and that the court should prefer the second construction as leading to a "sensible and just result complying with the statutory objective" ... instead of adopting a construction which would invalidate a counter-notice given in such circumstances.'

(ii) Co-owning landlords

As with a notice to quit, a counter-notice must be addressed to all co-owning landlords, although it may be effectively served on one on behalf of the others.

7.05 Restricting counter-notices: contracting out

The importance of the counter-notice in cases where a 'general' or 'simple' notice to quit is given is highlighted by Lord Salmon in *Johnson* v. *Moreton* (1980):

> 'as a rule, the landlord would be faced with a most daunting task were he to attempt to obtain the tribunal's consent to the operation of a notice to quit'.

Thus the right to serve an *effective counter-notice* is the tenant's primary source of security of tenure, a point which landlords and prospective landlords have readily appreciated. Is it possible to fetter this statutory right, and thus create agricultural tenancies without security for the tenant, leaving the landlord confident of regaining possession after the statutory period of notice has expired?

To date, two strategies which aimed to restrict the right to serve an effective counter-notice have been litigated, one to the highest level, the other, at the date of writing, to the Court of Appeal with consent to go further. Neither strategy has succeeded.

(i) Covenanting the right way

In *Johnson* v. *Moreton* (1980) the landlords granted an agricultural tenancy which included a clause whereby the tenant agreed

> 'to give possession of the whole of the farm to the landlords immediately upon the determination of the term hereby granted and not in any event to serve a counter-notice ... or take any steps to claim the benefit of any statutory provision granting security of tenure which may be in force ...'

In the event, when notice to quit was served on the tenant, he did serve a counter-notice. The landlord then served a notice to quit based on Case E: irremediable breach of covenant by the tenant, materially prejudicing the landlord's interest. When the tenant referred the notice to arbitration, the arbitrator stated a special case for the County Court as to whether the reasons given in the landlord's second notice to quit were good: was the covenant valid and enforceable against the tenant?

When the case reached the House of Lords it was conceded that the first part of this clause was unenforceable because it offended against section 3 of the 1948 Act (now section 3 of the 1986 Act). The last part was also conceded to be unenforceable as being against public policy. However, the landlords contended that the covenant not to serve a counter-notice was valid.

The House of Lords unanimously rejected this argument, and although the four reasoned judgments of the House vary slightly in emphasis, they are essentially encapsulated in the following quotation from Lord Salmon, at p. 51 D-F:

'I do not think any question of ambiguity arises in relation to section 24(1) (now section 26(1)). Its meaning is plain and unambiguous. It gives the tenant a statutory option to be exercised within one month of receiving a notice to quit. The option is to go voluntarily or to serve a counter-notice and remain in possession unless the Agricultural Land Tribunal exercises its very restricted powers of allowing the notice to quit to become effective. The option cannot be exercised any sooner or any later than the subsection prescribes. Nor can it, in my view, be renounced by the tenant in advance. The language of the section makes this plain. Moreover, the statutory option was conferred on tenant farmers, not for their personal protection alone, but for the public good.'

Public policy, the policy of the Act and the clear wording of the section all, therefore, rendered unenforceable an express agreement whereby the tenant purported in advance to contract out of the scheme of statutory protection.

(ii) *The captive co-owner*

Compared with the 'open, not to say brazen, attempt to get round the provisions of the legislation' the second technique designed to achieve a similar result was subtle and indirect. Here, an attempt was made to subvert the operation of the tenant's counter-notice by ensuring that the lease was held by joint tenants and that one co-owning tenant would always refuse to concur in a counter-notice. Since co-owning tenants must normally act unanimously, the belief was that such a reliable refusal would obviously be fatal to the tenants' security of tenure and would thus

in practice protect the landlord's right to repossession at any time after
due notice to quit had expired.

In *Featherstone* v. *Staples* (1986) three agricultural tenancies were
granted to a partnership comprising the two Staples brothers, and
Laughton Contracting Company Ltd (Laughton), a company wholly
owned by the plaintiff landlords.

Various provisions of the *partnership deed* bore directly on the issue of
security of tenure:

(a)   The deed provided that the partnership was to endure for an initial
      period of five years and thereafter unless and until it was terminated
      by twelve months' notice of dissolution from any partner (such
      notice of dissolution being required to expire on the anniversary of
      the *tenancy*).

(b)   Laughton alone was authorised by the deed to serve notice of
      dissolution during the initial five year period. Such a step could only
      be taken if notice to quit had been given and

      'either any report shall have been commissioned or published on
      the law relating to security of tenure of agricultural tenants or
      legislation or other governmental act shall have been announced
      or introduced in Parliament with a view to altering such law'.

(c)   After the initial five year period, no partner was permitted to serve
      a counter-notice under the 1948 Act without the consent of
      Laughton.

Laughton was, in effect, to play no part in the partnership business and
was to have no interest other than its 7.5 per cent share of the profits. The
only activity of Laughton was, apparently, trading with the Staples.

In 1983, the plaintiffs gave to the Staples and Laughton notices to quit
in respect of all three tenancies. Simultaneously, Laughton gave the
Staples notice of dissolution. Without Laughton's consent, the Staples
served on the landlords counter-notices in respect of each tenancy. The
counter-notices were signed by both Staples brothers 'on behalf of' the
partnership. The plaintiff landlords then issued proceedings in which
they sought a declaration that the counter-notices were invalid on the
grounds that 'the tenant' for the purpose of serving a counter-notice
meant all joint tenants and the Staples did not have authority to sign on
behalf of Laughton (indeed, were acting contrary to Laughton's wishes):
thus the counter-notices were inadequate. The Staples brothers counter-
claimed for a declaration to the opposite effect.

At first instance, Mr Justice Nourse accepted the argument put on
behalf of the defendant tenants that in cases where a joint tenancy is

involved, the word 'tenant' in the 1948 Act should be given flexible interpretation. In some cases it would fall to be read as meaning 'all the joint tenants'; in others it should be read as 'the joint tenants or any one or more of them'. The meaning in any particular case should ultimately be governed by the purpose of the section concerned and thus here by the protective purpose of section 24 of the 1948 Act, giving the right to serve counter-notices. Mr Justice Nourse recognised that normally joint tenants can only act effectively if they act unanimously, but was willing to accept that in some situations, and this was one, the normal rule of unanimity should not be imposed where it would destroy the substantive rights of the joint tenants and would pervert the effect of the statute. He drew support for this approach from *Howson* v. *Buxton* (1928) and *Lloyd* v. *Sadler* (1978) and distinguished *Newman* v. *Keedwell* (1977) where, he held, 'the fair reading' of 'tenant' had not, unlike the present case, required an exception to be made to the normal requirement of unanimity. Mr Justice Nourse thus upheld the counter-notices as valid, to avoid defeating the purpose of section 24.

The landlords appealed.

The Court of Appeal upheld the Staples' counter-notices as valid but on grounds which differed from those of Mr Justice Nourse. Rather than relying on 'exceptional' factors, the court's decision is based firmly on the orthodox application of two well-established principles.

Firstly, the court held that 'the tenant' in the case of any joint tenancy must mean 'the joint tenants' and not 'the joint tenants or any one or more of them'. Thus, to be valid, a counter-notice must be given by, or with the authority of, *all* joint tenants.

Secondly, it was held that in *Featherstone* v. *Staples* the counter-notices 'must be treated as having been served with the authority of Laughton, even though that authority was not given' because the 'restrictive condition' in the partnership agreement which required Laughton's consent to any counter-notice was void and unenforceable as being contrary to public policy. The court here applied *Johnson* v. *Moreton* (above), Slade LJ saying that

'if a landowner chooses to grant other persons a tenancy of agricultural land (whether or not including himself as a tenant) public policy (affirmatively) requires that those other tenants should have authority or be treated as having authority, to serve an effective counter-notice ... on behalf of all the tenants without his concurrence and thus (negatively) requires the avoidance of any contractual condition, whether express or implied and whether contained in the tenancy agreement itself or in a partnership agreement or elsewhere, which purports to deny those other tenants such authority.'

His Lordship added that

> 'any contrary decision of this court would be likely to open the door to
> widespread evasion of the 1977 Act to the detriment of the security of
> tenure which Parliament clearly intended to confer on agricultural
> tenants.'

Thus, once the restrictive condition had been struck down, the Staples
were authorised by section 5 of the Partnership Act 1890 and by the
(other) terms of their partnership agreement with Laughton to serve
counter-notices on behalf of the partnership. In addition, Laughton as a
co-owner-trustee of the assets of the partnership including the tenancy
was under a duty to preserve the tenancy, or, alternatively, was under a
duty to give effect to the wishes of the Staples as the ultimate
beneficiaries, by joining in the service of, or ratifying, any counter-notices
served by the Staples as in *Sykes* v. *Land* [7.04]. Had the restrictive
condition been valid, however, it would have been effective to deny these
remedies to the Staples.

(iii) Sham partnerships and artificial transactions

It is interesting to notice that in the course of his judgement, Slade LJ
made the point that

> 'arrangements are not infrequently made by virtue of which land-
> owners enter into a partnership with one or more other persons, on the
> basis that the partnership will be granted a tenancy of an agricultural
> holding and that the landowner himself will be what is colloquially
> known as a sleeping partner. Quite apart from any considerations
> relating to security of tenure, there may well be good and sufficient
> reasons (whether of a commercial, family, fiscal or practical nature)
> why all interested parties should regard such an arrangement as
> sensible and beneficial. There is nothing contrary to public policy in
> any arrangement of this nature as such.'

However, if it can be shown that such an arrangement is a mere sham, or
an artificial transaction whose only object is to avoid the security of
tenure provisions of the legislation then the court should strike it down.
The approach articulated by Lord Templeman in the House of Lords'
decision in *Street* v. *Mountford* (1985) should be applied in this context as
in the Rent Acts:

> 'although the Rent Acts must not be allowed to alter or influence the

construction of an agreement, the court should, in my opinion, be astute to detect and frustrate sham devices and artificial transactions whose only object is to disguise the grant of a tenancy and to evade the Rent Acts.'

To prove that, for example, a document is a 'sham device' the party alleging the sham must prove to the satisfaction of the court that the instrument in question, although purporting to express the parties' purpose in entering into their transaction, does not in fact represent their true purpose but has rather been designed to *conceal* the true nature of the transaction. The *prima facie* evidence of the document must therefore be controverted by the party alleging the sham and this is a heavy burden of proof to discharge, especially where that party has signed the instrument he is now seeking to overturn, as will frequently be the case in lease or licence situations. Parole evidence is rarely sufficient and yet it is inevitably the basis of the case for a sham. In a rare case where the argument of sham was upheld, *Walsh* v. *Griffith-Jones* (1978) two occupiers of accommodation who had signed documents individually, each of which purported to be a non-exclusive licence denying Rent Act protection on the occupier, were able to satisfy the court that the 'licences' were shams designed to conceal the true nature of their transaction, which was the creation of a single jointly-held Rent Act-protected tenancy. In that case, the court accepted that the circumstances surrounding the signing of the agreements were relevant and conclusive. Although both occupiers had signed separate agreements apparently making each severally liable for only half the rent due for the flat, the judge accepted that it had never been contemplated that one party alone would contract: the arrangement was that both tenants or neither would be bound. The tenants were also assured by the landlord's agent at the time of signing that the clause purporting to deny them exclusive occupation of the premises had no substance in reality. The only sharing would be with each other, not with the landlord or any third parties. In these circumstances the substance of the arrangement as a tenancy not a licence was accepted. The case however is a good example of the difficulty of establishing a sham: here the landlord was eager to avoid the security of tenure provisions of the Rent Acts if possible. (The fact that the occupiers were both law students should not be given undue weight!)

Where it is alleged that the arrangement is an 'artificial transaction', the party alleging this must show that there was a preordained series of transactions which constituted a single composite transaction *and* that the transaction contained steps which were inserted without any commercial or business purpose apart from the avoidance of liability under the statutory scheme of protection. This approach has not been widely used in the landlord and tenant field, but has been clearly articulated in connection with tax avoidance schemes by the House of Lords in *Furniss* v. *Dawson* (1984). As with the objection of 'sham' it invokes the court's scrutiny of the *substance* of a transaction regardless of the mere form in which it is presented. It may be much more widely available than the rather narrow objection of a technical 'sham'. If, in substance, a tenancy is created and given effect the artificial transactions disguising its existence will be disregarded and statutory protection will be available to the tenant as appropriate. Lord Templeman's judgment clearly indicates that this may be a valid and effective ground on which to challenge arrangements ultimately concerning the occupation of land and it may be that in future it will provide a fruitful source of litigation. There can now be no doubt to the courts' generally unsympathetic approach to such arrangements and landowners and their advisers should take notice accordingly.

The onus of proving that the arrangement is a sham lies on the tenants who seek to avoid it. In *Featherstone* v. *Staples* itself (despite the implications which might be drawn from the features of the partnership deed quoted above) no evidence was introduced concerning the motives for establishing the partnership structure and no argument was based on the 'sham' point.

(iv) After Featherstone

Where the joint tenants do not or cannot show that the arrangement was a sham or an artificial transaction, Slade LJ's judgment suggests that their position will be precarious. Although the *reality* of the situation will be that the landlord/partner may well not participate in a counter-notice, if there is no sham and no contractual provision expressly undermining the counter-notice mechanism, the arrangement may be beyond the scope of the courts' interference. However, even this is a little uncertain in the light of his lordship's statement that

> 'public policy (affirmatively) requires that (the) other tenants should have authority, or be treated as having authority, to serve an effective counter-notice ... on behalf of all the tenants without his (the landlord/partner's) concurrence'.

At the time of writing this case is still to go to the House of Lords. The position of partnerships and their manipulation in this way to avoid granting security of tenure therefore still awaits a final clarification but their popularity looks set to decline.

7.06 The landlord's application for Tribunal consent: introductory

Section 26(1)(b) of the 1986 Act provides that if the tenant serves an effective counter-notice, the landlord's notice to quit

'shall not have effect unless, on an application by the landlord, the Tribunal consent to its operation'.

Opportunities to obtain Tribunal consent are limited by

(i)   the need to make a formal application;
(ii) in good time, which
(iii) demonstrates that the landlord's case is within the few closely defined grounds for consent in section 27(3), and
(iv) also satisfies the Tribunal on the 'fair and reasonable landlord' test from section 27(2). Hence Lord Salmon's (perhaps overly) pessimistic generalisation that

'as a rule, a landlord would be faced with a most daunting task were he to attempt to obtain the Tribunal's consent to the operation of a notice to quit'.

7.07 Form and wording

Unlike the tenant's counter-notice, the form of the landlord's application for Tribunal consent to a notice to quit is closely prescribed by the Agricultural Land Tribunals (Rules) Order 1978, and applications *must* be in this form or 'substantially to like effect'. The form requires, in particular, that the landlord should identify the ground(s) from section 27(3) on which he relies. Where he has served a 'general' or 'simple' notice to quit without reasons this will be the first time that the tenant will have been notified formally of the case against him.

7.08 Time limit

The landlord's application for consent

'shall be made within one month of service of the counter-notice'.

This time limit is absolutely rigid. Service out of time will invalidate the application and the tenant's counter-notice will serve to protect the tenancy unless and until another notice to quit is served which is effective either through lack of challenge by the tenant or by efficient application to the Tribunal by the landlord. Failure to observe the time limit will therefore result in considerable loss of time to the landlord in his attempt to repossess.

7.09 The grounds for consent: approved purposes, section 27(3)

The first hurdle for the landlord is to demonstrate that the purpose for which he seeks repossession of the holding is within one or more of the six approved purposes in section 27(3).

7.10 Good husbandry

The landlord must show that

'the carrying out of the purpose for which (he) proposes to terminate the tenancy is desirable in the interests of good husbandry as respects the land to which the notice relates, treated as a separate unit'.

The rules of good husbandry have already been described[4.03].

To satisfy this ground the landlord must make a direct comparison between the existing scheme of husbandry on the land to which the notice relates and his intended future scheme: *Davies* v. *Price* (1958). He must also indicate why the projected scheme should result in a better standard of husbandry. Where, therefore, the landlord uses this ground to obtain possession from a bad tenant, he should bring evidence of the experience and standards demonstrated by the intended new farmer, be it himself or another tenant and contrast this with the present farming of the land. In *Lewis* v. *Moss* (1951), the Tribunal said of an application on this ground:

'the landlord must show that under the new regime he has in mind the farming would result in higher productivity and fertility'.

Section 27(3)(a) requires that the landlord's case should refer *only* to the area of land to which the notice to quit relates. It must be treated as a discrete farming area, whether it is the whole or merely part of a holding. The most important implication of this requirement is that arguments for possession with a view to amalgamating the land with other land should *not* be raised under this ground but under the following ground of 'sound management'.

7.11 Sound management

Here, the landlord must show

'that the carrying out of the purpose is desirable in the interest of sound management of the estate of which the land to which the notice to quit forms part or which the land constitutes'.

'Sound management' has not been defined. There are obvious echoes of 'good estate management' and the phrase may be slightly broader in import than the scope of the rules in section 10 of the 1947 Act. In *National Coal Board* v. *Naylor* (1972) Mr Justice Ashworth said that the phrase in its statutory context

'is directly ... related to the management of the farm in the physical sense of the word'.

Thus, in that case, an attempt to repossess, to agree and grant a new tenancy which was *financially* advantageous to the landlord because it omitted an existing burdensome covenant to supply cheap electricity to the tenant was not 'in the interest of sound management'. It did not affect the physical use of the land in any way.

The characteristic 'sound management' situation is where the landlord seeks to repossess the holding so that he can amalgamate it with other land and in this way reorganise the farming and physical management of his estate. In such cases, the application may well be in respect of a notice to quit part. In *Evans* v. *Roper* (1960) the landlord sought to repossess part of a holding to amalgamate it with other land of his so as to produce two more balanced efficient farming units which were both sound economic propositions. It was held that this was an appropriate case to bring under 'sound management', which required the Tribunal to consider the proposals from the point of view of the *estate* and each and every part of it. Hardship or difficulty caused to the *tenant* would be considered under the 'fair and reasonable landlord' test and not here. Where 'the estate' is in fact coterminous with the holding which the landlord seeks to repossess, difficult cases may arise which hover on the borders of 'good husbandry' and 'sound management'. The replacement of a bad tenant, for example, in such a case might seem to be either one or the other. Perhaps the safest course when this arises is to apply on both grounds in the alternative.

7.12 Agricultural research etc. and smallholdings

Where

> 'the carrying out of the purpose is desirable for the purposes of agricultural research, education or demonstration or for the purposes of the enactments relating to smallholdings'

the landlord must use section 27(3)(c).

These 'public interest' purposes are most likely to be of advantage to institutions such as agricultural colleges or local councils wishing to repossess smallholdings or parts of smallholdings so that a new tenant may be let in and started on the 'ladder'. However, there is no limitation to such institutional landlords and a private landowner could use the ground if it were relevant. Once the purpose has been shown to be 'desirable' within the section, the likelihood is that consent will be granted unless the tenant can argue sufficiently strongly on the 'fair and reasonable landlord' aspect to displace the public interest case: *Wilts County Council* v. *Habershon* (1952).

Where the 'education' ground is relied on, the landlord must be able to show that the intended purpose is directly educational. In *Home Office* v. *J.H. Williams* (1982) the Home Office sought to base a notice to quit on the educational ground, arguing that they aimed to use the land in question with other land for a prison farm. The Tribunal held that this was not a directly educational purpose. If research is intended it must be 'agricultural' research: a project to monitor water collected from agricultural land was found not to be appropriate in *North West Water Authority* v. *Taylor and os.* (1986).

7.13 Allotments

If the landlord shows that repossession is sought

> 'for the purposes of the enactments relating to allotments'

he is likely to obtain consent. Until the 1986 consolidation, this ground was part of the preceding 'education and smallholdings' ground. It is of similarly strong 'public interest' character and, again, the tenant is unlikely to succeed in contesting it where the purpose is made out.

7.14 'Greater hardship'

If the landlord can show

'that greater hardship would be caused by withholding than by giving consent to the operation of the notice'

he will be granted consent under section 27(3)(e), subject of course to satisfying the 'fair and reasonable landlord' test.

The ground clearly echoes Case 9 of Schedule 15 of the Rent Act 1977 where the County Court is placed in a similarly invidious position of having to balance the prospective hardships of the parties and others affected. *Bailey* v. *Purser* (1967) states that the Tribunal's approach under the agricultural holdings legislation should be the same as that of the courts under the Rent Act, and should take into account all the attendant circumstances. The onus is on the landlord to demonstrate that he, or his interests, will suffer the greater hardship if consent is withheld. Success in this case will depend entirely on the facts of the particular situation before the Tribunal. There is no objective standard imposed, the Tribunal is merely to avoid the 'greater' hardship. Obviously their assessment of this is necessarily subjective to some extent but from the wealth of case law available it is possible to indicate the broad boundaries of the relevant considerations.

(i) Hardship to whom?

In *Harte* v. *Frampton* (1948), Asquith LJ said that the judge

'should take into account hardship to all who may be affected by the grant or refusal of an order for possession—relatives, dependants, lodgers, guests, and the stranger within the gates'

but that they

'should weigh such hardship with due regard to the status of the persons affected and their 'proximity' to the tenant or landlord and the extent to which consequently hardship to them would be hardship to him.'

This statement was expressly adopted in the context of agricultural holdings by Lord Denning MR in *Bailey* v. *Purser*. In that case the landlord had served notice to quit but had died before the application for consent had been considered. He left heavy debts against his estate, leaving his widow in poverty and placing a great financial burden upon his son who was the administrator of his estate, his guarantor and also his heir. If consent were obtained to the notice to quit, the intention was to sell the holding with vacant possession, thus realising its maximum value to discharge as many debts as possible. The Court of Appeal held that in the circumstances, applying Asquith LJ's dictum, it was appropriate to consider the hardship to the widow and the son.

However, as Asquith LJ's dictum indicates, the weight given to the circumstances of individuals will reflect their 'proximity' to the parties to the lease. Thus whilst the parties' immediate family (even if not financially dependent: *Harte* v. *Frampton*) may be of some significance, in most cases more remote relatives such as cousins, nephews and nieces will be of little consequence unless a particularly close association can be shown: *R.* v. *Agricultural Land Tribunal for the South East Area ex parte Parslaw* (1979).

(ii) What kinds of hardship?

Giving his judgment in the Divisional Court in *Bailey* v. *Purser*, Lord Parker CJ said that the words of the statute.

> 'are wholly unrestricted as a matter of language and I can find no possible ground for limiting the word "hardship" in any way'.

In practice, aspects of *financial* hardship are most frequently pleaded. Although it is not usual for consent to be given to a notice to quit when the landlord wishes to evict the tenant so that he may sell with vacant possession, since in most cases it would be a greater hardship on the tenant in such a case to evict him, nevertheless if the landlord's financial hardship without such a sale is the greater, consent will be given. Thus in *Bailey* v. *Purser* the Court of Appeal agreed that the balance of hardship tipped in favour of consenting to the notice to quit so that the widow's and son's financial position could be eased.

Hardship caused through *disruption* and *disturbance* is, of course, frequently pleaded on behalf of tenants. In *Kinson* v. *Swinnerton* (1961), the tenant's considerable hardship stemmed from the substantial reduction which would be brought about to his dairy herd which he had built up over twenty-five years. Where the holding includes the tenant's family home, this will naturally be a potent argument. Where the holding is merely one of several farmed by the tenant, however, his argument may be based rather on financial hardship or on the depreciation of the value of his remaining land and the consequences to his overall *standards of husbandry* by eviction from one holding (or part), leaving his unit as a whole *uneconomic* or *difficult to farm*.

Hardship through *bad health*, whether physical or mental, may be pleaded, although evidence, especially of mental distress or illness, will be very carefully scrutinised: *Thomson* v. *Fryer* (1970)

(iii) Causation: 'Hardship caused by withholding consent'

In *Bailey* v. *Purser*, Lord Denning MR said:

'the word 'caused' in this section means 'done'. The question is whether greater hardship would be done by withholding consent.'

The tenant's counsel in that case had argued that the financial plight of the landlord's family pre-dated the notice to quit and the application for consent to it and therefore it was not a source of hardship 'caused by' withholding consent. The argument was rejected. In such a case, which admittedly was unusual in its extremity, the more appropriate analysis is that the Tribunal's withholding consent will cause the landlord hardship in preventing him from ameliorating his financial difficulties by realising the best (vacant possession) price for his asset (the tenanted holding). In this sense, withholding consent will 'cause' hardship which must be weighed against the tenant's situation.

In *Cooke* v. *Talbot* (1977) Lord Widgery CJ reiterated the need for a causal link between the Tribunal's decision and the hardship invoked under section 27(3)(d):

'If the Tribunal came to the conclusion that no hardship is going to arise in the path of anyone, then the paragraph ((d)) does not apply. There is no scope for its operation at all and the notice cannot go on that ground. But if, as is far more likely, there is the fairly formidable list of disadvantage or hardships which may follow a decision, ... then the Tribunal must look at those instances of hardship and they must take into account all the factors of hardship which can be said to be caused by the grant or withholding of permission for the notice to go. It is the causal element, that the hardship is caused by giving or refusing to give the notice to quit, which is the essential factor here.'

The court in that case held that the delay, loss and resentment caused to the landlord by the failure on procedural grounds of an earlier notice to quit, and the behaviour of the tenant's solicitor in contributing to such failure, were *not* considerations contributing to aspects of 'hardship' relevant to the second notice to quit. There was no causal link at all between them and the Tribunal's decision on the second notice. They could, however, have been relevant to the 'fair and reasonable landlord test'.

In some cases, it may be that although the landlord demonstrates 'greater hardship', he is yet refused consent on the 'fair and reasonable landlord' criteria: *Jones* v. *Burgoyne* (1963).

7.15 Non-agricultural user not within Case B of Schedule 3

This ground includes cases where

> 'the landlord proposes to terminate the tenancy for the purpose of the land's being used for a use, other than agriculture, not falling within Case B: section 27(3)(f)'.

Case B provides that *no* tribunal consent is required if the landlord either already has planning permission for the new use under the town and country planning legislation *or* 'otherwise than by virtue of those enactments' does not require such permission. Section 27(3)(f) therefore, is limited to those situations where *by virtue of* the town and country planning legislation, *no planning permission* is required for the proposed change of use. The section includes cases where, for example, development is permitted by reason of the General Development Order: in such a case Tribunal consent must be obtained.

Perhaps the most common change of use which requires Tribunal consent under this ground is a change to forestry, which is expressly not 'development' within the Town and Country Planning Act and therefore by virtue of that Act does not require planning permission.

Notice that planning permission for changes of use is not required by the *Crown*

> 'because it is the Crown: and not by virtue of any provision all the Town Planning Acts. The Crown is entitled therefore to the benefit of (Case B) and it is unnecessary for it to get the consent of the Agricultural Land Tribunal': Lord Denning MR in *Ministry of Agriculture, Fisheries and Food* v. *Jenkins* (1963).

7.16 Applying in the alternative

It is, of course, always possible to base an application for consent on more than one ground of section 27(3) and to argue them in the alternative as is frequently done in possession actions based on the discretionary cases of

Schedule 15 of the Rent Act 1977 in the case of residential accommodation. It is not at all unusual to find that good husbandry and sound estate management are being pleaded in the alternative. In recent years, a third alternative of educational or research purposes is sometimes added for good measure, although with a marked lack of success. Another fairly frequent combination is of one or two grounds and 'greater hardship', invoking the future consequences and context of a withholding of consent: *Cooke* v. *Talbot* (above), *Jones* v. *Wynn* (1986), *Barker* v. *Lampard* (1986).

7.17 Section 27(2): The fair and reasonable landlord test

Section 27(2) provides that

'Even if they are satisfied as mentioned in subsection (1) above, the Tribunal shall withhold consent under section 26 above to the operation of the notice to quit if in all the circumstances it appears to them that a fair and reasonable landlord would not insist on possession.'

Lord Widgery CJ in *Cooke* v. *Talbot* said:

'It seems to me that the proviso is quite deliberately inserted in this Act to comfort the tenant into this belief, that even if at some time in some way this landlord is able to prove one of the grounds of (section 27(3)) against him, yet the tenant knows full well that he still will not have to leave the holding if a fair and reasonable landlord would not require him to do so.'

If the Tribunal consider that in the circumstances, a particular application does not 'pass' the fair and reasonable landlord test they *must* refuse consent. The wording of the subsection makes this clear and emphasises that this consideration is as important to any application for consent as is the need to demonstrate that the intended purpose is within section 27(3)(a)-(f). However, standards such as that of a 'fair and reasonable landlord', although couched in objective terms, do permit of some flexibility in application and the context of any particular application as viewed by any particular Tribunal will be all important.

In some cases, this criterion will permit the Tribunal to consider factors which were not relevant to the section 27(3) aspects of the landlord's application. For example, in *Evans* v. *Roper* the 'sound management' ground was limited to considerations of the physical interest of the *estate*. However, the effect on the *tenant* of losing some of his holding was held to be relevant to the 'fair and reasonable landlord' consideration.

Similarly, in *Cooke* v. *Talbot* the court stressed that the Tribunal are required to look at *all* the circumstances of the case when deciding the 'fair and reasonable landlord' point, and might therefore consider such matters as the history of the relations between the particular landlord and tenant, including any previous litigation between them.

Matters pleaded (by both parties) in respect of the 'greater hardship' aspect of an application may also be relevant when the fair and reasonable landlord point is in issue. The interrelationship of the two aspects is seen quite clearly in *Jones* v. *Burgoyne* (1963) where the landlord sought possession of the holding so that he and his eighteen-year-old son could farm it in hand. Neither had experience of farming, nor any appreciable formal training but both were keen. The holding of approximately 207 acres formed a part of the tenant's 'farming empire' of 1136 acres, some of which was freehold. She had been on the land in question for eighteen years and had spent much money on it. The Tribunal were persuaded that the landlord had proved the greater hardship, *but* they also found that 'a fair and reasonable landlord' would consider amongst other things the comparative benefit of detriment to his *land* in insisting or not insisting upon possession and would have regard to the tenor of the Agriculture Acts (*sic*) as to efficient farming and productivity of agricultural land. They therefore withheld consent to the notice to quit.

7.18 'Sweeteners'

It is not unknown for the service of a notice to quit to be the result of a breakdown of informal negotiations between landlord and tenant in the course of which the landlord has offered the tenant money if he will surrender his tenancy (a 'sweetener'). Are such negotiations relevant to any later adjudication on the notice to quit?

The case law is not entirely clear but the position seems to be as follows:

(i)   If the negotiations were conducted clearly 'without prejudice' then no evidence of them should be allowed before the Tribunal. If such evidence is erroneously admitted, *certiorari* may be available to quash the Tribunal's decision: *R.* v. *A.L.T. for the South Eastern Area ex parte Bracey* (1960).

(ii) The earlier negotiations and any offers made or rejected are not directly relevant to the purposes specified in Section 27(3)(a)-(f): *R.* v. *A.L.T. for the Wales and Monmouth Area ex parte Davies* (1953). Lord Goddard stated very clearly in that case that the consent of the Tribunal to a landlord's notice to quit 'can only be given subject to the provisions of (Section 25(1)) ... and there is nothing in that subsection about a monetary bargain between the landlord and the tenant'.

(iii) However, where evidence of the negotiations is admissable it may in some cases contribute to the full appraisal of a 'greater hardship' claim.

(iv) Similarly, the offer of money by the landlord, and the amount offered, may be relevant in considering the 'fair and reasonable landlord' test in Section 27(2). In *Collins* v. *Spierway* (1967), for example, the landlord's offer of £100 was considered by the Tribunal.

(v) Where an agreement has been reached between landlord and tenant that in consideration of the tenant surrendering his lease and vacating the property the landlord will pay a specified amount of money, such an agreement is valid and enforceable as a contract. There is no issue of public policy, nor want of mutuality nor of an attempt to avoid the protective legislation which renders it void or unenforceable: *Rajben-back* v. *Mamon* (1955). If the landlord therefore subsequently denies the existence of a binding agreement before the tenant has moved out, the tenant can enforce the contract against him. If the tenant has already moved out in pursuance of his contractual undertaking in such a situation, his right to enforce the contract against the landlord is even clearer.

7.19 Separate issues

It is important that argument before the Tribunal and the Tribunal's decision itself observe a clear distinction between the two issues: section 27(3) and section 27(2). The grounds of section 27(3) must first be made out. If the landlord achieves this to the satisfaction of the Tribunal, they must secondly and separately consider the 'fair and reasonable landlord' point. A failure to follow this order of decision and to maintain this clarity of distinction may court the danger of review by *certiorari* with the result that the Tribunal's decision is quashed and remitted for reconsideration: *Evans* v. *Roper*; *R.* v. *Agricultural Land Tribunal for Wales and Monmouth Region ex parte Davies*.

7.20 Imposition of conditions on a consent by the Tribunal

The Tribunal, in granting consent to the landlord's notice to quit, are empowered by section 27(4) to impose

'such conditions as appear to them requisite for securing that the land to which the notice relates will be used for the purpose for which the landlord proposes to terminate the tenancy.'

Any such condition *must* therefore be designed to facilitate such intended purpose or to restrict the landlord to his claimed intention.

If circumstances change, the landlord may apply to the Tribunal to have any such condition varied or revoked: section 27(5).

If the landlord fails to abide by or fulfil any condition imposed by the Tribunal, then if an application is made to the Tribunal on behalf of the Crown proving

'that the landlord has acted in contravention of the condition or has failed within the time allowed ... to comply with it'

the Tribunal may impose a penalty on the landlord: section 27(6). A maximum penalty of two years' rent of the holding, or of the proportionate part of the holding, is specified. The penalty, if imposed, is due to the Crown and should ultimately be paid to the Consolidated Fund: section 27(8). Enforcement of a penalty order from the Tribunal is by the same methods as enforcement of similar County Court judgments: section 27(9).

7.21 Costs

Section 27(7) provides that the Tribunal may

'provide for the payment by any party of such sum as the Tribunal consider a reasonable contribution towards costs'.

Like penalty orders, a costs order may be enforced in the same way as County Court costs orders: section 27(9).

Chapter 8

Incontestable Notices to Quit

8.01 Introductory

As was explained in the previous chapter, where a 'general' or 'simple' notice to quit is served on the tenant of an agricultural holding, his right to serve a counter-notice in response provides him with a substantial degree of security of tenure. The counter-notice suspends the operation of the notice to quit and places considerable hurdles in the way of the landlord who seeks to make it effective. The landlord must first apply for Tribunal consent in good time. Then he must demonstrate to the Tribunal that he intends to use the land in question for one or more of only six 'approved' purposes, specified in section 27(3). Then he must also satisfy the 'fair and reasonable landlord' criterion. The burden of satisfying the Tribunal is entirely on the landlord. The balance in these cases therefore favours the tenant.

However, it is recognised that in a limited number of closely-defined circumstances the landlord should be more confident of regaining possession. The agricultural holdings legislation therefore includes provision for the service of so-called 'incontestable' notices to quit, which are not susceptible to challenge by the tenant's counter-notice. When an incontestable notice is served on him, the tenant will in some cases have the right to demand arbitration on the notice, but otherwise his only challenge will be on the validity of the notice. Such a challenge, for example, alleging ambiguity or an inadequate period of notice, would be raised in the courts, either as a defence to possession proceedings or as the basis for an action for a declaration that the notice to quit was invalid and of no effect.

The 'incontestable' notices therefore favour the landlord. Tribunal consent is not necessary for them to be operative; there is no 'fair and reasonable landlord' test, the landlord must simply be able to make out the facts which justify the particular 'incontestable' notice and must observe the appropriate formalities. Tenants are, of course, seriously prejudiced by the use of 'incontestable' notices, since repossession becomes much more likely and repossession by virtue of such a notice to quit disentitles the tenant from compensation to disturbance.

8.02 What are the 'incontestable' grounds?

Schedule 3 of the 1986 Act specifies the 'incontestable' grounds or Cases for notices to quit. Years ago they were known as the 'Seven Deadly Sins' and although this collective term is no longer numerically appropriate it conveys the general character of many of the cases, and the consequence of all.

The Cases A–H are:

Case A   : Retirement from a smallholding at age 65.
Case B   : Non-agricultural user, permitted or exempt.
Case C   : Certificate of bad husbandry.
Case D(a) : Failure to comply with a notice to pay rent due.
Case D(b) : Failure to comply with a notice to remedy.
Case E   : Irremediable breach materially prejudicing the landlord's interest.
Case F   : Insolvency of tenant.
Case G   : Death of tenant.
Case H   : Ministerial notice for amalgamation or reshaping of unit.

8.03 Construction of incontestable notices: landlord's watch points

(A)   It will be recalled that the general requirement that notices to quit are clear and unambiguous has two applications to incontestable notices to quit [6.05].

(1)   the notice must be so drafted that it is clear to the reasonable tenant whether it is a 'simple' or 'general' notice given under section 26 and therefore subject to a counter-notice, or an 'incontestable' notice given under Schedule 3 which admits of no such challenge. Ambiguity on this point renders the notice invalid: *Cowan* v. *Wrayford* (1953); *Mills* v. *Edwards* (1971).

It is, of course, possible to draft and serve a notice to quit expressed to be given under one or more Cases of Schedule 3 and *in the alternative* as a 'general' notice. Again, any ambiguity must be avoided. It is likely to be much safer for two separate notices to be served in such circumstances.

Where an 'incontestable' notice is served and fails because

the landlord when challenged does not make out the case alleged against the tenant, the notice will *not* then automatically operate as a 'simple' notice to quit: *Cowan* v. *Wrayford*. If the landlord wishes to protect this 'reserve' position he must have expressly given a general notice to the tenant, whether separately or as a part of a 'combined' notice to quit in the alternative.

(2) Where an incontestable notice is given, it must be clear and unambiguous *which* Case(s) from Schedule 3 are invoked: *Budge* v. *Hicks* (1951).

(B) It will also be recalled that since an effective incontestable notice is tantamount to a forfeiture of the lease, and particularly since there is no provision in these cases for relief from forfeiture, the courts will construe incontestable notice *strictly against* the landlord. Errors, whether slight or substantial, may invalidate such notices: mistakes in the landlord's name, the amount of rent owed and failure to address the notice to *all* co-owning tenants have all been held to invalidate incontestable notices to quit even though there was no evidence of prejudice or disadvantage to the tenant from the error.

Although Nicholls LJ in *Official Solicitor to the Supreme Court* v. *Thomas* (1986) appears to relax this rigorous standard to some extent, the precise import of the case is very unclear and it is unsafe to use the decision as an excuse for carelessness. Punctilious attention should still be paid to each detail.

(C) It should go without saying that 'incontestable' notices like 'general' notices to quit must satisfy the various common law and statutory requirements for validity. For example, the period of notice, date of expiry, authentication and addressees must conform with the various requirement specified in Chapter 6 above. If there is any element of invalidity the tenant is always at liberty to contest the notice on such grounds in possession proceedings in the courts and should his case be upheld, and the notice be found invalid, the landlord will need to start the whole process again, having lost both time and money to no effect by carelessness.

8.04 The tenant's challenges

The distinctive characteristic shared by the 'incontestable' Cases is that notice to quit based on them may *not* be challenged by the issue of a counter-notice. Tribunal consent is irrelevant to these notices. (There is one exception to this in Case D(b): failure to do work, but this will be discussed later and does not negate the general principle.)

The capacity for the tenant to challenge an 'incontestable' notice to quit is thus severely limited, and the likelihood of repossession by the landlord is much greater when a Schedule 3 Case is relied on. However, the term 'incontestable' exaggerates the invulnerability of the notice.

(1) Firstly, *all* incontestable notices to quit may be challenged by the tenant in the *courts* on the grounds of invalidity at law. Thus all notices may be challenged for ambiguity, inadequate period of notice, mistimed expiry, faulty service etc. The tenant wishing to challenge on these general grounds may wait until the purported notice has allegedly expired and the landlord brings possession proceedings to evict the recalcitrant tenant from the holding. The tenant's defence is that since the notice to quit was invalid for whatever cause, the tenancy continues and he is lawfully in possession as the landlord's tenant. Alternatively he might himself bring an action for a declaration to this effect rather than wait until possession proceedings are instituted unless the notice to quit is grossly and incontrovertibly inadequate. This latter pre-emptive course of action is to be preferred since in matters of construction of notices, reliance on relatively fine points may turn out to be an unsuccessful gamble and may result in the loss of the tenant's valuable rights.

(2) Secondly, incontestable notices based on Cases A, B, D or E may be challenged by the tenant demanding *arbitration*. The aim of the legislation here is to channel specifically 'agricultural' issues away from the courts to be resolved by expert arbitration. Where the tenant has a right to arbitration in these cases, by virtue of art. 9 of the Agricultural Holdings (Arbitration on Notices) Order 1978, SI 1978/257 (hence SI 1978/257) it is essential that he observes the strict statutory *time limits* imposed by arts. 9 and 9A of SI 1978/257 and that he restricts his challenge to the *appropriate issues* for arbitration described by art. 9 as 'any of the reasons' stated in the notice. These 'reasons' *cannot* be raised before the courts: challenge by arbitration under art. 9 is an *exclusive* right: *Harding* v. *Marshall* (1984). Thus the reasons alleged in a Case A, B, D or E notice to quit can *only* be challenged by arbitration. If, for whatever reason, the tenant misses his chance of referring the matter to arbitration he cannot then refer such a question to the court – for example, in possession proceedings.

Thus, imagine a tenant served with an incontestable notice to quit which is served under Case D(a): failure to comply with a notice to pay rent due. If the tenant wishes to challenge the notice on the reasons stated – for example, he wishes to claim that no effective notice to pay rent has been served, or that he did not owe the rent at the date the notice was served, or that he *has* paid the rent and complied with the notice – all these matters may *only* be disputed before an arbitrator. If the tenant fails to serve an arbitration notice within the appropriate time limit, he will lose altogether his opportunity to challenge on these matters. He cannot raise them before the court. Art. 9 is mandatory and exclusive and states that if 'the tenant wishes to contest any of the reasons ... stated, *he shall* within one month after the service of the notice (to quit) serve on the landlord notice in writing requiring the question to be determined by arbitration ...' (emphasis added). His only remaining possibility of challenge is to the validity of the notice during possession proceedings because, for example, it gave the wrong period of notice, or was ambiguous.

(3) In Cases C, F, G and H there is *no* right to arbitration and the *only* possibility of challenge is via the courts. In these cases, the tenant may defend possession proceedings either by challenging the validity of the notice to quit or by challenging its reason: for example he might wish to use the fact that the Certificate of Bad Husbandry was granted more than six months before the notice to quit was given under Case C. He may use the courts, therefore, in these Cases either to challenge the *reasons* for the notice or the *validity* of the notice. Alternatively, he may seek a declaration from the court on the matter rather than wait until possession proceedings are brought against him.

(4) Where the landlord serves a 'combined' notice which relies on incontestable grounds and *in the alternative* operates as a general notice to quit under section 26, or where he achieves the same result by serving two separate notices to quit, then the tenant *must* serve a *counter-notice* within the month allowed by section 26 to prevent the 'general' notice taking effect and terminating the tenancy regardless of the success or otherwise of the incontestable notice.

(5) Where the landlord serves a notice to quit and the tenant is *unsure* whether it is 'incontestable' or 'general' he is well advised in any event to serve an effective *counter-notice*. Whilst it seems likely, given *Cowan* v. *Wrayford*, that he could successfully defend a possession action on the grounds that such a notice was ambiguous and therefore totally invalid, the counter-notice will protect his security of tenure in the (unlikely) event that the court determines that the

notice is a general notice with reasons as in *Hammon* v. *Fairbrother* (1956) where the court admitted extrinsic evidence (correspondence between the parties' lawyers) to clarify an otherwise ambiguous notice.

8.05 Arbitration on Cases A, B, D and E

Whilst the details of arbitration procedures will be discussed in detail in Chapter 13, it seems both relevant and useful to consider at this point:

(i)   the scope of arbitrations on notices to quit;
(ii) arbitration notices;
(iii) the time limits applicable;
(iv) the arbitrator's power to postpone;
(v)   'combined' notices to quit.

(i) The scope of arbitration

Art. 9 of SI 1978/257 declares that:

'where it is stated in a notice to quit an agricultural holding or part thereof that the notice is given for one or more of the reasons specified in Case (A, B, D or E) and the tenant wishes to contest any of the reasons so stated, he shall ... serve on the landlord notice in writing requiring the question to be determined by arbitration.'

Where the tenant wishes to argue that the particular 'incontestable' case, A, B, D or E is in some way(s) not applicable to his circumstances, he must therefore refer the matter to arbitration. Art. 9 thus restricts arbitration to issues raised by the tenant on the reasons stated in the notice to quit. Examples of the types of dispute which should be submitted to arbitration are given in the detailed considerations of each case which follow below. Art. 9 also makes it clear by the words 'shall ... serve' that arbitration is the *only* method available to the tenant for resolving the types of dispute referred to. He '*shall*' refer them to arbitration; he may *not* therefore refer them to the court. The arbitrator's jurisdiction on these matters is exclusive.

(ii) Arbitration notices

Arbitration notices served by the tenant must be 'in writing' according to art. 9. There is no prescribed form for an arbitration notice but it should clearly identify the notice to quit to which it relates, the reason(s) which it seeks to refer to arbitration and the fact that it refers these matters to arbitration under the 1986 Act.

(iii) Time limits

Art. 9 states that the arbitration notice is to be served on the landlord *'within one month after'* service of the relevant notice to quit. This time limit is strict: if the tenant serves his arbitration notice out of time he has *completely lost* his opportunity to challenge the reasons for the notice to quit and may only challenge its validity at law.

In addition, art. 9A (added by the Agricultural Holdings (Arbitration on Notices) (Variation) Order 1984, SI 1984/1300 provides that the notice requiring arbitration will cease to be effective three months after the date of the service of that notice, unless before the expiry of those three months either

(a) an arbitrator has been appointed by agreement between the parties, or
(b) an application has been made to the President of the Royal Institution of Chartered Surveyors for the appointment of an arbitrator in default of agreement between the parties.

Thus the tenant must be alert not only to serve his arbitration notice within the month after service on him of the notice to quit but *also* to follow it up by ensuring that steps have been taken to name an arbitrator within the following three month period. It is advisable, even if agreement on an arbitrator seems likely, that he should protect his position in any case by applying to the President of the R.I.C.S. enclosing the appropriate fee, £70 at the time of writing (see paras. 1 and 2 of Schedule 11 of the 1986 Act) so that the three month time limit does not defeat him. If the tenant does *not* comply with art. 9A, then again, as with art. 9, his opportunity to challenge the reasons for the notice to quit is *irretrievably lost* and his only possible remedy is a challenge to the validity of the notice at law.

(iv) Postponing the operation of a notice to quit

The tenant's request for arbitration suspends the landlord's notice to quit: art. 11 SI 1978/257. If the notice would have taken effect during the period of the arbitration, the tenancy automatically continues until the arbitrator's decision is delivered to the tenant.

If the tenant fails to satisfy art. 9A and does not take steps to appoint an arbitrator within the three month time limit, so that his application for arbitration lapses, the landlord's notice to quit is only suspended until the end of that three month period.

If the arbitrator upholds the landlord's notice to quit, he has power under art. 12 to postpone its operation either of his own motion or after an application by the tenant if the tenant applies within fourteen days of the delivery of the arbitrator's decision at the latest. The tenant may alternatively apply for postponement during the arbitration hearing. The arbitrator's power is limited: if the notice to quit would come into effect on the termination of the arbitration or within six months of that date, then he may postpone the operation of the notice for a period not exceeding twelve months.

(v) 'Combined' notices

When the landlord serves a 'combined' notice to quit based clearly on both incontestable and 'general' grounds and the tenant seeks an arbitration on the incontestable reasons and '*wins*', in that the arbitrator decides that the incontestable ground does not apply and that the notice may *only* take effect as a general notice to quit, art. 10 of SI 1984/257 provides that

'the time within which a counter-notice may be served by the tenant on the landlord... shall be one month from the termination of the arbitration'.

This period is mandatory ('*shall* be one month from' etc.) Thus, even when the tenant has already served a counter-notice to protect himself from the 'general' aspect of the combined notice to quit (see above), he *must* now serve *another counter-notice* within the month after the arbitration if he is to challenge it effectively and invoke the need for Tribunal consent. The tenant must be astute not to miss this requirement, perhaps made overconfident by his success before the arbitrator and his earlier counter-notice. If he overlooks the second counter-notice he will lose his tenancy through his careless oversight of a rather devious requirement.

8.06 No relief in the courts

Whenever a valid 'incontestable' notice is served and the landlord can make out the facts of the Case(s) against the tenant, possession *will* ultimately be ordered. The court has no residual jurisdiction to grant relief from forfeiture. A particularly harsh example of this principle was shown in *Parrish* v. *Kinsey* (1983), where an aged tenant was served with a Case D(a) notice to quit. It was proved that although for years a 'model' tenant who had never previously been in arrears with rent, the tenant had in fact failed to comply with a valid notice to pay rent due. His sight was very poor and he could not read the various notices and it was certain that he had no idea of their implications. Nevertheless, the case was made out against him and the Court of Appeal held that there was no discretion available to be exercised in his favour. Possession was ordered. Whilst the procedures have changed slightly since that case was heard, in that notices to pay and to do work relevant to Cases D(a) and (b) are now required to include information warning the tenant of the consequences of a failure to comply with them, the principle of *Parrish* v. *Kinsey* remains: 'incontestable' notices to quit admit of no criterion of 'reasonableness' to mitigate their impact even in cases of 'mere' technical breach.

THE INCONTESTABLE CASES

8.07 Case A: retirement of smallholders at age 65

This case, formerly Case I, was introduced and added into the 1977 Act by the Agricultural Holdings Act 1984. It implements a recommendation of the Northfield Committee which aimed to increase the availability of smallholdings for new entrants to agriculture so that they could at least establish themselves on the first rung of the 'farming ladder' (even if the Case itself suggests that many make no further progress up that ladder before reaching the normal retirement age). To some extent it might be seen to complement the exclusion of pre-1984 smallholding tenancies from the succession provisions which is effected by section 38(4).

The necessary pre-conditions for Case A are:

(1) that the notice to quit states that it is given for Case A;
(2) that the holding is let (at the time of the notice to quit) by a smallholding authority or by the Minister pursuant to the Agriculture Act 1970. Thus, if a smallholding authority such as a County Council sells off parts of its smallholding estates subject to existing tenancies, the purchaser will *not* be able to use Case A unless it too is a smallholding authority;

(3)   the tenancy commenced on or after 12th September 1984 (the date the 1984 Act came into force);

(4)   the tenancy document contained an express acknowledgement that the tenancy was granted subject to Case A, *and* the tenant signed that acknowledgement;

(5)   the tenant has reached the age of 65 (i.e. before the notice to quit is served);

(6)   if the smallholding includes the tenant's living accommodation, 'suitable alternative accommodation' must be available for him either at the date notice to quit is served or at the date the notice will take effect.

'Suitable alternative accommodation' is further defined in Part II of Schedule 3, paras. 1-7, which are modelled closely on Part IV of Schedule 15 of the Rent Act 1977, and decisions reached under the earlier Act will be relevant here.

Where *council housing* is relied on as the 'suitable alternative accommodation', if a certificate can be produced from the local housing authority for the district in which the tenant's present accommodation lies, confirming that that authority will provide suitable alternative accommodation by a specified date, then their certificate will be 'conclusive evidence' that accommodation which is suitable will be available: para. 2.

Thus, one course for the smallholding authority seeking possession under Case A is to arrange council housing for the tenant with the appropriate district council in good time so that on reaching 65 the tenant is able to move.

If no certificate is available, however, either because *private rented accommodation* is relied on or the housing authority has not been approached sufficiently in advance or has no appropriate accommodation, then the smallholding authority must show that the alternative accommodation will be

(a)   subject to a protected tenancy under the Rent Act 1977 or equivalent secure tenancy; and

(b)   'reasonably suitable' to the needs of the tenant's family as regards proximity to work; and

(c)   *either* similar in rental and size to local council housing provided for people whose needs are similar to the tenant and his family (the council house standards may be conclusively proved by a certificate from the housing authority giving the appropriate information) *or* 'reasonably suitable' to the means of the tenant and the needs of the tenant and his family as regards extent and character. Thus, it is not necessary to use local council housing standards as the guide: the 'reasonable' test may be used instead. Notice, however, that as with the requirement of proximity of work, the size and character of the alternative accommodation must be suitable for the tenant *and his family* whose needs are expressly invoked in both these requirements. Thus not only the size of his family, but their ages and their special needs if any must also be provided for 'reasonably'. As under the Rent Act, 'family' will include those related to the tenant by marriage, his children and those to whom he is *in loco parentis* and will include, for example, a 'common law' partner: *Dyson Holdings Ltd* v. *Fox* (1976). The alternative accommodation will be 'reasonably suitable' if on balance it allows the family to enjoy at least an approximation of their accustomed standards and style of life. Notice that the *rental*, however, under this criterion is linked only to the *tenant's* income and not to that of the household as a whole.

(d) Finally, if furniture was provided by the smallholding authority under the tenancy which it is now seeking to terminate, furniture must also be provided in the alternative accommodation and must be either similar to that at present provided *or* 'reasonably suitable to the needs of the tenant and his family'. The second standard might of course be higher or lower than the first but will presumably only be relied on when lower.

Alternative accommodation which would be legally 'overcrowded' (Part X, Housing Act 1985) if occupied by the tenant and his family will never be 'suitable': para. 5.

Tenant's challenge

The tenant may challenge a Case A notice by effectively demanding arbitration [8.04, 8.05]. He must observe both the limits. He may use arbitration to challenge the 'reasons stated'—thus, for example, that he is 65, or that the accommodation is 'suitable' according to Schedule 3, Part II paras. 1-7. If he does not challenge such points by arbitration he cannot challenge them at all. The tenant may also challenge the validity of the notice to quit at law in possession proceedings or by an action for a declaration.

8.08 Case B: non-agricultural use

In two situations an 'incontestable' notice to quit may be served when land is required for a non-agricultural use. Unlike notices relying on non-agricultural use within section 27(3)(f), such notices (and thus, uses) do *not* require Tribunal consent.

The two situations are:

(a)   a non-agricultural use for which planning permission has already been obtained by the date of service of the notice and

(b)   a non-agricultural use for which planning permission is not required 'otherwise than by virtue of any provision of' the town and country planning enactments. This would include, for example, non-agricultural uses planned by the Crown in any of its various manifestations, since by virtue of *being* the Crown it is not subject to the town and country planning legislation: *Ministry of Agriculture Fisheries and Food* v. *Jenkins* (1963). It would *not* include non-agricultural uses authorised by, say, the General Development Order or other subordinate legislation made under the Town and Country Planning Acts.

The notice to quit must state that is is given on these grounds.

Paragraph 8 of Part II of Schedule 3 of the 1986 Act provides that any planning permission granted on an application by the National Coal Board relating to the working of coal by open cast operations which has been granted subject to 'restoration' and 'aftercare' conditions (as defined by Section 30A(2) of the Town and Country Planning Act 1971) specifying an agricultural or forestry use shall be ignored for the purposes of Case B.

This provision was introduced by the 1984 Act to protect tenants of agricultural land which was to be used for open cast coal working, since the planning requirements for such workings were altered in March 1984 and incidentally prejudiced such tenants. Now, if the land is ultimately to be restored to an agricultural or forestry use, as evidenced by the 'restoration' and 'after care' provisions, no 'incontestable' notice to quit may be served. Where, however, no such conditions apply, a Case B notice to quit may be served on the tenant in the normal way since, as in the other situations envisaged by that case, the land is passing permanently (or at least indefinitely) out of agricultural use and therefore should move out of the specific agricultural holdings scheme (see for an analysis *Rugby Joint Water Board* v. *Foottit* (1972)).

To avail himself of Case B the landlord must show that there is an immediate requirement of the land in question for a specified and non-agricultural use: a *future* intention so to use it if, for example, an interested purchaser should be found will not suffice: *Jones* v. *Gates* (1954). The land does not necessarily have to be required by the landlord for his own use, so long as the intention is to use it presently: *Rugby Joint Water Board* v. *Foottit*.

The relevant planning permission does not need to be obtained by the landlord. If the landlord has a particular purchaser in view and wishes to regain possession in order to sell, the purchaser in question must have a genuine and realistic plan to develop the land: *Paddock Investments Ltd* v. *Lory* (1978).

If planning permission has been obtained for one of the 'public interest' uses detailed in Section 31 (erection of labourers' cottages, provision of gardens etc. [6.07]) then repossession of *part only* of the holdings may be obtained under Case B if that is appropriate.

It should also be recalled that *if* the contract of tenancy so provides, repossession of the holding for any specified non-agricultural use may be obtained after a *shorter period of notice* than the normal statutory twelve months, by virtue of Section 25(2).

Tenant's challenge

The tenant may challenge a Case B notice by effectively demanding arbitration [8.04 and 8.05]. He must observe both time limits. In challenging 'the reasons stated' he may, for example, dispute whether the land concerned is really 'required' for the specified non-agricultural use proposed, whether planning permission has been granted or is truly necessary as the Case states. If he does not challenge such points by arbitration he cannot challenge them at all. The tenant may also challenge the validity of the notice to quit at law in possession proceedings or by an action for a declaration.

8.09 Case C: certificate of bad husbandry granted

Under Case C an incontestable notice to quit may be served on the tenant if:

(1)   not more than six months before the giving of the notice, the Agricultural Land Tribunal granted a certificate of bad husbandry against the tenant in respect of his farming of the holding, or part-holding, in question and

(2)   the notice to quit expressly states this fact.

Certificates of bad husbandry

(i) Applications

Applications for certificates of bad husbandry may be made by the landlord to the Agricultural Land Tribunal using the prescribed form: Form 3 of SI 1978/259. Rule 17 requires that on receiving such an application the Secretary to the Tribunal must serve a copy of the application on all other parties involved. Thus the tenant will be served with a copy of the landlord's application and has *one month* from the date of such service to oppose the application using the prescribed Form 3R. Thus the tenant is given an opportunity to contest or defend himself from the landlord's allegations at the Tribunal hearing.

(ii) Standards

If the Tribunal is satisfied, on any such application, that the tenant is not 'fulfilling his responsibilities to farm in accordance with the rules of good husbandry' then para. 9 of Part II of Schedule 3 states that they 'shall grant' the certificate. Once they are satisfied that the standard of farming is inadequate, therefore, the Tribunal has no discretion, they *must* grant the certificate applied for.

In assessing whether or not the tenant is farming to the appropriate standard, para. 9(2) directs the Tribunal to *disregard* any measures

(1)　taken in pursuance of an agreement between the landlord and the tenant, whether the agreement is within the contract of tenancy or is independent of it, where

(2)　the agreement indicates that its object is the furtherance of one or more of the following purposes, *viz*.

    (a)　the conservation of flora or fauna or of geological or physio-graphical features of special interest;

    (b)　the protection of buildings or other objects of archaeological, architectural or historic interest;

    (c)　the conservation or enhancement of the natural beauty or amenity of the countryside or the promotion of its enjoyment by the public.

This 'disregard' provision was introduced by the 1984 Act and is clearly intended to protect tenants who pursue agreed conservation aims from the charge of 'under farming' and any loss of security which might be contingent on such a charge. It thereby encourages, or at least reinforces, the voluntary conservation code of the Wildlife and Countryside Act 1981. Notice that the measures taken must be in pursuit of an *agreed* conservation policy. Unilateral conservation measures taken by the tenant without consultation or agreement will not be protected by this provision. The agreements concerned are defined sufficiently broadly to include management agreements in addition to terms included in, or collateral to, the tenancy itself. There is no requirement that the Tribunal should make any judgement on the substance or value of any agreement invoked under this paragraph: it is sufficient to protect the tenant if the agreement *declares itself* to have conservation as described in para. 9 as its object.

(iii) Duration

Notice that a certificate of bad husbandry granted by the Tribunal has a very limited life: any notice to quit which relies on such a certificate must be given within six months of *the grant* of the certificate. This time limit was introduced in 1984. It replaced a period of six months running from the date of the landlord's application for a certificate which was found to pose very real practical problems. The landlord cannot, under the Act, obtain a certificate of bad husbandry and then hold it in reserve indefinitely against the tenant: any notice to quit which relies on such a certificate but which is served out of time will be *invalid*.

(iv) Short notice

In granting a certificate of bad husbandry, the Tribunal may specify a minimum period of notice which is less than the normal twelve months imposed by Section 25(1) of the 1986 Act. Section 25(4) provides that the Tribunal may specify any period of 'not less than two months' and may direct that such a period shall apply to any notice to quit given in reliance on their certificate. If the Tribunal do specify such a period of short notice in a particular case, the validity of a notice to quit given in accordance with their direction will not be affected if the period of notice does not then expire on the anniversary of the tenancy or the day preceding the anniversary. In these circumstances the usual common law requirement is overriden. Thus, where a tenant is 'guilty of' bad husbandry, not only is he vulnerable to an incontestable notice to quit but he is also liable to particularly rapid eviction/repossession.

(v) Case C or Case D?

Notice that it may be simpler in many cases for a landlord to serve an incontestable notice under Case D(b), as a tenant who is guilty of bad husbandry may well also be in breach of other aspects of his tenancy agreement. A Case D(b) notice avoids the necessity of an application to the Tribunal for a Certificate since it can be served directly on the tenant if he fails to comply with a notice to remedy 'within a reasonable period'. On the other hand there is no provision for 'short notice' under this Case.

The pros and cons of each approach should be weighed by the landlord in the particular circumstances he is faced with.

Tenant's challenge

The tenant has *no* right to demand arbitration on a Case C notice. His challenge will be through the courts by arguing either that the notice to quit is invalid or that it is not applicable at all, perhaps because the six months' life span of the certificate of bad husbandry expired before the notice was served. These issues would normally be raised as a defence in possession proceedings. (It is, of course, open to the tenant to 'defend himself' at the earlier stage, when a certificate is being sought from the Tribunal.)

8.10 Case D(a): failure to pay rent due

This Case allows the landlord to serve an incontestable notice to quit when, at the date of the notice to quit, the tenant had failed to comply with a notice in writing served on him by the landlord which requires him, within two months from the service of the notice, to pay any rent due in respect of the agricultural holding to which the notice to quit relates.

Thus, under Case D(a), a tenant may lose his security of tenure if

(a)   he is in arrears with his rent and
(b)   the landlord serves on him a valid written notice requiring him to pay the rent due (the arrears) within two months from the date of service of the notice and
(c)   the tenant fails to comply within the stated time and
(d)   the landlord then serves on him a valid notice to quit which expressly states that it is given by reason of the tenant's failure to comply with a notice to pay rent due. Notice that Case D(a) is based on the tenant's failure to comply with a valid *notice to pay*, not merely on his being in arrears with his rent.

Because no relief against forfeiture is available to a tenant who is served with a valid notice to quit based on Case D(a), landlords may find this a more attractive means of terminating an agricultural tenancy than forfeiture for non-payment of rent at common law. However, since the case will in substance effect a forfeiture, any notice served by the landlord will be construed strictly against him: *Pickard* v. *Bishop* (1975). Landlords must therefore take care that they observe punctiliously the following requirements where this Case is relied on:

(1)   Rent, not other debts, must be in issue: *Buck* v. *Hallet* (1969)

(2)   The rent must be *due* and *owing* (i.e. must not have been paid) at the time of *service* of the notice to pay: *Urwick* v. *Taylor* (1969). That is, the tenant must be in arrears at the time the notice is served. A premature notice will be invalid, but since service is achieved at delivery rather than despatch of the notice, a notice to pay posted on the last day for paying rent which arrives and is therefore served the next day, will be valid: *French* v. *Elliott* (1959) (see also section 92 of the 1986 Act). So, for example, if rent is due on 29th September, a notice to pay posted on that day will be assumed to be served (if first class post is used) the next day and will thus be valid, assuming that no payment has been made after posting on 29th.

(3)   The amount specified in the notice must be the correct amount. Even if the tenant is not misled by the error, a mistake in the amount owing which appears in the notice to pay will render it, and any subsequent notice to quit which relies on it, invalid: *Dickson* v. *Boucher* (1983).

(4)   The notice to pay must be in the prescribed form or 'a form substantially to the same effect'. The prescribed form for notices to pay rent was introduced in 1984. The requirement is now found in para. 10(1)(a) of Schedule 3 of the 1986 Act, and the prescribed form itself is Form I in the Schedule to the Agricultural Holdings (Forms of Notice to Pay Rent or to Remedy) Regulations 1984, SI 1984/ 1308.

(5)   The notice to pay must be served by or on behalf of the landlords (*Pickard* v. *Bishop*) and must accurately state the tenants at the date of service and where there are joint tenants must be addressed to all of them and effectively served on all of them: *Jones* v. *Lewis* (1973)

(6)   Before a notice to quit is served under Case D(a) the tenant must have failed to comply with the notice to pay. Thus he must have either

   (i)   not paid *all* the rent owing. If he pays a substantial proportion, but not all, this will not satisfy the notice to pay: *Price* v. *Romilly* (1960) and/or

   (ii)   not made payment of the rent due *in time*, i.e. in the two months permitted by the notice to pay. This time limit is strictly observed, and if the tenant pays *after* the period has expired he will nevertheless be liable to have an incontestable notice under Case D(a) served on him by his landlord: *Stoneman* v. *Brown* (1973)

Payment should be made directly to the landlord. Tendering payment on the land itself, as in *Flint* v. *Fox* (1956) where the rent was left on the holding during the two month period is not satisfactory. Where the tenant pays by cheque and the landlord has previously been willing to accept payment by cheque which, although posted on or before the date due, has regularly arrived after that date, a payment in this way will be treated as within the period: *Beevers* v. *Mason* (1979).

However, tenants 'paying' by cheque should take careful note of *Official Solicitor to the Supreme Court* v. *Thomas* (1986). There it was pointed out by Nicholl LJ that it was not sufficient that a tenant had put the cheque in the landlord's possession. For the rent to be 'paid' the cheque had to have been cashed and the money had to have left the tenant's account and passed to the landlord. Receipt and retention by the landlord of a cheque for rent which he did not present for payment might have afforded a defence that the rent had been *tendered* and, Nicholl LJ said, in a case where the cheque had expired, might have precluded the landlord issuing a notice to pay until he had asked for a further cheque and given the tenant a reasonable opportunity to send one, but merely tendering the rent must be distinguished from actually *paying* the rent, on which Case D(a) hinges. The onus therefore appears to be on the tenant to check his bank statements and ensure that the landlord has presented the rent cheque. It is obviously important, therefore, that the cheque should be despatched to the landlord in good time.

It is essential that a valid notice to pay has been effectively served and not complied with before a notice to quit under Case D(a) may be served.

Tenant's challenge

The tenant may challenge a Case D(a) notice by effectively demanding arbitration [8.04 and 8.05]. He must observe both time limits. He may use arbitration to challenge the 'reasons stated'—thus, for example, that he had not paid, that an appropriate notice to pay in the prescribed form was served, that the rent was 'due and owing' at the date of the notice to pay. If he does not challenge such points by arbitration he cannot challenge them at all. The tenant may also challenge the validity of the notice to quit at law in possession proceedings or by an action for a declaration.

8.11 Case D(b): failure to comply with a notice to remedy

A landlord may serve an incontestable notice to quit on his tenant where the tenant has, at the date of service of the notice to quit, failed to comply with a written notice requiring him within a specified 'reasonable period' to remedy any breach by the tenant that was capable of being remedied of any term or conditions of the tenancy which was not inconsistent with his responsibilities to farm in accordance with the rules of good husbandry. Para. 10(1)(d) of Part II of Schedule 3 provides that, in effect, breaches of conservation agreements may be the subjects of notice to remedy.

(A) The general scheme

In practice this Case is complex, both in the variety of statutory provisions which govern its procedures and in the various rights of challenge given to the tenant. The general scheme may be outlined as follows:

(1)   Is the breach in question remediable or irremediable? If irremediable, the landlord should rely on Case E (below).

(2)   If remediable, does its remedy involve the performance by the tenant of any work of repair, maintenance or replacement or not? For example, does it merely require the insuring of the property?

(3)   If remedying the breach involves work by the tenant then the landlord should serve a notice to remedy in the prescribed Form 2.

    (a)   The tenant may challenge *the notice to remedy* by requiring *arbitration* on

        (i)   his liability to do the work required in the notice to remedy, or

        (ii)   the necessity for or justification of any particular item of work which if not necessary or justified he may seek to have deleted, or

        (iii)   the substitution of a method or material in the case of any item of work in place of the method or material required in the notice

        If the tenant refers *any* of these three aspects of the notice to remedy to arbitration he *must also* at the same time refer other points regarding the notice which he wishes to dispute. If he fails to include these other points at this stage he loses his right to refer them to arbitration altogether [see D below].

    (b)   If no such reference to arbitration is made, or on a reference the arbitrator upholds the notice to remedy with or without extending the time limits for the completion of the work, then, if the tenant fails to complete the work in time, the landlord may serve on him a notice to quit under Case D(b)

    (c)   The tenant may challenge the *notice to quit* by demanding *arbitration*. It is now too late for him to dispute his liability to do the works specified (see (a) above) but he may nevertheless wish to challenge, for example, the assertion that he has not done the necessary work.

(d) As an alternative *or additional* challenge, the tenant may serve a *counter-notice* after receipt of the Case D(b) notice to quit, requiring that the landlord obtains the consent of the Tribunal before the notice to quit can be effective. If by the time this stage is reached the tenant has substantially performed the requisite work, even if well out of time, the Tribunal may refuse consent to the landlord's notice to quit on the 'fair and reasonable landlord' test and thus thwart his possession action right at the last moment.

(4) If the breach may be remedied without work then a notice to remedy in Form 3 should be reserved.

(5) If the tenant fails to comply with such a notice, a notice to quit may be served under Case D(b).

(6) The tenant at this point may demand arbitration to challenge the validity of the notice *to remedy* and his liability to comply with it.

(7) The tenant may in some circumstances apply to the Tribunal for the postponement of the termination of the tenancy for a period not exceeding twelve months.

(B) The essential distinction: remediable and irremediable breaches

It is necessary firstly to consider the basic distinction between remediable and irremediable breaches of terms of the tenancy.

There is no comprehensive test for the classification of breaches of leasehold covenants as remediable or irremediable breaches. Nor are there exhaustive lists of the two categories. The essence of the distinction is whether the damage suffered by the landlord's interest is capable of being remedied and this suggests that breaches of negative conditions will normally be irremediable: *Scala House and District Property Co. Ltd* v. *Forbes* (1974). Breaches of positive covenants, or continuing covenants on the other hand will normally be remediable even if the tenant 'remedies' the breach late: the nature of the breach itself is important here rather than the tenant's response.

From decided authorities the following relevant decisions may be quoted:

(i) *remediable breaches*: failure to use as a private residence only: *Segal Securities Ltd* v. *Thoseby* (1963); failure to reside continuously in the farmhouse: *Lloyd's Bank* v. *Jones* (1955) (even in a case where absence was caused by an appreciable period in prison: *Sumnall* v. *Stott*

(1984)); failure to observe the rules of good husbandry; failure to keep the property adequately insured: *Farimani* v. *Gates* (1984).

(ii) *irremediable breaches*: breach of condition against subletting and assigning: *Scala House etc. Properties Ltd* v. *Forbes* (above); serious breaches of the rules of good husbandry which severely prejudice the conditions of the land such as breaches of proper rotation which would take an inordinate or an unreasonable time to remedy: *Peach* v. *Partridge* (1953).

Where an irremediable breach has occurred, the landlord's possession proceedings should be brought under Case E (see below).

(C) Notices to do work: Form 2

Where a remediable breach of the tenancy agreement has occurred which may be remedied by the tenant undertaking work of repair, maintenance or replacement, a notice to remedy in, or substantially similar to, Form 2 prescribed by the Agricultural Holdings (Forms of Notice to Pay Rent or to Remedy) Regulations 1984, SI 1984/1308 should be served on the tenant. It is not always completely clear whether the breach is remediable by work or not: is weed control, for example, 'work of maintenance, repair or replacement?' It has been suggested that it may be 'maintenance': *Hereford and Worcester C.C.* v. *Newman* (1975). The notice must state the breach(es) complained of and must indicate the work necessary to remedy each. It must also indicate a specific period of time within which the work must be completed. Case D(b) itself indicates that the notice to remedy must require the work to be done within a specified 'reasonable period' and para. 10(c) of Part II of Schedule 3 stipulates that any period of less than six months

'shall not be treated as a reasonable period within which to do any such work.'

If a further notice to remedy is served on the tenant 'less than twelve months' after the preceding notice, it shall be disregarded unless the earlier notice was withdrawn with the tenant's agreement in writing: para. 10(1)(b).

(D) Challenging the notice to do work: arbitration

As has been indicated in the outline of procedures under Case D(b) above, the Case is unusual in giving the tenant the right to challenge the proceedings at several points. The first opportunity comes after the service of a notice to do work. The right is given in the Agricultural Holdings (Arbitration on Notices) Order 1978, SI 1978/257 which allows the tenant to require matters to be referred to arbitration if he wishes

(a)   to dispute his liability to do the work or any part of it specified in the notice and/or

(b)   to request that an item or items be deleted from the notice to do work on the ground that it or they are unnecessary or unjustified and/or

(c)   to request that a different method or material be substituted for those specified in the notice to do work.

If the tenant seeks arbitration at this point he must refer to arbitration not only the matter(s) specified in (a) to (c) which he wishes to dispute but also any other issue he wishes to refer to arbitration. The tenant seeking arbitration on these points or any of them must serve on the landlord a written notice requiring the matters which he is challenging to be referred to arbitration within one month of the service on him of the notice to do work: art. 3(1), (2). There is *no* prescribed form for the tenant's notice.

If the tenant fails to challenge these matters at this point he has lost the chance to do so altogether: he may not argue on these grounds at a later stage.

If the tenant does challenge the items of work in the notice to do work at this stage, he need not undertake those items of work until the arbitration has been concluded and the matters resolved. However, any unchallenged items of work do not benefit in the same way from a suspension of the time limit and therefore the tenant must take steps to perform any such unchallenged items of work within the period specified in the landlord's notice. If he does not do so, a valid notice to quit may be served on the grounds of this default.

The arbitrator has wide powers of deletion and amendment in considering the notice to work but must have regard in reaching his decision(s) to the overriding interests of good husbandry as regards the holding and sound estate management as regards the estate which it constitutes or of which it forms a part: art. 5(a). He may decide that the work specified is not the tenant's responsibility. He may delete items on the ground that they are unnecessary or unjustifiable or he may substitute different methods or materials from those specified in the notice if he is persuaded that those specified are likely to involve undue difficulty or expense, so long as the substitutes are as effective for the purpose as the methods or materials originally specified: art. 5(b)

Although the time for completion of the work is extended to the conclusion of the arbitration in respect of those items of work in dispute, the tenant may nevertheless find it more convenient to put all the work in hand before the arbitrator has reached a decision on his liability to do the disputed items of work. If the arbitrator subsequently determines that in so doing the tenant has completed work which was not his responsibility the arbitrator may determine the reasonable cost of the work done and this amount will be recoverable from the landlord: art. 8.

If the arbitrator finds that the tenant *is* liable to do the work(s) specified he may extend the period for completing the work as he thinks fit: art. 6. The arbitrator in such a case may *also* set a fixed date for the termination of the tenancy in the event that the tenant does not complete the work within the now extended period allowed: art. 7(1). The arbitrator is constrained in setting this new fixed termination date: it cannot be earlier than *either* the date when the tenancy would have been terminated by an effective notice to quit served on the tenant when the time originally allowed for the works to be completed expired *or* six months after the expiry of the extended period given for compliance, whichever is the later: art. 7(2). If the landlord seeks such a fixed date from the Tribunal the matter will usually surface during the arbitration but otherwise the landlord may specifically apply for such a date to be set and must notify the tenant that he has made such an application and the tenant's representations may be heard.

(E) The notice to quit

If the tenant fails to comply with the notice to do work, the landlord may then serve a Case D(b) notice to quit. (Like the Case D(a) notice, the 'ground' is the failure to comply with the previous notice and not the substantial breach itself.)

If there has been an arbitration on the notice to do work which has resulted in an extended period being granted for the completion of the work and, in default, a fixed date set for the termination of the tenancy, the landlord must serve his notice to quit *within one month* of the expiry of the extended period. As long as he observes this requirement, the notice will be valid even if it is of less than twelve months' duration and does not expire on the term date or anniversary of the tenancy – although the notice of course *must* in such circumstances expire on the fixed date set by the arbitrator.

(F) The tenant's right to arbitration on the notice to quit

The tenant has the right to challenge issues raised by the notice to quit by referring them to arbitration: Agricultural Holdings (Arbitration on Notices) Order 1978, SI 1978/257, art. 9. Although he may *not* at this stage raise questions as to his liability to do the work and the other matters properly arbitrated in respect of the notice to do work, discussed above, the tenant may nevertheless, wish to dispute, for example, the assertion in the notice to quit that he has not completed his work. Or he may argue that the time period specified for completing the work, although originally reasonable, has been rendered inadequate and unreasonable by the turn of events.

If the tenant seeks arbitration he must serve written notice on the landlord within one month of the notice to quit being served, specifying the matters and requiring that they be referred to arbitration: art. 9. The operation of the notice to quit is then suspended until the arbitration is completed: art. 11.

If the tenant alleges that he has completed the work required in the original notice to remedy, he must show that he has completed *all* such work: *Price* v. *Romilly* (1960). *Any* failure will provide the basis for a Case D(b) notice to quit. A failure to satisfy any item in the notice to quit may be fatal to the tenant: *Shepherd* v. *Lomas* (1963). It is of course crucial that the period specified in any 'multiple' notice to remedy is reasonable at the outset for the completion of *all* the work specified; if it is not, the notice to remedy and any notice to quit dependent on it are invalid.

If the tenant alleges that the period specified for the completion of the work, although originally reasonable, has become inadequate by reason of changed circumstances, the arbitrator has powers similar to those he enjoys in relation to a notice to remedy: he may extend the period, bearing in mind the time which has already elapsed since the service of the notice to remedy: art. 13. He may fix a termination date for the tenancy in the event of the tenant's non-compliance on the same basis as for a notice to remedy: art. 14. If this should become relevant through the tenant's default, the landlord should serve a second notice to quit, and if he decides to take this course, he must serve such second notice within one month of the expiration of the extended period to do work set by the arbitrator. As in the case of an unsatisfied notice to remedy which was 'reinforced' by a fixed termination date from the arbitrator, it will not invalidate the notice to quit if it is of less than twelve months' duration and does not expire on a term date of the tenancy so long as it was served within the month allowed *and* expires on the date fixed by the arbitrator.

(G) The final challenge: the tenant's right to serve a counter-notice

Uniquely for an 'incontestable' notice to quit, the tenant is expressly given a right to serve a counter-notice in response to a notice to quit based on Case D(b). The tenant's right is now stated in section 28 of the 1986 Act. As with notices to quit under section 27(3), the service of a valid counter-notice results in the notice to quit not having effect unless the consent of the Agricultural Land Tribunal is given in response to an application by the landlord: section 28(2).

The counter-notice must be served within one month of the giving of the notice to quit: Section 28(3). There is no prescribed form, but the counter-notice must be 'in writing' and must require 'that this subsection shall apply to the notice to quit': section 28(2).

Section 28 makes it clear that the right to challenge a Case D(b) notice to quit by the service of a counter-notice is *additional to* the right to refer matters relating to the efficacy of the notice to quit to arbitration. Section 28(4) establishes that arbitration is the primary remedy where the tenant seeks to invoke both. In such a situation, if the tenant seeks arbitration then

(i)   any counter-notice already served shall be of no effect but
(ii) if the arbitration upholds the notice to quit, the tenant may *then* serve a counter-notice which will render the notice to quit ineffective unless and until Tribunal consent is sought and obtained. In these circumstances, the tenant's counter-notice must be served within one month 'from the date on which the arbitrator's award is delivered to him': section 28(4).

It is, of course, always possible for the tenant to use *only* the counter-notice as a challenge to the notice to quit: there is no obligation on him from Section 28 or elsewhere to use both arbitration and counter-notice in tandem, merely the clarification that if he does decide to use both he must give precedence to the arbitration. His counter-notice must make clear which procedure he is using, both challenges or only the one.

When Tribunal consent is applied for under section 28(2) the criteria governing their decision are those in section 28(5), and they differ markedly from the criteria applicable to cases brought before the Tribunal under Sections 26 and 27(3). Section 28(5) provides that the Tribunal

'shall consent ... to the operation of the notice to quit unless it appears to them ... that a fair and reasonable landlord would not insist on possession,'

having regard to

'(a)   the extent to which the tenant has failed to comply with the notice to do work,
(b)   the consequences of his failure to comply with it in any respect and

(c)   the circumstances surrounding such failure.'

The onus is thus clearly on the *tenant* to establish the 'fair and reasonable
landlord' ground as a defence. The Tribunal's discretion is broad and they
may take into account *all* relevant circumstances: *Clegg* v. *Fraser* (1982).

The Tribunal's attention is particularly drawn by Section 28(5)(a) to
the matter of 'substantial' compliance by the tenant: an issue which as
explained above is not open to adjudication by arbitration. If the Tribunal
find that by the date of the hearing the tenant has completed the works
specified, or has substantially completed them, even though out of time
(whether the period was specified by the notice to remedy or the
arbitrator) it is difficult to see how they could give consent to the notice
to quit.

(H) Notices to remedy: Form 3: no work required

Where the breach of the tenancy can be remedied *without* 'work of
maintenance, repair or a replacement' – for example, where a tenant is in
breach of a covenant to insure – then a notice to remedy in Form 3
prescribed by the Agricultural Holdings (Forms of Notice to Pay Rent or
to Remedy) Regulations 1984 SI 1984/1308 should be served. The
procedures consequent on such service are, thankfully perhaps, considerably less complex than those relating to Form 2 discussed immediately
above.

There is no requirement that the 'reasonable period' in these cases must
be at least six months. Neither is there any restriction (such as the twelve-
monthly intervals imposed on Form 2 by para. 10 of Schedule 3) on the
frequency with which further notices may be served.

The tenant has no right to demand arbitration after the receipt of a
Form 3 notice to remedy. If he fails to comply with it and a notice to quit
based on Case D(b) is subsequently served, however, he may then
demand arbitration either on matters arising from the notice to remedy,
or from the notice to quit. If he intends to demand arbitration he must
serve a notice referring the validity of the notice to remedy, and his
liability to comply with it, to arbitration within one month of service on
him of the notice to quit. If he fails to seek arbitration effectively, he has
lost his *only* opportunity to challenge the substance of the landlord's
claim.

During the arbitration, the notice to quit is suspended: Agricultural
Holdings (Arbitration on Notices) Order 1978 SI 1978/257, art. 11.
However, if the arbitration ultimately upholds the notice to quit, and it
thus would come into effect again but would expire on or within 6 months
after the termination of the arbitration, the tenant has fourteen days after
the end of the arbitration in which to apply for its operation to be

postponed. The arbitrator may postpone the termination of the tenancy for a period not exceeding twelve months: art. 12.

The tenant may apply to the arbitrator to extend the period specified for compliance, where this was originally reasonable but no longer is so. In such a case, the arbitrator has power to extend the period by such amount as he considers reasonable: art. 13. He may also specify a fixed date for the termination of the tenancy, if so requested by the landlord, in the event of non-compliance by the tenant with the notice to remedy in its extended period to remedy.

There is no right for the tenant to issue a counter-notice in response to a notice to quit based on a Form 3 notice to remedy. Thus, in clear contrast with situations subject to Form 2, the tenant has only one opportunity to challenge: the *arbitration* after *notice to quit* has been served.

8.12 Case E: irremediable breach

An incontestable notice under Case E may be served when

'at the date of the giving of the notice to quit, the interest of the landlord in the agricultural holding had been materially prejudiced by the commission by the tenant of a breach which was not capable of being remedied, of any term ... of the tenancy that was not inconsistent with the tenant's responsibilities to farm in accordance with the rules of good husbandry.'

Para. 11(2) of Part II of Schedule 3 of the 1986 Act provides, in effect, that breach of a conservation agreement may be treated as a breach on which to base a Case E notice if the other requirements of the Case are satisfied.

In addition, para 11(1) makes special provision where smallholdings are concerned and the landlord is a smallholding authority or the Minister. In such cases where a Case E notice is served, when considering whether the landlord's interest has been 'materially prejudiced',

'regard should be had to the effect of the breach in question not only on the holding itself but also on the carrying out of the arrangements made by the smallholding authority or the Minister ... for the letting and conduct of smallholdings.'

As with all the 'incontestable' notices, a notice to quit given under Case E must state its grounds: that it is given by reason of the irremediable breach. The landlord must make clear in his notice that it is given under

Case E and not, say, Case D. Any ambiguity on this point will render the notice invalid: *Budge* v. *Hicks* (1951).

The most frequent 'irremediable' breach met with in practice is probably assignment, subletting or parting with possession without the landlord's consent. Notice, however, that the landlord must be able to demonstrate if necessary not only that the breach in question was irremediable, but also that it had 'materially prejudiced' his interest in the holding.

The tenant's challenge

The tenant may challenge a Case E notice by effectively demanding arbitration [8.04 and 8.05]. He may use arbitration to challenge the 'reasons stated' – thus, for example, whether there has been a breach, whether the breach is irremediable, whether he is responsible for the breach, whether there has been 'material prejudice' to the landlord's interest. If he does not challenge such points by arbitration he cannot challege them at all. The tenant may also challenge the validity of the notice to quit at law in possession proceedings or by an action for a declaration.

Johnson v. *Moreton: questioning the terms of the tenancy*

In *Johnson* v. *Moreton* (1980) an alleged breach of a covenant gave rise to a notice under what is now Case E which was incorporated in a complex design of arguments intended to avoid the security of tenure measures of the agricultural holdings legislation. In that case, a clause in the tenancy agreement obliged the tenant not to serve a counter-notice in response to any notice to quit served on him by the landlords. When in fact such a counter-notice was served, the landlords used that act as the basis of a Case E 'incontestable' notice to quit, saying that the service of the counter-notice was an irremediable breach of a condition of the tenancy which had materially prejudiced their interest in the holding. Thus, by using Case E they aimed to oust the security of tenure provisions. After 'the stately minuet of notices and counter-notices' the issue was referred to arbitration and since it raised a question of law, the arbitrator, with the parties' agreement, stated a question for the court in the form of a special case: whether the reason for the notices stated by the landlords was good or not. The House of Lords struck down the tenancy clause as being against public policy and against the Act itself which does not, they held, countenance contracting-out. Thus, the tenant's arbitration in this case raised the most fundamental point on the validity of the clause and the possibility of contracting out of the legislation [7.05]

8.13 Case F: insolvency of the tenant

Where the tenant is insolvent an incontestable notice to quit may be served. This is so whether the tenant is an individual (or joint tenants) or a body corporate. Section 96(2) of the 1986 Act provides that for the purposes of the Act a tenant is insolvent if

'(a) he had been adjudged bankrupt or has made a composition or arrangement with his creditors, or

(b) where the tenant is a body corporate, a winding-up order has been passed with respect to it (other than a resolution passed solely for the purposes of its reconstruction or its amalgamation with another body corporate).'

Thus a Class F notice may be served on a farming company if a winding-up order has been made against it or a voluntary winding-up resolution has been passed in respect of it. This avoids the necessity of the landlord resorting to forfeiture proceedings in such a case as he had to when the corporate insolvency provision was introduced in 1984. Where the tenant is insolvent a short notice to quit of less than the usual twelve months' duration may be served by virtue of section 25(2)(a) of the 1986 Act.

A notice to quit based on Case F must state that it is given by reason of the tenant's insolvency.

The landlord will have a choice of procedure in many cases since agricultural tenancies regularly include a proviso for re-entry on bankruptcy. The court's usual limited power to suspend forfeiture in cases of bankruptcy does not apply to agricultural property: section 146(9) of the Law of Property Act 1925. However, it is difficult to see what advantages such proceedings can now offer over the Case F notice to quit.

The tenant's challenge

No arbitration or counter-notice is available where a Case F notice to quit is served. The tenant's only challenge is to claim that the notice to quit is invalid in some aspect or that the Case does not apply because he/it is not in fact insolvent. Such challenges must be made through the courts and may be raised, for example, in possession proceedings brought by the landlord at the expiry of the notice to quit.

8.14 Case G: death of the tenant

An incontestable notice may be given under Case G

'following the death of a person who immediately before his death was the sole (or sole surviving) tenant under the contract of the tenancy.'

In these situations the landlord must ensure that

(i)   the notice states that it is given by reason of the particular person's death *and*
(ii) the notice must be served within the time limit laid down in Case G read with para. 12 of Part II of Schedule 3 of the 1986 Act. Case G itself states that notice must be served 'not later than the end of the period of three months beginning with the date of any relevant notice'.

The date of any relevant notice is defined in para. 12 as the date on which a notice in writing was served on the landlord by or on behalf of an executor or administrator of the tenant's estate, informing the landlord of the tenant's death *or* the date on which the landlord was given notice of any application for succession to the holding under section 39 or 41 of the Act. If both notices are given to the landlord, the three month period runs from his receipt of the first of them.

Para. 12 further defined 'tenant' as *not* including

'an executor, administrator, trustee in bankruptcy or other person deriving title from a tenant by operation of law'.

Thus, for a Case G notice to be served effectively it must be served within three months of the date *when the death of the actual tenant of the holding was notified to the landlord.* There is no direct duty imposed on the executors or administrators to notify the landlord when the tenant dies but in cases where there is no succession application time will not begin to run against the landlord in the context of a Case G notice until they have informed him of the death. If this time limit is not observed and the landlord fails to serve a Case G notice within the three months he has lost altogether his opportunity to use the tenant's death as reason for termination. The tenancy will continue in the estate and may be prolonged indefinitely whilst the tenant's estate is being administered. Time limits are in practice difficult to impose on this process, especially if the persons interested in the estate (beneficiaries, heirs etc.) are content to prolong the *status quo* and not to challenge the actions of executors and administrators and thus retain the tenancy for the benefit of the estate.

Service of a Case G notice to quit should be made on the personal representatives of the deceased tenant, and/or on the person responsible for the control of the management or the farming of the holding: Section 93(3) of the 1986 Act. If the landlord is uncertain, in particular circumstances, of the appropriate parties for service, the notice should be served on the President of the Family Division of the High Court, c/o the Treasury Solicitor, Queen Anne's Chambers, 28 Broadway, London SW1H 9JS [Practice Direction [1985] 1 All ER 832].

Since the interplay of the incontestable Case G notice to quit and the succession application can be somewhat convoluted, it is probably clearer to consider Case G notices firstly given in relation to tenancies commencing on or after 12th July 1984 (to which in general no succession rights attach) and then, separately, to earlier tenancies.

Recent tenancies (post 12th July 1984) without succession rights

Where the landlord serves a Case G notice to quit stating that it refers to the tenant's death and he serves it within the three month time limit imposed by the Case, the notice will be incontestable. The validity of the notice is of course open to challenge in the courts and if, in fact, it were found to be invalid, the situation could only be 'saved' for the landlord if time remained within the three period for a second, valid, notice to be served. Since the likelihood is that any such challenge would only be raised at the expiry of the notice to quit, well outside the three month time limit, it is extremely important that every effort is made to ensure that Case G notices comply with all the statutory and common law requirements. There is no provision for short notice to be given on the death of the sole or sole surviving tenant, so the normal statutory period of twelve months, terminating on the term date or anniversary of the tenancy, will apply.

Tenant's challenge

The tenant's estate has *no* right to demand arbitration on a Case G notice to quit. The only possible challenge available is through the courts by arguing either that the notice to quit is invalid or that it is not applicable at all (surely rare in this context?).

Pre-12th July 1984 tenancies

(i) When no succession application is made

If no succession application is made within the statutory period of three months beginning with the day after the tenant's death (section 39(1)), then the Case G notice to quit shall have effect: section 43(1). The time limit for succession applications is rigid. How far the two periods of three months overlap will depend, of course, on the date on which the landlord received notice of the tenant's death. In many cases it will be possible for the landlord to wait until the expiry of the period for succession applications to see whether there will be a contest on that front or whether his notice to quit would be immediately effective. Any such delay must, however, be most carefully timed so that the landlord's own three month period for service is not exceeded and the opportunity to serve the notice lost.

(ii) Where succession applications are made

When one or more applications for a succession tenancy is lodged in time under section 39, then the landlord's Case G notice to quit will not have effect by virtue of section 43 unless *either* the Tribunal determines that none of the applicants is a suitable person to become tenant of the holding *or* the Tribunal consent under Section 44 to the operation of the notice to quit in relation to the whole or part of the holding.

Thus, the application for a succession tenancy will be disposed of first. Regardless of his notice to quit, the landlord of course has the right to make representations to the Tribunal in the context of such an application, especially on the 'suitability' aspects of the candidate(s) [10.15].

If the Tribunal decide that the applicant is not suitable, then the notice to quit will take effect: section 43(1)(G). If the Tribunal decides that the applicant is suitable, then Section 44(1) provides that before giving a direction that the successor shall have a new tenancy of the holding, the Tribunal 'shall afford the landlord an opportunity of applying for their consent ... to the operation of the notice to quit.' The landlord may therefore, as a last attempt to regain possession, seek consent to his notice to quit even when a suitable successor has been identified. In considering the notice to quit, the Tribunal are required by section 44(2) to apply the considerations of section 27 to it: the fair and reasonable landlord test and the six grounds for consent. The landlord's application for consent in these circumstances *must* be made in pursuance of section 44(1): section 44(3). If the Tribunal do give consent to the notice they 'shall dismiss the application or each of the applications' for succession tenancies: section 44(4). Where this occurs, the tenant may apply to the Tribunal for an extension of the period of notice if their consent is given to the notice to quit either within three months of the date on which the notice to quit would have expired ('the original operative date') or their consent is given after the notice would have expired: section 44(7), so that they may only grant an extension to either a date not more than three months after the 'original operative date' or a date no more than three months after their consent was given, whichever is the later. It is possible, under the succession provisions of the Act, for eligible and suitable successors to opt for a tenancy of *part only* of the original holding (section 39(10)). Where this occurs and the landlord has served a Case G notice to quit in respect of the holding, then assuming that the landlord applies for Tribunal consent under section 44(1), 'the Tribunal *shall* give their consent to the operation of the notice to quit' as regards the part of the holding which is *not* taken by the successors: section 44(5). This subsection is unqualified: there is no ground on which the Tribunal is able to refuse to consent to this effective notice to quit part. No criteria need be satisfied other than the successors' agreement that they do not want the tenancy of that part of the holding.

Finally, section 43(2) gives the Tribunal a general power to consent to the partial operation of a Case G notice to quit, without invalidating the notice but instead causing it to operate only as a notice to quit part.

8.15 Case H: Ministry amalgamation

An incontestable notice to quit may be given by the Minister for the purposes of amalgamating or reshaping any agricultural unit.

For this Case to be relevant, the following three criteria must be satisfied:

(i) the notice must be given by the Minister and
(ii) he must certify in writing that the notice to quit is given for the purpose of enabling him to amalgamate (as defined in the Agriculture Act 1967, section 26(1)) or reshape any agricultural land and
(iii) the tenancy instrument contained an acknowledgment, signed by the tenant, that the tenancy is subject to Case H.

The written certificate does *not* need to be in the notice to quit, indeed it should be, from the wording of the Case, a separate document.

Tenant's challenge

The tenant has *no* right to demand arbitration on a Case H notice to quit. The only possible challenge available is through the courts by arguing either that the notice to quit is invalid or that it is not applicable at all – perhaps because no signed acknowledgement of its applicability appeared in the tenancy document, or no certificate is available.

Chapter 9

Termination Otherwise Than By Notice To Quit

9.01 Introductory

The prominence given to notices to quit agricultural holdings because of their statutory importance should not be allowed to eclipse totally the other methods available for ending the lease. All tenancies may be terminated in a variety of ways and agricultural leases are no exception. This chapter does *not* purport to rehearse in full the law relevant to each alternative means of termination: for such basic detail the reader is referred to the usual landlord and tenant authorities such as *Woodfall: Landlord and Tenant* or *Hill and Redman's Law of Landlord and Tenant*.

The aim here is simply to point up aspects of the other methods of termination which have a particular significance where the lease in question is a tenancy of an agricultural holding.

9.02 Effluxion of time

Where a fixed-term tenancy is granted it will at common law end automatically at the expiry of the term. In the context of agricultural leases, significant modifications are made to the common law position by section 3 and 2 of the 1986 Act.

Section 3 provides, in effect, that on the expiry of a fixed term agricultural tenancy, a tenancy from year to year will arise automatically and will endure unless and until it is terminated by notice to quit or otherwise.

Section 2(1) provides that fixed terms granted for one year or less will be treated (from the outset) as tenancies from year to year and therefore, similarly, will not end automatically at the expiry of the contractual period but will continue until effectively terminated by notice to quit or otherwise.

Thus, the only fixed term tenancies of agricultural holdings which *will* terminate 'normally' at the expiry of the term are:

(1) terms of between one and two years: *Gladstone* v. *Bower* (1960)
(2) fixed terms of one year or less granted with prior ministerial approval under section 2(1), 2(2);
(3) fixed terms of between two and five years granted with prior ministerial approval under section 5.

These points are all discussed in detail in Chapter 2 to which the reader is referred.

9.03 Surrender of the tenancy

A surrender of the lease is a bilateral act whereby the lease is ended prematurely by agreement between the landlord and tenant. No tenant has a right to surrender and the landlord may always refuse to accept a surrender if, for example, he considers it advantageous to continue to hold the tenant responsible under the lease. Where a lease is surrendered it merges into the landlord's reversion and is thus extinguished.

Surrender may be express or implied.

Express surrender

Express surrender must be by deed where the original term was for three years or more: Law of Property Act 1925 section 52(1), 52(2)(a), 54(2). These provisions would clearly apply in the case of a surrender of many fixed term agricultural tenancies. In the case of lesser grants, however, surrender in writing signed by the tenant(s) will suffice and will bind so long as it is supported by consideration: Law of Property Act 1925, section 53(1)(a). Thus, agricultural tenancies from year to year, including those arising by virtue of sections 2 and 3 of the 1986 Act may be surrendered in writing.

Implied surrender by operation of law

This will occur where the parties manifest some intention to terminate the lease, evidencing their apparent intention by some act or statement which makes it inequitable to rely on the absence of a deed to deny the surrender: for example *Foster* v. *Robinson* (1951). In some cases, variation of the terms of the tenancy may be so substantial as to be effectively a surrender and regrant of the land.

Where joint tenants hold a lease including an agricultural tenancy, *all* must concur in the surrender: *Leek and Moorlands Building Society* v. *Clark* [1952] 2 All ER 492.

Surrender and subtenants

Where the tenant has granted a sublease, whether or not such a grant was permitted by the terms of his tenancy, a surrender of the tenant's own tenancy will *not* extinguish the subtenancy which survives and may be enforced directly against the head landlord for its full term by virtue of the Law of Property Act 1925 Section 139(1). This may be of relevance to agricultural tenancies, given the fashion in some quarters for granting simultaneous subtenancies with at least half an eye on security of tenure considerations.

Surrender and statutory compensation

Where an agricultural tenancy terminates by surrender, this will be a 'termination' for the purposes of section 96 of the 1986 Act, and both landlord and tenant may therefore claim compensation for improvements and dilapidations. Since no notice to quit has been served the tenant will not be eligible for compensation for disturbance under section 60.

9.04 Forfeiture

(a) The right

The landlord may be entitled to forfeit the lease, that is, to take or re-enter the premises by reason of an express proviso for re-entry, right of re-entry or forfeiture clause included in the lease which is activated by a breach or breaches of covenant on the part of the tenant. There is *no* implied right of re-entry or forfeiture. It must be expressly reserved to the landlord.

When an agricultural tenancy has been reduced into writing to conform with section 6 and Schedule 1 of the 1986 Act some provision concerning re-entry must have been included: para. 8, Schedule 1. In other cases where there is a formal tenancy a proviso for re-entry is usually included. The great majority of formal agricultural leases will therefore reserve to the landlord the right to forfeit the lease in the event of the tenant's breach of covenant.

It is unlikely that the express reservation of a right of re-entry could be proved where the lease is merely oral.

(b) Enforcing the right

Theoretically the landlord may choose between two procedures to enforce his right of re-entry consequent on a breach of covenant by the tenant. He may either make a peaceable entry himself upon the premises or may bring an action for possession. The first option is *not* recommended. There is a considerable risk that force used by the landlord will render him liable under the Criminal Law Act 1977. The Act also makes *illegal* any enforcement of forfeiture otherwise than by court proceedings where the premises include premises let as a dwelling and any person is at the time lawfully residing in or on the premises. Finally, it is as well to remember that direct enforcement usually leads to a deteriorating confrontation and in the heat of the moment relatively little attention will be paid to the finer points of legal argument. In *R.* v. *Hussey* (1924), for example, a landlord took two friends to assist her in repossessing a room. In the *mêlée* which ensued the tenant shot both the assistants. He was subsequently found not guilty of unlawful wounding. His active defence of his home was lawful as, in the circumstances, it was found that the landlord had no right to repossess and was thus a trespasser attempting to take with force. There is no suggestion that tenants do, or should, turn with impunity on their re-entering landlords, but there is no doubt that the enforcement of forfeiture rights by the instituting of possession proceedings is in several respects a safer and preferable course. The writ in such proceedings brings about a forfeiture when it is served on the tenant: *Calabar Properties Ltd* v. *Seagull Autos Ltd* (1969)

(c) Relief against forfeiture

Traditionally it has been said that 'the law leans against forfeiture' and in certain circumstances looks sympathetically on the tenant, who may be able to obtain relief against the enforcement of the landlord's rights. A major distinction must be made from this point onwards in the discussion between forfeiture for non-payment of rent and forfeiture for breaches of other covenants. In both cases the landlord is put to a strict proof of his case. However, in the case of non-payment of rent, relief against forfeiture may be available to the tenant from the court's inherent equitable jurisdiction, as amended by statute. In other cases only the distinct statutory jurisdiction is available, although in *Shiloh Spinners Ltd* v. *Harding* (1973) the House of Lords made clear that even there in appropriate cases the equitable relief may be available. The two aspects will now be considered separately, and a 'comparison of convenience' made between them and Cases D(a) and D(b) under Schedule 3 of the 1986 Act.

9.05 Forfeiture for non-payment of rent

(a) The landlord's formal demand

Before forfeiting a lease for non-payment of rent the landlord must make a formal demand for the rent due (unless he benefits from one of the two exceptions to this requirement – see (b) below). This in an inconvenient (and somewhat anachronistic) technicality. For an effective formal demand of rent, the landlord must demand from the tenant the exact sum due, on the day it falls due, at the premises which are the subject of the lease, at a time before sunset which will allow sufficient time for the counting of the money: *Duppa* v. *Mayo* (1669).

(b) A formal demand is unnecessary

(i)   Where the lease contains an *express* provision that it may be forfeited if rent is a specified number of days in arrears 'whether formally demanded or not', the landlord will be saved the trouble and technicality of the formal demand. It is important that the lease should therefore include such provision.
(ii) The Common Law Procedure Act 1852, section 210 and, in County Court cases, section 139(1) of the County Courts Act 1984, dispense with a formal demand even if no express provision is made in the lease if
   ●   half a year's rent is in arrear *and*
   ●   any goods on the premises available for distress are insufficient to satisfy the arrears due. In the case of an agricultural lease, the goods available for distress will be restricted by Section 18 of the Agricultural Holdings Act 1986. [5.15]

(c) The Court

Possession proceedings may be brought in either the County Court or the High Court. The current limit on the County Court's jurisdiction is a rateable value of £1000: section 147(1)(b) County Courts Act 1984.

(d) The tenant's statutory right to terminate proceedings

Where proceedings are brought in the County Court, section 138(2) of the County Courts Act 1984 states that if the tenant pays into court all the rent in arrears and the costs of the action not less than five clear days before the return day then the action 'shall cease'. The tenant will then continue to hold under the original lease. Where proceedings are brought in the High Court, section 212 of the Common Law Procedure Act 1852 gives the tenant a similar right to terminate the proceedings by paying (directly, not into court) the arrears and costs. However, this right is exercisable *at any time* before trial but *only* if the tenant is at least half a year in arrears.

(e) The tenant's claim to relief against forfeiture

If the case is not terminated by the tenant paying the arrears and costs as appropriate, then the tenant may be able to claim relief.

(i)　If the action is brought in the County Court, section 138 of the County Courts Act 1984, as amended by section 55 of the Administration of Justice Act 1985 provides that the court, when satisfied that the landlord is entitled to enforce the right of re-entry or forfeiture, shall order possession to be given to him at the expiry of not less than four weeks from the date of the court order: section 138(3). During this period of four or more weeks, the tenant may pay the rent and costs into court, thus avoiding repossession: section 138(3), or the tenant may apply for an extension of the period between the order and repossession, in order that payment may be made and repossession avoided: section 138(4). If, however, no payment is made and the landlord quite properly recovers possession of the land in accordance with the court order, the lessee may still apply for relief from forfeiture at any time within six months from the date of repossession, and on any such application the court may, if it thinks fit, grant him such relief as it thinks fit: section 9A of the 1984 Act, added by section 55(4) of the Administration of Justice Act 1985.

In addition, although some doubt has been raised on this point, it seems that the tenant may also, and finally, invoke the residual equitable jurisdiction of the High Court to give relief against forfeiture: *Jones* v. *Barnett* (1984), not following *Di Palma* v. *Victoria Square Property Co. Ltd* (1984). However, since the amendment of section 137, such an approach seems likely to be unprofitable.

(ii)　Where a lessor has repossessed the premises by peaceable re-entry without litigation, section 139(2) of the 1984 Act gives the tenant the right to apply for relief against forfeiture to the County Court within six months from date of re-entry. The court, on such an application, 'may grant such relief as the High Court could have granted'.

(iii)　Where the possession proceedings are brought in the High Court, and the tenant does not terminate the action by payment (above), or is not entitled to do so, for example, because less than half a year's rent is owing, then he is dependent on the inherent jurisdiction of the High Court to grant relief.

Where judgment was obtained by the landlord in circumstances which allowed him to dispense with the formal demand for rent (see above), the tenant must apply for relief within six months of execution of the judgment: sections 210-212 of the Common Law Procedure Act. In all other cases there is no statutory time limit for applications, but the six months period acts as a guideline: *Thatcher* v. *C.H. Pearce and Sons (Contractors) Ltd* (1968). In any event 'delay defeats equity'.

In exercising the residual equitable jurisdiction, the court will tend to grant relief where all arrears and costs are paid – equity seeing the reservation of a right of re-entry as merely a security for the payment of rent.

(f) Forfeiture and subtenants

Where the tenant has sublet, the subleases will automatically come to an end if the lease is forfeited: *Great Western Railway* v. *Smith* (1876). However, the subtenant, or indeed any mortgagee of the tenant, may apply for relief against the forfeiture of the head lease in the same way as the tenant directly concerned: Common Law Procedure Act 1852, section 210; County Courts Act 1984, section 9C.

(g) The effect of relief

If relief against forfeiture is granted, the original lease continues in existence regardless of the point at which relief was sought.

From the landlord's point of view, therefore, the two procedures would seem to have equal but differing advantages and disadvantages.

Forfeiture may be much quicker but is always subject to the tenant claiming and being granted relief, even after judgment has been given and executed.

Case D(a) is lengthy and riddled with formal traps but has no capacity for relief even in a 'deserving' case, e.g. *Parrish* v. *Kinsey* (1983).

9.06 Forfeiture for breaches other than non-payment of rent

In cases other than non-payment of rent, the landlord's right to forfeit the lease is subject to two restrictions: the obligation to serve a notice under

Forfeiture	Case D(a)
− Formal tenancy necessary. − Must include express proviso for re-entry. − Landlord may need to make 'formal demand' for rent (this is avoided by good drafting). + If rent is in arrears, landlord may institute proceedings immediately and request summary grant. − Tenant has right to apply for relief up to six months after execution.	+ No formal lease required. − Notice to pay must be served and must be accurate and in due form. − Notice to pay must give 2 months to pay. − If tenant defaults, notice to quit may be served: 12 months expiring on a term date. − On expiry of notice to quit, tenant may seek arbitration. + If all notices are good and no payment made by due date, arbitrator has no discretion to relieve tenant. + Strict time limits for payment and arbitration may 'catch' tenant. − Requisite accuracy and/or time limits may 'catch' landlord.

the Law of Property Act 1925 section 146 on the tenant and the tenant's right to apply for relief from forfeiture at any time before re-entry.

(a) The statutory notice: section 146

The landlord must serve on the tenant before instituting proceedings to enforce forfeiture, a notice which

(i)   specifies the breach complained of; and
(ii) requires that it is remedied if possible; and
(iii) requires the tenant to compensate the landlord in money for the breach (if he wishes to obtain such compensation). If no such notice is served, the forfeiture will be *void*: *Re Riggs* (1901).

Since the problem of whether the breach complained of is remediable or irremediable may be substantial it is wise for any section 146 notice to be expressed that the breach specified be remedied 'if it is capable of remedy'.

Where there are joint tenants, the section 146 notice must be served on them all: *Blewett* v. *Blewett* (1936).

(b) Time to remedy

After service of the section 146 notice, the landlord must allow the tenant a 'reasonable' period of time to remedy the breach and comply with the notice. No statutory period is prescribed. Even where the breach is irremediable, a period must be allowed for the tenant to consider his position: *Horsey Estate Ltd* v. *Steiger* (1899). A short period such as a fortnight may well suffice in such cases.

If, after a reasonable period has expired since the service of the statutory notice, the tenant has not remedied the breach and paid compensation when demanded, the landlord may take action to enforce the forfeiture. As explained above, he may either enter peaceably upon the premises or institute possession proceedings. The latter course of action is infinitely preferable.

(c) The tenant's right to apply for relief

Under section 146(2) (or in County Courts, section 146(12)) the tenant may apply to the court for relief against forfeiture. He may do so at any time when the landlord 'is proceeding' to enforce the forfeiture *before* he actually re-enters. This may include a period after judgment before possession has been granted: *Egerton* v. *Jones* (1939). The tenant's application may be made in and during the landlord's possession action, or separately. Where joint tenants are involved, the application must be made by or on behalf of them all: *Fairclough & Sons Ltd* v. *Berliner* (1931). There is *no power* in the court to grant relief from forfeiture *after* the landlord has re-entered.

In considering the tenant's application, the court may grant relief at its discretion and on such terms as it thinks fit: section 146(2). Where the tenant has remedied the breach it is likely that he will be granted relief, but since the remedy remains in the discretion of the court he has no right to relief, merely a right to apply for the remedy. If, therefore, the landlord can demonstrate, for example, that the individual personal qualifications of the tenant are of importance in the context of the particular tenancy (as may be the case with an agricultural holding) and the tenant has shown himself to be a bad tenant in the past then relief may be refused: *Bathurst* v. *Fine* (1974).

(d) A notable exception

In general, section 146 concerning forfeiture and relief from forfeiture will apply in *all* cases of breach of covenant other than non-payment of rent. The rights cannot be excluded or avoided: *Plymouth Corporation* v. *Harvey* (1971). However, section 146(8) and (9) do in fact detail exceptions to this general rule. The important exception in the agricultural holdings area is in section 146(9), which refers to a breach of a condition against insolvency. In several specified cases where the tenant has been declared insolvent (or, in the case of a company, wound up) section 146 is declared to have *no application at all*: the landlord may therefore immediately forfeit the lease without statutory notice and without any possibility of relief for the tenant. One of these cases quite beyond the protection of the statute is of a tenant declared insolvent where the lease is of agricultural or pastoral land.

(e) Subtenants and mortgagees

The Law of Property Act 1925 section 146(4), as amended by the Law of Property (Amendment) Act 1929 section 1 gives subtenants (including mortgagees whose security is a sub-demise or legal charge) the right to apply for relief against the forfeiture by the head landlord of their landlord's lease, even in cases where the landlord himself cannot claim relief (for example, the insolvent tenant of agricultural land: *Re Good's Lease* (1954)).

The court will not grant the subtenant a longer term than his original lease, but it may make an order vesting the whole or any part of the demised premises in the subtenant on such conditions as it thinks fit. These may include making good any existing breaches of covenant: *Ewart* v. *Fryer* (1901) or covenanting with the head landlord to perform the covenants of the forfeited lease: *Gray* v. *Bensall* (1904).

Although, as with the previous chart, this is only a fairly crude comparison, from the landlord's point of view, it can be seen that in these cases forfeiture proceedings compare quite favourably with proceedings under Cases D(b) and E, and particularly favourably with Case D(b) where a notice to do work is involved. The ever-present threat of relief up to and after re-entry is a drawback with forfeiture, however, compared with the more obviously 'incontestable' notices to quit for Case E and Case D(b) when a notice to remedy not involving work is concerned, although the landlord (or his agent) must be prepared here, as ever with notices to quit, to take punctilious care that the notices are correct and perfected in all details.

Forfeiture	Case D(b)	Case E
– S.146 notice must be served.	– Landlord must determine whether breach remediable or not.	– 'Incontestable' notice to quit.
+ Notice may be drafted to cover both remediable and irremediable breaches.	– Must serve correct notice to remedy.	– Must be 'material prejudice' to landlord's interest.
	– If notice to do work, tenant may arbitrate.	– Arbitration available to tenant on 'reasons'.
– Reasonable time allowed to remedy.		
– Tenant may apply for relief until landlord re-enters.	– Notice to quit: tenant may arbitrate.	– Court challenge to validity of notice possible.
– Tenant who has remedied *likely* to get relief.	– If subsequent to notice to do work, tenant may finally serve *counter-notice*.	+ Strict time limits for tenant to observe.
+ Relatively speedy.		+ Speedy process.
	– Landlord must then get tribunal consent: pass 'fair and reasonable landlord test' (notice to remedy not requiring work only subject to *one* arbitration).	+ Straightforward but beware formalities of notices.
	– Very involved (for both parties).	
	– Potentially very long.	
	– Control with tenant.	

9.07 Waiver of breach

If the landlord waives the breach of covenant, he will not subsequently be able to proceed to enforce his right of re-entry. Waiver may be express, or it may be implied if the landlord is aware of the breach and still does some unequivocal act recognising the continued existence of the lease. Such an act, for example, would be to demand, accept or sue for rent due after the breach. Any demand or acceptance of rent will be treated as a waiver of the breach, even if expressed by the landlord to be 'without prejudice': as Somervell LJ stated in *Oak Property Co. Ltd* v. *Chapman* (1947):

'The acceptance of rent being, in the circumstances, an unequivocal act, waiver of the breach followed ... as a matter of law; and so unequivocal was the act of acceptance of rent that the landlord was held disentitled to get the best of both worlds by attempts to qualify his acceptance, for example, by stating that he accepted the rent without prejudice to his rights of forfeiture.'

Mr Justice Sachs expressed the same principle in *Segal Securities Ltd* v. *Thoseby* (1963):

'Where forfeiture is involved, in essence once the landlord has knowledge of a past breach the law thus treats the rent as a piece of cake: its nutritional qualities in the landlord's hands being unaffected by attaching to it the label "without prejudice", the law treats the attachment as having no effect.'

Later in his judgment, Mr Justice Sachs held that a demand operates in exactly the same fashion as an acceptance of rent. Where the rent is payable in advance, a demand or acceptance of rent, however expressed, will operate as a waiver of all breaches occurring before the date of the demand or acceptance and will also operate as a waiver of continuing breaches of covenant known to the landlord at the time of his demand or acceptance for such period as he knew they would continue into the new rental period: in other words where rent is payable in advance the landlord's demand or acceptance of rent will in some cases operate as a *prospective* waiver of a *continuing* breach (for example, non-residential user) but this will depend on whether in the circumstances of the case it can be shown that the landlord *knew* the breach would continue.

9.08 Forfeiture and compensation in agricultural leases

Forfeiture will effect a 'termination' of the tenancy for the purposes of section 96 of the 1986 Act, so that the parties can claim compensation for improvements and dilapidations in the usual way. Compensation for disturbance is not available, however, since no notice to quit has been served as required by section 60. Where relevant, compensation for high farming may be claimed by the tenant under section 70, but he must serve notice of his intention to make such a claim at least one month before the tenancy ends. Since a possession judgment consequent on forfeiture proceedings terminates the tenancy on judgment and dates back to the date of service of the writ, it is necessary for any proviso for re-entry to provide for at least one month's notice of forfeiture proceedings to be given to the tenant so that an effective claim may be made.

Part IV

Succession Tenancies

Introduction

The Agricultural (Miscellaneous Provisions) Act 1976 greatly streng-thened the rights of the family of the tenant of an agricultural holding by providing two generation succession rights. The result of the Act was that in certain circumstances a holding could be kept in the tenant's family for three generations without the landlord having a free choice of tenant after the initial letting. Indeed, when 'succession' tenancies were in issue, the successor was to be chosen by the Agricultural Land Tribunal and not effectively by the landlord at all. A 'succession tenancy' may be granted pursuant to a direction from the Agricultural Land Tribunal if

(1) succession rights apply to the tenancy held by the deceased tenant *and*
(2) an applicant has satisfied the Tribunal that he is 'eligible' *and*
(3) he has also satisfied them that he is 'suitable' *and*
(4) the Tribunal has not consented to the operation of a Case G notice to quit served by the landlord.

The aim of the statutory requirements of 'eligibility' and 'suitability' is to restrict occasions of succession to those situations where the holding in question has been of primary importance to the livelihood of the applicant, a member of the deceased tenant's close family, for a period of time before the death.

The succession provisions were particularly unpopular with landlords and were thought to have encouraged the trend away from agricultural tenancies which has been observable in recent years. In 1984, as a major part of the N.F.U./C.L.A. 'package', the Agricultural Holdings Act provided that *no* statutory succession rights would apply to any tenancy granted on or after 12th July 1984, *unless* the parties *expressly included* them. The Act, however, was not retrospective: rights arising by virtue of the 1976 Act in respect of tenancies granted up to and on 11th July 1984 were left untouched. Thus, although the number of 'new' tenancies to which the succession provisions will be relevant is always likely to be small, decisions on succession arising from 'old' grants will continue to form a substantial, but slowly declining, part of the workload of Tribunals for several decades yet.

In addition to the statutory scheme for succession on death, the 1984 Act introduced major provisions establishing a parallel mechanism for succession on the retirement of a tenant who had reached the age of 65 or, being younger, had become permanently incapable of farming the holding by reason of infirmity. This scheme, like that governing succession on death, entitles an applicant who fulfils the statutory criteria and satisfies the Tribunal on all counts to be granted a direction for a succession tenancy even if the landlord opposes his application. In both cases the Tribunal is the ultimate arbiter and may override the landlord's expressed wish or preference.

It is, however, by no means inevitable that there will be disagreement between the landlord and potential successor. The final aspect of the statutory succession schemes which should be noted, therefore, is the provision made for successions arranged *by agreement* between the parties to count as statutory successions within the scheme.

The two following chapters review the details of the succession provisions, considering firstly the various provisions for succession on the death of a tenant and secondly succession on his retirement.

Chapter 10

Succession on Death

10.01 Introduction: when do succession rights apply?

The Agriculture (Miscellaneous Provisions) Act 1976 provided that succession rights would apply to all existing and future agricultural the enactment of the Agricultural Holdings Act 1984, on 12th July 1984. Thus, rights to succession tenancies exist in relation to *all* tenancies of agricultural holdings granted before 12th July 1984 but to *no* tenancies granted on or after that date, *subject* in each case to a very limited number of excepted situations. The relevant provisions are now Sections 34, 37 and 38 of the 1986 Act.

(i) Section 34: the basic structure

Where the tenant of an agricultural holding dies, and his tenancy was a tenancy within section 34, close relatives may apply for a succession tenancy unless section 37 or 38 serves to exclude the succession provisions in the particular case. Section 34 tenancies include:

(a)   any tenancy of an agricultural holding granted before 12th July 1984: section 34(1)(a).

(b)   a tenancy obtained on or after that date by virtue of a direction of the Agricultural Land Tribunal: section 34(1)(b)(i) (i.e. a succession tenancy. As we shall see this is limited by section 37 to *first* succession tenancies only).

(c)   a succession tenancy granted by the landlord: section 34(1)(b)(ii). The only difference between this and the previous tenancy is in the mode of vesting. The tenancy will similarly be the result of a

Tribunal direction. It must be a *first* succession tenancy: section 37.

(d)   any tenancy granted by a *written* contract which expressly indicated that the statutory succession provisions were to apply: section 34(1)(b)(iii). In such a case the parties have clearly 'contracted in' to the succession scheme which, because the tenancy was granted on or after 12th July 1984, would not otherwise apply. Although such cases are likely to be rare, they may occur for example in sale and lease-back arrangements with institutional landlords.

(e)   a tenancy granted to a person who immediately before 12th July 1984 was the tenant of the same agricultural holding, or a substantial part of the land comprised in it: section 34(1)(b)(iv). This clearly accommodates cases of surrender and regrant and incidentally prevents such a technique from being used to avoid the consequences of the 1976 legislation.

The first question regarding succession rights to be asked on the death of a sole or sole surviving tenant, therefore, is whether his tenancy fell into any category in section 34. If it did *not*, then no succession rights apply to it. If, on the other hand, it was within one of the classes of section 34, the next point to check is whether succession rights are *excluded* by any other provision of the 1986 Act.

(ii) Exceptions

Even if the deceased's tenancy was within section 34, *no* succession rights apply to it if:

(a)   it was a tenancy for a fixed term of years, of which more than twenty-seven months remained unexpired at the date of death: section 36(2)(a). Such a tenancy will continue automatically since, with that period unexpired, no effective notice to quit could be served, and when the contractual term expires, it will continue as a tenancy from year to year by virtue of section 3.

(b)   it was a tenancy for a fixed term of between one and two years: section 36(2)(b). Such *Gladstone* v. *Bower* tenancies do not enjoy security of tenure and are therefore logically excluded also from the succession provisions.

(c)   it was the second consecutive succession tenancy of that particular agricultural holding. The statutory succession rights extend to two successions only and therefore once those two are exhausted no more will remain. In defining the tenancies which constitute successions, section 37 includes tenancies granted or obtained in pursuance of a Tribunal direction: section 37(1); and tenancies granted by agreement to a nominated close relative successor, so that the 'succession' occurs in fact when the earlier tenant retires rather than when he dies: section 37(2). In respect of tenancies commencing after 12th July 1984, the section also includes as successions assignments of the tenancy to an *inter vivos* successor on retirement effected with the landlord's agreement section 37(2)(b); tenancies granted or obtained of *part only* of the holding section 37(4); tenancies granted or assigned to joint tenants one of whom is a statutory 'close relative' as a nominated successor: section 37(5); and also where there has been an *inter vivos* succession by a nominated successor under section 53(7): section 37(6).

(d) it was a tenancy subject at the date of the tenant's death to a valid notice to quit which would *inevitably* terminate the tenancy. Section 38(1), (2), (3) describe and include the following situations:

- At the date of death a 'general' notice to quit had been served under section 26, and the month for the tenant's service of a counter-notice had expired without a notice being served *or* the Tribunal had consented before the date of death to the operation of the notice to quit.
- At the date of death the tenancy was subject to a valid notice to quit falling within Case C (Certificate of Bad Husbandry) or Case F (insolvency).
- At the date of death the tenancy was subject to a valid notice to quit within Cases B, D or E and *either* the period for seeking arbitration (and serving a counter-notice: Case D) had expired without either procedure being invoked *or* the arbitrator had upheld the notice to quit *or* the Tribunal had consented to the notice to quit.

(e) The holding consists of a smallholding, regardless of the date the tenancy was created: section 38(4);

(f) The tenancy was granted by trustees of a charity whose sole or principal object is the settlement in agriculture of former forces personnel.

10.02 When must applications be made?

Section 39(1) provides that an application for a succession tenancy must be made to the Tribunal

'within the period of three months beginning with the day after the date of death.'

Rule 5(1) of the Agricultural Land Tribunals (Succession to Agricultural Tenancies) Order 1984 provides that at the time of making his application to the Tribunal, the applicant shall notify the landlord of his application. He is also to notify anyone else who to his knowledge has made such an application, or may make one. All these notifications are to be in statutory form, Form 3, prescribed by the Order. The applicant in his application must indicate to the Tribunal the names and addresses of all the people he has notified.

10.03 Who may apply?

Section 36(1) of the 1986 Act provides that any

'eligible person may apply ... to the Tribunal for a direction entitling him to a tenancy of the holding.'

An '*eligible person*' is

(i)   a 'surviving close relative' of the deceased who
(ii) satisfies the 'principal source of livelihood' test and
(iii) satisfies the 'commercial unit occupation' test.

These various criteria are set out in detail in sections 35 and 36 and in Schedule 6 of the Act, which is introduced by section 35(5).

Section 41 allows close relatives who satisfy the commercial unit test and satisfy the livelihood test 'to a material extent' to apply to the Tribunal to be *treated* as 'eligible'.

10.04 Who is a 'surviving close relative?'

Section 35(2) states that the phrase 'close relative' of the deceased tenant means the wife or husband, brother, sister or child of the deceased and also includes any person who is not included in these classes of relative who

'in the case of any marriage to which the deceased was at any time party, was treated by the deceased as a child of the family in relation to that marriage.'

Not surprisingly the last category is usually abbreviated to 'treated child'.

It is this last category which poses some difficulties in practice, and fortunately these are not frequent. In most cases, relatives such as a distant cousin (*Williams* v. *Lady Douglas* (1980)) and a stepson (*Ashby* v. *Holliday* (1983)) who have lived with the deceased tenant and his wife as members of their family are accepted without demur as a 'treated child'. However, the Tribunal treats strictly the requirement in the definition of an ongoing 'marriage' as a basis for the 'family'. Thus in *Berridge* v. *Fitzroy and os.* (1980), the applicant was found not to be eligible. He was the nephew of the deceased tenant and was found to have been treated as his child. However, the deceased tenant had been a single man, and since there was no marriage as the section required, the applicant could not be a 'treated child' for the purposes of the Act. The Tribunal were not impressed by arguments on the familiar concept of one-parent families and it may be that the specific statutory reference to 'marriage' excludes *de facto* rather than *de jure* relationships. The 'marriage' issue was also central to *Varley* v. *Marquess of Northampton* (1984) where the applicant was the great-nephew of the deceased tenant's wife. However, he had only been close to the tenant *after* his wife (the great-aunt) died. The Tribunal held that at this period there was no 'marriage' as required by the Act and thus no 'family': 'one man does not make a family'. The applicant was not a 'treated child' for the purposes of the Act and therefore not eligible. On the facts, the Tribunal preferred the description of 'favoured relatives' as representing the applicant's status.

Notice that where a holding is farmed by brothers or cousins as joint tenant lessees, one of whom has children and the other does not, a rather arbitrary situation arises regarding the children's rights to apply as 'eligible persons'. If their uncle predeceases their father, they will be eligible as close relatives of the sole surviving tenant at their father's death. If their father is the first to die, however, they will be neither children nor 'treated children' of their uncle, the sole survivor, and therefore not eligible to apply for a direction. Clearly, this is a result which should be avoided and the retirement succession provisions discussed in the next chapter should be used to that end.

10.05 The principal source of livelihood test

The second criterion of eligibility is that the applicant's agricultural work on the holding has provided his sole or principal source of livelihood for a total of not less than five years out of the seven years preceding the tenant's death.

Perhaps one of the more surprising points to notice about this 'test' is that its major terms are undefined in the Act. 'Agricultural work', 'principal source', 'livelihood' – all crucial to an applicant's eligibility – have been wrestled with by Agricultural Land Tribunals since 1976, but very rarely by the courts. The 1984 Act included only one refining definition, with the result that the operation of the section is largely to be deduced from the practice of the Tribunals, although their decisions, of course, do not bind.

'Agricultural work'

This seems clearly to include manual work on the holding in the furtherance of 'agriculture', Tribunals have considered that it includes such work as cleaning dairy equipment (*Hayward* v. *Marshall* (1983)), helping with a retail milk round (*ibid*); erecting a farmhouse (*Hooper* v. *Hooper* (1982). However, whilst physical or manual work is perhaps the most clearly 'agricultural', the word may also include secretarial or managerial work undertaken on or in relation to the holding: *Dagg* v. *Lovett* (1979) where the Divisional Court described the Tribunal's construction of various aspects of the eligibility tests as 'a model for dealing with this kind of application'.

'Livelihood'

'Livelihood' is a broader term than 'income' and in *Dagg* v. *Lovett* (above) it was said that the ordinary meaning, i.e. 'means of living' or 'subsistence' should be applied. In *Trinity College* v. *Caines* (1984) Webster J said:

> 'I conclude that the expression 'source of livelihood' means what the applicant spends or consumes on her ordinary living expenses from time to time in money and/or kind.'

Undrawn profits, he held, were not therefore a 'source of livelihood'.

'Source of livelihood'

This includes benefits in kind which may be derived from the work on the holding: somewhere to live, a car, petrol and food, for example, and in many cases this overall view of the returns to the applicant from his agricultural work is vital to his eligibility, especially where the income from that work is relatively small. On the other hand, as we shall see in assessing the 'principal source of livelihood' of any applicant, the financial returns from the holding form the initial and often conclusive matter for examination.

'Principal source of livelihood'

Whilst Tribunals have looked at the whole of the benefit derived from the applicant's work on the holding, in cases where benefits in kind are inconsiderable the Tribunal's attention will inevitably focus on whether the income from the work on the holding forms the principal source of livelihood. As a guideline, they have looked to see whether it constitutes over 50 per cent of the applicant's total income: *Hall and Hall* v. *Shadingfield Pty* (1982) and *Tunstall* v. *Cresswell* (1982).

In *Trinity College* v. *Caines* (above), Webster J identified the applicant's 'sources of livelihood' throughout the relevant seven year period as

'her husband's drawings from the farm and almost certainly his private income; secondly, her private income, and, thirdly, her drawings from the farm.'

Since the evidence showed that during that period the applicant's private income averaged about £2,000 per year whereas her drawn profits averaged only about £1,500 per year, the learned judge found that

'even without taking into account her husband's resources therefore, it could not be said that her drawings from the farm constituted the 'principal source of livelihood', even if some allowance is made for benefits in kind.'

In any particular case the applicant's circumstances must be considered as a whole, and the primacy or otherwise of the returns from his agricultural work must be assessed in that general context. In some cases informal financial arrangements between husband and wife may lead to difficulties on this point because of the problems in proving the relative importance of individual contributions to the household accounts. In *Moses* v. *Hurst* (1983), for example, the applicant had worked on the tenancy but in addition his wife had earned money from hairdressing and had arranged vegetable piece-work gangs. Together they also grew contract crops on land away from the holding. No separate accounts had been kept, their total earnings had been pooled and the Tribunal felt that there was not sufficient reliable evidence to show that the applicant had satisfied the livelihood test.

'Work on the holding or on the agricultural unit of which the holding forms part'
An 'agricultural unit' is defined in section 109(2) of the Agriculture Act 1947, incorporated into the 1986 Act by section 96(1). The precise meaning of that definition, at least in this context, has not yet been decisively explained. The wording of section 109(2) tends to imply that the various parcels of land which go to make up the 'unit' must all be occupied by the same person or persons. Thus where an applicant seeks a direction from the Tribunal he must be able to show that the land from which he derives his principal source of livelihood *and* the agricultural unit of which that land is a part (where relevant) are occupied by the same person. This approach has found favour with several Tribunals: *Evans* v. *Rudge Trustees* (1977); *Heal* v. *Sidcot School* (1978). However, in *Scott* v. *Durham County Council* (1979) and *Hall & Hall* v. *Shadingfield Pty Ltd* (above) the opposite approach was taken. Where parcels of land are farmed in conjunction, therefore, ostensibly as one enterprise, but some are occupied and worked by the applicant and the others by, say, his father, a tenant, if the former interpretation is given to 'agricultural unit' the son will not be eligible to apply for a succession tenancy, since his work was not on his father's holding(s), nor can they be aggregated with his own holdings into one unit since the occupation is separately enjoyed by his

father and himself. Whilst on balance the tendency of section 109(2) seems to favour such an interpretation, it is not satisfactory in many cases in practice.

Five years

Para. 2 of Schedule 6 provides that attendance for up to three years at a university, college or other establishment of further education

> 'shall be treated as a period throughout which (the applicant's) only or principal source of livelihood derived from his agricultural work on the holding.'

The subject studied is not relevant to the applicant's case: there is no requirement that his studies were related in any way to agriculture. It may seem bizarre that three years spent at the University of X studying astrophysics or classics will thus count towards an applicant's eligibility whereas three years of working on a farm abroad (or indeed on any farm other than the holding in issue) will *not* help his case at all. The Act, however, if bizarre, is clear on the point. The words 'or other establishment of further education' are to be constructed *sui generis* with 'university, college'. In *Littlewood* v. *Rolfe* (1980) the Tribunal doubted whether training as a nurse in a hospital is 'a full-time course of further education'. Their doubts are probably well founded: to quote from their decision:

> 'the mere fact that educational training is conducted in an establishment does not of itself make that establishment another "establishment of further education".'

The applicant's work on the holding

Until 1984, widows who applied to succeed to their husband's tenancies had a considerable difficulty to overcome posed by the construction placed on these words by the Tribunals. In the majority of cases the principal source of livelihood of such women was seen not to be derived from their agricultural work on the holding, but rather from their marital status. This difficulty has now been removed by the inclusion since 1984 of an explanatory subsection, currently section 36(4), which provides that

> 'in the case of a deceased's wife, the reference in subsection 3(a) above to the relative's agricultural work shall be read as a reference to agricultural work carried out by either the wife or the deceased (or both of them).'

Direct experience of working and managing the holding will, of course, continue to contribute to the widow/applicant's 'suitability' even though the 'eligibility' test is now relaxed in this respect. Where it is anticipated that she should take a succession tenancy, therefore, her active participation in the business of farming the holding during her husband's life continues to be of prime importance.

In as far as the landlord's interest is better served by a succession tenancy being granted to someone of the same generation as the deceased tenant rather than, say, his child, this relaxation may seem to benefit both 'sides' in succession cases.

10.06 Person 'treated as eligible': section 41

If a potential applicant for a succession tenancy cannot precisely satisfy the principal source of livelihood test by demonstrating that for five of the seven years immediately prior to the tenant's death at least 51 per cent of his livelihood (in cash or kind) was derived from his agricultural work on the holding in issue, he may nevertheless apply to the Tribunal to be 'treated as eligible' in this respect by virtue of section 41.

The section provides that the Tribunal shall relax the full rigour of the principal livelihood test if they are satisfied that the person

(a)   is a 'close relative' who
(b)   satisfies the 'commercial unit' test (see below [10.08]) and
(c)   was for *some part* of the seven years ending with the tenant's death engaged in agricultural work (whether full or part-time) on the holding in question and
(d)   satisfies the principal source of livelihood test 'to a material extent' (section 41(1))

and if they are also satisfied that

(e)   'in all the circumstances it would be fair and reasonable for the applicant to be able to apply ... for a direction entitling him to a tenancy of the holding' (section 41(3)).

If the Tribunal are satisfied on all these matters, they have no discretion but must determine that the person be treated as an eligible person: section 41(3).

Notice that section 41 only provides for a relaxation of the principal source of livelihood test. The prospective applicant must satisfy *all* the other criteria to the full in the normal way. Notice also that the applicant's work even under section 41 must have been on the holding in issue: the section does not relax this aspect of the test so 'external' agricultural work remains irrelevant to his claim under the Act.

'A material extent'
The applicant must satisfy both parts of the principal source of livelihood test at least 'to a material extent' to benefit from section 41. Thus the *period* during which he was engaged in agricultural work and the *extent* to which his livelihood was derived from such work must both be 'to a material extent' the 5 years and 51 per cent required by section 36(3). How far do these words allow the Tribunal to relax the letter of the law in section 36(3)? What is 'a material extent'? The interpretation of the phrase, ('that strange, almost weird subsection' as Hodgson J described it in *Wilson* v. *Earl Spencer's Settlement Trust* (1985)) caused considerable difficulty for Tribunals, until the first instance decision in *Littlewood* v. *Rolfe* (1981) provided guidance. In that case, a widow applied to be treated as eligible, there being no doubt that she satisfied the other conditions for eligibility. She had worked on the holding for 44½ months prior to her husband's death for some periods full-time, for others part-time only. Over the 44½ months the couple's income had been from their work on the farm and at times also from part-time nursing posts each had taken. Judge Edgar Fay QC, sitting as a deputy judge of the High Court, after rehearsing the various Tribunals' approaches to the matter of interpretation decided that as a matter of definition he would adopt the approach of the Northern Area Agricultural Land Tribunal in *Dagg* v. *Lovett* (1979):

'"material" means "substantial in terms of time and important in terms of value".'

He declined to impose a straightforward mathematical formula which might provide a cut-off point for eligibility:

'percentages of fulfilment, when worked out, are a useful guide to put the facts of finance or of time in perspective and to help judge their weight'

but they are not to be treated as decisive in themselves. The Tribunal, in considering this case had implicitly considered that any applicant hoping to benefit from the provision needed to have worked on the holding for at least 75 per cent of the statutory 5 year period. This continues to be a useful *guide* in such applications, but as Judge Fay stated:

'I can envisage that 50 per cent could well, in some circumstances, be satisfaction to an extent that was material in the sense of substantial.'

Thus in some cases a mere 2½ years' work in the 7 years preceding the tenant's death may suffice if other factors are appropriate. In *Cooke* v. *Bateman* (1983) 60 per cent (3 years) was found adequate. A relatively generous interpretation of the phrase 'to a material extent' was encouraged in his honour's view by the existence of the second hurdle for an applicant under what is now section 41: the 'fair and reasonable' test.

> 'I find some assistance in ... the paragraph setting up the further hurdle to the successor tenant of whether the order is fair and reasonable. I think this points to a wide interpretation of the words 'material extent'. If the "not quite" view were right and the let-out consisted of what may be called the "hard luck cases" (where the applicant had 59 months instead of 60, or 49 per cent in livelihood instead of the 51 per cent which would make it the principal source) then it is difficult to see how any tribunal could find that it was not fair and reasonable to make the order bearing in mind that the applicant has still the final hurdle of suitability to surmount. On the other hand, if jurisdiction is given over a wide spectrum of facts by a beneficial interpretation of the word "material", the tribunal will have a real task in deciding where lies fairness and reasonableness.'

Littlewood v. *Rolfe* has subsequently been followed in *Wilson* v. *Earl Spencer's Settlement Trustees* (above) and *Trustees of James Raine (Senior)* v. *Raine* (1985).

'Fair and reasonable'
The quotation above from Judge Fay indicates the relationship between the Tribunal's consideration of the 'material extent' aspect of the applicant's case to be treated as eligible under section 36(3) and the 'fair and reasonable' test in such cases. In *Trustees of James Raine (Senior)* v. *Raine* (above), Forbes J was required to consider the role of this test a little further. The landlords argued that, amongst other points, the Tribunal had been in error when applying the 'fair and reasonable' criterion to the applicant's application to be treated as eligible, in that the Tribunal at this point had not taken into account the consequences of their decision for other beneficiaries under the settlement. Forbes J pointed out that this provision was concerned

> 'not so much with the merits themselves as with the question of overcoming a procedural bar (if I can call it that). That is why the Tribunal have to consider what is fair and reasonable in this situation. They have to consider it against the background that it has to be fair and reasonable for the applicant to be able to apply to be treated as eligible;

in other words to be able to apply for a direction entitling him to the tenancy.'

The application under section 41 is to be treated as a preliminary matter. If the applicant is 'deemed eligible', he must then satisfy the Tribunal that he is 'suitable', as required by section 39. If he passes that hurdle, the landlord may apply to the Tribunal for consent to his Case G notice to quit, where one has been effectively served. At *this* stage it would seem appropriate for the landlord to seek an adjudication on the merits of the case by arguing the 'greater hardship' justification from section 27(3)(e), relevant at this point by virtue of section 44(2). Such factors as the landlords in *Raine* were seeking to introduce would certainly be appropriate here. They might also be borne in mind by the Tribunal at the same stage when applying the 'fair and reasonable landlord' test to the notice to quit.

In practice, it seems rare for the fair and reasonable test to play a crucial role in the outcome of the application under section 41.

Ineligible because of small holding: section 41(6)
As an example of a case where the tenant may not be eligible under the normal test, section 41(6) specifically refers to

'cases where the close relative's agricultural work on the holding fell short of providing him with his principal source of livelihood because the holding was too small.'

This example, however, is totally 'without prejudice to the generality of' section 41(1)(b). It is, in fact, a fairly common cause of applications to the Tribunals for 'deemed eligibility'.

Time limit for applications under section 41
Any potential applicant who seeks a determination of 'deemed eligibility' from the Tribunal under section 41 must apply to them in that respect

'within the period of three months beginning with the day after the date of death.'

This time limit is *identical* with that prescribed under section 39(1) for applications for a direction, and this is not merely a coincidence. An application under section 41 for deemed eligibility *must* be made *on the same form and at the same time* as the application for a direction to succeed to the tenancy made under section 39(1): rule 3(2) of the Agricultural Land Tribunals (Succession to Agricultural Tenancies) Order 1984, SI 1984/1301. The form is prescribed by that Order: ALT Standard Form 1.

Where there is the *slightest doubt* as to the prospective applicant's ability to satisfy either the 'extent' aspect of the test (51 per cent of 'livelihood' from the holding) or the five year 'period' requirement, or both then an application *in the alternative*, both as an eligible applicant using Part A of the prescribed form, and as an applicant for deemed eligibility under section 41 using Part B of the form, should *always* be submitted. It is not possible for the Tribunal to accept any application under section 41 *after* the substantial succession application has been submitted. The two *must* be *simultaneous* and the wise adviser or applicant errs on the side of caution rather than risk, entering a section 41 (Part B) application in the alternative to avoid defeat by uncertainly or hairsbreadth ineligibility.

10.07 The commercial unit test

The final, but currently most complex, requirement for eligibility is introduced by the disarmingly brief section 36(3)(b): the applicant must satisfy the Tribunal

'that he is not the occupier of a commercial unit of agricultural land.'

The aim of this requirement is to limit the grant of succession tenancies to applicants who do not already have a secure beneficial interest in what is deemed by the Act to be a commercially viable unit. At the very least, the test should serve to prevent individuals using statutory succession rights to expand farming 'empires'. At its most effective, perhaps it should in the words of another commentator

'fulfil the original intention of the 1976 Act that succession should be granted as a privilege to those in need' (D. Troup: *Agricultural Holdings Act 1984*: RICS (1984)).

There are clearly two main points to consider with this 'commercial unit' aspect of eligibility:

(i)   What is a *commercial unit* for the purposes of the Act?
(ii) What constitutes '*occupation*' by an applicant for the purposes of the test?

10.08 What is a commercial unit?

A commercial unit is defined in para. 3(1) of Schedule 6 of the Act as 'a unit of agricultural land which is capable, when farmed under competent management, of producing a net annual income of an amount not less than the aggregate of the average annual earnings of two full-time male agricultural workers aged twenty or over.'

Thus one is looking to see whether the applicant occupies as an agricultural unit agricultural land with the assessed productive capacity of at least twice the current average annual wage of a male agricultural worker aged twenty or more.

The test is ostensibly *objective*: is the unit in question *capable*, under competent management, of producing at least that level of net income? The net income actually produced by the holding under the existing regime is not the yardstick.

The assessment of productive capacity is based on figures published annually by the Minister in the appropriate Agricultural Holdings (Units of Production) Order: para. 4 Schedule 6. This prescribes the net annual income to be attributed to specified 'units of production' for the current year. The awkward phrase 'unit of production' means an animal, or a hectare of specified crop, or 1000 square metres of horticultural crops and the net income per animal, hectare or 1000 square metres which is prescribed in the Order as the net income deemed to result from that 'unit of production' in a regime of 'competent management'.

Thus, the productive capacity of a unit may be calculated by considering the *potential* farming enterprises which could be undertaken there without major re-investment being undertaken, identifying and counting the 'units of production' involved (how many hectares of which crop, how many head of sheep/cattle/goats, are the cattle dairy/beef etc.) and then using the relevant current Order, to produce the total net annual income of which the unit is objectively capable.

Para. 5 of Schedule 6 provides that for the purposes of succession proceedings, any 'close relative' of the deceased tenant, whether or not they are the applicant, or the landlord or the Tribunal themselves may request from the Minister a determination of his assessment of the productive capacity of any 'land which the applicant occupies' or is deemed to occupy or of the holding which is the subject of the possession proceedings ...'. The Minister (acting normally through Divisional Surveyors) is to furnish such a requested assessment in writing, giving the grounds on which his final assessment is reached. If, after he has provided an assessment in response to a particular request, an Order is published before the Tribunal hearing, the surveyor may revise his determination in the light of the new values and issue a revised statement accordingly to the original requesting party: para. 5(4).

This document will be evidence 'of any facts stated in it', i.e. it will prove how the ministerial decision on the productive capacity was reached. It is *not*, however, conclusive on the issue of the productive capacity and in a Tribunal hearing, for example, the Divisional Surveyor may be cross-examined on the choice of 'units of production' applied to the unit and on the information contained in the ministerial statement. He cannot, however, be challenged on the adequacy or otherwise of the current net income values stipulated by the appropriate Order.

10.09 'Occupation' of a commercial unit

In 1984 the details of the 'occupation' test were considerably refined, partly in an attempt to deny effect to some of the less subtle manoeuvres which had until then succeeded in maintaining an applicant's formal eligibility for a succession tenancy whilst in reality also allowing him to enjoy the secure beneficial occupation of other agricultural land. These relatively modest anti-avoidance provisions are now contained in paras. 6-10 of Schedule 6 of the 1986 Act. Two strategies may be discerned: permitted disregards of genuinely precarious 'occupation' and 'deemed occupation' in specified situations where the Act presumes beneficial enjoyment by the applicant.

Firstly, where an applicant occupies land under various specified *precarious*, short-term or non-beneficial arrangements, these interests may be *disregarded* or *ignored* in assessing his eligibility. Occupation in such circumstances would not be appropriate even where a 'commercial unit' was involved as the basis of an established independent enterprise, and thus the applicant remains eligible for a succession tenancy.

Secondly, and by contrast, the Act treats with great suspicion arrangements concerning holdings of agricultural land which concern the applicant's spouse, or any company controlled by the applicant (known collectively as 'connected persons'). In effect, their occupation of agricultural land is treated as that of the applicant himself and such '*deemed occupation*' is to be brought into account in assessing his eligibility and will serve to disqualify him where a commercial unit or more is involved.

The Schedule also deems the applicant to be in occupation of any holding in respect of which he has already obtained a direction from the Tribunal for a succession tenancy, where the tenancy of that holding was also previously held by the deceased tenant.

Finally, Schedule 6 makes specific provision for cases of *joint occupation*, and explains how the 'share' of a joint occupier applicant should be calculated and brought into account.

These anti-avoidance provisions do not affect arrangements with family members *other than* the spouse nor do they affect arrangements with trusted third parties. To date there has been no litigation on the new aspects of the occupation condition nor on any challenge to an applicant's eligibility on this ground.

10.10 Occupation: interests which may be disregarded

Para. 6 of Schedule 6 directs the applicant's occupation of agricultural land may be *disregarded* where he occupies such land 'only'

(a) under an 'insecure' tenancy approved by the Minister under section 2 [3.03] or under a grazing/or mowing agreement for a specified period of the year [3.05];

(b) under a *Gladstone* v. *Bower* tenancy [3.07];

(c) under any other tenancy which apart from (a) and (b) above is not an 'agricultural tenancy' – for example where the applicant's tenancy of agricultural land is excluded by section 1(1) from the Act because it is held of his employer during his employment;

(d) under a section 5 fixed term tenancy without security of tenure [2.05; 3.04];

(e) as a licensee;

(f) as an executor, administrator, trustee in bankruptcy or other person deriving title by operation of law.

The only circumstance in which any such interest will *not* be ignored but will be brought into account against the applicant's eligibility is where the occupation is by reason of such a grant to the applicant made *by* a 'connected person': para.6(1)(b) The Act here raises a presumption that in such circumstances the legally precarious characteristics of the grant are belied by the reality. This presumption of the Act is irrebuttable and cannot be displaced by contrary evidence.

Para. 6(1) thus puts the occupier in the unusual position of occasionally needing to prove that his occupation is precarious—normally, of course, occupiers of agricultural holdings who dispute or litigate are attempting to prove quite the opposite. Although from time to time quite difficult problems of evidence may arise—for example, in showing that an arrangement was in fact limited to grazing and/or mowing for a specified period of the year—nevertheless, with one exception, the precarious grants in para. 6(1) are unambiguously identified and conceptually clear. The exception which has provoked many disputes before Tribunals and latterly has been the subject of litigation at first instance is 6(1)(e): occupation 'only as a licensee'.

'Licensee only'

The occupation of agricultural land as a 'licensee only' has never counted against an applicant in assessing his eligibility for a succession tenancy. Before the 1986 Act, the provision for disregarding such interests was contained in section 18(2)(c) of the Agriculture (Miscellaneous Provisions) Act 1976. In the consolidation the wording has changed in order, from 'occupies as licensee only' to 'occupies only ... as a licensee'. This change does not alter the substance of the exclusion, nor does it remove the source of uncertainty, since the difficulty experienced by Tribunals and ultimately by the Queen's Bench Division has been in deciding precisely what significance should be given to the word '*only*'.

Guidance must now be taken on this point from the decision of the late Forbes J in *Brooks* v. *Brown* (1986). In that case the applicant, Mr Brown, had farmed three holdings in partnership with his father who had been the tenant of all three, and had held them of different landlords. The tenancies were not partnership property.

After his father died, Mr Brown established a new partnership with his mother and sister who had both been granted letters of administration of the father's estate. The applicant was from this point onwards the only working farmer in that particular family farming partnership. He applied for a direction from the Tribunal for a tenancy of one of the holdings previously held by his father and the landlords contested his eligibility under section 18(2)(c) of the 1976 Act saying that he did not occupy as a 'licensee only'.

The transcript of the Tribunal decision indicates the clearest possible exposition of the problem raised by this wording. For the applicant it was contended that there were only four 'classes' of occupation: owner, tenant, licensee or trespasser and that the applicant, as a partner of the tenant, had been in occupation during his father's lifetime as a licensee of his father and after his father's death as a licensee of the personal representatives, his new partners. This analysis was based on *Harrison-Broadley* v. *Smith* (1964). 'Licensee only' was thus to be contrasted simply with owner, tenant, or trespasser. For the landlords on the other hand it was contended that the distinction was between the status of 'licensee *only*' and, as it were, 'licensee *plus*'. The landlords contended that on his father's death the applicant was a licensee who enjoyed partnership rights, rights under the intestacy and also rights under the 1976 Act and that therefore he could not be said to be a licensee *only*. The Tribunal, deciding in favour of the applicant's eligibility, said:

'as at the date of death and as at the date of hearing the applicant had no security of tenure in relation to (the unit) ... our conclusion is that the term 'occupies as a licensee only' means that he does not occupy by virtue of being the owner, a tenant or a licensee whose licence would be converted into a letting from year to year by virtue of section 2 of the

Agricultural Holdings Act. In our judgment the applicant occupied
(the unit) as a licensee only.'

The landlords appealed by way of case stated to the Queen's Bench
Division where Forbes J gave what is presently the decisive judgment on
this point. He adopted the more restrictive interpretation and found for
the landlords that the quality of the applicant's occupation was not merely
that of a 'licensee only', since his partnership rights gave him a degree of
security beyond that which could be disregarded. (The other two
arguments put forward by the landlords do not seem to have contributed
appreciably to the learned judge's decision.) The following rather lengthy
passage may usefully be quoted from Forbes J's judgment since it will
govern the position for many other applicants who find themselves in Mr
Brown's situation of being on the land because they farm it 'as a working
partner in a family farming partnership': a very common situation.

Forbes J held that, partly by reason of section 38 of the Partnership Act
1890,

'a farming partner who is on the land is ... there (particularly if he is a
family farming partner) not as a mere licensee or as a licensee only, he
has rights and duties if he is the working partner which mean that he
has more security of tenure than a mere licensee. His position will be
protected ... in the Chancery Division as a partner in the operations he
wants to carry out on the land ... This is a situation which it seems to
me gives him some security of tenure, using that expression with a very
wide meaning as I am sure Lord Russell intended to use it ... As long
as it can be shown that the occupier occupies because he is either the
working farmer or one of the working farmers in a family farming
partnership it really ... cannot with any sense of reality be said that he
is there in occupation as a licensee only. His position, ... his rights
deriving from occupation as a working farmer will be protected in a way
that they could not be ... if he was a licensee only. The position of the
respondent, as the only family farmer left farming the land in the new
family partnership ... means that his occupation of the land carries with
it a greater security of tenure (using that word in its broadest sense as
I think Lord Russell intended it to be used) than that possessed by a
licensee only.'

The case was not appealed further. Whether or not an appeal court would
uphold this very restrictive interpretation of the 'licensee only' exception,
Brooks v. *Brown* must be taken as stating the law for the guidance of
Tribunals and applicants until subsequent litigation pursues the point.
Where an applicant claims that he occupies agricultural land 'only as a
licensee' he must be able to show that he is a 'mere' licensee or a bare

licensee. It seems from *Brooks* v. *Brown* that if, for any reason, the licence is not revocable at the will of the licensor, the licensee is in danger of enjoying 'a greater degree of security of tenure' than para. 6(1)(e) permits. Any partner-licensee will clearly be ineligible where the partnership rights relate to a commercial unit, and thus where succession rights are in view it is especially important that attention be given to the position of partner-applicants.

10.11 Deemed occupation: arrangements concerning connected persons

In the following situations the applicant will be deemed to be in occupation of the relevant land:

(1)   Where land is occupied by his spouse or by a body corporate controlled by the applicant: para. 9 of Schedule 6. The applicant 'controls' a body corporate if he and/or his spouse have the constitutional power to secure that the affairs of that body are conducted in accordance with 'his her or their wishes': para. 1(2) of Schedule 6.

(2)   Where the applicant or a 'connected person' (spouse or controlled body corporate) is entitled to occupy the land 'otherwise than under a tenancy' or otherwise than under one of the 'precarious etc. interests' specified para. 6(1)(a)-(f), and they then grant to a third party the right to occupy the land under an interest falling within para. 6(1)(a)-(d).

Thus, if an owner-occupier grants an 'insecure' interest in a third party, and during the third party's tenure the grantor applies for a succession tenancy of another holding, he will be deemed to be in occupation of his land and the third party interest will be ignored for the purposes of the eligibility test: para. 10 of Schedule 6.

(3)   As mentioned above, where the applicant holds under an 'insecure' grant specified in para. 6(1)(a)-(e) which was *granted by* a 'connected person', that apparently insecure grant *will* count against him when eligibility is assessed.

10.12 Deemed occupation: applicant's existing Tribunal direction

Where the applicant has already applied for and obtained a Tribunal direction entitling him to a succession tenancy of *another* holding previously held *by the deceased tenant*, he will be deemed to be in occupation of that holding for the purposes of any subsequent eligibility assessment.

10.13 Occupation: joint occupiers

Para. 7 of Schedule 6 makes provision for the allocation of 'shares' in the net income of jointly occupied land so that for the purposes of ascertaining whether or not an applicant already occupies a commercial unit, although the applicant will be deemed to be in occupation of the whole, only his appropriate share of any jointly held land will be counted against him.

Where the applicant is a joint tenant, whether a beneficial joint tenant (of the fee simple) or a joint tenant of the lease, or where he is a joint licensee, his 'appropriate share' of the net annual income of that land will be an equal part with his co-owners/occupiers: thus if there are three beneficial joint tenants or three licensees, each will be treated as entitled to one third of the net annual income of the land. If this one third share is itself equivalent to 'the aggregate of the current average earnings of two full-time male agricultural workers aged twenty or more' then the applicant will be ineligible since his deemed share of the jointly occupied land will constitute a 'commercial unit'.

Where the co-owners are tenants in common of their interest, then the total net annual income of the land will be divided so as to give effect to the 'proportionate share' of the applicant in that property and its income.

The intention of para. 7 is to clarify the position where joint occupation is involved and thus fill the gap which previously existed in the legislation and was exposed by the litigation of *Williamson* v. *Thompson* (1980). The paragraph deals expressly but exclusively with four only of the most frequently encountered types of joint occupation.

10.14 When must the applicant be eligible? Section 39(2)

Before 1984 there was a degree of doubt as to *when*, in the sense of at what points in the application procedures, an applicant had to demonstrate that he was eligible. The present law on this matter is now to be found in section 39(2) of the 1986 Act which provides that the Tribunal must be satisfied that the applicant (i) was an eligible person at the date of the previous tenant's death and (ii) has not subsequently ceased to be such a person. Thus the applicant's eligibility must endure from the date of death to the date of the Tribunal's determination of his suitability.

10.15 Suitability

When the Tribunal are satisfied that the applicant is eligible under section 36, or is to be treated as eligible under section 41, they must then determine whether he is in their opinion a 'suitable' person to become the tenant of the holding: section 39(2). In making their determination, they must

(i)   give the landlord an opportunity to state his views on the suitability of the particular applicant: section 39(7), and
(ii) themselves have regard to 'all relevant matters', including, from section 39(8),
   (a)   the applicant's training or practical experience in agriculture,
   (b)   his age, physical health and financial standing, and
   (c)   the landlord's views on his suitability.

The standard required
In considering 'suitability' Tribunals will normally consider whether a reasonable and prudent landlord would consider the applicant suitable as a tenant of the particular holding in question. This avoids the extremes of either demanding that the applicant be the tenant who would be chosen by a landlord under open market conditions, or alternatively of agreeing that any tenant who could produce a bare living from the holding would be 'suitable'.

No factor relevant to the tenant's suitability should be overlooked, so that all the circumstances of each case should be considered. Whilst section 39(8) directs the attention of Tribunals to the aspects of each application specified there, it must not be read as limiting them only to those considerations. Each application will turn on its own particular facts.

Training and experience
Evidence of the applicant's 'track record' will be particularly relevant where he had already been actively involved in farming the holding in question. If the landlord criticises his standards of husbandry, the Tribunal's view and inspection of the holding will enable them to assess the validity of the criticism. In *Adams* v. *Harris* (1982), for example, the landlord produced considerable evidence of the applicant's poor standards of husbandry including poor returns and the bad condition of fencing and animals on the holding. After viewing the holding, the Tribunal could not agree with the landlord's opinion and a direction for a tenancy was given in favour of the applicant. On the other hand, in *Franklin* v. *Duncombe* (1986) there was strong evidence of poor husbandry and pernicious weed infection and the Tribunal found that the poor present

condition of crops followed a long build-up of weeds and poor soil fertility for which the applicant was substantially responsible and they held him unsuitable.

Where the applicant's training and experience has been acquired largely on the holding in question under the guidance of a parent or relative whom he now seeks to succeed, the Tribunal may be faced with difficult decisions in attempting to identify their respective responsibilities and capacities. In *Mason* v. *Leigh Ltd* (1986), for example, the applicant son had virtually run the holding during his father's tenancy, but the father was found to have been very dictatorial and not to have discussed the policy of the enterprise with his son. On the facts, the Tribunal found that the problems experienced on the holding were essentially attributable to the father rather than the son and they held that although in his own right the son was 'only average as a farmer' nevertheless they (the Tribunal) 'could not seek perfection' and they held him suitable. However, in *Ponsford-Raymond* v. *Bahamas International Trust Co Ltd* (1984) and *Hewitt* v. *Gardner* (1983), although the parents concerned were seen by the Tribunal to be dictatorial and to have exerted a strong influence on the applicants, this reflected also on the applicants' own capacities and indicated in each case that they were ineffectual and unlikely to be suitable.

In *Brooks* v. *Magdalen College Oxford* (1982), the applicant, aged 51, had worked under his father's old-fashioned methods and had gained his training and experience under that regime. The Tribunal found that the farm was in poor condition and that the applicant could not fully appreciate the detailed plan produced by a business consultant to improve the position. The applicant was found in these circumstances to have neither the will nor the ability to improve the farming and was held unsuitable.

In considering the applicant's training and experience it is important to remember that the Tribunal is looking for a background appropriate to a *tenant* and not merely for an agricultural worker. In *Hewitt* v. *Gardner* (1983), this point was clearly to the fore. The applicant in that case had farmed the holding with his father and subsequently with his mother who had taken a first succession tenancy by agreement. The Tribunal agreed with the landlord that the applicant was 'as a farm worker, first class' but his capability and competence as a farmer, especially in respect of a holding of 168 acres was seriously doubted. The Tribunal found that the applicant lacked

'drive and determination and in an era when farming in a farm of 168 acres or so is 'big business' the Applicant's admitted lack of understanding of farming accounts and matters financial cannot but be a severe disadvantage to him ... and is a deficiency which cannot quickly (if at all) be improved.'

The Tribunal accepted that the applicant's ability to do better

'may well have been handicapped by the presence over the greater part of his farming career of a somewhat dominant father' but felt that 'this is no reason for requiring that the landlord ... should have to accept these failings.'

Where a wife seeks to succeed to her husband's tenancy it is of course important that her experience on the holding has equipped her to take control of the enterprise. This continues to be crucial even now that the 'eligibility' test has been relaxed for widows in respect of the principal source of livelihood test. Where it is hoped that such a succession will take place it is therefore *vital* that the wife should be involved in the policy-making administrative side of the business during her husband's life as well as in the more purely laborious tasks. In some circumstances it may be relevant to the Tribunal that a widow will have the support and help of other members of the family to call on. In *Broadwith* v. *Parkinson Trustees* (1984), for example, the applicant widow aged 61 had been in control of her husband's farming enterprise for the seven years prior to his death as he had been incapacitated in an accident. She had farmed the holding with her two sons and the Tribunal took their future support into account in finding her suitable to succeed to the tenancy.

Age, health and financial standing

Of these three, the financial standing of the applicant is most frequently questioned by the landlord or the Tribunal. The reasonable and prudent landlord must necessarily be assured that the tenant will be able to pay the rent, fulfil the covenants and farm the holding so as to realise its full potential. The applicant's existing capital, credit-worthiness and acumen and the quality of his financial advisers may all, therefore, be relevant to this consideration. It may also be necessary to consider any major claims pending against the applicant. In *Turner* v. *Greenwell and Shreiber* (1983), for example, one factor considered by the Tribunal was the likely effect on the applicant's financial position of an outstanding claim for capital from his former wife.

Age and health seem only rarely to play a crucial role. In *Smith* v. *Chambers* (1982), the applicant was aged 58 and suffered badly from arthritis. These factors in conjunction with poor evidence from his past farming ability seem to have rendered him unsuitable. It may be that this case, like *Brooks* v. *Magdalen College Oxford* both tacitly recognise that the teaching of new tricks to an old dog is likely to be unfruitful.

Other considerations

Whilst other relevant considerations are infinitely various, the *size* of the

holding seems often to affect the standard required from the tenant. This
was referred to as a central issue in *Hewitt* v. *Gardner* whilst in *Mason* v.
Leigh the Tribunal indicated that in the case of a small acreage the
suitability test might be applied less severely.

The *distance* of the holding from other land farmed by the applicant
may be relevant: in *Yardley* v. *Evans* (1980) a distance of 3.5 miles and a
Draper v. *Tiffin* (1979) 8 miles were both held reasonable.

Finally, in *Raine* v. *Raine* (which was subsequently litigated in the
Queen's Bench Division on another point), the Tribunal considered the
bad feeling which existed between the applicant and another beneficiary
under the family trust but found that it was not a factor which rendered
him 'unsuitable' to succeed.

10.16 The Tribunal's duty

In *Skelton* v. *Cholmley Trustees* (1984) the applicant's case was supported
by the landlord and the applicant contended that, where the landlord
agreed, the Tribunal should automatically give a direction for a succession
tenancy in his favour and he asked for a ruling from the Tribunal to that
effect. The Tribunal declined, and stated that they had a duty in every
case to satisfy *themselves* as to the applicant's eligibility and suitability. In
the event, they were satisfied here on both counts and after appropriate
consideration, gave the direction.

Similarly, the Tribunal in *Carr* v. *Berrisford* (1982) themselves raised
the question whether the applicant satisfied the 'commercial unit' test of
eligibility. Since neither counsel had prepared argument on this point, the
Tribunal reserved judgement pending lodgement by counsel of supplemental observations regarding the eligibility point within a specified time
limit.

The wording of the 1986 Act seems clearly to support the approach
illustrated by these two cases in requiring in section 39(2) that 'the
Tribunal, if satisfied' on the issue of eligibility 'shall determine whether
(the applicant) is in their opinion a suitable person to become the tenant
of the holding'. The landlord's support of an applicant is not conclusive,
any more than the landlord's adverse comments on his suitability would
be. It is merely one factor in the decision on *suitability* to which the
Tribunal is specifically required by section 39(8) to have regard. In
examining the applicant's claim to *eligibility* the landlord's opinion is not
even of advisory importance to the Tribunal, who alone are the arbiters of
the matter by virtue of the Act.

10.17 Procedure when there are several applicants

Where several competing applications are effectively lodged before the Tribunal, sections 39 and 40 indicate the procedures to be followed.

Priority to the will
Where one of the applicants is indicated in the deceased tenant's will or a codicil to it as his desired successor, then the Tribunal must consider that person's application first: section 39(4). Only if they determine that that applicant is *not* suitable may they progress to consideration of the other contenders' applications.

A person is 'designated' for the purposes of the Act if the deceased tenant's will, or a codicil to it, contains an effective specific bequest to that person of the holding or contains specific mention of the holding and exclusively designates that person as the person whom the deceased tenant wished to succeed him as tenant of the holding. The will must be subject of a grant of probate or administration but any direction given in favour of an applicant by reason of his being a 'designated person' will continue to be valid even if the probate or administration is subsequently revoked or varied: section 40(3).

No designated successor
If there is no designated successor, or if the designated successor is found by the Tribunal not to be suitable then the Tribunal must consider the eligibility and suitability of each of the (other) applicants. If only one person satisfies them as being a suitable person, then the Tribunal must give a direction entitling him to a tenancy of the holding (subject as below to the landlord's notice to quit): section 39(5). If, on the other hand, two or more applicants are found to be suitable by the Tribunal, then the Tribunal is required by section 39(6) to determine which applicant is

'in their opinion the more or most suitable person to become the tenant of the holding'

and shall then, subject to any landlord's notice to quit, make a direction accordingly.

Joint grants
As an alternative to this procedure, section 39(9) permits the Tribunal to make a direction entitling two, three or four applicants to a joint succession tenancy. Any such direction can only be made *with the consent of the landlord*.

10.18 Multiple holdings

Where the deceased tenant in fact held several tenancies, and on his death either one person applies for several succession tenancies, or several people apply for the various succession tenancies, then section 42(2) provides that the order in which the various successions shall be considered is as follows:

(a)   if there is only one applicant, in the order chosen by the applicant;
(b)   where there is more than one applicant, in the order agreed by them or, in default of their agreement, as decided by the chairman of the Tribunal, who is required by subsection (3) to deal with the holdings in order of size, beginning with the largest.

It will be recalled that anyone who is granted a direction for a succession tenancy of a holding will be deemed to be in occupation of it [10.13]. If the holding is therefore a commercial unit, the successor will become ineligible for any subsequent holding under consideration and in this way an attempt has been made to maintain the limit of succession rights to one holding only.

10.19 The landlord's notice to quit

Where a landlord has served a notice to quit under Case G in the three months after notification to him of the tenant's death, the notice *will* be effective without more if *either* no application for a succession tenancy is made *or* no applicant is held 'suitable' by the Tribunal.

Where an applicant or joint applicants *are* found suitable to succeed, however, the Case G notice will *not* have effect *unless* the landlord applies to the Tribunal under the provisions of section 44 for their consent to its operation whether in whole or in part and obtains it. Section 44(1) provides that the Tribunal must afford the landlord an opportunity to apply for their consent before they give a direction for a succession tenancy.

Application for consent
The procedure for applying for consent in these circumstances is presently prescribed by the Agricultural Land Tribunals (Succession to Agricultural Tenancies) Order 1984, SI 1984/1301.

Where only *one* application for succession has been lodged in the period of three months from the day after the death, the landlord must apply for consent in the statutory Form 2 within four months of the service on him of notice of the succession application: section 1 1984/1301 p.4. Where *more than one* succession application has been lodged the landlord must apply for consent either within that same four month period after the service of notice on him of the first of the applications *or* within one month of these several applications being reduced to one, whichever is the later date: r.4(4). The Secretary to the Tribunal must notify the landlord of the start of any four month or one month period.

The landlord's application for consent is treated as being subject, as normal 'contestable' notices are, to section 27 of the 1986 Act. The landlord must therefore satisfy the Tribunal that one or more of the grounds specified in section 27(3)(a)-(f) is appropriate to his case *and* that a fair and reasonable landlord would seek possession, as required by section 27(2). He must indicate in his application for consent which ground(s) he is relying on and give the main facts on which his case is to be based. If he intends (as is often the case) to rely on the greater hardship ground of section 27(3)(e), and his case relies on hardship to persons other than himself he must identify them in his Form 2 application and indicate the nature of the alleged hardship: r.4(2).

The Case G notice, therefore, loses its 'incontestable' nature where a viable succession application is made and in such a case the landlord must persuade the Tribunal that the notice should have effect.

If the Tribunal are satisfied as to the grounds claimed and as to the fair and reasonable landlord criterion then they must consent to the operation of the notice and shall dismiss the applications for succession tenancies: section 44(4). The notice to quit will then come into operation in the normal way, unless the tenant successfully applies for its postponement to a 'new operative date': section 44(6). This new operative date must be a date not later than three months after the original operative date or the date of Tribunal consent to the notice, whichever is the later.

10.20 Succession to part only of a holding and the Case G notice to quit

Section 39(10) makes provision for a direction to be given for a succession tenancy for *part only* of a holding. This may occur if the suitable applicant (or applicants if there is to be a joint succession tenancy) *agrees* to accept a tenancy of part only of the holding. Such an arrangement cannot be forced on the applicant. He cannot be obliged to accept part only of the holding but may voluntarily do so.

Where such a 'partial' succession is agreed, this will have important repercussions for the landlord's Case G notice to quit, where such a notice has been effectively served.

As we have seen [10.10], the landlord must apply to the Tribunal under section 44(1) for consent to the notice to quit coming into operation when there is at least one suitable succession applicant identified. Where a direction is to be given which will concern part only of the holding, the landlord is still required to apply for consent under that section.

However, as regards the part of the holding which is *not* to be the subject of the direction (i.e. which is *not* required by the successor(s)) the Tribunal *must* give their consent, *without* any further argument. The landlord does *not* need to 'justify' the notice under section 27(3)(a)-(f), nor is he required to satisfy the fair and reasonable landlord test, in respect of the 'unwanted' part of the holding: section 44(2) does not apply to that part.

As regards the part of the holding which *is* to be the subject of the succession, however, the usual requirements of section 44 will apply and thus to obtain consent to the operation of the notice to quit in respect of the land wanted by the successor the landlord must show grounds under section 27(3)(a)-(f) and must satisfy the fair and reasonable landlord test of section 27(2).

A grant of a tenancy of part only of a holding will count as one succession occasion for the purposes of section 37(1). That section refers throughout to 'the tenancy of the holding or a related holding' having been obtained or granted. 'A related holding' is defined in section 35(2) as 'any agricultural holding comprising the whole or a substantial part of the land comprised in the holding.'

10.21 Effect of a direction for a tenancy: the new tenancy

Commencement

Where a direction is given for a new tenancy in favour of a successor or joint successors, the rights under that direction (as opposed to rights under the consequent tenancy) are not capable of assignment: section 45(7).

The new tenancy is deemed to be granted by the landlord and accepted by the persons entitled under the direction: section 45(1). It is deemed to take effect either

(a)   at the end of twelve months following the end of the tenancy year in which the deceased died; or

(b)   if a Case G notice was served, then at the time that notice would have expired. Section 46(1) and 47(2).

However, where the Tribunal's direction is given in the last three months before these commencement dates, the tenant may apply for a postpone-ment of the new tenancy for a period of up to three months from the so-called 'original date'. If, on the other hand, the direction itself is given after the 'original relevant date' the Tribunal must specify a commencement date which is within three months of the giving of the direction.

The terms of the tenancy

The new tenancy will be in the same terms as that held by the deceased tenant before his death: section 47(1). However, section 47(2) provides that in any case where the deceased tenant held under a fixed-term lease, this shall be treated as having been converted into a tenancy from year to year before his death and the new tenancy will therefore also be a tenancy from year to year. Section 47(3) provides that in any event the new tenancy will include a covenant against assignment subletting and parting with possession. Section 48 provides that a tenancy dependent on a direction may be submitted to arbitration by either party within the three months after the Tribunal's direction or the first three months of the tenancy, whichever is the later. The issues which may be submitted to arbitration are:

(a)   what variations in the terms of the existing tenancy are justifiable with regard to the circumstances of the holding and the length of time elapsed since the holding was first let on those terms; and

(b)   what rent should be payable or should have been payable at the relevant time. Either or both of these questions may be referred to arbitration but notice that even when only question (a) alone is referred by the parties, the arbitrator may, if he considers it equitable, vary the rent: section 48(b).

The rent properly payable is to be assessed on the same basis as is used under section 12 and Schedule 2: the rent reasonably to be expected by a prudent and willing landlord from a prudent and willing tenant, taking into account all the factors specified in Schedule 2: section 48(9). This provision was introduced by the 1984 Act. Under the previous legislation, succession tenancy rents were *not* tied to rent review levels. However, it is quite clear that succession tenancies are now to be treated in precisely the same way as 'original' grants and the older differential no longer exists. This, of course, makes succession tenancies even less attractive to landlords.

The arbitrator shall also include in his award any necessary compensation provisions, treating the old and new tenants in effect as outgoing and incoming tenants respectively. Compensation between landlord and tenant must be calculated and paid or allowed in the normal way as if a straightforward change of tenant had occurred: section 48(5), (8).

10.22 Concurrent leases

Section 45(2), (3) and (4), derived from the 1984 Act, were introduced to overcome a difficulty encountered with the statutory succession machinery where the original grantor had granted a lease of his reversion to a third party *after* granting the deceased tenant his agricultural tenancy. In such a situation the lessee of the reversion is effectively the assignee of the reversion for the duration of his lease. He thus becomes the agricultural tenant's 'landlord', entitled to the rents of the holding and subject to the rights and liabilities of the lease. The concurrent lessee thus takes the place of the grantor in these respects and at the same time reduces the agricultural tenant to a status similar to that of a subtenant, although the agricultural lease is not dependent on the concurrent lease and will not end when the concurrent lease terminates. For example, where G grants an agricultural tenancy to A, and subsequently grants a lease of the reversion to R, R effectively becomes A's landlord for the duration of his (R's) lease.

The problem for the succession machinery, which surfaced in *Cheshire* v. *Elwes and the Colesbourne Estate Co.* (1979) was to identify correctly the person in such a situation who was to be deemed to grant the succession tenancy. Section 45(2) now resolves this difficulty by providing that the succession tenancy will be 'deemed to be granted by the person for the time being entitled to the interest from which the deceased's tenancy was derived', i.e. in the example above, by G. Any 'supervening interest' defined by section 45(3) as 'an interest created subsequently to (the deceased's) tenancy and derived (whether immediately or otherwise) from the interest from which that tenancy was derived' (i.e. R's interest) is to be ignored for the purposes of the succession grant. Section 45(4), however, makes it clear that 'the landlord's' (R's) rights and liabilities are not to be affected. The effect of section 45 is to protect the successor from becoming a true subtenant as one whose tenancy took effect *after* the lease of the reversion. As we have already seen, subtenants are in an extremely precarious position since the legislation does not substantially protect them and they remain vulnerable to notices to quit which operate outside the statutory time limits and Tribunal control [6.17].

However, section 45 has not entirely prevented landlords from contriving by the use of concurrent leases to deny successors any substantial benefit from the Act. The section's definition of 'supervening interest' is admittedly wide. However, it is not all-encompassing. Consider, for example, the case where a landlord creates a string of concurrent and dependent tenancies and then *finally* grants a concurrent lease which intrudes a new head-tenant between himself and the original head-tenant of the string. This final concurrent lease will *not* be a 'supervening interest' as regards any successor to a dependent tenancy because it was not 'derived from the interest from which' the dependent tenancy was derived but was itself taken from the landowner's interest rather than the earlier concurrent lease. Thus, such a strategy would cause successors to be 'genuine' subtenants and thus to lose the substance of their statutory rights.

10.23 Agreed succession on death

Notice that one of the 'occasions of succession' described in section 37 is the situation of the landlord granting a tenancy to a person who

'being a close relative of the tenant who died on that occasion was or had become the sole remaining applicant'

for a Tribunal direction: section 35(1)(b).

This is an occasion where *no* Tribunal direction has actually been given. Instead, the landlord has directly granted a new tenancy to a person who

(i)   is a close surviving relative within section 35(2)(a)-(d); and
(ii) has *applied* for a Tribunal direction; and
(iii) is by the date of the grant of the new tenancy the *only* or only remaining applicant for a direction.

There is *no* requirement in such a situation that the new tenant should satisfy the 'eligibility' requirements of section 36(3): he merely needs to fulfil the three requirements specified above. This clarification was introduced in 1984.

As long as the successor in such a case does *apply for* a Tribunal direction, such a grant will constitute one of the two permitted statutory successions. This minimal involvement of the Tribunal is essential if the landlord is to have the 'benefit' of such an agreed succession counting towards the statutory scheme. However, the absence of a direction and the relaxation of the 'eligibility' requirement characterise it as a succession by agreement comparable in some ways with the *inter vivos* agreed successions to be considered in the following chapter.

Chapter 11

Succession on Retirement

11.01 Introductory

Under the 1976 Act a facility was provided for *agreed* successions effected when a tenant *retired* to be treated as 'succession occasions' for the purposes of the statutory scheme.

In 1984, the 'retirement' facility was extended in some circumstances, so that even if the landlord did *not* agree, a retirement and succession could be effected through the machinery of a Tribunal application and direction. The new machinery is very closely modelled on the procedures for succession on death now contained in sections 36–48 of the 1986 Act.

This chapter compares and explains the two modes of succession on retirement.

(A) AGREED RETIREMENT

11.02 Agreed succession during the lifetime of the tenant

The Agriculture (Miscellaneous Provisions) Act 1976 provided that where all the parties agreed, the transfer of an agricultural tenancy to a successor during the current tenant's lifetime would constitute one of the two succession occasions of the statutory succession scheme. This provision made it possible, where the parties were in agreement, for the tenant to retire and in effect it accelerated one succession. Such an arrangement is convenient for the tenant, who might prefer to retire rather than die 'in harness', for the successor, whose interest is advanced, and for the landlord, since it hastens his ultimate resumption of possession.

The provisions for agreed retirement successions were slightly modified in 1984. The present provision is found in section 37(2) of the 1986 Act, which provides that

(i) where there is an *agreement* between the landlord and the current tenant and

(ii) consequently the holding is *let* or *assigned* to

(iii) someone who is a '*close relative*' of the current tenant, then such an occasion will constitute one succession within the statutory scheme, as it will be 'deemed to be an occasion ... on which a tenancy ... was obtained by virtue of a direction under section 39.'

(i) Agreement

The retirement envisaged by section 37(2) is one taking place as a result of an agreement freely reached between landlord and tenant. The section does *not* provide for a situation where the landlord is to be obliged to accept an unwelcome successor, nor where the tenant is being compelled to retire, so if landlord and tenant cannot agree on a retirement and a successor who is eligible under the section, the provision is of no assistance.

The section imposes no age requirements on the tenant: he may choose to retire when he wishes – again, so long as the landlord agrees to the subsequent arrangement.

In both respects the situation provided for in section 37(2) differs from that governed by sections 49-59, which is discussed below.

(ii) 'Let or assigned'

The successor's tenancy may be vested in him either by the grant of a new tenancy to him by the landlord or 'by virtue of an assignment of the current tenancy'.

The possibility of an assignment was introduced in 1984. It is attractive because a direct assignment will avoid the normal consequences of a changeoever of incoming/outgoing tenants: valuations claims for dilapidations and counter-claims. It is likely that an assignment will be in breach of the terms of the current tenancy, however, and therefore if this technique is adopted the 'agreement' must include the agreement of the landlord to waive any such restrictions.

It seems from the wording of section 37(2)(a) and (b) that if the landlord grants a new lease to the successor, it may be for part only of the holding. Where the tenant assigns the 'current tenancy', however, it is of necessity the tenancy of the *whole holding* which is *assigned*. This distinction will need to be carefully observed in cases where the successor is intended to succeed to part only of the original holding.

(iii) The successor a 'close relative'

The *only* eligibility requirement imposed by section 37 on the successor to a retiring tenant is that he is a person 'who, if the tenant had died immediately before the grant or assignment would have been his close relative'; that is, the successor must be the wife or husband, brother or sister, child or 'treated child' of the current tenant, as defined in section 35(2). This requirement has already been discussed at length in the previous chapter [10.10]. Notice, therefore, that a successor taking the holding *by agreement* on the retirement of the tenant does *not* need to satisfy the 'principal source of livelihood' test nor the 'commercial unit occupation' test. His position is therefore similar to that of a successor *by agreement* on death, described above [10.24].

(B) RETIREMENT WITHOUT THE LANDLORD'S AGREEMENT

11.03 The scheme of the statutory retirement provisions

Sections 49-59 of the 1986 Act and Part III of the Agricultural Land Tribunals (Succession to Agricultural Tenancies) Order (SI 1984/1301) establish a scheme for succession on the retirement of the tenant which closely resembles the statutory scheme for succession on the tenant's death, set out in sections 36-48 and considered in Chapter 10 above. The aim of the scheme is to enable tenants whose tenancy enjoys succession rights and who wish to retire for reasons of age or infirmity to do so and to be succeeded at that point by an 'eligible' and 'suitable' successor whose claims have been assessed by the Agricultural Land Tribunal. This scheme is *not* dependent on the landlord's agreement and is therefore radically different from section 37(2) situations. The Tribunal must give the landlord an opportunity to comment on the nominated successor's suitability and, if he so wishes, to oppose the proposed retirement and succession on 'greater hardship' grounds, but his voice is not decisive: the final outcome rests with the Tribunal.

The initiative under the statutory retirement scheme is with the tenant. He initiates the procedure by serving a retirement notice on the landlord which states that he wishes to retire on a specified date when he will be at least 65 years old or will be permanently incapable of farming the holding in accordance with the rules of good husbandry by reason of physical or mental infirmity. The retirement notice must also name a 'nominated successor'. The nominated successor should then apply to the Tribunal for a direction entitling him to a tenancy of the holding, normally beginning at the retirement date. Before granting such a direction, the Tribunal must be satisfied as to the successor's eligibility and suitability and must consider any case put to them by the landlord to persuade them that greater hardship would be caused by granting than by declining to grant such a direction.

If the Tribunal do grant a direction, the new grant of tenancy will constitute one 'succession occasion' of the two statutory successions permitted. If the Tribunal decide against granting a direction in favour of the nominated successor then

(i)   the tenant will have lost his only opportunity to retire and pass on the tenancy to his relative, unless he can negotiate an *agreed* retirement and succession under section 37(2). The statutory retirement scheme only permits *one* retirement application to be made in respect of any particular tenancy. If, however, the nominated successor does not pursue his application to the decision stage, but prematurely abandons or withdraws it, his application will be treated as if it had never been made and he will have preserved the tenant's right to serve a subsequent retirement notice which may then be followed by an application by the relevant nominated successor, whether that is the original applicant or another.

(ii) the nominated successor will have lost his chance of applying for a succession tenancy on the tenant's death under the provision of sections 36-48. This is so regardless of the reason for the Tribunal's decision against his application and regardless of the lapse of time between the attempted retirement and the subsequent death. An unsuccessful nominated successor is denied the right to apply for a succession tenancy on the tenant's death by section 57(4).

Where there is serious doubt as to the outcome of an application, therefore, the nominated successor is well advised under this scheme to withdraw before the decision is given and thus preserve a chance of a further application in the future.

As with the provisions for successions on death, a direction will entitle the successor to a new tenancy, which may be subjected to arbitration on terms and/or rent. There are also detailed provisions designed to avoid the deployment of retirement notices as effective counter-measures to notices to quit which have been served or set in train by the landlord.

The introduction of the statutory retirement scheme was hoped to aid the interests of efficient agriculture. Notice that the scheme is set in motion by the tenant and is designed essentially to accommodate his plans. The landlord may be obliged by the Tribunal's decision to accept in the nominated successor a tenant whom he would not have chosen if given a free hand. The aim and practice of the statutory retirement succession scheme therefore should not be confused with the aim underlying Case A notices to quit, where the landlord of a smallholding may in certain circumstances effectively oblige a tenant to retire and move on. In the succession situation the tenant acts, the landlord merely reacts if he wishes and in any event is never allowed to take the initiative nor to have the decisive voice in the proceedings.

The following paragraphs consider the details of the scheme.

11.04 The retirement notice

The statutory scheme for retirement successions is set in motion by the service on the landlord, of a retirement notice by the existing tenant or tenants under the provisions of section 49(1)(b). The retirement notice must indicate that the tenant or tenants wish a single 'eligible person' who is named in the notice and who is known as the 'nominated successor' to succeed him or them to the tenancy from a date specified in the notice. The following points should be noted from section 49(1).

(i) No prescribed form for the retirement notice
Neither section 49(1) nor SI 1984/1301 prescribe either the form or the wording of the retirement notice.

(ii) A tenancy from year to year
A retirement notice may only be served if the existing tenancy is a tenancy from year to year. The procedure dependent on a retirement notice does *not* apply to a fixed term tenancy, although it will apply once the fixed term has expired and section 3 has caused the continuation of the tenant's interest as a tenancy from year to year.

(iii) A tenancy granted before 12th July 1984
The retirement notice procedures *only* apply to tenancies endowed with statutory succession rights. For the most part these are either tenancies granted before 12th July 1984 or succession tenancies dependent on such a grant or those rare cases where a written tenancy granted after 12th July 1984 has been expressly made subject to the succession provisions, i.e. the parties have consciously 'contracted into' the succession scheme. Section 49(1) expresses this requirement by limiting the retirement notice procedure to tenancies from year to year which are tenancies falling 'within paragraph (a)-(b) of section 34(1)' [10.02].

(iv) Joint tenants
Section 49(1) expressly states that a retirement notice must be given by *all* the tenants in the case of a joint tenancy. (This is so even though only one needs to satisfy the age requirement, although apparently all must satisfy the infirmity alternative where that is relied on.)

(v) Period of notice

In specifying the date from which the named eligible person, the nominated successor, is to succeed as tenant, the notice must specify a date on which the tenancy of the holding could have been determined by notice to quit and which falls 'not less than one year but not more than two years after the date of the notice'.

11.05 The eligible person/nominated successor

The person named in the retirement notice as the intended successor, referred to in this part of the Act as 'the nominated successor' is to be an 'eligible person'. Section 50(2), (3) and (4) defined 'eligible person' in the terms similar to section 36(3) with necessary deletions or amendments but with the important difference that there is no provision here parallel to section 41 and thus no possibility of an applicant being 'deemed eligible' on the livelihood test. A nominated successor therefore *must* satisfy this test in every detail. The nominated successor must be:

(i) a 'close relative' who satisfies
(ii) the principal source of livelihood test exactly both as to time and extent and
(iii) the commercial unit occupation test.

The criteria have all been considered at length above: [10.04-10.17].

The 'eligible person'/nominated successor is entitled by section 50(1) to apply to the Tribunal under section 53 for a direction entitling him to a tenancy of the holding.

11.06 Situations where the right to apply to the Tribunal is excluded

Section 51 identifies various specific situations where, even if the requirements of sections 49 to 50 have been satisfied, the nominated successor's right to apply to the Tribunal will be excluded. They are:

(i) Situations defined in sections 37 and 38
These are cases where two successions have already occurred, cases where a notice to quit served before the retirement notice will inevitably take effect, smallholdings and charity land held by trustees for the settlement of former forces personnel. All these matters are discussed in detail above [10.02].

The problems of notices to quit and retirement notices are also considered further below [11.07].

(ii) A prior notice and application

The nominated successor may not apply to the Tribunal if the retiring tenant has already given an earlier retirement notice and the person who was the nominated successor in that notice made an application for a succession tenancy which was pursuant to a decision of the Tribunal: section 51(2). Notice, however, that where a nominated successor abandons or withdraws his application it is treated as if it had never been made: section 53(10). This leaves the possibility of future applications, so that the mere service of an earlier retirement notice will not of itself prevent later notices and application. The later 'nominated successor' must ascertain the *consequences* of the earlier notice(s).

(iii) Age or infirmity

The nominated successor may not apply to the Tribunal if the retiring tenant will not have reached the age of 65 at the retirement date specified in the retirement notice as the date at which the succession is to take place: section 51(3). The only alternative to the age requirement is to claim that a younger tenant is retiring because he is, or will be by the retirement date,

> 'incapable by reason of bodily or mental infirmity of conducting the farming ... in accordance with the rules of good husbandry'. section 51(3)(a)' *and* 'any such incapacity is likely to be permanent': section 51(3)(b).

Thus, the statutory retirement provisions, in contrast with the case of an agreed retirement and succession under section 37(2), only relate to retirement at age 65 and above, or earlier *if* permanent ill-health and consequent incapacity to farm can be proved.

Notice that where the tenancy is presently held by *joint tenants*, section 51(3) will be satisfied if any *one* of them will have reached the age of 65 by the retirement date. However, if neither or none of the joint tenants will have satisfied the age condition by the appropriate date, the retirement provisions will only be available if they can show that they will *all* be permanently infirm and incapable of farming by that date. This requirement of comprehensive ill-health is expressly and unambiguously stated in section 51(3)(a), but is no less bizarre for its clarity.

(iv) Notice to quit in train

Where a valid notice to quit given under Cases B, D or E has been given before the date of the retirement notice then no application may be made for a succession tenancy unless and until the notice to quit is held ineffective in arbitration proceedings or, if a counter-notice is served, either the Tribunal withhold their consent to the operation of the notice to quit or no application for consent is made within the time limit: section 53(4)(5). Thus the succession right is effectively postponed in these Cases until the result of a pending notice to quit is ascertained. The relevant notices to quit all depend on preliminary moves (such as the obtaining of planning permission or the service of a notice to remedy) which alert the tenant at an early stage to the possibility of further action by the landlord. This provision suspending retirement notices in such cases is to avoid their (mis)use as instruments of sabotage. If the notice to quit 'dies', however, the nominated successor has one month from the arbitrator's decision, or the Tribunal's refusal of consent or the expiry of the period for an application for consent in which to apply to the Tribunal under section 50(1), depending on whichever of these three occurrences was in the particular case fatal to the notice to quit: section 51(5)(b).

11.07 Notice to quit and the retirement notice procedures

The interplay of notices to quit with the retirement notice procedures is somewhat complicated, although the underlying intention is clear. It may be helpful at this point to draw together the rather scattered sections which are relevant so that the picture may be seen as a whole.

There are four distinct situations:

(i) Inevitably operative notices to quit: section 38
Section 51(1) applies section 38 with the necessary minimal amendments to the retirement notice procedures. It will be recalled [10.02] that the effect of section 38 is to exclude the right to make a succession application to a holding which is *already*, at the time the retirement notice is given, subject to an inevitably operative notice to quit. Where, at the date the retirement notice is served on the landlord, an earlier notice to quit served by him has already passed beyond challenge or has received Tribunal consent to its operation, that notice to quit will take effect unhindered. Thus, if the various time limits for service of a counter-notice or referral to arbitration have passed without the tenant effectively challenging the notice to quit, or alternatively, Tribunal consent to it has been obtained, then *no* succession application can be made: sections 38/51(1) exclude the nominated successor's right under section 50(1) to apply to the Tribunal.

Sections 38/51 therefore relate to situations where a notice to quit, whether given under section 26 or Schedule 3, has already gone *beyond challenge* by the date the *retirement notice* is served and *excludes* the successor's right to apply in such cases.

(ii) Notice to quit pending when retirement notice is given: section 51(4)(5)(6)

As described above, section 51(4)(5)(6) apply where an incontestable notice under Case B, D or E has been given *before* the retirement notice but its effectiveness is still uncertain at that date because there still remains time to challenge it by arbitration or counter-notice. In such a case the nominated successor's rights under section 50(1) are *postponed* until the fate of the notice to quit is clear. If the notice to quit is ultimately *not* effective or operative (being held ineffective by the arbitrator or because the Tribunal withhold consent to its operation, or because no application for consent is effectively made) then the nominated successor *will have* the right to apply for a direction, and will have *one month* from the date on which the fate of the notice to quit became certain to do so: section 51(b).

If, however, the notice to quit is ultimately effective, the nominated successor's rights are excluded.

In situations under section 57(4), therefore the nominated successor will have to wait and see the fate of a notice already given *before* the succession procedures were triggered by the giving of the retirement notice.

(iii) Notice to quit under Cases C, F, B or D given after retirement notice: section 52

Section 52 contains two separate provisions, each dealing with a notice to quit given *on or after* the date of the retirement notice but both relating to notices to quit heralded long in advance of their service by preliminary moves such as the service of a notice to remedy or the obtaining of a certificate of bad husbandry.

If the notice to quit is given under Case C *after* the retirement notice has been served and the necessary certificate of bad husbandry was granted in response to an application made *before the date of the retirement notice*, the retirement notice 'shall be of no effect': section 52(1)(a).

If the notice to quit is given under Case F, similarly, the retirement notice is nullified without any further condition: section 52(1)(b).

If, however, a notice to quit under Case B or D is given *on or after* the date of the retirement notice the successor must wait to see the ultimate fate of the notice to quit, whose various procedures will be given priority and permitted to run their natural course. Both of these cases require preliminary steps: for Case B the obtaining of planning permission (usually) and for Case D the service of a notice to remedy or pay, which section 52(c)(a) requires to have been served *before* the retirement notice. Neither, therefore, takes the tenant by surprise. If the notice to quit *is* ultimately effective, it will nullify the retirement notice and destroy the rights of the nominated successor. If, on the other hand, the notice to quit under Case B or D is ultimately not effective, by reason of the arbitrator's decision, or the Tribunal's withholding consent to its operation or no application for consent being effectively made, then the nominated successor has *one month* from the date of the decision or expiry of the time limit to apply to the Tribunal, exercising his right under section 50(1).

Thus in these cases a *subsequent* notice to quit based on *preliminaries* which *pre-date* the retirement notice may nullify the retirement notice and its dependent procedures.

(iv) Notices to quit in any other case: section 54

Where a notice to quit is served which does *not* fall within one of the three classes described above, section 54 provides that the *retirement notice* procedures take *priority* regardless of the date on which the notice to quit was served, whether before, simultaneously with, or after, the retirement notice.

A notice to quit within section 54 will not take effect within a month beginning with the day after the date of the giving of the retirement notice, even if it would normally come into effect at that time: section 54(2)(3). Thus, the effect of the notice to quit is held in suspense during that period in which the nominated successor may apply to the Tribunal. If he does make an application, section 54(2)(b) provides that the notice to quit will not be effective whilst the application is still before the Tribunal and has not been 'finally disposed of ... or withdrawn or abandoned'. The notice to quit is therefore kept in further suspense until the termination of the Tribunal proceedings. Finally, where the Tribunal does grant the nominated successor a direction for a tenancy, section 54(2) provides that the notice to quit 'shall in any event not have effect'.

Ideally, therefore, a landlord who foresees a retirement notice being given should be astute to serve *any* notice to quit so that it is effective *before* the retirement notice is given or is at least beyond challenge by that date and thus is within sections 38/51. This is certainly so where he intends to rely on a 'general' section 26 notice. In some circumstances incontestable notices to quit under Cases B, C, D, E and F may suffer relatively little interruption from the retirement notice procedures, but this should not be allowed to detract from the desirability of prompt service where retirement is in view.

11.08 The application to the Tribunal

Assuming that no excluding situation is in question, the nominated successor should apply under section 53 and SI 1984/1301 to the Tribunal for a direction entitling him to a tenancy of the holding.

Time limit

The nominated successor's application must be made within *one month* beginning with the day after the date of the giving of the retirement notice: section 53(2), r.23(2) of SI 1984/1301. At the same time he must notify the landlord of his application using Form 6: r.24 SI 1984/1301.

Form
The application must be in Form 5 prescribed by r.23 of SI 1984/1301 and

(a)   accompanied by a copy of the retirement notice *and*
(b)   signed by the nominated successor and the retiring tenant or tenants: section 53(3).

The landlord's reply
The landlord's reply, in Form 5 R, must be submitted within one month of service on him of the application: r.25 1984/1301.

Tribunal scrutiny
Where the retirement notice is expressly based on the impending or present permanent infirmity and consequent incapacity, the Tribunal must *first* be satisfied that this statement is supported in all respects and, where there are joint tenants, that it is true in the case of each one. The Tribunal must be satisfied in these matters before proceeding further with the application: section 53(4). No guidelines are provided for the Tribunal's approach to this matter but medical evidence is clearly crucial on the degree of infirmity and its effect and its likely permanence.

   If they are satisfied on these points, where relevant, the Tribunal should then proceed to consider the applicant and to satisfy themselves on the two 'standard' criteria of 'eligibility' in the same fashion as they would in the case of succession on death. Thus, the Tribunal must be satisfied in any case that the nominated successor

(i)   was an eligible person at the date of the giving of the retirement notice and has not subsequently ceased to be eligible: section 53(5), and
(ii) is in their opinion a suitable person having regard to his training or experience, age, health, financial standing and the views expressed on the matter by the landlord: section 53(6) [10.04-10.17].

If the Tribunal is satisfied that the applicant is suitable; they shall give a direction entitling him to a tenancy: section 53(7).

Landlord's challenge
The only challenge available to the landlord once the tenant has been found 'suitable' is under section 53(8). The landlord may apply to the Tribunal claiming that 'greater hardship would be caused by giving the

direction than by refusing' to grant it. This challenge is the equivalent in some respects of the landlord's application for consent to a notice to quit under the succession on death procedures. However, he has only the *one* specified ground of 'greater hardship' available and the onus is on him to show greater hardship. The ambit of 'greater hardship' was discussed above [7.14]. The 'greater hardship' relied on may be to *any* person (e.g. to the landlord's family who require the holding). The landlord must explain the nature of his greater hardship argument in his reply on Form 5R (SI 1984/1301). If the Tribunal accept the landlord's argument, of course, the retirement plans of the tenant will be thwarted and he will be obliged to remain subject to the tenancy. Since his retirement notice was followed by an application which was not prematurely withdrawn or abandoned it will serve to exclude any possibility of a second retirement notice being effective.

11.09 The unsuccessful nominated successor

Where the Tribunal decline to grant a direction for a tenancy in favour of the 'nominated successor' because they do not find him eligible, or suitable, or because they are persuaded by the landlord's greater hardship argument, the unsuccessful applicant will *not* be permitted to apply for a succession tenancy on the tenant's death: section 57(4).

If, however, the nominated successor withdraws or abandons his application, the application is treated 'as if it had never been made': section 53(10), and his right to apply at the tenant's death is thus preserved. Similarly, any application made in retirement proceedings which is invalidated by a Case G, F, B or D notice to quit coming into operation within section 52(1) or (2) is also treated as if it had never been made and thus again the applicant's opportunity of applying for a succession tenancy on the tenant's death endures, although this seems to confer little benefit on the applicant in reality.

11.10 Effect of the death of the retiring tenant

Depending on the point reached by the retirement proceedings, the tenant's death may have more or less effect on them. Section 57 specifies the position when the tenant dies *after* giving the retirement notice.

(i) No application made
If at the time of death either no application has been made by the nominated successor *or* his application has not been finally disposed of, section 57(2) provides that no proceedings (or no further proceedings)

shall be taken under section 53 but instead the matter should proceed as a succession on death. This opens the field to other prospective successors and also gives the landlord other grounds in addition to greater hardship on which to contest the application, assuming he serves a valid Case G notice to quit.

(ii) Direction given but tenancy not commenced
Where the retiring tenant dies after the Tribunal has granted a direction in favour of the applicant but before the new tenancy has begun, the provision of sections 55 and 56 continue to apply and the matter is concluded as a retirement succession. The provisions for succession on death are not relevant in such a case: section 57(3).

(iii) Death after refusal of direction
If the tenant dies after the Tribunal have refused to grant a direction in favour of the applicant then the tenancy is 'available' for succession applications under section 36 to 48, and the matter will proceed anew as a case of succession on death: section 57(4). The unsuccessful nominated successor may *not*, however, apply in such proceedings: section 57(4).

(iv) Joint tenants
Where the retirement notice was given by joint tenants and one of them dies leaving survivor(s) this will *not* affect the retirement proceedings, irrespective of the precise stage at which the joint tenant dies: section 57(5). This holds true regardless of the age of the deceased joint tenant or of the survivor(s). Their joint notice continues to be given effect and the retirement proceedings run their normal course.

11.11 Effect of Tribunal direction

Section 55 explains the effect of a Tribunal direction in favour of the 'nominated successor'. The section is modelled precisely on section 45 [10.22] and includes similar provisions to resolve the difficulties posed by concurrent leases: section 55(2), (3), (4) [10.23].

Notice that the direction will normally entitle the successor to a tenancy as from the retirement date stipulated in the tenant's retirement notice: section 55(1), (8). However, where the direction is given within the three months before that date, the Tribunal is given the discretion to postpone the new tenancy's commencement to a date within three months after the retirement date, if the retiring tenant applies to them to do so: section 55(8)(a). If the Tribunal direction is given *after* the retirement date, then it must specify a commencement date for the succession tenancy which is within the three months following the date of the direction: section 55(8)(b).

The rights of the successor deriving from the Tribunal's direction, as opposed to the new tenancy, 'shall not be capable of assignment': section 55(6)

11.12 Tribunal direction: 'deemed occupation'

Where the nominated successor is entitled to a tenancy by virtue of a direction given under section 53(7) but, before the commencement of that succession tenancy, the retiring tenant dies, the nominated successor will be deemed to be already in occupation of that holding for the purposes of assessing his eligibility to apply for a succession tenancy of any other holding *held by the deceased tenant* at the time of death: section 58.

This provision dealing with multiple applications essentially mirrors para. 8(1) of Schedule 6 [10.13].

11.13 Terms of the succession tenancy

Section 56 applies the provision of section 48(3)-(12) concerning arbitration on new tenancy terms to retirement successions: section 56(3) [10.22].

The terms of the new tenancy apart from arbitration are to be the same as the tenancy held by the retiring tenant and in any event are to include a covenant against assignment, subletting or parting with possession: section 56(1), (2).

Part V

Compensation Rights and the Resolution of Disputes

This last Part concerning agricultural holdings deals with two important areas. The first is compensation. The parties' rights to compensation at the end of a tenancy, in particular, when the tenant quits the holding, have long been a matter for statutory intervention. These are discussed in Chapter 12.

The second is the resolution of disputes concerning tenancies of agricultural holdings, which is divided amongst several possible procedures. Chapter 13 discusses the jurisdictions of each forum and considers the procedure applicable. It deals with *all* disputes, not just those which may arise over compensation on quitting.

Chapter 12

Compensation Entitlement at the Termination of a Tenancy

12.01 Introductory

Parts V and VI of the 1986 Act consolidate the statutory provisions for compensation for both landlord and tenant on the termination of the tenancy of an agricultural holding. In nearly every case, the statutory provisions are now the exclusive source of entitlement to such compensation and they replace the pre-existing customary provisions. The only situations in which customary entitlements remain relevant are in relation to 'old' improvements begun before 1st March 1948 and in respect of tenant right claims where the tenant was in occupation of the holding before 1st March 1948 and has *not* effectively elected to take advantage of the statutory compensation provisions in respect of those claims: Schedule 9, para. 4; Schedule 12, paras. 6 and 7.

The statutory compensation provisions may in general not be avoided: contracting out from them, modifying or excluding their application is prohibited by section 78 unless the statute elsewhere expressly permits such variation.

This chapter is intended merely as a guide through the compensation provisions. The detailed heads of compensation available appear in the relevant Schedules to the Act. To avoid repetition the reader is at appropriate points merely referred to the relevant Schedule.

12.02 The tenant's claims

The Act identifies several types of compensation which may be available to a tenant when he quits the holding at the termination of the tenancy. It may be remarked at this point that the tenant is *only* entitled to such compensation when the tenancy has been terminated *and* he has quit the holding. In the case of compensation for disturbance, the availability of compensation is further restricted to those situations where the tenancy has been terminated by an appropriate notice to quit. Note that specific provision for compensation for milk quotas is now included with the Agriculture Act 1986. The statutory classes of compensation for the tenant are:

(1) Compensation for disturbance
This is designed to cover or contribute towards compensating 'the tenant's actual loss' directly attributable to the quitting of the holding which is unavoidably incurred by the tenant in selling or removing his items from the holding.

(2) Long-term improvements begun on or after 1st March 1948
These enure for the benefit of the holding rather than merely for the benefit of the next incoming tenant.

(3) Short-term improvements begun on or after 1st March 1945
These have only a limited continuing benefit and are essentially only of advantage to the tenant or tenants taking the holding in the years soon after their completion.

(4) 'Old' improvements begun before 1st March 1948
There is a distinct statutory scheme to provide for compensation arising from this now declining class of early improvements which are rarely encountered in practice.

(5) 'High farming'
Separate provision is made for claims that the continuous adoption of a specially advantageous system of farming has led to an enhancement of the value of the holding.

(6) Tenant right matters
These are also compensated by a separate statutory scheme designed to accommodate claims by the quitting tenant for the value of sown and harvested crops left on the holding which he has no right to remove and for established flocks of hill sheep left in appropriate areas.

(7) Market gardens
Market gardens are subject to some special additional compensation provisions found in Part VI of the Act.

(8) Milk quotas
Milk quotas are compensated through the provisions of section 13 and Schedule 1 of the Agriculture Act 1986.

12.03 Compensation for disturbance

The tenant's entitlement to statutory compensation for disturbance was introduced by the Agriculture Act 1908 and, at a time when there was no security of tenure, served to mitigate to some extent the tenant's precarious position. The statutory scheme was retained after security of tenure was introduced in 1947 and is now contained in sections 60-63 of the 1986 Act.

Compensation for disturbance is available *in addition* to any other compensation which the tenant may claim on quitting. The parties cannot, directly or indirectly, contract out of the entitlement to compensation for disturbance. In *Coates* v. *Diment* (1951) it was held that any clause in a tenancy whose effect was to give the landlord the right to resume possession without giving the tenant time to serve the requisite statutory compensation notices would be invalid as excluding the tenant's right to compensation.

Compensation for disturbance is *only* available to the tenant according to section 60 when the tenancy is *terminated by reason of a notice to quit served by the landlord* or by the *service of a counter-notice by the tenant* in accordance with section 32, converting a notice to quit part into a notice to quit the entire holding. Not all notices to quit are appropriate: the detailed provisions as to which notices to quit may be used to found claims for compensation for disturbance are explained below.

The tenant must be able to show, if necessary, that he quitted the holding 'by reason of' the notice to quit. If that essential causal link exists, a delay on the tenant's part is not important to his claim. For example, where he holds over whilst the validity of a notice to quit is determined. If the tenant does act on an invalid notice to quit, his claim to compensation for disturbance seems to be unaffected. Section 60's predecessor, section 34 of the 1948 Act, was interpreted as meaning that compensation for disturbance is payable where the tenant quits 'by reason of this document, good, bad or indifferent, namely the notice to quit served by the landlord': *Kestell* v. *Langmaid* (1950)

12.04 The amount of compensation for disturbance

The Act provides in section 60(2) for both 'basic' and 'additional' payments for compensation for disturbance. In appropriate cases the tenant will be entitled to both, and will then be entitled to a *maximum* sum equivalent to six years' rent at the rate payable immediately before the termination of the tenancy. In any case where compensation for disturbance is payable, a *minimum* of one year's rent, similarly calculated, will be payable.

Basic compensation Wherever compensation for disturbance is available to the tenant because he has quit as the result of an appropriate notice to quit or counter-notice, he will be entitled in any case to one year's rent: section 60(2)(a), (3)(a).

A *higher amount* of basic compensation, equal to either two years' rent or the amount of his 'actual loss' on removal, whichever is the *lower* will be available if the tenant serves the appropriate notices on the landlord in good time: section 60(3)(b).

His 'actual loss' is defined by section 60(5) as

'the amount of the loss or expense directly attributable to the quitting of the holding which is unavoidably incurred by the tenant upon or in connection with the sale or removal of his household goods, implements of husbandry, fixtures, farm produce or farm stock on or used in connection with the holding and includes any expenses reasonably incurred by him in the preparation of his claim for basic compensation, (not being the costs of an arbitration ...)'

Thus, the tenant could include here any valuer's fees incurred in preparing his claim and any loss incurred by a forced sale of stock or goods provoked by the notice to quit.

To claim this advantageously higher rate of 'basic' compensation the tenant must satisfy the two requirements of section 60(6):

(a)   he must serve notice in writing on the landlord at least one month before the tenancy ends, indicating his intention of claiming the higher rate *and*

(b)   he must also give the landlord a 'reasonable opportunity' of valuing the stock and goods as described before they are sold.

If these conditions are satisfied the tenant will be entitled to a maximum of two years' rent, or to his 'actual loss' if that is a lower sum, as basic compensation.

Additional compensation is an amount equal to four years' rent which is payable essentially when the holding is repossessed for a non-agricultural purpose: its precise availability is discussed below.

12.05 When is compensation for disturbance payable?

Although as we have seen from section 60, compensation for disturbance is only payable when the tenancy terminates by reason of a landlord's notice to quit or tenant's counter-notice, not every notice to quit will carry entitlement. The situation may be summarised as follows:

(1)   *No compensation for disturbance* (neither basic nor additional) is payable when the notice to quit is an incontestable notice given under Case C, D, E, F or G of Schedule 3. Thus where the notice to quit is based on a certificate of bad husbandry, a notice to pay or remedy, an irremediable breach of covenant, the tenant's insolvency or the tenant's death, *no* compensation for disturbance is available to the tenant.

(2)   *Basic compensation only* will be payable
      (i)   where the notice to quit is an incontestable notice given under Case A or Case H of Schedule 3, i.e. where it relies on the retirement of a smallholding tenant at 65 or on a Ministry amalgamation of holdings.
      (ii)   when the notice to quit is a 'general' notice subject to sections 26 and 27 *and* is stated to rely on one or more of the purposes in section 27(a) (b) (c) or (e) and, where Tribunal consent to its operation is sought, the Tribunal are satisfied that one or more of the stated purposes applies. Thus basic compensation *only* will be available where the landlord retakes possession for the purpose of good husbandry or sound estate management or educational or research purposes or because hardship will ensue to him if possession is not retaken. It is important to the landlord that his notice to quit *should state* the purpose for which he seeks possession if he wishes to limit his liability to basic rate compensation.

(3)   *Basic and additional compensation* (the maximum possible entitlement) will be payable when
      (i)   the notice to quit is an incontestable notice given under Case B of Schedule 3: non-agricultural use for which planning permission has been obtained or is unnecessary;
      (ii)   the notice to quit is a 'general' notice under sections 26 and 27 and is stated to be given so that the landlord can resume possession of the land for a non-agricultural purpose outside Case B (section 27(7)) and the Tribunal are satisfied that this is so;
      (iii) the notice to quit is a 'general' notice subject to sections 26 and 27 and is stated to rely on a purpose or purposes within section 27(a) (b) (c) or (d) as above (2(ii)) *and* in giving their consent to the notice, the Tribunal indicate that they are satisfied that *additionally* the landlord requires the land for a non-agricultural purpose within section 27(f), *whether or not* this was claimed by the landlord;
      (iv)   the notice to quit was a general notice to quit subject to section 26 which contained *no indication* of the purpose(s) for which

repossession was sought, i.e. a 'general' notice given at large without reference to any of section 27(a)-(f).

Whilst these provisions are somewhat intricate their general pattern is fairly clear: incontestable notices to quit mostly *disentitle* the tenant to compensation for disturbance; other notices will entitle him to 'basic' compensation apart from those notices terminating the tenancy so that the land can be turned to a non-agricultural use, when the quitting tenant will normally be entitled to claim the maximum disturbance compensation available – both 'basic' and 'additional' payments. It must be remembered that the higher rate of basic compensation depends on the tenant serving the appropriate notice on the landlord and giving an opportunity for a valuation of his goods.

The anomalous notice to quit is the 'general' notice given 'at large' which does not state any purpose. Although such drafting may avoid the pitfalls of ambiguity it may be expensive to the landlord as it may result in him paying 'additional' compensation to the tenant and it should therefore be avoided [see also 6.05]

12.06 Compensation for disturbance in cases of early termination

Many tenancies include a 'short notice' provision whereby the landlord reserves the right to resume possession of the holding for a stated non-agricultural purpose without needing to give the normal statutory minimum of twelve months' notice required by section 25. Short notice in such cases is expressly authorised by section 25(2)(b). Where an agricultural tenancy is terminated by a notice to quit given under such a 'short notice' provision, section 62 provides the tenant with a statutory entitlement to compensation for disturbance which he enjoys *as well as* his rights under sections 60 and 61. The further entitlement from section 62 is to an amount

'equal to the additional benefit (if any) which would have accrued to the tenant if the tenancy had, instead of being terminated as provided by the notice been terminated twelve months from the end of the current tenancy year.'

In other words, the tenant may claim benefit, such as loss of profits, which he would have enjoyed from the holding had the normal period of notice been given. A tenant in such circumstances will therefore be entitled to a maximum of six years' rent *plus* any 'loss of benefit' payment under section 62 as is appropriate.

12.07 Subtenancies and compensation for disturbance

Section 63 now clarifies the position concerning compensation for disturbance in cases where the tenant has sublet the holding and is served with a notice to quit by his own (head) landlord. In such a situation an effective notice to quit served on the tenant will cause the subtenancy to terminate by operation of law. The precarious position of subtenants of agricultural holdings is discussed above [6.17].

Section 63(1) provides that in such a case the *subtenant* is entitled to compensation for disturbance from the tenant. Thus, where his subtenancy is ended by operation of law consequent on the termination of his grantor's interest the subtenant is in precisely the same position as he would have been if the tenant, his grantor, had independently served him with notice to quit.

Where a subtenancy has been created, it could be argued that the tenant, not being himself physically in possession of the holding, does not 'quit' it in consequence of the notice to quit. Section 63(2) overcomes this difficulty by providing that where a subtenancy has been granted and, as a result of the head landlord's notice to quit the tenant becomes liable to pay his subtenant compensation for disturbance, the *tenant* himself is entitled to recover such compensation under the Act from the head landlord.

12.08 Notice to quit part

Where the tenant serves a counter-notice under section 32 in response to a notice to quit part only of the holding, he is able to treat the notice as notice to quit the entire holding. However, he will not always be able to claim compensation based on the rent of the entire holding: his entitlement is restricted by section 63(3). The section provides that where the notice to quit part *or* any series of notices to quit part given by the same person *or* any notices to quit part given by several owners of severed parts of the reversion affect, when aggregated, less than one-fourth of the original holding, *and* the unaffected part would be reasonably capable of being farmed as a separate holding, then the tenant may only claim such compensation for disturbance as is proportional to the part or parts of the holdings to which the notice(s) referred.

12.09 Compensation for long-term improvements begun on or after 1st March 1948: Schedule 7

Where an improvement specified in Schedule 7 has been effected on or after 1st March 1948 the tenant will be entitled to compensation when he quits the holding on the termination of the tenancy, *regardless* of how the tenancy terminates. Section 96(1) defines 'termination' as

'the cesser of the contract of tenancy by reason of effluxion of time or from any other cause.'

A notice to quit is *not* therefore a necessary prerequisite for a claim under Schedule 7.

However, the tenant must be able to show that the appropriate *consent* to the improvement had been obtained: section 64(1), 67(1). Normally this will be the consent of the landlord and must be given in writing. It does *not* necessarily need to be given *before* work is commenced on the improvement. The consent may be conditional or unconditional. The conditions may relate to the compensation payable and will be effective to vary the statutory level of compensation payable so long as the agreement between landlord and tenant on the matter is in writing. Conditions which in effect denied the tenant's entitlement to compensation, however, would be invalid: *Coates* v. *Diment* (1951) and section 78.

The landlord may, however, refuse consent. There is no direct challenge to such a refusal. The landlord is not, for example, limited to a 'reasonable' refusal of consent, his refusal may be totally arbitrary and yet go unchallenged. Where the improvement in question is within Part I of Schedule 7, the landlord's refusal will, without more, deny compensation to the tenant who, if he undertakes the improvement in question, does so entirely at his own uncompensated expense. Such improvements include the making of osier beds, planting hops and providing underground tanks (see Schedule 7 in Appendix I for the complete list). However, where the improvement in question is in Part II of Schedule 7 and the tenant is

'aggrieved by the refusal of his landlord to give his consent ... or is unwilling to agree any terms subject to which the landlord is prepared to give his consent'

then

'the tenant may apply to the Tribunal for approval of the carrying out of the improvement': section 67(3).

Thus for Part II improvements the tenant may overcome the landlord's refusal by approaching the Tribunal. The Tribunal may approve the work in question conditionally or unconditionally. They may also withhold their approval: section 67(5). The effect of their approval to an improvement is that the landlord may, within one month of being notified of it, serve notice on them and on the tenant that he intends to carry out the improvement *himself*. If the landlord does not serve such a notice, or serves it out of time, or having opted to do the work fails to carry out the work in a 'reasonable' time, then the tenant may go ahead and carry out the work and the Tribunal's consent will have effect as if it were the consent of the landlord: section 67(6)(7). Thus the landlord's refusal is not automatically fatal to the tenant's right to compensation where a Schedule 7 Part II improvement is in question but instead opens the door to a Tribunal consent and the possibility of the landlord himself undertaking the work. Part II includes erection of buildings, reclaiming of wasteland, provision of electric light or power and provision of facilities for the storage or disposal of sewage or farm waste: the Schedule is reprinted in full in Appendix I.

The amount payable

Subject to the written agreement of the parties (section 67(2)) the amount of compensation payable for a Schedule 7 improvement is

'an amount equal to the increase attributable to the improvement in the value of the holding as a holding, having regard to the character and situation of the holding and the average requirements of tenants reasonably skilled in husbandry': section 66(1).

This sum may be arrived at by considering the increase in rental value attributable to the improvement and multiplying it by a number of years to reflect the anticipated useful life of the work, thus achieving a capital sum payable to the tenant. Where the tenant has received any grant aid from central or local government for the work, this must be brought into account in assessing his compensation: section 66(5).

12.10 Limited owners: consents from landlords

Notice that where the landlord of an agricultural holding has only a limited interest in the property (for example, he may be a tenant for life under a settlement) he can nevertheless give a perfectly valid consent for the purposes of the Act and his limited interest will not affect the tenant. Section 88 of the 1986 Act provides that a limited owner may 'give any consent, make any agreement or do or have done to him any other act' as if he were an absolute owner in fee simple, or of a leasehold interest.

12.11 Limited owners and Schedule 7 improvements

Section 89 ensures that in most cases where a limited owner (for example a life tenant) uses capital money on Schedule 7 improvements there will be no need for that capital to be repaid out of income. Where the limited owner is acting under powers in either the Settled Land Act 1925 or the Law of Property Act 1925, the Schedule 7 improvement will be deemed to be within Part I of Schedule 3 to the Settled Land Act and not for income repayment. Where the 'improver' is an institution using powers within the Universities and College Estates Act 1925 and 1964, however, the Minister of Education or the institution itself may consider such repayment to be appropriate under section 26(5) of the 1925 Act.

12.12 Subtenants and Schedule 7

Where a subtenant has applied to the Tribunal under section 11 for a direction that his immediate landlord should carry out work to provide fixed equipment to satisfy existing statutory requirements, it may be that the work in question also constitutes a Schedule 7 improvement. In such circumstances, section 68(2) provides that the immediate landlord will *not* be entitled to compensation on quitting for such improvement from his (head) landlord but the section further provides that if the immediate landlord fails to comply with the Tribunal direction and the subtenant *himself* undertakes the work, then the tenant will be able to claim compensation for that improvement from his (head) landlord on quitting as if he had done the work himself. These provisions take into account the rentals payable as a result of such work and prevent the tenant of the holding from either benefiting twice over or, alternatively, losing money from the work.

12.13 Hill farming

Section 68(3) dovetails the provisions of the Hill Farming Act 1946 with the Schedule 7 compensation scheme. The result is that where a tenant carries out work which constitutes an improvement within Schedule 7 and which also was undertaken because the tenant was responsible for doing that work in a hill farming land improvement scheme under section 1 of the 1946 Act, then if the work was included in the scheme at the instance of or with the consent of the landlord, the compensation provisions of section 67 will apply. The landlord will be deemed to have consented and any agreement made between the landlord and tenant concerning compensation (or otherwise) will be effective under section

67(2). Where such a hill farming improvement is involved, however, section 67(5) and (6) do *not* apply. Thus the landlord is *not* able to refuse consent to the work and yet ultimately do it himself.

12.14 Short-term improvements begun on or after 1st March 1948: Schedule 8, Part I

Part I of Schedule 8 specifies six short-term improvements for which the tenant may be paid compensation if they were begun on or after 1st March 1948. The scheme of compensation for these improvements differs from that governing Schedule 7 improvements in two important ways.

Firstly, *no consent* is required from the landlord or the Tribunal to protect the tenant's eligibility for compensation. Section 68(1) provides that if the tenant intends to carry out 'mole drainage and works ... to secure its efficient functioning' then he must *notify* the landlord in writing at least one month beforehand if he is to protect his entitlement to compensation but the landlord has no right to disentitle the tenant by refusing him permission to do the work. Secondly, the measure of compensation for Schedule 8 Part I improvements is, subject to any expressly agreed varying terms,

'the value of the improvement or matter to an incoming tenant calculated in accordance with such method if any as may be prescribed': section 66(2)

The 'prescribed method' is presently laid down in the scale of values included in Part I of the schedule to the Agriculture (Calculation of Value for Compensation) Regulations 1978 (SI 1978/809 as amended). In assessing compensation, any grant aid received by the tenant from central or local government funds must be brought into account. In addition, any 'benefit' given or allowed to the tenant by the landlord in consideration of the tenant's effecting the improvement(s) in question where the 'benefit' is the result of an agreement in writing between parties must also be brought into account: section 66(3). This is most usually some arrangement such as a reduction in the rent payable.

As with Schedule 7, it is the date on which the improvement work was begun which is the vital qualifying date. The work must not pre-date 1st March 1948. The date of the tenant's entry into occupation of the holding, however, is irrelevant. As with Schedule 7, however, the tenant will *not* be entitled to compensation for an improvement which he was required to carry out by the terms of his tenancy where that contract of tenancy was made before 1st January 1921: para. 5, Schedule 12.

12.15 'Old' improvements begun before 1st March 1948: Schedule 9

Schedule 9, introduced by section 64(4), provides a scheme of compensation for improvements *begun before* 1st March 1948, referred to in the Schedule as 'old' improvements. The scheme is complementary to the other schemes of compensation. It is, of course, of declining importance and is encountered only rarely in practice.

Schedule 9 will not entitle the tenant to compensation for any improvement required by a contract of tenancy made before 1st January 1921: para. 3. Similarly, it does not entitle the tenant to compensation for work done on land which was not an agricultural holding within the Agricultural Holdings Act 1928 nor treated as such at the time the work was done.

Para. 4 of Schedule 9 makes it clear that compensation under the schedule is additional to any compensation to which the tenant may be entitled 'by custom or agreement or otherwise': a rare case where customary entitlement may coexist with the statutory provisions.

The amount of compensation available under the Schedule is, as for Schedule 7 improvements,

'an amount equal to the increase attributable to the improvement in the value of the agricultural holding as a holding, having regard to the character and situation of the holding and the average requirements of tenants reasonably skilled in husbandry.'

Any benefit (for example, a reduced rent) allowed by the landlord to the tenant for the improvement shall be brought into account in assessing the compensation payable, whether or not the benefit was expressly identified in the contract of tenancy.

Under Schedule 9 the tenant must have obtained his landlord's consent in writing to the work 'before the execution of the improvement'. The consent may have been conditional or unconditional. Any terms agreed as to compensation will override the statutory formula. There is only one exception to this: where drainage works were planned, the tenant was required to give the landlord not more than three months' and not less than two months' notice in writing of his intention to execute the improvement and he must have given details of the manner in which he proposed to effect it, in accordance with section 3 of the Agricultural Holdings Act 1923. If the parties cannot agree on the details of the work, the landlord is entitled to effect the improvement himself within a reasonable time. If he does not do so, or in default the tenant does the work, he (the tenant) will be entitled to compensation. However, the parties may expressly agree to dispense with the need for a section 3 notice and with the rest of those procedures.

Finally, Schedule 9 provides that the tenant's claim for compensation for improvements on the holding will not be prejudiced by his having remained on the holding during successive tenancies and effected the improvements during an earlier tenancy. He is also entitled to be compensated for any payment made in entering the holding to the outgoing tenant in respect of any Schedule 9 improvement, so long as such payment was made with the consent in writing of the landlord.

12.16 Compensation for tenant right matters

The statutory provisions giving compensation for tenant right matters replace the earlier customary provisions. Part II of Schedule 8, introduced by section 65, details the matters for which compensation may be obtained under this head, including growing crops and severed or harvested crops and produce; seeds sown and fallows and acts of husbandry performed at the expense of the tenant; acclimatisation, hefting or settlement of hill sheep and the residual fertility value of the sod of the excess qualifying leys as defined in para. 11.

The tenant will not, however, be entitled to compensation for any tenant right matter which is in contravention of a written contract of tenancy unless the tenant can justify such practices either by a direction under the Agriculture Act 1947 or as being necessary to satisfy his responsibility to farm in accordance with the rules of good husbandry, despite the tenancy agreement.

The amount of compensation payable for tenant right matters is stated in section 66(2) to be

'the value of the matter to an incoming tenant calculated in accordance with such method if any as may be prescribed.'

The 'method' presently 'prescribed' is to be found in Part II of the Schedule to the Agriculture (Calculation of Value for Compensation) Regulations 1978, SI 1978/808. However, section 66(4) makes it clear that the parties may if they wish substitute any other method of compensation for that 'prescribed' so long as the alternative formula is contained in a written contract of tenancy.

Section 65(3) provides that compensation for tenant right matters is available, with two exceptions, to a tenant regardless of the date at which he entered into occupation of the holding. The two exceptions are specified in paragraphs 6 and 7 of Schedule 12 of the Act and relate to older tenancies.

Paragraph 6 of Schedule 12 provides that where the tenant entered into occupation of the holding before 1st March 1948 the statutory provisions for compensation regarding all matters of tenant right except qualifying leys will *only* be available if the tenant elects by notice in writing served on the landlord that section 65 is to apply to him. Such election must be made, and the notice served, before the termination of the tenancy. Where the tenancy terminates by reason of a notice to quit from the landlord, the landlord may hasten the tenant's election by requiring him by a notice in writing to elect whether section 65 should apply. In such circumstances the tenant *must* elect within one month of the landlord's 'election notice' or, if the notice to quit in the case depends on proceedings under section 27 or 27 in Schedule 3, then within one month of the termination of those proceedings.

Paragraph 7 provides a similar procedure of election in respect of compensation for hill sheep where the tenant of the holding entered into occupation of the holding before 31st December 1957 and was immediately before that date subject to section 47(1) of the Agricultural Holdings Act 1948.

12.17 Improvements: successive tenancies

Where a tenant remains in occupation of *the same holding* under successive tenancies, he may claim compensation as his final tenancy terminates for an improvement or improvements regardless of when he effected them. Section 69(1) provides that

'he shall not be deprived of his right to compensation under this Act ... by reason only that the improvements were made during a tenancy other than the one at the termination of which he quits the holding.'

For the tenant to retain claims through a succession of tenancies, the holding must remain the same. It must not, for example, be expanded by the addition of further land. The section would easily cover a series of grants, surrenders and regrants, however, or a series of fixed term tenancies to take just two examples.

12.18 Improvements: Crown compensation

Section 95 makes provision for the raising and paying of compensation money by the Duchy of Lancaster and the Duchy of Cornwall and preserves the operation of the Duchy of Cornwall Management Act 1982.

12.19 Tenant's payment on entry for improvements

Section 69(2) and (3) protect the tenant who has as an incoming tenant, paid compensation directly either to the landlord or to the outgoing tenant in respect of an improvement within the statutory schemes. The section provides that the tenant shall be able to claim such compensation at quitting the holding so long as he had the landlord's consent in writing where he paid money directly to his predecessor tenant as he entered the holding. The tenant is enabled by the section to claim the improvements as if they were his own.

12.20 'High farming': section 70

Section 70 provides for compensation for a very particular form of 'improvement' of the holding: 'high farming' or in the words of section 70:

'the continuous adoption of a system of farming which has been more beneficial to the holding

(a)   than the system of farming required by the contract of tenancy or
(b)   in so far as no system of farming is so required, then the system of farming normally practised on comparable agricultural holdings.'

The amount of compensation payable for high farming is the amount equal to the increase in value of the holding as a holding, as specified in section 70(1) which echoes section 66(1).

To protect his eligibility for such compensation the tenant must comply with the two requirements of section 70(2):

• he must give the landlord notice in writing of his intention to claim such compensation at least one month before the tenancy terminates; and
• a record must have been made under the provisions of section 22 of the 1986 Act of the condition of the fixed equipment on the holding and of the general condition of the holding. No compensation will be paid for any work which predated the record, or if several records have been made, the first of these.

Claims for high farming under section 70 are dovetailed into the schemes of Schedules 7 and 8 by sections 70(4) and (5) which both aim to prevent occasions of double compensation. No compensation will be paid under section 70 for any improvement falling within the other statutory schemes of compensation. In assessing the value of the holding for section 70, allowance must be made for compensation agreed or awarded under Schedule 7, 8 or 9. This final provision ensures that claims for 'high farming' are relatively rare since in most cases they will largely rely on improvements eligible for compensation under the other schemes.

12.21 Termination of tenancy of part of a holding and the severed reversion

Section 74 makes provision for the situation where a landlord resumes possession of part only of the holding. When this occurs, the compensation provisions of the Act will apply but where he resumes partial possession in pursuance of a term of the contract of tenancy (as opposed to his powers under section 31 or section 43(1) of the Act) then the arbitrator is specifically directed to take into account

> 'any benefit or relief allowed to the tenant under the contract of tenancy in respect of the land'

which the landlord has resumed possession of. This 'relief' is not to be brought into reckoning, however, in assessing additional compensation for disturbance which may be payable.

Where the owner of a severed part of the reversion resumes possession of a part of the holding by virtue of a notice to quit, the tenant will be eligible for compensation on quitting as if that were a separate holding: section 74(3).

If the tenant quits an entire holding and the reversionary estate is vested in several persons in several parts, the tenant is entitled by virtue of section 75(1) to require that any compensation payable to him under the Act shall be determined as if the estate were not so severed. Where necessary, however, the arbitrator shall apportion any such compenstion amongst the owners of the reversion and shall similarly apportion any additional costs of the award caused by the apportionment amongst the owners of the reversion in proportion to their shares.

12.22 Exclusion of certain improvements

Section 76 provides that no compensation will be available to the outgoing tenant for any work effected in order to comply with an arbitrator's order under section 14(4) (land to be maintained as permanent pasture). Similarly, any work done to comply with section 15(4) is outside the compensation scheme (returning the manurial value of crops sold off the land).

12.23 Market gardens

Part VI of the 1986 Act makes special provision for agricultural holdings which, either by express agreement in writing between the parties or by a direction of the Agricultural Land Tribunal, are to be treated as 'market gardens'. Such holdings carry particular additional rights for the tenant to remove fixtures on quitting the holding, they entitle the tenant to additional heads of compensation on quitting and they may be subject to the 'Evesham custom' if the tenant terminates the tenancy by giving notice to quit or by becoming insolvent. Notice that special compensation provisions apply to some market gardens leased *before* 1st January 1896: para 10, Schedule 12.

12.24 What is a 'market garden'?

The term 'market garden' is not defined in the Act, nor with any great precision elsewhere. As we have seen, a description of a market garden was given in *Bickerdike* v. *Lucy* [1.03]. The essence is that it is an agricultural holding, or part of such a holding, being a trade or business which produces goods characteristic of a greengrocer's shop which normally reach that shop via an early morning wholesale market: *Watters* v. *Hunter* (1972).

For the particular provisions of Part IV to apply to a holding, the parties must have agreed in writing that the holding is to be treated as a market garden: section 79(1). If, after the tenant has requested such an agreement, the landlord refuses or fails to agree within a reasonable time, then the tenant may apply to the Tribunal for a direction that it is to be so treated: section 80(1)(2). The agreement or direction may apply to the entire holding or merely to a part of it. Where a holding is so divided as a result of a Tribunal direction, the rent of each part of the divided holding shall be settled in arbitration if necessary but otherwise, by reference to the terms and conditions on which the entire holding was formerly held.

12.25 Improvements and compensation

Where the holding is classified as a market garden, Schedule 10 lists five particular improvements for which the tenant may claim compensation on quitting in addition to those generally applying. The five are: planting of standard or other fruit trees permanently set out; planting of fruit bushes permanently set out; planting of strawberry plants; planting asparagus, rhubarb and other vegetable crops which continue to be productive for two or more years and finally the erection, alteration or enlargement of buildings for the purpose of the trade or business of a market gardener.

Where such improvements were begun on or after 1st March 1948 they are to be treated as Schedule 8 Part I improvements (i.e. short-term improvements not requiring consent) and compensated accordingly. Where work to erect or enlarge buildings for the purpose of a market garden was begun *before* 1st March 1948, then such an improvement will be treated as if it were included amongst Part II of Schedule 9 ('old' improvements).

Where the parties agree in writing that the tenant should be paid

'fair and reasonable compensation, having regard to the circumstances existing when the agreement was made'

then that amount of compensation shall be substituted for the statutory measure: section 81(1).

12.26 Removal of tenants' fixtures from market gardens

Where the holding is technically a market garden the tenant may remove from it any building erected or acquired by him for the purpose of his trade or business as a market gardener and any fixture or building affixed or erected before 1st January 1884 if it was also there for the purpose of his business. Section 79(3) modifies section 10(2) in these respects. If he exercises this right, the tenant must comply with the normal requirement of section 10(1) and remove the item(s) during his tenancy or within two months of its termination and he must also observe the conditions of section 10(3) of having fulfilled all his obligations under the lease and having given the landlord notice in writing of his intention to remove the fixtures.

The tenant may also, by virtue of section 79(4) remove all

'fruit trees and fruit bushes planted by him on the holding and not permanently set out'

but these *must* be removed by the end of his tenancy; otherwise they will remain the property of the landlord and the compensation will be payable in respect of them.

Where an incoming tenant to a market garden 'purchases' an improvement from his predecessor he does not require the landlord's consent in writing to the purchase to be able to exercise his own right to compensation for that improvement on quitting the holding: section 79(5).

12.27 The 'Evesham custom' for market gardens

Section 80(3) (4) and (5) incorporates into the Act the so-called 'Evesham custom' which modifies the parties' rights in respect of tenancies of market gardens which terminate by reason of the tenant's giving notice to quit or becoming insolvent. The 'Evesham custom' will *automatically* apply to those holdings accorded the status of market gardens by reason of a direction of the Tribunal: section 80(3). It may also be *expressly* made to apply to those holdings which landlord and tenant agree should be treated as market gardens if it is substituted in writing for any alternative compensation scheme which would otherwise apply.

The Evesham custom modifies the *tenant's right to compensation* for improvements when the tenancy ends by reason of his notice to quit or his insolvency. Compensation will *only* be available to him if two conditions are satisfied: section 80(4)

(a)   that the tenant produces an offer in writing from a 'substantial and otherwise suitable person' to accept a tenancy of the holding when the existing tenancy terminates, to hold it on the same terms and to pay all compensation to the outgoing tenant which is payable under the Act or under the contract of tenancy. The offer must be produced to the landlord not later than *one month* from the date of the notice to quit being given or of the tenant's insolvency and it must be expressed to hold good for three months from the date it is produced;

(b)   that the landlord fails to accept the offer within the three month period.

Thus the *landlord's* position is modified by the custom in that he may avoid paying any compensation when the tenant quits *but* only if he accepts the substitute tenant proposed by the outgoer. The custom will normally apply in those cases where the holding has been designated a market garden against the wishes of the landlord by reason of the tenant's application to the Tribunal. The custom will therefore prevent the landlord being liable to pay considerable compensation in such cases so long as he accepts the new tenant.

12.28 Compensation for milk quotas

Section 13 of the Agriculture Act 1986 states that compensation 'may be payable to certain agricultural tenants' on the termination of their tenancies in respect of milk quota. The section invokes Schedule 1 of the Act. The Schedule essentially provides that compensation will be payable to tenants, 'succession' tenants holding by virtue of section 39, 53, 45(6) or 37(1)(b) of the Agricultural Holdings Act 1986, assignees of agricultural holdings and sublandlords of such holdings. The amount payable will be calculated in accordance with the detailed provisions of Part II of the Schedule. For convenience, Schedule I is reprinted in full in Appendix I.

THE LANDLORD'S CLAIMS

12.29 Introductory

In the 1986 Act the landlord is given two specific claims for compensation from the tenant when he quits the holding. Firstly, by section 71 he is entitled to claim compensation for the deterioration during the tenancy of *specific parts* of the holding. Secondly, in section 72, the landlord is given a claim for compensation for the *general deterioration* of the holding. In addition to these two grounds for claiming compensation at the end of the tenancy, the landlord may be entitled to bring an action for damages for breach of contract or covenant *during* the tenancy when the tenant by failure to repair maintain or reinstate has been in breach of the tenancy agreement and has thereby reduced the value of the landlord's reversion.

12.30 Compensation for specific deterioration

Section 71(1) provides the landlord with an entitlement to claim compensation from the tenant when the tenancy terminates and the tenant quits, in respect of

'the dilapidation or deterioration of, or damage to, any part of the holding or anything in or on the holding caused by non-fulfilment by the tenant of his responsibilities to farm in accordance with the rules of good husbandry.'

There are four points to notice about this claim.

(i) A *specific* part of the holding. This claim must be carefully distinguished from the second statutory right to compensation (for the *general* deterioration of the holding). Thus the landlord must be able here to identify particular specific breaches of the rules of good husbandry: for example, a failure to repair or as a 'deterioration' a failure to maintain the fertility of particular fields.

(ii) *The standard of care.* The tenant will only be liable to pay compensation if he has been in breach of 'the rules of good husbandry'. As we have seen, these rules which underlie other aspects of the 1986 Act are expressed in section 11 of the Agriculture Act 1947. They must be read together with the contract of tenancy and in some cases the Agriculture (Maintenance, Repair and Insurance of Fixed Equipment) Regulations 1973, SI 1973/1473 to discover where the burden of maintenance falls in any particular tenancy. The Regulations will impose the burden of repair on the tenant when the lease is silent on the matter, but they will not contradict a contractual provision which places the burden on the landlord. Their role is complementary not contradictory.

(iii) *The measure of damages.* Section 71(2) provides that *prima facie* the landlord's measure of damages will be

'the cost, as at the date of the tenant's quitting the holding of making good the dilapidation, deterioration or damage.'

This is modified however, by the upper limit imposed in every case by Section 71(5) which provides that the amount of compensation payable under the section

'shall in no case exceed the amount (if any) by which the value of the landlord's reversion in the holding is diminished owing to the dilapidation, deterioration or damage in question.'

Thus the ultimate loss in value to the reversion constitutes the 'ceiling' of the tenant's liability where such a sum is less than the actual cost of reinstatement when the tenancy ends.

(iv) Section 70(3) provides that, as an alternative to the statutory basis of claim in section 70, the landlord may base his claim instead on the terms of a *written* contract of tenancy. Section 70(4) makes it clear that if the contractual action is used the compensation shall *only* be claimed when the tenant quits the holding, and for any one holding, the landlord's specific compensation claims must either *all* be made under the contract or *all* be made under the statutory entitlement of section 70; the two bases of claim must *not* be mixed in respect of any single holding. The case in prospect here is where the contract imposes additional burdens on the tenant and is therefore an advantageous basis of claim for the landlord. The landlord, however, must be entirely consistent in the form of his claim, and must rely *either* on statutory rights *or* on contractual rights without mingling them together in his claim.

12.31 Compensation for general deterioration

Section 72(1) provides the landlord's second entitlement to compensation on quitting. He will have a claim where he can show

> 'that the value of the holding generally has been reduced by reason of ... dilapidation, deterioration or damage ... or otherwise by non-fulfilment by the tenant of his responsibilities to farm in accordance with the rules of good husbandry.'

Here the landlord is claiming compensation for *an overall* decline or reduction in the value of the holding by reason of the tenant's failings. The claim must be carefully distinguished from the *specific* claims possible under section 71, although in some circumstances it may be possible to show that specific breaches *also* contribute to an additional overall decline in value which is not compensated simply by the specific claims under section 71: *Evans* v. *Jones* (1955)

The standard of care

As with the earlier claim, the tenant is liable where it is his failure 'to form in accordance with the rules of good husbandry' which has resulted in loss to the landlord.

The measure of damages

Section 72(3) provides that the landlord is entitled to recover compensation under the section 'in so far as the landlord is not compensated' by any claim under section 71. The quantum of compensation, as expressed in section 72(3)

> 'shall be equal to the decrease attributable to the matter in question in the value of the holding as a holding, having regard to the character and situation of the holding and the average requirements of tenants reasonably skilled in husbandry.'

The reduction in rental value will be a guide to this.

Notice of the claim

Compensation under section 72 is *only* available when the tenant quits the holding. In addition, section 72(3) provides that the landlord *must* give notice in writing to the tenant of his intention to claim such compensation and must give such notice not later than one month before the tenancy ends.

Clearly, for the landlord to substantiate a claim under section 72, it will be most necessary that a record of the holding's condition should have been made.

Successive tenancies

Section 73 provides that the landlord will not be deprived of his statutory rights to compensation if the tenant remains on the holding during two or more successive tenancies. When the tenant quits he will be subject to claims arising at any period of his occupation as tenant of that holding. The section mirrors section 69 [12.15].

12.32 Landlord's claim during the tenancy

It may be that the landlord wishes to take action against a defaulting tenant *during* the period of the tenancy, rather than wait until the tenant quits. Apart from any other consideration, such a tactic may provoke the tenant into a better observance of his responsibilities during the later period of his tenancy by providing a salutary shock to the tenant. As we have seen, there are various actions intended as preliminaries to a landlord's notice to quit which may be invoked to serve this purpose. For example, the landlord may serve a notice to remedy or obtain a certificate of bad husbandry – both of which precede and threaten the issue of an incontestable notice to quit.

Alternatively, he may serve a repairing notice under the 1973 Regulations. However, as a final alternative he may choose to institute an action for damages for breach of contract *during the currency of the tenancy*. The tenant's liability will depend on the terms of the contract of tenancy, as amplified if necessary by the 1973 Regulations. The measure of damages available to the landlord will be the diminution of the value of the landlord's reversion. This is imposed by section 18(1) of the Landlord and Tenant Act 1927 in respect of breaches of repairing covenants and by the common law for breach of non-repairing covenants.

Kent v. *Coniff* (1953): viability of the claim
Although the damages available under an action such as this may be quite small and the procedure therefore not especially attractive, its tactical value may be more substantial. It is important, therefore, to explain the relationship between the action and those statutory claims for compensation from the quitting tenant established in sections 71 and 72. It will be recalled that section 78(1) provides that

'in any case for which ... the provisions of this Act provide for compensation a tenant or landlord shall be entitled to compensation *in accordance with those provisions and not otherwise*, and shall be so entitled notwithstanding any agreement to the contrary' (emphasis added).

In *Kent* v. *Coniff* it was held that since the statutory entitlements are purely for compensation *at the termination* of tenancies, the action for breach during the currency of the tenancy did not impinge upon the Act's exclusive jurisdiction. The only situation in which the Act was truly exclusive, it was held, was in the effect of what is now section 15(5). Where a tenant injures or deteriorates the holding by the manner in which he exercises his rights of disposal of produce and cropping the holding, then the section provides that the landlord's remedies 'but no other' will be to obtain an injunction and to recover damages from the tenant when he quits the holding. Such abuse of his rights by the tenant may *not* be checked by an action for damages during the tenancy.

12.33 Termination of tenancy of part only of the holding

As we have seen in the context of the tenant's claims, section 74 makes detailed provision ensuring that a resumption of possession of part only of the holding shall be treated as if the part repossessed were a separate holding and claims for compensation made by the landlord are included within its scope.

12.34 Transfer of the landlord's interest during the tenancy

Where the landlord transfers his interest, or a part of it during the currency of the tenancy, it may be important to know whether the new owners of the reversion will be entitled to compensation for dilapidations *whenever caused* when the tenant quits the holding. Does an assignee of the reversion enjoy the benefit of repairing covenants which will entitle him to recover even for breaches of covenant arising *before* his interest?

Section 141 of the Law of Property Act 1925 provides the answer in stating that the assignee of the reversion *is* entitled to the benefit of covenants and conditions of the lease. In *Re King, Robinson* v. *Gray* (1963) it was held that a breach of a repairing or reinstatement covenant gives rise to a liability on the tenant which runs with the landlord's reversion and thus a breach during the period of the original reversioner's ownership will endure for the benefit of any assignee, who becomes exclusively entitled to exercise any rights of action resulting from such breach.

12.35 Making the claim

It is important to notice that, where either landlord or tenant intends to make a claim for compensation at the end of a tenancy, they are required to notify the other party of such claim, in some cases by two separate notices, and if the claim(s) cannot be settled by agreement within eight months of the termination of the tenancy it must be settled by arbitration under the 1986 Act: section 83(4).

Notices
A party, whether landlord or tenant, intending to claim for compensation whether by reason of custom, agreement, or statutory right, *must* serve notice on the other party of such claim(s) *within two months* of (i.e. after) the termination of the tenancy. The notice must specify the claims to be pursued: section 83(2). Section 83(3) provides that it will be sufficient merely to identify the claim by reference to the statutory provision, custom or term of the agreement under which the claim is to be made.

However, for some specific claims, an earlier notice is *also* required: it is important to remember that in such cases *both* notices must be appropriately served: the earlier notice will *not* suffice for the later.

The earlier notices are needed where

- *the tenant* intends to claim compensation for the higher rate of basic compensation (up to two years' rent) or for 'high farming': in either case he must serve notice of his intention at least *one month before* the termination of the tenancy; or
- *the landlord* intends to claim for general deterioration of the holding: again the notice must be served at least one month before termination.

Arbitration
Section 83(4) provides that the parties have eight months from the termination of the tenancy to settle any compensation claims by agreement in writing. If they cannot achieve agreement within this period, outstanding claims 'shall be determined by arbitration' under the Act: section 83(5).

'Termination'
For the purposes of calculating the two month post-termination period for settlement of claims, 'termination' is to be read as 'termination *of occupation*' where the tenant lawfully remains in occupation of the holding after the tenancy ends: section 83(6).

Enforcement
If the parties agree an amount of compensation or an award is finally made by an arbitrator, it should be paid by the party liable. If he has not paid within 14 days of the sum becoming due, then it is recoverable through the County Court as if it were money ordered to be paid by the court under its ordinary jurisdiction: section 85(1).

The *tenant* is given a second method of enforcement by sectio 85(2). If the landlord has not paid compensation within *one month* from the date on which payment was due, the tenant may obtain from the Minister an order charging the holding with payment of the amount due. Such a charging order may also be made where the landlord holds the reversionary estate as trustee and is not therefore personally liable to pay compensation: section 85(3).

Jurisdiction Over Disputes Concerning Agricultural Holdings

13.01 Introductory

Throughout the earlier chapters of this book it has been made apparent that some disputes which arise from the agricultural holdings legislation are within the exclusive jurisdiction of specialist decision-making forums whereas other issues which may arise are appropriately submitted to the courts for adjudication. The purpose of this chapter is to identify the respective jurisdiction of agricultural land tribunals, arbitrators and the courts and give an indication of the procedures appropriate to the first two.

The chart in Table 13.01 illustrates the division of jurisdictions at a glance.

13.02 Arbitration

As is indicated in the 'jurisdiction chart', arbitration under the 1986 Act is reserved for those matters which can benefit from the valuation or surveying expertise rather than the lawyer's skills, and in particular those disputes or issues concerning the terms of the tenancy, the state of the holding and related matters such as the amount of compensation payable when the tenant quits. The 1986 Act reserves such issues for resolution by arbitration, and further stipulates in section 84 that such matters 'shall, notwithstanding any agreement (under a contract of tenancy or otherwise) providing for a different method of arbitration, be determined by the arbitration of a single arbitrator in accordance with the provisions of any order under this section, together with the provisions of Schedule 11'. Thus both the jurisdiction and form of agricultural arbitrations under the Act are prescribed. The 'order' giving specific effect to section 84 is the Agricultural Holdings (Arbitration on Notices) Order 1978, SI 1978/257.

The parties are, of course, at liberty to resolve such issues by agreement between themselves, but the statutory provisions provide a scheme of

Table 13.1 Jurisdictions: (a) arbitration (b) Agricultural Land Tribunals (c) the courts.

Arbitration

Schedule 11, 1986

1.	Operation of section 2 to any arrangement	s.2(4)
2.	Obtaining *written* tenancy	s.6
3.	Inclusion of 'model clauses'	s.8
4.	Rent review	s.12
5.	Rent increase for landlord's improvements	s.13
6.	Reduction of permanent pasture	s.14
7.	Damage from freedom of cropping	s.15
8.	'Fair value' of tenant's fixtures on quitting	s.10
9.	Compensation for damage by game	s.20
10.	Compensation on quitting	s.23; Pt. V
11.	Disputes on notices to remedy/pay	SI 1978/257
12.	Disputes on notices to quit, Cases A, B, D, E	SI 1978/257
13.	Milk quotas	Ag. Act 1986 Sch 1

Agricultural Land Tribunals

1.	Grant of certificate of bad husbandry	Schedule 3 Part I
2.	Consent to notice to quit	ss. 26, 27
3.	Modification of condition on notice to quit	s.27(5)
4.	Enforcing condition on notice to quit	s.27(6)
5.	Provision of necessary fixed equipment	s.11
6.	Consent to long-term improvements	s.67(3)(4)
7.	Direction to treat as market garden	s.80
8.	Succession applications under Part IV	s.36 ff

also

Relaxation of covenant against burning	Hill Farming Act 1946 s.21
Determination of treated owner	Agriculture Act 1947 s.21
Directions as to ditching	Land Drainage Act 1961 s.40

The courts

1.	Relevance/application of section 2	*Goldsack* v *Shore* (1960)
2.	Damages for breach of repairing covenant *during* tenancy	*Kent* v *Conniff* (1953)
3.	Enforcement of covenant to pay outgoings	*Lowther* v *Clifford* (1927)
4.	Possession proceedings	
5.	Forfeiture proceedings	
6.	Construction of tenancy contract	
7.	Validity of notices	
8.	All other claims where jurisdiction is not expressly allocated elsewhere by the Act: section 97. Would include, for example, actions for injunctions, for trespass, negligence etc.	

dispute resolution for those situations where such agreement is not possible. Notice that section 84(1) expressly states that the Arbitration Act 1950 does *not* apply to arbitrations conducted under the provisions of Schedule 11 of the 1986 Act and the 1978 Order.

13.03 Seeking an arbitration: preliminary notices

In most cases where the Act prescribes arbitration for the resolution of disputes, it also requires that a preliminary notice or notices be served, either notices specifically referring to the arbitration or other relevant notice referring to the issue between the parties. Strict time limits based on the service of these notices then apply for the initiation of an arbitration and the appointment of an arbitrator. The chart in Table 13.02 identifies any preliminary notices and indicates time limits which apply in the case of the individual arbitration jurisdictions.

Any notices required must be clear and unambiguous: precedents for many of these documents are given in Appendix IV. Note that where no relevant preliminary notice is served, or the notice is served out of time, or is invalid for ambiguity or mis-service, the arbitrator will be without jurisdiction for that matter and any award which he might make would be voidable: *Stiles* v. *Farrow* (1977).

13.04 The appointment of the arbitrator

In many cases the parties can and do agree on the appointment of an arbitrator and also agree between themselves and with him the award of his fee and costs for the arbitration. If they can agree on an arbitrator but cannot reach agreement on his fee, then the county court registrar may determine an appropriate fee, and an appeal is possible from his decision on this point to the county court judge: Schedule 11, paragraph 6. Such an agreed procedure is perfectly appropriate, but it must of course conform with the various statutory requirements (for example, simple arbitration, written appointment) prescribed by Schedule 11.

Where the parties *cannot* agree on an arbitrator (or, in the case of rent reviews, as an additional precaution [5.06]) Schedule 11 of the 1986 Act provides a scheme of appointment by the President of the Royal Institution of Chartered Surveyors. Either party may apply to him at 12 Great George Street, Parliament Square, London, SW1P 3AD, for him to appoint an arbitrator for the matter(s) in dispute. He will select from a panel (or list of suitably experienced valuers, surveyors, agents or auctioneers nominated for such purposes by the Lord Chancellor: paragraph 1(5)). If the holding in question is in Wales, the appointment must be of an arbitrator familiar with Welsh farming practices and, if either or both of the parties so request, he must also be familiar with the Welsh language which may be the principal language of the arbitration: paragraph 1(4). Where the President is requested to make an appointment, a fee of £70 is payable to the RICS which will cover any work done by them in relation to the appointment of an arbitrator for that matter; it

Table 13.2 Preliminary notices required before arbitration.

Issue	Preliminary notice	Time limit	Authority
1. Operation of section 2	None	None	Section 2(4)
2. Preparation of written tenancy agreement	Request for written tenancy agreement	None	Section 6(1)
3. Inclusion of 'model clauses'	Request to include	None	Section 8(2)
4. Rent review	Written notice	As for notice to quit	Section 12(1),(4)
5. Rent increase for landlord's improvement	Notice of rent increase	Within 6 months of improvement completed	Section 13(1),(7)
6. Reduction of pasture	Written demand for arbitration	None	Section 14(2)
7. Damage from freedom of cropping	None	None	Section 15(6)
8. 'Fair value' of tenant's fixture	(i) Tenant's notice of intent to remove	(i) Month before termination of tenancy and before removal intended	Section 10(6) Section 10(3)
	(ii) Landlord's counter-notice to purchase	(ii) During currency of (i)	Section 10(4)
9. Damage by game	(i) Written notice of damage	(i) Within 1 month of its discovery	Section 20(2)(b)
	(ii) Written notice of claim	(ii) Within 1 month of tenancy year's end	Section 20(2)(c)
10. Compensation on quitting	Notice of claim	Within 2 months of tenancy term	Section 83(2)
N.B. (i) 'High farming' (ii) High 'basic' compensation	Additional notices necessary	1 month before tenancy term	Section 70(2) Section 60(6)
11. Notice to remedy or pay	Demand for arbitration	Within 1 month of notice to remedy/pay	S.I. 1978/257, art.3,4,9
12. Notice to quit A, B, D, E	Demand for arbitration	Within 1 month of service of notice to quit	S.I. 1978/257, art.9

would, for example, cover the appointment of a second arbitrator should the initial appointee fail or be unable to act for any reason. The £70 fee is non-returnable, however. It is also *additional* to the fee and costs payable to the arbitrator himself.

When the President is requested to make such an appointment, he shall do so 'as soon as possible after receiving the application': paragraph 1(3). The only modification of this requirement is in cases of rent review under section 12, where the appointment 'shall in any event not be made by him earlier than four months before the next termination date': paragraph 1(3) (5.8). If the original appointee has to be replaced for any reason, a second arbitrator will be appointed as if no earlier appointment had taken place. However, in the case of rent reviews, the date of the reference from which the new rent is calculated will be the date of the original appointment: paragraph 2.

After an appointment has been made (whether by agreement or by the President) neither party has the power to revoke that appointment without the consent of the other party: paragraph 2(4). All stages of the appointment, the application, appointment, and where relevant, consent to revocation and revocation *must* be in *writing*: paragraph 2(5). Notice that this requirement of writing applies equally to all stages of an appointment by agreement as to an appointment by the President.

13.05 Initiating proceedings: particulars of claim

Once the arbitrator's appointment has been effected (i.e. from the time the President executes the instrument of appointment: paragraph 31) the parties have *35 days* to submit to him their particulars of claim: paragraph 7. During this 35 day period they may also submit amendments, additions and alterations to their originally submitted claim, defence or counter-claim as they wish. The 35-day period is mandatory, inflexible and is not capable of modification or extension by the arbitrator. If, when that period expires, a party has failed to submit his particulars of claim, he will *not* be allowed to plead, although he will be allowed to attend the subsequent hearing and to put the other party's evidence to the test by cross-examination. Thus it is *essential* that the parties both submit their basic claims within the statutory period. There is no statutory form for such claims but it is clear that they must identify the substantive claims made and issues relied on so that the particular issues between the parties may be identified, allowing both parties to define their inquiries and address their responses with appropriate precision. There is no requirement from the statute or from practice for the same degree of precision or technicality as is needed for litigation in court: the parties' claims are 'in general sufficient if the document ... which contains the particulars gives an indication to the landlord or the tenant, as the case may be, of the particular kind of claim which is going to be made in order that he may have an opportunity of himself examining the subject matter and seeing what evidence he will have to adduce or what information he will have to give the arbitrator': Warrington LJ in *Jones* v. *Evans* (1920).

Once particulars have been lodged, the arbitrator should secure the exchange of particulars between the parties and at this stage one or both parties may well wish to amend their own submissions in the light of the other's claims.

The arbitrator, although *not* empowered to admit claims after the 35-day period *may* admit *amendments* to claims properly lodged after that 35-day period. He must ensure that the claim itself is lodged in time, and that it discloses an issue for decision. He should then consider whether to allow the proposed amendment would unfairly prejudice the other party. If no such disadvantage can be identified, his consent to the amendment will normally be forthcoming.

Once particulars are finally settled, the parties will be confined to matters stated there and in any amendment duly made with the arbitrator's consent: paragraph 7(b)

13.06 The hearing and the view

The arbitrator is required by paragraph 14(1) of Schedule 11 to make and sign his award within 56 days of his appointment, although this period may be extended by the President of the RICS at any time in a particular case. At first sight, therefore, and in any case where no extension of time applies, there will normally be only a three week period between the last date for the parties' submissions of claim and the arbitrator's decision. It is imperative, therefore, that no time is lost in arranging the hearing and if necessary the view or inspection of the holdings, so that the arbitrator may be apprised of all relevant facts in good time. A view or inspection will be particularly necessary where the condition or state of the holding is fundamental to the issue, such as in claims for compensation on quitting or where a notice to do work is being pursued.

In all proceedings, both the hearing and the view, despite their relative informality, it is essential that their *quasi-judicial* character is observed, and that the arbitrator gives effect to the rules of natural justice, with both parties being clearly treated equally and justly. Any failure in this respect will leave the arbitrator open to a challenge by the aggrieved party which, if successful, may result in the award being set aside—for example, on the grounds of 'misconduct' under paragraph 27.

The hearing

Having set a date for the hearing which is agreeable to both parties, the arbitrator may require the parties to give evidence on oath or affirmation, and to produce before him any documents or samples which are pertinent to the arbitration: paragraph 8. Similarly, he is empowered to call witnesses to give evidence on oath, and may compel them to attend if necessary by witness summons obtainable through the county court and enforceable by normal county court procedures: paragraphs 10, 11. If a witness fails to answer a summons or refuses to give evidence then he may be directed by the county court judge to forfeit a fine of not more than £10 which, on the judge's direction, may be applied towards indemnifying the party injured by the witness' default: paragraph 11. Notice, however, that such a penalty is only to be imposed if the person summoned has been paid or had tendered to him such a sum of money for his expenses as is prescribed for the purposes of the County Court Act 1984: paragraph 11(3).

In conducting the hearing itself, the normal rules of evidence will apply and the order of the proceedings will mirror normal court proceedings with the party on whom the burden of proof lies opening the case: for example, the landlord in matters concerning notices to remedy or notices to quit. If a party fails to appear, after due notice, it is possible for the arbitrator to continue *ex parte* in his absence, but the preferable (and safer) course of action is to adjourn the proceedings and use the award of costs as an appropriate sanction if the failure to appear was in any way beyond excuse.

In giving evidence, the parties to the arbitration will be subject to the normal rules of civil evidence. The arbitrator is required to reach a decision based on the evidence of the parties, although as an expert appointed by reason of his expertise he may, in limited circumstances, rely on his experience of other comparable situations to supplement the evidence presented to him.

Ultimately, the arbitrator must decide in accordance with the evidence presented before him.

If a view or inspection of the holding is required, the arbitrator must continue to observe good judicial practice on that occasion. Both parties, with their advisors if they so desire, should be enabled to attend – an inspection in the presence of only one of the parties is *prima facie* partial: *Re O'Connor and Whitlaw's Arbitration* (1919).

It may be that during the arbitration the arbitrator desires to seek independent legal advice on his own account. He is entitled to retain an advisor to sit in with him and advise on points of procedure and law and on the presentation of his final award. He may include the cost of such advice as his expenses to be defrayed by the parties. Any such legal advice must be quite independent of the parties' advisors. There is no need for the parties to consent if the arbitrator wishes to take this course: *Giacomo Costa fu Andrea* v. *British Italian Trading Co. Ltd* (1961).

13.07 The award and costs

After the hearing the arbitrator is required to make and sign his award within the 56-day time limit imposed by paragraph 14(1), unless this has been extended by the President of RICS. An interim award on account may be made if he thinks fit. The form of the award is specified in the Agricultural Holdings (England and Wales) Rules 1948. In addition, Schedule 11, paragraph 16 requires that the arbitrator shall state separately in his award the amounts awarded in respect of the various claims made in the arbitration and if any party applies to him to do so, he must also specify the amount of any particular improvement. Thus, depending on the parties, the arbitrator *must* indicate separate awards for, for example, tenant right, high farming and tenant's improvements and *may* particularise each improvement.

The arbitrator is required to state, orally or in writing, the reasons for his award if requested to do so by any party. The statement given 'on or before' the award will form a part of it and is an item of record which may later be the subject of review: paragraph 21 applies section 12 of the Tribunals and Inquiries Act 1971. Reasons may be requested from the arbitrator whether his appointment was by agreement between the parties or was, in default to such agreement, made by the President.

The amount of the award will carry interest from the date of the award at the same rate as a judgment debt.

With regard to *costs*, paragraph 23 gives the arbitrator complete discretion as to amount, allocation between the parties and the manner of payment. In reaching his award of costs, he is directed by paragraph 25 to take into account the reasonableness of the claims in respect of amount or otherwise, any unreasonable demand for or refusal of particulars and generally all the circumstances of the case. He may also disallow the costs of any witness or other costs which he considers to have been unnecessarily incurred. If either party so wishes, the costs allowed may be taxed in the county court on the prevailing county court scale: paragraph 24. Normally costs will follow the case.

The award must name a day 'not later than one month after the delivery of the award' for the payment of the money awarded as costs, compensation or for any other cause: paragraph 18. The award may be enforced by proceedings in the county court and if the court orders the recovery of the amount due it is recoverable in the same way as money ordered to be paid by the court in the exercise of its ordinary jurisdiction: section 85(1).

13.08 Review of the arbitration and award by the county court

Three situations are specified where review of an agricultural holdings arbitration in the county court is possible.

(1) A special case: during the proceedings

Paragraph 26, Schedule 11 provides that at any time during the proceedings the *arbitrator* may state any question of law or any question as to his jurisdiction which arises out of the arbitration. Alternatively, either *party* may apply to the county court judge for a direction that such a special case should be stated. Jurisdictional points which may foreseeably arise include, for example, whether the requisite preliminary notices (as detailed above, 13.03) have been properly served, and this may be used by either party to challenge the proceedings. This procedure, stating a case *during* the arbitration, is an interlocutory procedure. If follows, therefore, that it cannot be used after the award has been made.

When this procedure is employed, the arbitrator must identify the relevant facts, summarise the parties' arguments and then outline the questions of law on which an opinion is required. Legal assistance may be obtained by the arbitrator in drafting the special case, but ultimately it is the arbitrator's sole responsibility to decide the scope of the case to be submitted whether the reference was intiated by him or by one of the parties. The arbitrator will, however, normally show a draft of the case stated to the parties and may, indeed, consult with them as to the final form.

The procedure for stating a case is to be found in Order 44 of the County Court Rules 1981 and the procedure for a party to apply to the court for a direction that the arbitrator should state a case is that of an originating application as provided in Order 3, rule 4 of the County Court Rules, to which the reader is referred.

Stating a case is a fairly expensive and long procedure, the costs of which will fall on both parties. It may be that a preferable alternative is for the arbitrator's award to indicate clearly his decision on the point of law (or jurisdiction) which has been in contention, which may then be challenged subsequently as an error on the face of the record if either party should wish to proceed further.

(2) Arbitrator's misconduct

Paragraph 27 of Schedule 11 gives the county court powers to be exercised 'where the arbitrator has misconducted himself'. The court may remove him in such circumstances and they may also set aside the award. This latter power may also be exercised by the court where an arbitration or award has been improperly procured or there is an error of law on the face of the award.

'Misconduct' in this context is not defined in the Act. It has been held to include numerous misdoings covering a wide spectrum of veniality. For example, it can range through fraud, bribery, and corruption, and apparent partiality: *Re O'Connor and Whitlaw's Arbitration* (1919); failing to make his award within the permitted time: *Halliday* v. *Semple* (1960) and failure to comply with the rules of evidence: *Re Plews and Middleton* (1854). In one noted case an arbitrator who accepted hospitality from one side to the point of intoxication, was held to have participated in 'unbecoming' conduct but since there was found to be no intention to corrupt, he was not guilty of 'misconduct'. Whether in such circumstances accepting hospitality from *both* parties would have cured the fault must be left for decision!

Misconduct by an arbitrator can be waived by the parties but the evidence of waiver must be very clear.

'Improper procurement' in this context is more limited than 'misconduct' and has been held to imply some moral fault—fraud, bribery or corruption, for example: *Wood* v. *Durose* (1958). The procedure for invoking the court under paragraph 27 is for the aggrieved party to apply to the county court for the removal of the arbitrator or the setting aside of his award within 21 days of the award being made: Order 44, rule 3, County Court Rules 1981. If the arbitrator is removed or the award is set aside, the arbitration is at an end and a new arbitrator may then be appointed.

(3) Error of Law on the face of the record

The final 'appeal' to the county court available under the 1986 Act against the award of the arbitrator is to invoke that court's jurisdiction where there is an error of law on the face of the record. In such circumstances, paragraphs 27 and 28 provide that the court may:

(i)   set the award aside: paragraph 27(2(;
(ii) remit the award, or a relevant part of it, to the arbitrator for his reconsideration: paragraph 28(1); or

(iii) vary the award by substitution of 'such award as the court considers that it would have been proper for the arbitrator to make in the circumstances': paragraph 28(2).

This statutory power in the county court to remedy an error of law has been held to exclude entirely the inherent jurisdiction of the High Court where there is an error of law on the face of the record and to transfer all such power to the lower court: *Jones* v. *Pembrokeshire County Council* (1967). The procedure is restricted to errors of law apparent from the award itself, including, of course, any reasons given for the award. It may be, for example, that the contract of tenancy has been misconstrued, the statutory provisions misunderstood or the statement of decisions may be inadequate to comply with the Tribunals and Inquiries Act 1971.

As with the previous challenge, an application to the county court based on an error on the face of the record must be made by originating application within 21 days after the date of the award. If the court remits the award to the arbitrator, he must normally make and sign his award within 30 days of the making of the order: paragraph 28(3), although where the court is satisfied that such a time limit is 'for any good reason insufficient' it may extend or further extend that time limit 'for such period as it thinks proper': paragraph 28(4).

AGRICULTURAL LAND TRIBUNALS

13.09 Introductory

The second specialist forum dealing with disputes under the agricultural holdings legislation (and several miscellaneous matters under other legislation) is the agricultural land tribunal. These tribunals were first established under the Agriculture Act 1947 and at that stage served an appellate function, hearing appeals from the County Agricultural Executive Committees. The Agriculture Act 1958, however, transformed them by giving them an important first instance jurisdiction which was greatly enhanced by the succession jurisdiction which arose from the Agriculture (Miscellaneous Provisions) Act 1976 which has been their primary source of applications in recent years and can be expected to retain the same importance for years yet whilst the succession provisions gradually exhaust themselves. Their jurisdiction is summarised in Table 13.2.

13.10 Constitution

England and Wales are served by eight tribunals whose addresses and geographical jurisdictions are given in Appendix II. The constitution of individual tribunals is governed by Schedule 9 of the Agriculture Act 1947, paragraphs 13-16 of which were substituted by the Agriculture Act 1958, Schedule 1 part 1, paragraph 5(1)(2).

A panel of suitable persons is appointed to each area tribunal, including a chairman and several deputy chairmen. For any individual case, a panel of three is constituted, to include the chairman of the tribunal, or one of the deputies, together with 'a representative of the landlord's interest' nominated by the Country Landowners' Association and a representative of the tenant's interest nominated by the National Farmers' Union. The chairman and deputy chairmen must be a qualified lawyer, a barrister or solicitor of at least seven years' standing who is appointed by the Lord Chancellor. If in any area there is a shortfall of appropriate nominations from the two nominating bodies the Lord Chancellor may appoint persons of his own choice to make up the deficiency.

In addition to the three 'usual' members of the tribunal, the chairman may also nominate two assessors to assist at the hearing. They are to be selected from a panel of surveyors nominated by the President of the RICS.

The decision of the tribunal need not be unanimous. It will not be invalidated by any technical fault in the appointment of any of the members nor even by the discovery that one of the appointed members was technically disqualified from sitting.

13.11 Tribunal procedure

The procedure to be followed by agricultural land tribunals is governed by the Agricultural Land Tribunals (Rules) Order 1978, SI 1978/259, made under the authority of section 73(3) of the Agriculture Act 1947. The Order is reprinted in full in Appendix II and the forms prescribed by it appear in the precedents of Appendix III. The form, or forms 'substantially to like effect' should be used in connection with all tribunal applications, although a failure to do so will not necessarily invalidate the proceedings unless the chairman of the tribunal directs that this should be so: paragraph 38 of SI 1978/259.

The Rules also govern the other essential procedural matters such as time limits, applications for extensions and interlocutory applications.

The hearing of an application or other matters before a tribunal takes place in public, unlike arbitration proceedings which are characteristically private. The hearing itself, again unlike an arbitration, is *not* subject to the rules of evidence which apply to proceedings in court: rule 28, SI 1978/259. Evidence may be given orally, on oath or affirmation, or by affidavit if the parties to the proceedings consent. Evidence is subject to examination, cross-examination and re-examination in the usual (court) fashion. Where an unsworn document or written statement is introduced as evidence, the author or deponent may be called to attend the hearing in person so that he may be subjected directly to examination and cross-examination.

It is within the power of the tribunal to call a witness or witnesses of its own motion: rule 29(2). Attendance and disclosure of documents may similarly both be required by the tribunal.

Parties to the application may appear in person or by counsel or solicitor or by any other representative appointed in writing: rule 25. It is quite usual for a surveyor experienced in agricultural valuation to appear. Normally the party making the application will be heard first unless the tribunal directs otherwise. If an applicant fails to appear, his application can be dismissed. If the respondent fails to appear, the matter may be decided by the tribunal in his absence: rules 26 and 27.

In many cases a view or inspection of the holding(s) concerned will be at least desirable and often necessary for the due decision of the application. Where a view is to be held, the tribunal must give all parties at least twenty-four hours' written notice, unless oral notice is given during the hearing itself. The parties, their advisors or representatives and expert witnesses may attend the view: rule 28.

In practice, once tribunal proceedings have been instituted, it is quite usual for the secretary of the tribunal, a permanent civil servant of the Ministry of Agriculture, Fisheries and Food, to notify the parties of the procedural steps to be taken.

13.12 Time limits

SI 1978/289 lays down strict time limits for the service of all documents connected with an application before the tribunal. The time limits *must* be complied with but rule 37 provides that the chairman *may extend* the time limit for any step in connection with tribunal proceedings, 'on such terms and conditions, if any, as appear to him just'. The chairman's discretion whether to allow, conditionally or unconditionally, or refuse such an extension is *absolute. Moss* v. *National Coal Board* (1982) decided that he must permit the parties to make written submissions when exercising this power if he is to comply with the rules of natural justice. No such requirement extends to oral submissions, however, and the chairman's decision may only be challenged if he can be shown to have erred *in law*. Retrospective authority, i.e. condoning or authorising a failure to meet a time limit which is already past, is not envisaged.

13.13 The tribunal's decision

The tribunal's decision must be given in writing and must explain the reasons for the decision. As mentioned above, it need not be unanimous. Rule 31 requires the secretary to send a certified copy of the decision and reasons to all parties and he may be required to send a further copy 'to any party who appears reasonably to require it'. Mere clerical, as opposed to substantive, errors may be corrected by the tribunal.

13.14 Challenge to the tribunal's decision

Two modes of challenge are available to parties wishing to contest the decision of a tribunal. They are:

(1)   Reference of a point of law to the High Court by way of case stated: a procedure which may be used either *during* tribunal proceedings or *after* their conclusion;
(2)   Judicial review of the tribunal proceedings by way of the prerogative orders.

(1) Case stated

The procedure for referring a matter to the High Court for review by way of case stated is to be found in section 6 of the Agriculture (Miscellaneous Provisions) Act 1954 and the Rules of the Supreme Court. The case must be stated following the request of one of the parties: the tribunal may *not* refer a case or point to the High Court on its own initiative. The party seeking a reference may make his request during the course of proceedings or after the tribunal's decision has been given but, if the latter, the request must be made not later than 14 days from the date that a copy of the tribunal's decision was sent to him. If this later request is made, it must be in writing and must be accompanied by sufficient copies for all the other parties to the proceedings. If the tribunal agrees to the request, their statement of the case must be sent to the requesting party within two months of the date of his request.

If, on the request of a party, the tribunal refuses to state a case, their refusal must be notified to all parties to the proceedings within 14 days of the request being received. Section 6(2) of the 1954 Act empowers any party aggrieved by such a refusal to apply to the High Court for an order directing the tribunal to state a case. The party aggrieved must notify the secretary of the tribunal in writing within 7 days of receiving their decision of his intention to apply for a directing order from the court. The secretary must then serve copies of this notice on all parties to the tribunal proceedings. Application is made to a divisional court of the Queen's Bench Division by originating motion and the motion must be entered for hearing and notice of it be served on all other parties within 14 days of the applicant's having received the tribunal's refusal to state a case.

If, after such an application, the High Court orders a case to be stated *or*, in the party's original request the tribunal agrees to state a case for the High Court, the case stated must set out the question of law and the facts found by the tribunal and it must be signed by the chairman. Proceedings must commence by way of originating motion in the divisional court of the Queen's Bench Division. Notice of motion must be served on the secretary of the tribunal and on any other parties to the proceedings and it must be entered for hearing within 14 days of the case stated being served on the applicant: RSC 0561.10.

If the case stated proceedings take place during the tribunal hearing, the tribunal hearing is suspended for their duration. When the High Court has given its ruling, the tribunal must, if necessary, modify their decision to accommodate the Court's findings. Where appropriate, this modification may be effected by the chairman on behalf of the tribunal, without reconvening the tribunal.

If the party aggrieved is unable to draft his case from the reasons given by the tribunal for its decision, the court may amend the case stated or may return it to the tribunal for amendment. At this stage the parties may elaborate any statements or propositions already submitted but they may not introduce new evidence. *Moses* v. *Hurst* (1983) makes it clear that the tribunal is under an overriding duty to provide both parties with the materials which will enable them to know whether an error of law has been made in reaching findings of fact.

(2) *Judicial review: the prerogative orders*

The prerogative orders of *certiorari, mandamus* and prohibition are available, within their very restricted spheres, to challenge a tribunal decision by way of an application for judicial review under Order 53 of the Rules of the Supreme Court. Leave of the court must be obtained before an application for judicial review may be brought and applications for leave should be obtained from a single judge of the Queen's Bench Division.

Although relatively rare in practice, judicial review, especially *certiorari*, is not unknown in relation to agricultural holdings matters. Cases such as *R.* v. *Agricultural Land Tribunal for the Wales and Monmouth Area ex parte Davies* (1953) [7.19] and *R.* v. *Agricultural Land Tribunal for the*

South Eastern Area ex parte Bracey (1960) [7.18] are good examples which have already been discussed in their substantive context.

13.15 Costs

Agricultural land tribunals have only a very limited power to award costs. Section 5 of the Agriculture (Miscellaneous Provisions) Act 1954 gives them merely a power to award costs against a party who has 'acted frivolously, vexatiously or oppressively' in pursuing a cause. The power may be used, for example, to penalise harassment of a tenant by the landlord serving repeated notices to quit in rapid succession but in any event the power is rarely exercised.

13.16 The courts

Section 97 of the 1986 Act provides that apart from express provision elsewhere in the Act,

> 'nothing in this Act shall prejudicially affect any power, right or remedy of a landlord, tenant or other person vested in or exercisable by him by virtue of any other Act or law or under any custom of the country or otherwise in respect of a contract of tenancy or other contract or of any improvements, deteriorations, waste, emblements, littages, away-going crops, fixtures, tax, rate, tithe, rent charge or other thing.'

Thus the courts retain jurisdiction except in those cases which are expressly allocated to arbitration or to the tribunals and subject to any clear restriction on their powers—for example, the limitation of remedies in section 15(5) available to the landlord for deterioration of the holding from the tenant's exercise of his right of freedom of cropping.

It has been emphasised by courts in cases such as *Goldsack* v. *Shore* (1960) and *Kent* v. *Conniff* (1953) that the courts' jurisdiction can only be ousted by the clearest possible words. The result seems to be that the jurisdiction remaining to the courts in respect of agricultural holdings includes:

(i)   matters under section 2 concerning the operation of that section to convert a licence or short-term lease into a tenancy from year to year: *Goldsack* v. *Shore*:

(ii)   actions during the tenancy for damages for breach of repairing covenants brought by either landlord or tenant: *Kent* v. *Coniff*;

(iii)   actions by the landlord and forfeiture based on the right of re- entry;

(iv)   actions for breach of covenant to pay outgoings: *Lowther* v. *Clifford* (1923):

(v)   actions to determine the construction of the contract of tenancy;

(vi)   actions for possession;

(vii)   actions to determine the validity of a notice to quit. (For example, was it properly served? Is it ambiguous?);

(viii) all other matters not governed by the legislation. (For example, nuisance, negligence, trespass actions).

Part VI

Agricultural Tied Cottages: An Overview

Introduction

The provision of accommodation by farmers for their workers has long been a characteristic of English and Welsh farm management. Such 'tied cottages' or 'units of service accommodation' are provided as an integral part of the contract of employment and are usually made available to workers (and their families) at low rent or at no rent. The offer of such accommodation is often of prime importance in recruiting a new worker. Now as in the past, agricultural wage levels make it unlikely that he will be an owner-mortgagor and the demands of the work usually require him to live within easy access of the farm. The provision of conveniently sited housing by the employer is therefore the traditional convenient solution to this problem.

However, under the common law, the agricultural worker in a tied cottage, like other 'service occupiers' was in a precarious position. Since his right to occupy the cottage was *inextricably* linked to his contract of employment, once his employment ended his right to occupy his home ended too. Being in nearly every case a mere licensee or a tenant at a low rent, the occupier was not protected by the Rent Acts. Regardless of the cause, once the worker ceased to work for the person providing the cottage, his right to occupy the cottage was at an end. Thus, if the worker resigned or retired or was made redundant or was dismissed, he was also subject in every case to peremptory possession proceedings requiring him to leave his home. This situation was modified slightly by section 33 of the Rent Act 1965 which gave him a 'breathing space' of six months' security of tenure after his employment ended. It was only with the enactment of the Rent (Agriculture) Act 1976 that the position changed radically. This Act applies a scheme of protection broadly similar to the Rent Acts to agricultural workers and former agricultural workers who occupy tied cottages. It thus confers on them a uniquely privileged and protected status in comparison with other service occupiers, whose tenure remains precariously linked with their employment.

Chapter 14

The Rent (Agriculture) Act 1976

14.01 The scheme of the Act

The 1976 Act seeks to cut the 'tie' between the worker's contract of employment and the agreement by his employer to provide his housing. The aim is to preserve the worker's security of occupation in his home even when he no longer works for the employer who provided the cottage. An attempt is also made, however, to resolve the inevitable difficulties which will arise when there are insufficient cottages available to house former workers who qualify for statutory protection and the new workers recruited to replace them.

The Act protects the occupying worker by causing a statutory tenancy to arise in his favour immediately the contractual agreement for his occupation of the cottage ends. This normally occurs when his employment ends – if he resigns or retires or is dismissed or made redundant or if he 'dies in harness'. He (or his family) will then occupy the cottage as a statutory tenant under the terms of the statutory tenancy as prescribed by the Act and so long as he continues to occupy the cottage as his residence he can only be obliged to leave if the landlord obtains a possession order from the County Court. The Act provides that possession orders are only to be granted in certain specified situations which are derived from the Rent Act scheme. Where the worker qualifies for protection under the 1976 Act he is, therefore, quite secure in his accommodation.

The former worker's security may, of course, be inconvenient to his ex-employer who may want to offer the cottage to a new worker. The Act recognises that situations will arise where such conflicting needs must somehow be resolved and it provides a scheme to achieve this. If the employer himself has, or could reasonably provide, alternative accommodation he is expected to make it available. However, where he has no such alternative housing and can show that the 'interests of agricultural efficiency' justify the employment (and consequent housing) of the new worker, then the local housing authority is placed under a duty by the Act

to use its 'best endeavours' to rehouse the statutory tenant and thus to
liberate his tied cottage for the new worker. Where such an application for
rehousing is made to the local authority an ADHAC (Agricultural
Dwelling House Advisory Committee) may be convened and its opinion
sought on the 'agricultural efficiency' aspect of the case, so that the key
plank of the landlord's claim to impose a rehousing duty on the authority
is well tested. To date, the part of the Act seems to have worked
reasonably well. In most cases, the councils' 'best endeavours' seem to
produce alternative housing. However, the reduction of council housing
stock, especially in rural areas, as a result of council house sales and
reduced building programmes suggests that in the future the pressure on
this scarce resource will increase to a point where the 'remedy' provided
in the Act will no longer be effective.

14.02 The 1976 Act: an exclusive jurisdiction

The 1976 Act is drafted to avoid overlaps with other statutory landlord
and tenant codes and to retain for itself an exclusive jurisdiction over
agricultural tied cottage requirements. Paragraph 2 of Schedule 2 of the
Act dovetails it into the other schemes by providing that it will not apply
to tenancies which fall within the protection of:

- the Rent Act 1977 as amended (residential tenancies)
- Part I of the Landlord and Tenant Act 1954 (long leases at low rents);
- Part II of the Landlord and Tenant Act 1954 (business tenancies);
- The Agricultural Holdings Act 1986 (agricultural holdings).

In 'tailoring' the Rent Act scheme to meet the needs of agricultural
tenants, the 1976 Act incorporates by reference parts of what is now the
Rent Act 1977, as amended. Although this technique shortens the Act
considerably, it is inconvenient to the reader as both statutes need to be
read together. The commentary which follows describes the resulting
code of protection.

14.03 The 'protected occupancy' and the 'protected occupier'

The beneficiary of the 1976 Act is described there as a 'protected
occupier', whose occupation constitutes a 'protected occupancy' as
defined by the Act. The three essential features of such an arrangement
are:

(i)   a 'qualifying worker' who has

(ii) a 'relevant licence or tenancy' of

(iii) a 'dwelling house in qualifying ownership' (section 2(i)).

14.04 The 'qualifying worker'

The Act does not automatically protect every agricultural worker who occupies a tied cottage. To be within the Act's protection, the occupier must be a 'qualifying worker', a concept defined by Schedule 3 as someone who has been employed in agriculture whole-time (i.e. for at least 35 hours per week) for at least 91 of the previous 104 weeks, or has been working as a 'permit worker' in agriculture for a similar period. The periods are calculated from the date protection is sought – usually the date at which the landlord suggests that the worker should vacate his property or the contract of employment is ended. The following points should be noted:

(a) Employed in agriculture

The Act does not protect self-employed agricultural contractors: there must be a contract or contracts of employment. Informal contracts will be perfectly adequate: para. 11 of Schedule 3 includes contracts 'whether express or implied and if express whether oral or in writing'.

'Agriculture' is defined for the purposes of the 1976 Act in section 1(1) The definition is the same as that used in the Agricultural Wages Act 1948 which has become well-known within the industry and is well understood, despite its inelegant drafting.

This definition differs in important respects from the definition of agriculture in the Agricultural Holdings Act [1.03] and the two should not be confused. Examples of the difference include the definition of 'livestock' (narrower in the 1976 Act, which is based on 'animal' rather than 'creature' and thus excludes fish farming as well as excluding more esoteric activities such as snail farming) and the inclusion in the 1976 Act of the reference to the

> 'production of consumable produce ... in connection with a trade or business or for any other undertaking (whether carried on for profit or not)'

which clearly includes arrangements other than the 'purposes of a trade or business' essential to the 1986 Act [1.05].

It has been held in *Normanton* v. *Giles* (1980) that persons employed as gamekeepers in raising game such as pheasant are *not* employed in agriculture: the activity here is essentially the promotion of a recreational activity, not the production of consumable produce [1.03 (i)]

(b) *Whole time for 91 weeks*

Schedule 3 provides that the worker must have worked 'whole-time' in agriculture for at least 91 weeks in the previous 104 if he is to claim the protection of the Act. 'Whole-time' means at present at least 35 hours per week. In calculating his entitlement, the occupier may include:

(i)   any week in which he has worked 35 hours or more;
(ii) any week in which he has worked less than 35 hours with his employer's permission;
(iii) any week in which he has taken holiday leave to which he was entitled;
(iv) any week in which he has taken time off with his employer's consent; and
(v)   any week in which he has taken time off because of any illness or injury.

The shortfall of 13 weeks (91/104) in the two years before protection is sought is intended to allow for periods when the worker was out of work or was absent without leave.

The 91 weeks may have been worked in a number of different jobs: the Act does *not* require that the worker qualifies only by working for two years for his present employer/landlord. It may also be worked anywhere in the E.E.C. and still be counted towards the occupier's entitlement. It is therefore of paramount importance that an employer who offers accommodation to a new worker has an accurate record of that worker's previous employment history so that his status under the Act is clear from the outset. Many new workers will already be 'qualifying workers' when engaged by a new employer.

(c) *Permit workers*

Work as a 'permit worker' may be counted towards a worker's eligibility. The Agricultural Wages Committee may grant a permit in respect of a particular worker. This is a recognition that because of physical injury, mental deficiency or infirmity of whatever origin he may be paid at less that the current minimum agricultural wage and the provisions relating to 'standard hours' (requiring 35 hours per week) do not apply to such a worker. Thus weeks worked as a permit worker may be counted towards the 91 weeks, and weeks interrupted by contractual holiday leave, approved absence or sickness and injury may be included.

Persons suffering from a 'qualifying injury or disease'

In addition to whole time work and work as a permit worker, a third possibility exists under the Act for an individual to include periods of time towards his eligibility. This is where he suffers from a 'qualifying injury or disease'. Weeks missed because of such indisposition may be counted towards the 91 weeks necessary for eligibility. These diseases or injuries are essentially conditions arising out of and caused by the occupier's work in agriculture: in other words, time off because of an 'industrial illness or injury' may be counted.

In addition, it is important to note that section 2(2) provides that a person who is incapacitated by such 'industrial illness', will, if he has at that time a relevant licence or tenancy of a dwelling house in qualifying ownership be a protected occupier during his illness or incapacity *regardless* of the length of time he had worked in agriculture before he became ill or was injured. Thus, the Act ensures that an occupier who suffers from an industrial illness or injury from his work in agriculture will benefit from the Act's protection even if he was made ill or suffered his injury right at the beginning of his agricultural career, and his residential security will be ensured whilst he recovers his health. When (or if) he returns to whole-time or permit work in agriculture the weeks off will be counted towards his entitlement and he may therefore effectively qualify by illness in some more serious cases.

14.05 A relevant licence or tenancy

For protection under the 1976 Act, the worker's interest in his tied cottage must be a 'relevant licence or tenancy' as defined by Schedule 2. The Act here aims to apply a scheme directly modelled on the Rent Act to tied cottages, but appropriately modified to take account of features of the tied system – in particular, the fact that most tied cottages are subject to licences or to leases at very low rents and that in many such arrangements the employer-landlord agrees to provide the worker with some meals where to do so encourages an efficient working routine. Since the Rent Act applies only to leases granted at a more than nominal rent and expressly excludes arrangements which provide board and attendance, that 'model' clearly required modification if it was to protect tied cottage occupants effectively. Unfortunately, the drafting of Schedule 2 relies heavily on the incorporation of Rent Act sections by reference and their subsequent modification and the provisions are therefore especially unclear.

Relevant licences

Since *Street* v. *Mountford* (1986) the distinction between leases and licences of residential property has become very faint: where an occupier is granted exclusive possession of premises in exchange for a money rent the arrangement is likely to be construed as a lease. However, since many agricultural tied cottages are held on gratuitous licences where no rent is paid it is important to notice that the 1976 Act extends to protect 'relevant licences', which are defined by para. 1 of Schedule 2, as licences

> 'under which a person has the exclusive occupation of a dwelling house as a separate dwelling'

and which in all other respects are similar to the tenancies protected under the Act. Where a licence grants exclusive possession, therefore, even if it is gratuitous and no 'rent' is charged, it is likely to be a 'relevant licence'.

Relevant tenancies

A 'relevant tenancy' is defined by the 1976 Act as one which would be protected by what is now the Rent Act 1977 as modified to take account of agricultural practice by the 1976 Act. Reading the resulting compound statutory requirements, the following features should be noted.

(a)   The lease (or licence – see above) must grant exclusive possession of a separate dwelling. *Exclusive possession* is an inherent characteristic of a leasehold interest and, as we have seen, to qualify for protection under the Act 'relevant licences' must also grant exclusive possession. The occupier must therefore be entitled to exclude all third parties from the premises by reason of his grant, be it lease or licence. The premises themselves must constitute a *'separate dwelling'* – a requirement from section 1 of the Rent Act 1977 in respect of leases and of Schedule 2 in respect of 'relevant licences'. The essence of this requirement is that the occupier should have possession of premises which include space for all the recognised essential living activities of normal life: eating, sleeping, and sitting and that these facilities should not be subject to being shared with anyone claiming a right to them under a separate grant. If the occupier has, say, a bed-sitting room with some cooking facilities in it this will be sufficient to constitute a 'separate dwelling' which may be a part rather than the whole of a house. Washing and toilet facilities are, perhaps oddly, *not* usually seen by the courts as essential living facilities and shared use of these in addition to exclusive occupation of the bed-sitting room would not prejudice the occupier's protection under the statutory codes.

One statutory exception applies, however. Section 23 of the 1976 Act expressly provides that in one closely defined situation even the sharing of essential living accommodation will not deny protection to an agricultural worker. If several workers together share a tied cottage, and each has exclusive occupation of a living area (say, a separate bedroom each) but they share the kitchen and living room/ lounge, in addition to sharing the use of the bathroom, section 23 provides that each will have the full protection of the Act in respect of his separate accommodation (his bedroom) so long as it is not an arrangement whereby more than four people are sharing the building and each only has one room of his own. In other words, up to four workers may share in the manner described above and each will enjoy that degree of protection. If more than four share, *none* will be protected. Alternatively, two families may share a larger house, each family having a number of rooms for their exclusive use (perhaps one storey each) but sharing the kitchen and bathroom. Again, the 'exclusive' areas would be protected under section 23. The aim of the section is to avoid giving protection to workers housed in hostel-style accommodation.

(b)   To retain statutory protection, the lease or licence must *not*

(i)   be the subject of protection under any of the other statutory codes;

(ii)   grant accommodation in a building in which the landlord also lives, unless this is a purpose-built block of flats (an almost unimaginable situation in the agricultural context). The 'resident landlord exception' is taken from the Rent Act 1977 and would exclude from the 1976 Act a worker who is allowed to live in a flat within the farmhouse, for example. This is *not* dependent on his sharing any facilities with the landlord, but simply the presence in the same building of the two parties, even where each has a 'separate dwelling' within the meaning of the Act;

(iii) include a *bona fide* term whereby the landlord provides the tenant with board, other than meals provided in the course of his employment in agriculture, or substantial attendance. Although neither of these qualifying phrases is especially clear, meals provided by the employer/landlord in order to structure an efficient working regime on the farm or holding are unlikely to affect his worker/tenant's protection under the Act;

(iv)   be granted by any one of the landlords specified in sections 13–16 of the Rent Act 1977 including, for example the Crown, statutory authorities and other bodies.

(v)   be for a property above the current Rent Act rateable value
       limits.

Notice that the rent payable under a tied cottage arrangement is not of
crucial importance unless it is so high as to take the arrangement outside
Rent Act protection (i.e. more than two-thirds of the rateable value of the
property: a situation which is most unlikely to arise). The 1976 Act
expressly provides in para. 3(2) of Schedule 2 that low rents or grants at
no rent are still within the protection of the statute.

14.06 Qualifying ownership

The third aspect of the 'protected occupancy' is that the dwelling house
concerned must be in 'qualifying ownership'. Para. 3 of Schedule 3
defines this term. The essence of it is that the tied cottage either belongs
to the worker's employer or was provided to the worker as a result of an
arrangement to that effect made by his employer with the owner of the
cottage.

14.07 When must the criteria be satisfied?

The question of whether or not a particular occupier is protected under
the Act will, of course, normally only arise if his landlord/employer
requires him to leave his job or his cottage. The occupier *must* then be able
to show that he is a 'qualifying worker', i.e. that he satisfies the '91 week'
test. Most cases which arise under the Act are straightforward: at the date
on which protection is sought the worker and his family are living in a
cottage owned by his employer and the worker has worked whole-time in
agriculture for more than two years. It is important to notice, however,
that in the interests of extending protection to all who may need it, the Act
also includes some more unusual cases within its scope.

One such case is where the worker has satisfied the 91 week test and has
thus obtained the *enduring* status of 'qualifying worker', even though at
the date protection is sought he no longer satisfies the test because he has,
for example, begun to work only part-time in preparation for his
retirement: section 2(2).

Similarly, so long as the house has been in qualifying ownership 'at any
time during the licence or tenancy' that condition will have been satisfied
even if at the time the licence etc. was not a 'relevant' licence.

For example, if a worker is given a bedsitting room in his employer's
own home (not a relevant licence or tenancy because of the 'resident

landlord' exception) and the landlord then moves out, the licence will become a relevant licence and the conditions as to licence and ownership will be satisfied. If the worker has completed his 91 week working period he will be a protected occupier. If the landlord/employer were then to sell the property, thus terminating the licence, the occupier, having been a protected occupier, would as against the third party purchaser be a statutory tenant unless he was granted a new licence in which case his status would remain that of a protected occupier.

These situations are relatively rare and unlikely but the aim of section 2 is to include all tied cottage tenants who have or have had the necessary qualifications.

14.08 Protected occupier by transfer

Section 2(3) defines a further category of protected occupier as opposed to those who qualify by work or by industrial illness. If a worker has been a protected occupier he will retain his protected status if he is required to move into any other house under a 'relevant licence or tenancy' or where a new licence is granted to him. For example, if a worker is a protected occupier of a tied cottage and on his retirement is moved by his employer into another cottage, assuming that the arrangement continues under a 'relevant licence or tenancy' as is likely, he will continue to be a protected occupier.

Alternatively, if he is a protected occupier of a tied cottage which is then sold to a third party, so long as he is again granted a 'relevant licence or tenancy' he will continue as a protected occupier.

14.09 Protected occupiers by succession

The conditions discussed above are those which must be satisfied if the occupier is to be accorded the status of a 'protected occupier in his own right'. When such an occupier dies, if he leaves a spouse who has a relevant licence or tenancy of the cottage in his or her own right, the spouse will become a 'protected occupier by succession'. If no spouse survives the original occupier, then any member of his family who has a relevant licence or tenancy and was residing with him for six months before his death may be the protected occupier by succession of the cottage and if several members of the family qualify, then they should decide which one is to enjoy protected status. In default of their agreement, the county court should nominate the successor from amongst those who are eligible. 'Family' has the same extended meaning here as we have already encountered under the Agricultural Holdings legislation

[7.18], derived similarly from cases on the Rent Acts.

Section 3 will not apply in many cases. Normally, succession rights under the 1976 Act will be enjoyed by *statutory tenants*, not by protected occupiers by succession. The section will apply in those cases where *either* the original occupier was entitled to an interest in the property which did not terminate with his death and has therefore passed with his estate, such as a yearly tenancy, *or* where a successor, either as protected occupier or statutory tenant, is granted a tenancy or licence of the property anew in their own right. The second of these situations may be more frequent than the first, since most interests in tied cottages terminate with the end of employment (or death). The second situation, however, may be encountered where after the original occupier's death, the employer offers the surviving spouse or family the occupation of another cottage and the section would then serve to protect their interest in moving. Notice, however, that as 'succession' interests, protected occupancies by succession will *not* themselves give rise to any succession rights: once the successor dies or moves from a tied cottage the landlord/employer will be entitled to vacant possession.

14.10 Statutory intervention during the contractual period

During the period of the protected occupancy, when the worker's right to occupation of the cottage is found in the contractual arrangement between himself and his employer, the 1976 Act has only a peripheral role: its main purpose is the protection of the occupier *after* the contractual arrangement has ended.

However, three provisions of the 1976 Act do affect the contractual occupation agreement:

(1)   Section 20 prevents the landlord from lawfully demanding rent in advance. Any such demand will be void. In addition the section provides that any demand that rent be paid more than six months before the end of the tenancy will also be void when the lease is for more than a six month period.

(2)   As mentioned above [14.6(a)], where no more than four workers share a cottage and each has an area which he occupies separately and exclusively, that separate area will be fully protected as a protected occupancy. Sections 23(4) and (5) also give the tenants some protection for their rights over the shared areas, where those include shared 'living accommodation'. The section provides that the landlord may not vary or modify the tenants' rights over the shared 'living accommodation'. The only exception to this is to permit the landlord to vary the number of people who share, *if* there is an

express term to that effect in the tenancy. 'Living accommodation' is defined in such a way as to include kitchens, bedrooms and living rooms but to exclude bathrooms and toilets (following the case law: [14.6(a)].

(3)   Section 6(1) provides that

'a Court shall not make an order for possession ... except in the Cases in Schedule 4'

where premises are subject to a protected occupancy. The landlord's right to resume possession is heavily restricted.

14.11 The statutory tenancy

When does it arise?

Section 4(1) provides that a statutory tenancy will arise where a person

'ceases to be a protected occupier of a dwelling house on the termination, whether by notice to quit or by virtue of section 16(3) of this Act or otherwise, of his licence or tenancy', and it will last 'if and so long as he occupies the dwelling-house as his residence'.

Thus, the protected occupier automatically and instantly becomes a statutory tenant when the contractual arrangement under which he occupies the cottage is ended. In most cases, since the right to occupy the property depends on the worker's employment, the licence will be terminated by the ending of the contract of employment, whether it is ended by the worker or by the employer. Thus, if the worker resigns or retires or is dismissed or made redundant the contractual licence will normally terminate automatically and the occupier will enjoy the status of statutory tenant of his cottage.

In some situations, although the purpose of the licence or tenancy is to facilitate the worker in his job, its terms are to some extent independent of the contract of employment. It may, for example, confer on him an annual tenancy or some other periodic interest which may not necessarily terminate with his employment. In such cases, the original protected occupancy will continue until specifically terminated. This may be by notice to quit or notice to vacate (if a licence). Where notice to quit is given the usual rules as to notice will apply.

The 1976 Act also provides that a notice of increase of rent served on a protected occupier may operate as a notice to quit and will terminate the protected occupancy and cause a statutory tenancy (subject to the new rent) to arise. For this result to be achieved, section 16(3) of the Act specifies that the notice of increase must be served during the protected occupancy and that the period of notice given must exceed the period appropriate to a notice to quit were one to be served on the same terms. Thus, for example, where a worker/occupier is about to retire, and his employer intends him to remain in his cottage but subject to an increased rent during retirement, a notice of increase of rent might be served which, if appropriately timed, would end the contractual licence at the retirement date and cause a statutory tenancy at the newly increased rent to arise from that time. Similarly, if a worker leaves the landlord/employer's employment for another job and the cottage is not immediately required, a notice of increase would be appropriate and would clearly terminate the contractual protected occupancy.

14.12 Statutory tenants by succession

In addition to the statutory tenancies which arise when an erstwhile protected occupancy is terminated, a statutory tenancy also arises to protect the *successor* to a protected occupier/statutory tenant in those circumstances where there is a successor as defined by the Act (surviving spouse or resident member of the deceased's family: section 4(2), (3), (4)) who is not a 'protected occupier by succession' under section 3. There is only a one generation succession entitlement under the 1976 Act and after the original occupier dies the interest will pass to a protected occupier by succession or to a statutory tenant.

14.13 The terms of the statutory tenancy

Unlike the Rent Act, which merely continues the terms of the contractual tenancy into the period of statutory protection, the Rent (Agriculture) Act prescribes with some precision the terms of the statutory tenancy both with respect to rent and other matters. This is to ensure that, especially in cases where the original arrangement was not a tenancy but a mere licence, there is certainty regarding the terms of the ultimate statutory tenancy.

Apart from the detailed provisions regarding rent, the terms are contained in Schedule 5, which is introduced by section 10. Notice that paragraph 2 of Schedule 5 maintains the benefit of the terms of the *original* contract for the statutory tenant, so long as he remains in residence. Paragraph (2), however, makes it clear beyond doubt that any term in the original contract under which the right of occupation depended on employment in agriculture or any other employment is to be entirely left out of account: the statutory tenancy protects *occupation* rights alone.

14.14 Transition terms

To effect the transition from licence to statutory *tenancy*, Schedule 5 provides that where the original contract was a licence the statutory tenancy shall be a weekly tenancy (paragraph 3) and it shall include any terms including the normal covenants for quiet enjoyment and use in a tenant-like manner which are implied into any tenancy (paragraph 4).

In addition, paragraph 6 provides that section II of the Landlord and Tenant Act 1985 (formerly section 32 of the Housing Act 1961) will apply during the statutory tenancy, whether or not it was relevant to the preceding contractual arrangement, thus establishing on the landlord the statutory repairing duty. Paragraph 7 restricts the tenant's use of the property to the purposes of a private dwelling house and imposes on him during the statutory tenancy a condition against assignment, subletting or parting with possession.

Where the landlord has contractually provided the occupier with 'reasonably necessary' facilities during the protected occupancy, which the occupier could not reasonably have been expected to provide for himself (such as, say, water or electricity supply) paragraph 5 ensures that the landlord will continue to provide these during the statutory tenancy. This will apply if the services were provided at any time during the protected occupancy.

Paragraphs 8 and 9 ensure the parties' respective rights of access to the premises. Paragraph 8 imposes a condition that the statutory tenant shall offer access and reasonable facilities to the landlord so that he can effect repairs. Paragraph 9 protects the tenant's right of reasonable access to the cottage. The paragraph also expressly permits the landlord to restrict access to the house if this becomes necessary to inhibit the spread of disease, or where such restriction of access is 'reasonably necessary in the interests of efficient agriculture', but in either of these situations the landlord must ensure that the tenant has suitable alternative access.

Paragraph 10 provides for the rare situation where the tenant wishes to terminate the statutory tenancy. The paragraph provides that the tenant in such a case must give at least four weeks notice to quit.

Paragraph 11 provides that the landlord may recover the *rates* of the tied cottage from the tenant if he gives the tenant *notice in writing* of such liability. The notice will only have retrospective effect for four weeks prior to its service, so the landlord who can foresee a statutory tenancy arising on retirement, for example, should be alert to give notice of rates liability at the earliest possible stage. Notice that if an appropriate notice is served on the tenant, he will be liable to pay rates even if he is expressly *not* required to pay rent under the statutory tenancy. However, it must always be remembered that a notice of rates liability is absolutely necessary to establish such a duty on the statutory tenant. 'Rates' includes water rates.

Finally, paragraph 12 gives a restricted right to the parties to *vary* the terms of the statutory tenancy by *an agreement in writing*. This may be made between them at any time – even before the beginning of the statutory tenancy. Again, therefore, when a statutory tenancy is forseeable it is possible for the parties to arrange well in advance the precise terms on which it will take effect. These terms will be a combination of those expressly agreed by the parties and those necessarily imposed by the Act. Section 12 provides that *no* agreement between the parties may result in:

(1) a substantial addition to the land or premises occupied by the tenant;
(2) any breach of an obligation implied by law, and in particular a breach of the landlord's repairing liability under section 11 of the Landlord and Tenant Act 1985;
(3) any modification of the circumstances in which the statutory tenant may give notice to quit; or
(4) the inclusion of any term unrelated to the occupation of the dwelling house and, in particular, the inclusion of any term relating to the employment of the tenant by the landlord.

Any agreement under this paragraph will bind successors in title to the original parties, as will agreements relating to the payment of rates and the basic agreements relating to the payment of rent discussed below.

14.15 Payment of rent during the statutory tenancy

Because so many service occupancies of tied cottages are free of rent or are at only minimal rentals, special attention is paid in the Rent (Agriculture) Act to terms providing for liability to pay rent during the statutory tenancy. The relevant provisions are sections 10–16 and Schedule 6.

The first important point to note is that there is *no automatic statutory liability* to pay rent during the statutory tenancy: any duty to pay rent will necessarily be the result of *express agreement* or notification between the parties: section 10(2). The duty to pay rent may be imposed by an agreement subject to section 11 or by a notice of inrease of rent served subject to section 12 or 14.

By agreement: section 11

The parties may agree, before or during the statutory tenancy, what rent shall be payable, subject to a statutory maximum which is either the registered rent for the cottage, where one has been registered, or in default of registration, a rent of 1.5 × the rateable value of the property. The parties may agree on any rent up to the appropriate limit, or they may agree that no rent should be payable. Where a statutory tenancy is foreseeable, therefore, the wise landlord will arrange the agreement regarding rent well in advance and will arrange the registration of a fair rent by the rent officer at the earliest possible time, as the rateable value maximum is likely in any case to fall noticeably short of the fair rent. If a rent is agreed which exceeds the appropriate statutory limit, the amount of the excess will not be recoverable from the tenant who can be sure of his maximum rental liability.

Normally such an agreement would be used for a period before the fair rent had been established. Section 11(9) was enacted with this assumption in mind and provides that if an express agreement concerning rent is terminated the rent payable under the agreement will nevertheless remain payable unless and until a notice of increase in rent takes effect. This important provision ensures that an agreed rent will be payable throughout the statutory tenancy unless a higher rent is sought through the appropriate procedures.

If in a situation where a fair rent has not been registered in respect of a tied cottage, and the rent agreed to be payable is not equal to the provisional rent based on 1.5 × rateable value, the landlord may increase the rent payable to the provisional rent by the service of an appropriate notice of increase which conforms with section 12. Such a notice must specify the rent based on the rateable value and must show how the landlord has calculated it. The notice must also specify the date from which the provisional rent will apply. The notice can apply the increased rent retrospectively for up to four weeks.

A provisional rent payable after service of a notice under section 12 will replace the rent payable under any section 11 agreement. Either the new 'provisional' rent will be expressly and clearly stated on the notice to replace the agreed rent or alternatively, if the notice of provisional rent gives at least four week's notice of the increase, then it will itself be treated as ending the express agreement as from the operative date of the notice of increase.

The provisional rent provisions were really intended to provide a reasonable income for the landlord during the period when he was waiting for a fair rent to be registered. Section 13 provides for a fair rent to be registered for a tied cottage, such registrations being recorded in a special part of the rent register maintained by rent officers. As with residential registered rents under the Rent Acts, such registered rents may be reviewed and revised at three-yearly intervals. Any increase on the second and subsequent valuation shall be phased over the three-year period according to the formulae set out in Schedule 6. Section 14 provides that where a rent is registered for a cottage subject to a statutory tenancy, the existing rent payable may be increased to the level of the registered rent by the serving of a notice on the tenant which specifies the rent registered and the date on which it is to take effect. The notice may be retrospective, but only for a maximum period of four weeks. It must not purport to take effect from the termination of a section 11 agreement. If it gives the necessary four weeks' minimum notice, it may itself serve to terminate the section 11 agreement. Schedule 6 is reprinted in full in Appendix III.

Notices advising the tenant of increase in rent whether under section 12 or section 14 may, if convenient and appropriate, be served before the statutory tenancy arises. If this is done, the notice of increase in rent will itself serve as a notice to terminate the protected occupancy if a notice to quit served at the same time as the notice of increase would have been effective (i.e. if at least four weeks' notice is given, in most cases). Thus the registered rent will be payable right from the beginning of the statutory tenancy. This method of termination may be desirable, for example, if the tenant is known to be leaving the landlord's employment.

Notice that where a *bona fide* mistake on the part of the landlord results in an error in a notice of increase, the County Court may amend the notice to avoid it being denied effect. If such an amendment involves an increase in the rent payable, the court may devise just and reasonable conditions to accommodate this: paying the arrears of increase by instalments, for example. In any case the landlord is limited by section 16(7) to recovering a maximum of 6 months' arrears of increase by reason of any such order.

14.16 Obtaining possession from a protected occupier or statutory tenant

A crucial aspect of the security of tenure provisions of the Rent (Agriculture) Act is the requirement that a court order for possession of the tied cottage may only be obtained from the county court if the landlord is able to prove one or more of the thirteen Cases for possession specified in Schedule 4 and, where Cases 1–10 are relied on, he must also be able to satisfy the court that it would be reasonable in all the circumstances to make an order for possession in the particular case.

The thirteen Cases for possession mirror those in the Rent Act which are appropriate to agricultural tied cottages. As with the Rent Act, there are 'discretionary' Cases in which the 'reasonableness' test as mentioned above must be satisfied (Cases 1–10) and also 'mandatory' Cases where the advantage is more clearly with the landlord, who has merely to prove that the relevant Case applies to obtain possession. The three 'mandatory'

Cases under the 1976 Act are: (i) Case 11: letting the landlord's own home; (ii) Case 12: letting the landlord's retirement home; (iii) Case 13: criminal overcrowding by the tenant of the tied cottage. If any of these three Cases is proved, the court has no discretion but must grant a possession order against the tenant. The tenant's security of tenure in such situations is therefore minimal.

The Cases reflect various difficulties which may arise between landlord and tenant. Cases 1 and 2 can cast the county court in the role of arbiter between the tenant and his landlord or another provider of housing such as the local housing authority where the matter in dispute between them is whether or not the alternative accommodation which has been offered is suitable and appropriate. Where the tenant has accepted the 'new' accommodation and has then refused to move, of course, the court's task may be much more straightforward but in practice cases are not unusually brought under this head because several offers of alternative housing have been made and rejected by the occupier. The Cases provide the court with the criteria which should be satisfied by the new accommodation and thus allow the impasse to be resolved. It may be that the use of these two Cases, and particularly Case 2 will become more frequent in the future as the stocks of council housing available are reduced through tenants' purchases and less ambitious building programmes. The courts' view of the tenant's behaviour in refusing the accommodation may become less tolerant in the light of such changing circumstances, thus acknowledging the authorities' difficulties and recognising that 'best endeavours' to rehouse may not produce a perfect result. The particular difficulty for the landlord under these two Cases will be showing that the tenant's refusal has been unreasonable. If he can achieve that, it is likely that the court's discretion will be exercised in his favour and an order for possession will be granted.

Cases 3–8 all depend on aspects of the tenant's default. Here it is much less likely that even if the Case is proved against the tenant the court will make an order for possession, at least on the first approach. It is much more probable that the order for possession will be suspended subject to conditions that the tenant remedies his default by, for example, paying by instalments the arrears of rent, repairing or improving the deteriorations, or undertaking in future to avoid causing a nuisance. When these Cases are relied on by the landlord it is as well to ensure that any Case which the evidence will support is pleaded with and as an alternative to others. For example, behaviour amounting to a nuisance may also lead to the deterioration of the premises and possibly also of the furniture and may also be a breach of the implied duty to occupy in a tenant-like manner. In such a situation the landlord's claim might be based on Case 3 and/or Case 2 and/or Case 5 and/or Case 6. Similarly, given the likelihood of a suspended order on the first approach, where possession is sought from an

unreliable or untenant-like tenant it is advisable to persevere with several
'return' applications. Either of these approaches will begin to establish the
character of the tenant's possession of the property and to increase the
'reasonableness' of an order for possession in the eyes of the court in a later
application.

Case 9 is based on the landlord's, or his family's, reasonable need for the
property and the 'greater hardship' consideration. Although more
clumsily phrased than under the Agricultural Holdings legislation, the
greater hardship criterion here is similar to that encountered in the
succession and possession aspects discussed earlier [7.18]. Under the 1976
Act, the court has to be satisfied that

'no greater hardship would be caused by granting the order than by
refusing to grant it',

the onus being therefore on the landlord to show that the hardship to his
family if they were deprived of possession would be at least as great as the
hardship caused to the evicted tenant.

Case 10 penalises the tenant for subletting at illegally exhorbitant rents.

As mentioned previously, Cases 11–13, the 'mandatory' grounds only
require the landlord to make out their very precise facts and the court *must*
grant him an effective possession order.

Schedule 4 of the Act is reprinted in full in Appendix III.

14.17 Subtenants' security

As we have seen, there is an absolute prohibition on subletting by a
statutory tenant under the Rent (Agriculture) Act. Any subtenant whose
interest began at that stage in his landlord's tenure would therefore be an
unlawful subtenant and would not enjoy protection if the landlord himself
were to be made the subject of a possession order.

However, particular attention is paid by the Act to the cases of *lawful*
subtenants who themselves are protected occupiers or statutory tenants
under the Rent Act 1977 (Schedule 18 para. 19) and whose landlord, also
the object of protection under one of the statutory tenancy codes, is made
the subject of a possession order. Normally, in such a case, if the head
tenancy falls the subtenancies fall too. However, section 9 and Schedule
18 para. 19 provide that where a possession order is made against the
'landlord' (the head-tenant), the subtenant will hold directly of the head
landlord, who cannot therefore free himself of the subtenant's interest
unless he can also obtain a possession order against him directly, having
made out one or more of the Schedule 4 Cases (or Rent Act Schedule 15
cases) and, if necessary, convinced the court that it is reasonable to make
the order.

Section 9 provides for the security of lawful subtenants who themselves are protected occupiers or statutory tenants under the Act and whose immediate landlord is either a protected occupier or statutory tenant under the Act, or a protected or statutory tenant under the Rent Act or a tenant under the Agricultural Holdings Act 1986 or under Part I of the Landlord and Tenant Act 1954. The only exception to this position is where the landlord holds under the 1954 Act and a notice to terminate his interest has been given under section 4(1) if that Act or his tenancy was being statutorily continued and he at that stage grants the subtenancy. If the head landlord agreed in writing to the subtenancy, the subtenant will be protected as in other cases, but if no consent in writing is obtained the subtenancy in those two situations will be vulnerable to a possession order being obtained against his landlord. Para. 19 of Schedule 18 makes parallel provision where the subtenant is protected under the Rent Act.

The effect of these protective provisions may be seen in the following examples. Where a tenant of an agricultural holding leases cottages to workers who are protected under the 1976 Act, then if for any reason the tenancy of the agricultural holding is determined, the workers will nevertheless still enjoy security of tenure in their accommodation as against the head landlord unless they were joined as defendants in a possession action and a case made out against them directly. Similarly, if an agricultural worker sublets a part of his accommodation to another worker each may then have protected occupier status *vis-à-vis* their respective landlords. In such a case, section 9 would be effective to protect the subtenant if an order for possession was obtained against the original tenant of the tied cottage.

It is relevant at this point to notice the effect of section 24 which provides that a tenant protected by the 1976 Act will not lose his protection if he lawfully sublets a part of his accommodation to subtenants who share facilities with him or who pay him for board and attendance included in their rent. Obviously, such a subletting may be in contravention of the terms of the statutory tenancy, but those terms themselves may, as we have seen, be altered by the parties. In such a subletting situation, however, although section 24 will preserve *the tenant's* protected position, the *subtenants* will necessarily be outside the scope of the Act: the 'resident landlord', shared living facilities and board and attendance factors may all serve to exclude them.

14.18 The rehousing provisions

As mentioned in the introduction to this Part, a distinctive feature of the Rent (Agriculture) Act is its attempt to resolve the difficulty of conflicting claims to tied cottages presently occupied by secure occupiers protected by the Act but needed to house new agricultural workers to whom the accommodation is a necessary adjunct of their work. Where the employer has no stock of 'spare' accommodation the Act directs him to look to the local housing authority to resolve the difficulty by using their 'best endeavours' to find alternative accommodation for the worker who is being replaced. The aim is therefore to ensure that a protected occupier or statutory tenant under the 1976 Act may be guaranteed accommodation either in a tied cottage or in council housing which is suitable to his needs. The council may only be required to act to find accommodation, however, if the landlord can show that

(1)   vacant possession will be required of the tied cottage to house a person who is or who will be employed in agriculture by the applicant;
(2)   the applicant himself is unable reasonably to provide suitable alternative accommodation for the present occupier of the cottage; and
(3)   the housing authority ought to provide suitable alternative accommodation 'in the interests of efficient agriculture': section 27.

Once the landlord has made a written application to the housing authority in the appropriate form or some substantially similar form then the local authority must within seven days notify the occupier of the tied cottage that the application has been made. It would be extraordinarily bad management if this was the first notification which he had received of the impending move and clearly the employer/landlord should ensure that the worker is aware in advance of such developments.

Any of the three parties – landlord, tenant or authority – may then obtain advice on the 'agricultural efficiency' aspect and on the urgency of the application by applying for the services of an ADHAC (an Agricultural Dwelling House Advisory Committee). These Committees, a creation of the Act, are composed of three members appointed by the local chairman. Any particular ADHAC which is convened should include a chairman, one member representing or at least reflecting the interests of employers and a third member reflecting the interests of workers in agriculture. Both parties may make representations to the ADHAC, which is encouraged to be both informal and astute to possibilities of being misled. The Committee essentially has to give an opinion on the need for the new worker planned by the landlord, and the strength of the consequent claim that the present occupier of the tied cottage should be moved out and rehoused by the Council. If the ADHAC decides that the landlord's application is indeed in the interests of efficient agriculture then the local authority is highly likely to accept this: section 28(5) requires them to 'take full account of advice tendered to them by the Committee'. Notice that ADHACs are subject in some instances to judicial review: *R* v. *ADHAC for Bedfordshire, Cambridgeshire and Northamptonshire* (1986).

The authority's decision on any application must be notified to the applicant and the occupier within 3 months of receiving the application, or within 2 months of the report of the ADHAC if one has been called for. Since ADHACs are expected to report back within 28 days, in practice an attempt is made to observe the 3 month period from application to decision in all cases. Where a local authority accepts that the landlord satisfies the statutory conditions, then they must use their 'best endeavours' to find new housing, a duty which, in appropriate cases, may expressly be enforced by an action for damages for breach of statutory duty: section 28(8). The duty may also, of course, be enforced by an action for judicial review.

Although the demands of such a duty are unclear, the reality of local council housing availability, in most cases, will make the council's position clear. Where the council offers alternative housing to the existing tenant of the tied cottage and he declines it on the ground that it is not appropriate, and where further negotiations fail to produce a satisfactory result, the dispute as to the appropriateness of the council's offer(s) and the reasonableness of the tenant's refusal of them may be resolved by submitting it to the county court in the form of an action for possession of the cottage brought under Case 2 of the Act. As mentioned earlier, the court here may be influenced by the context of the case, and in particular by the choice available to the council (and therefore to the tenant) and by the background of 'the interests of efficient agriculture' which underlie the projected move.

14.19 Power to obtain information

Part 5 of the Act contains miscellaneous powers which the Minister may use to obtain information about housing provision in agriculture and forestry. These powers are not of direct interest to farmers or tenants and seem, to date, to have been only little exploited.

Agriculture Act 1986, Schedule 1 Tenants' Compensation for Milk Quota

PART I

RIGHT TO COMPENSATION

Tenants' right to compensation

1.—(1) Subject to the following provisions of this Schedule, where on the termination of the tenancy of any land the tenant has milk quota registered as his in relation to a holding consisting of or including the land, the tenant shall be entitled, on quitting the land, to obtain from his landlord a payment—

(*a*) if the tenant had milk quota allocated to him in relation to land comprised in the holding ("allocated quota"), in respect of so much of the relevant quota as consists of allocated quota; and

(*b*) if the tenant had milk quota allocated to him as aforesaid or was in occupation of the land as a tenant on 2nd April 1984 (whether or not under the tenancy which is terminating), in respect of so much of the relevant quota as consists of transferred quota transferred to him by virtue of a transaction the cost of which was borne wholly or partly by him.

(2) In sub-paragraph (1) above—

"the relevant quota" means—

(*a*) in a case where the holding mentioned in sub-paragraph (1) above consists only of the land subject to the tenancy, the milk quota registered in relation to the holding; and

(*b*) otherwise, such part of that milk quota as falls to be apportioned to that land on the termination of the tenancy;

"transferred quota" means milk quota transferred to the tenant by virtue of the transfer to him of the whole or part of a holding.

(3) A tenant shall not be entitled to more than one payment under this paragraph in respect of the same land.

Succession on death or retirement of tenant

2.—(1) This paragraph applies where on the termination of the tenancy of any land after 2nd April 1984 a new tenancy of the land or part of the land has been granted to a different tenant ("the new tenant") and that tenancy—

(a) was obtained by virtue of a direction under section 39 or 53 of the Agricultural Holdings Act 1986 (direction for grant of tenancy to successor on death or retirement of previous tenant);

(b) was granted (following a direction under section 39 of that Act) in circumstances within section 45(6) of that Act (new tenancy granted by agreement to persons entitled to tenancy under direction); or

(c) is such a tenancy as is mentioned in section 37(1)(b) or (2) of that Act (tenancy granted by agreement to close relative).

(2) Where this paragraph applies—

(a) any milk quota allocated or transferred to the former tenant (or treated as having been allocated or transferred to him) in respect of the land which is subject to the new tenancy shall be treated as if it had instead been allocated or transferred to the new tenant; and

(b) in a case where milk quota is treated under paragraph (a) above as having been transferred to the new tenant, he shall be treated for the purposes of any claim in respect of that quota—

(i) as if he had paid so much of the cost of the transaction by virtue of which the milk quota was transferred as the former tenant bore (or is treated as having borne); and

(ii) in a case where the former tenant was in occupation of the land on 2nd April 1984 (or is treated as having been in occupation of the land on that date), as if he had been in occupation of it on that date.

(3) Sub-paragraph (1) above applies in relation to the grant of a new tenancy before the date on which the Agricultural Holdings Act 1986 comes into force as if the references in that sub-paragraph to sections 39, 53 and 45(6) of that Act were references to section 20 of the Agriculture (Miscellaneous Provisions) Act 1976, paragraph 5 of Schedule 2 to the Agricultural Holdings Act 1984 and section 23(6) of the said Act of 1976 respectively.

Assignments

3. Where the tenancy of any land has been assigned after 2nd April 1984 (whether by deed or by operation of law)—

(a) any milk quota allocated or transferred to the assignor (or treated as having been allocated or transferred to him) in respect of the land shall be treated as if it had instead been allocated or transferred to the assignee; and

(b) in a case where milk quota is treated under paragraph (a) above as having been transferred to the assignee, he shall be treated for the purposes of any claim in respect of that quota—

(i) as if he had paid so much of the cost of the transaction by virtue of which the milk quota was transferred as the assignor bore (or is treated as having borne); and

(ii) in a case where the assignor was in occupation of the land on 2nd April 1984 (or is treated as having been in occupation of the land on that date), as if he had been in occupation of it on that date;

and accordingly the assignor shall not be entitled to a payment under paragraph 1 above in respect of that land.

Sub-tenancies

4. Where the sub-tenancy of any land terminates after 2nd April 1984 then, for the purposes of determining the sub-landlord's entitlement under paragraph 1 above—

(*a*) any milk quota allocated or transferred to the sub-tenant (or treated as having been allocated or transferred to him) in respect of the land shall be treated as if it had instead been allocated or transferred to the sub-landlord;

(*b*) in a case where milk quota is treated under paragraph (*a*) above as having been transferred to the sub-landlord, he shall be treated for the purposes of any claim in respect of that quota—

(i) as if he had paid so much of the cost of the transaction by virtue of which the milk quota was transferred as the sub-tenant bore (or is treated as having borne); and

(ii) in a case where the sub-tenant was in occupation of the land on 2nd April 1984 (or is treated as having been in occupation of the land on that date), as if he had been in occupation of it on that date;

(*c*) if the sub-landlord does not occupy the land after the sub-tenancy has ended and the sub-tenant has quitted the land, the sub-landlord shall be taken to have quitted the land when the sub-tenant quitted it.

Part II

Amount of Compensation Payable

Calculation of payment

5.—(1) The amount of the payment to which the tenant of any land is entitled under paragraph 1 above on the termination of his tenancy shall be determined in accordance with the following provisions of this paragraph.

(2) The amount of the payment to which the tenant is entitled under paragraph 1 above in respect of allocated quota shall be an amount equal—

(*a*) in a case where the allocated quota exceeds the standard quota for the land, to the value of the sum of—
(i) the tenant's fraction of the standard quota, and
(ii) the amount of the excess;

(b) in a case where the allocated quota is equal to the standard quota, to the value of the tenant's fraction of the allocated quota; and

(c) in a case where the allocated quota is less than the standard quota, to the value of such proportion of the tenant's fraction of the allocated quota as the allocated quota bears to the standard quota.

(3) The amount of the payment the tenant is entitled to under paragraph 1 above in respect of transferred quota shall be an amount equal—

(a) in a case where the tenant bore the whole of the cost of the transaction by virtue of which the transferred quota was transferred to him, to the value of the transferred quota; and

(b) in a case where the tenant bore only part of that cost, to the value of the corresponding part of the transferred quota.

"Standard quota"

6.—(1) Subject to the following provisions of this paragraph the standard quota for any land for the purposes of this Schedule shall be calculated by multiplying the relevant number of hectares by the prescribed quota per hectare; and for the purposes of this paragraph—

(a) "the relevant number of hectares" means the average number of hectares of the land in question used during the relevant period for the feeding of dairy cows kept on the land or, if different, the average number of hectares of the land which could reasonably be expected to have been so used (having regard to the number of grazing animals other than dairy cows kept on the land during that period); and

(b) "the prescribed quota per hectare" means such number of litres as the Minister may from time to time by order prescribe for the purposes of this sub-paragraph.

(2) Where by virtue of the quality of the land in question or climatic conditions in the area the amount of milk which could reasonably be expected to have been produced from one hectare of the land during the relevant period ("the reasonable amount") is greater or less than the prescribed average yield per hectare, then sub-paragraph (1) above shall not apply and the standard quota shall be calculated by multiplying the relevant number of hectares by such proportion of the prescribed quota per hectare as the reasonable amount bears to the prescribed average yield per hectare; and the Minister shall by order prescribe the amount of milk to be taken as the average yield per hectare for the purposes of this sub-paragraph.

(3) Where the relevant quota of the land includes milk quota allocated in pursuance of an award of quota made by the Dairy Produce Quota Tribunal for England and Wales which has not been allocated in full, the standard quota for the land shall be reduced by the amount by which the milk quota allocated in pursuance of the award falls short of the amount awarded (or, in a case where only part of the milk quota allocated in pursuance of the award is included in the

relevant quota, by the corresponding proportion of that shortfall).

(4) In sub-paragraph (3) above the references to milk quota allocated in pursuance of an award of quota include references to quota allocated by virtue of the amount awarded not originally having been allocated in full.

(5) In this paragraph—

    (*a*) references to land used for the feeding of dairy cows kept on the land do not include land used for growing cereal crops for feeding to dairy cows in the form of loose grain; and

    (*b*) references to dairy cows are to cows kept for milk production (other than uncalved heifers).

(6) An order under this paragraph may make different provision for different cases.

(7) The power to make an order under this paragraph shall be exercisable by statutory instrument and any instrument containing such an order shall be subject to annulment in pursuance of a resolution of either House of Parliament.

"Tenant's fraction"

7.—(1) For the purposes of this Schedule "the tenant's fraction" means the fraction of which—

    (*a*) the numerator is the annual rental value at the end of the relevant period of the tenant's dairy improvements and fixed equipment; and

    (*b*) the denominator is the sum of that value and such part of the rent payable by the tenant in respect of the relevant period as is attributable to the land used in that period for the feeding, accommodation or milking of dairy cows kept on the land.

(2) For the purposes of sub-paragraph (1)(*a*) above the rental value of the tenant's dairy improvements and fixed equipment shall be taken to be the amount which would fall to be disregarded under paragraph 2(1) of Schedule 2 to the Agricultural Holdings Act 1986 on a reference made in respect of the land in question under section 12 of that Act (arbitration of rent), so far as that amount is attributable to tenant's improvements to, or tenant's fixed equipment on, land used for the feeding, accommodation or milking of dairy cows kept on the land in question.

(3) Where—

    (*a*) the relevant period is less than or greater than 12 months; or
    (*b*) rent was only payable by the tenant in respect of part of the relevant period,

the average rent payable in respect of one month in the relevant period or, as the case may be, in that part shall be determined and the rent referred to in sub-paragraph (1)(*b*) above shall be taken to be the corresponding annual amount.

(4) For the purposes of sub-paragraph (2) above "tenant's improvements"

and "tenant's fixed equipment" have the same meanings as in paragraph 2 of Schedule 2 to the 1986 Act, except that—

(*a*) any allowance made or benefit given by the landlord after the end of the relevant period in consideration of the execution of improvements wholly or partly at the expense of the tenant shall be disregarded for the purposes of sub-paragraph (2)(*a*) of that paragraph;

(*b*) any compensation received by the tenant after the end of the relevant period in respect of any improvement or fixed equipment shall be disregarded for the purposes of sub-paragraph (3) of that paragraph; and

(*c*) where paragraph 2 above applies in respect of any land, improvements or equipment which would be regarded as tenant's improvements or equipment on the termination of the former tenant's tenancy (if he were entitled to a payment under this Schedule in respect of that land) shall be regarded as the new tenant's improvements or equipment.

"Relevant period"

8. In this Schedule "the relevant period" means—

(*a*) the period in relation to which the allocated quota was determined; or

(*b*) where it was determined in relation to more than one period, the period in relation to which the majority was determined or, if equal amounts were determined in relation to different periods, the later of those periods.

Valuation of milk quota

9. The value of milk quota to be taken into account for the purposes of paragraph 5 above is the value of the milk quota at the time of the termination of the tenancy in question and in determining that value at that time there shall be taken into account such evidence as is available, including evidence as to the sums being paid for interests in land—

(*a*) in cases where milk quota is registered in relation to the land; and

(*b*) in cases where no milk quota is so registered.

Part III

Supplemental Provisions

Determination of standard quota and tenant's fraction before end of tenancy

10.—(1) Where, on the termination of a tenancy of any land, the tenant may be entitled to a payment under paragraph 1 above, the landlord or tenant may at any time before the termination of the tenancy by notice in writing served on the other demand that the determination of the standard quota for the land or the tenant's fraction shall be referred to arbitration.

(2) On a reference under this paragraph the arbitrator shall determine the standard quota for the land or, as the case may be, the tenant's fraction (so far as determinable at the date of the reference).

(3) Section 84 of the Agricultural Holdings Act 1986 (arbitrations) shall apply as if the matters mentioned in this paragraph were required by that Act to be determined by arbitration under that Act.

Settlement of tenant's claim on termination of tenancy

11.—(1) Subject to the provisions of this paragraph, any claim arising under paragraph 1 above shall be determined by arbitration under the Agricultural Holdings Act 1986 and no such claim shall be enforceable unless before the expiry of the period of two months from the termination of the tenancy the tenant serves notice in writing on his landlord of his intention to make the claim.

(2) The landlord and tenant may within the period of eight months from the termination of the tenancy by agreement in writing settle the claim but where the claim has not been settled during that period it shall be determined by arbitration under the Agricultural Holdings Act 1986.

(3) In any case where on the termination of the tenancy in question a new tenancy of the land or part of the land may be granted to a different tenant by virtue of a direction under section 39 of the Agricultural Holdings Act 1986 then, as respects any claim in respect of that land or part, references in sub-paragraphs (1) and (2) above to the termination of the tenancy shall be construed as references to the following time, namely—

(a) in a case where no application is made under that section within the period within which such an application may be made, the expiry of that period;

(b) in a case where every such application made within that period is withdrawn, the expiry of that period or the time when the last outstanding application is withdrawn (whichever is the later);

(c) in a case where the Agricultural Land Tribunal refuse every such application for a direction under that section, the time when the last outstanding application is refused; and

(d) in a case where the Tribunal give such a direction, the relevant time for the purposes of section 46 of that Act;

and no notice may be served under sub-paragraph (1) above before that time.

(4) Where a tenant lawfully remains in occupation of part of the land subject to the tenancy after the termination of the tenancy or, in a case where sub-paragraph (3) above applies, after the time substituted for the termination of the tenancy by virtue of that sub-paragraph, the references in sub-paragraphs (1) and (2) above to the termination of the tenancy shall be construed as references to the termination of the occupation.

(5) Section 84 of the Agricultural Holding Act 1986 (arbitrations) shall apply

as if the requirements of this paragraph were requirements of that Act, but paragraph 18 of Schedule 11 to that Act (arbitration award to fix day for payment not later than one month after award) shall have effect for the purposes of this paragraph as if for the words "one month" there were substituted the words "three months".

(6) Where—

(a) before the termination of the tenancy of any land the landlord and tenant have agreed in writing the amount of the standard quota for the land or the tenant's fraction or the value of milk quota which is to be used for the purpose of calculating the payment to which the tenant will be entitled under this Schedule on the termination of the tenancy; or

(b) the standard quota or the tenant's fraction has been determined by arbitration in pursuance of paragraph 10 above,

the arbitrator determining the claim under this paragraph shall, subject to sub-paragraph (7) below, award payment in accordance with that agreement or determination.

(7) Where it appears to the arbitrator that any circumstances relevant to the agreement or determination mentioned in sub-paragraph (6) above were materially different at the time of the termination of the tenancy from those at the time the agreement or determination was made, he shall disregard so much of the agreement or determination as appears to him to be affected by the change in circumstances.

Enforcement

12. Section 85 of the Agricultural Holdings Act 1986 (enforcement) and section 86(1), (3) and (4) of that Act (power of landlord to obtain charge on holding) shall apply to any sum which becomes due to a tenant by virtue of this Schedule as they apply to the sums mentioned in those sections.

Termination of tenancy of part of tenanted land

13. References in this Schedule to the termination of a tenancy of land include references to the resumption of possession of part of the land subject to the tenancy—

(a) by the landlord by virtue of section 31 or 43(2) of the Agricultural Holdings Act 1986 (notice to quit part);

(b) by the landlord in pursuance of a provision in the contract of tenancy; or

(c) by a person entitled to a severed part of the reversionary estate in the land by virtue of a notice to quit that part given to the tenant by virtue of section 140 of the Law of Property Act 1925;

and in the case mentioned in paragraph (c) above this Schedule shall apply as if the person resuming possession were the landlord of the land of which he resumes possession.

Severing of reversionary estate

14.—(1) Where the reversionary estate in the land is for the time being vested in more than one person in several parts, the tenant shall be entitled, on quitting all the land, to require that any amount payable to him under this Schedule shall be determined as if the reversionary estate were not so severed.

(2) Where sub-paragraph (1) above applies, the arbitrator shall, where necessary, apportion the amount awarded between the persons who for the purposes of this Schedule together constitute the landlord of the land, and any additional costs of the award caused by the apportionment shall be paid by those persons in such proportions as the arbitrator may determine.

Powers of limited owners

15. Notwithstanding that a landlord of any land is not the owner in fee simple of the land or, in a case where his interest is an interest in a leasehold, that he is not absolutely entitled to the leasehold, he may for the purposes of this Schedule do anything which he might do if he were such an owner or, as the case may be, were so entitled.

Notices

16.—(1) Any notice under this Schedule shall be duly served on the person on whom it is to be served if it is delivered to him, or left at his proper address, or sent to him by post in a registered letter or by the recorded delivery service.

(2) Any such notice shall be duly served on an incorporated company or body if it is served on the secretary or clerk of the company or body.

(3) Any such notice to be served on a landlord or tenant of any land shall, where an agent or servant is responsible for the control of the management or farming, as the case may be, of the land, be duly served if served on that agent or servant.

(4) For the purposes of this paragraph and of section 7 of the Interpretation Act 1978 (service by post), the proper address of any person on whom any such notice is to be served shall, in the case of the secretary or clerk of an incorporated company or body, be that of the registered or principal office of the company or body, and in any other case be the last known address of the person in question.

(5) Unless or until the tenant of any land has received—

    (*a*) notice that the person who before that time was entitled to receive the rents and profits of the land ("the original landlord") has ceased to be so entitled; and

    (*b*) notice of the name and address of the person who has become entitled to receive the rents and profits,

any notice served on the original landlord by the tenant shall be deemed for the purposes of this Schedule to have been served on the landlord of the land.

Crown land

17.—(1) The provisions of this Schedule shall apply to land which belongs to Her Majesty in right of the Crown or to the Duchy of Lancaster, the Duchy of Cornwall or a Government department or which is held in trust for Her Majesty for the purposes of a Government department, subject in each case to such modifications as the Minister may by regulations prescribe.

(2) For the purposes of this Schedule—

(*a*) as respects land belonging to Her Majesty in right of the Crown, the Crown Estate Commissioners or the proper officer or body having charge of the land for the time being, or, if there is no such officer or body, such person as Her Majesty may appoint in writing under the Royal Sign Manual, shall represent Her Majesty and shall be deemed to be the landlord,

(*b*) as respects land belonging to Her Majesty in right of the Duchy of Lancaster, the Chancellor of the Duchy shall represent Her Majesty and shall be deemed to be the landlord;

(*c*) as respects land belonging to the Duchy of Cornwall, such person as the Duke of Cornwall or the possessor for the time being of the Duchy of Cornwall appoints shall represent the Duchy and shall be deemed to be the landlord and may do any act or thing which a landlord is authorised or required to do under this Act.

(3) Any sum payable under this Schedule by the Duke of Cornwall (or any other possessor for the time being of the Duchy of Cornwall) may be raised and paid as if it were an expense incurred in permanently improving the possessions of the Duchy as mentioned in section 8 of the Duchy of Cornwall Management Act 1863.

(4) Any sum payable under this Schedule by the Chancellor of the Duchy of Lancaster may—

(*a*) be raised and paid as if it were an expense incurred in the improvement of land belonging to Her Majesty in right of the Duchy within section 25 of the Duchy of Lancaster Act 1817; or

(*b*) be paid out of the annual revenues of the Duchy.

(5) The power to make regulations under this paragraph shall be exercisable by statutory instrument and any statutory instrument containing such regulations shall be subject to annulment in pursuance of a resolution of either House of Parliament.

Interpretation

18.—(1) In this Schedule—

"allocated quota" has the meaning given in paragraph 1(1) above;

"holding" has the same meaning as in the 1986 Regulations;

"landlord" means any person for the time being entitled to receive the rents and profits of any land and "sub-landlord" shall be construed accordingly;

"milk quota" means—

(*a*) in the case of a tenant registered in the direct sales register maintained under the 1986 Regulations, a direct sales quota (within the meaning of the 1986 Regulations); and

(*b*) in the case of a tenant registered in the wholesale register maintained under those Regulations, a wholesale quota (within the meaning of those Regulations);

"the Minister" means—

(*a*) in the case of land in England, the Minister of Agriculture, Fisheries and Food; and

(*b*) in the case of land in Wales, the Secretary of State;

"registered", in relation to milk quota, means—

(*a*) in the case of direct sales quota (within the meaning of the 1986 Regulations) registered in the direct sales register maintained under those Regulations; and

(*b*) in the case of a wholesale quota (within the meaning of those Regulations) registered in a wholesale register maintained under those Regulations;

"relevant quota" has the meaning given in paragraph 1(2) above;

"standard quota" has the meaning given in paragraph 6 above;

"the 1986 Regulations" means the Dairy Produce Quotas Regulations 1986;

"tenancy" means a tenancy from year to year (including any arrangement which would have effect as if it were such a tenancy by virtue of section 2 of the Agricultural Holdings Act 1986 if it had not been approved by the Minister) or a tenancy to which section 3 of that Act applies (or would apply apart from section 5 of that Act); and "tenant" and "sub-tenant" shall be construed accordingly;

"tenant's fraction" has the meaning given in paragraph 7 above;

"termination", in relation to a tenancy, means the cesser of the letting of the land in question or the agreement for letting the land, by reason of effluxion of time or from any other cause;

"transferred quota" has the meaning given in paragraph 1(2) above.

(2) In this Schedule references to land used for the feeding of dairy cows kept on the land and to dairy cows have the same meaning as in paragraph 6 above.

(3) The designations of landlord and tenant shall continue to apply to the parties until the conclusion of any proceedings taken under or in pursuance of this Schedule.

Forms and Precedents

Forms and precedents for use in agricultural tenancy matters are divided into two categories. There are prescribed forms and unofficial forms.

The prescribed forms are prescribed by Statutory Instrument. Some of the Statutory Instruments allow for minor variation and others insist upon the forms being reproduced in their entirety including notes without variation of any kind. Failure to comply with this requirement may lead to the notice given in the wrong form being invalid. Any kind of variation to a prescribed form is therefore to be regarded as highly undesirable and only to be made after careful examination of the Statutory Instrument which prescribes the form in question.

At the moment of delivery of this book to the publishers the position with regard to prescribed forms was in a state of flux. The necessary new Statutory Instruments had not all been passed and as a result the correct forms referred to primary legislation which had been repealed by the 1986 Act. For this reason it was decided that the prescribed forms would not be included in this appendix. It is in any case good practice for the draftsman always to have the up to date Statutory Instrument before him when preparing statutory notices. The main matters covered by statutory forms are as follows:

Notice to pay rent due.
Notice to remedy or repair.
Notice to remedy not requiring work.
Application for consent to operation of notice to quit.
Reply to application for consent to operation of notice to quit.
Application to postpone operation of notice to quit.
Reply to application to postpone operation of notice to quit.
Application for certificate of bad husbandry.
Reply to application for certificate of bad husbandry.
Application for direction to provide fixed equipment.
Reply to application for direction to provide fixed equipment.
Application for approval of long term improvement.
Reply to application for long term improvement.
Application for appointment of arbitrator as to variation of rent.
Application for appointment of arbitrator for general purposes.
Application for extension of time for award.
Form of arbitrator's award.

Application for direction giving entitlement to tenancy – succession on death.
Reply to application for direction giving entitlement to tenancy – succession on death.
Application for consent to operation of notice to quit – succession on death.
Reply to application for consent to operation of notice to quit – succession on death.
Notice of application for entitlement to tenancy – succession on death.
Reply to application for direction giving entitlement to tenancy – succession on death.
Application for direction giving entitlement to tenancy – succession on retirement.
Reply to application for direction giving entitlement to tenancy – succession on retirement.
Notice of application for entitlement to tenancy – succession on retirement.
Notice of hearing of application to the Agricultural Law Tribunal.

The precedents which are set out below are for guidance purposes and may be amended to meet the requirements of the individual case. When preparing any of these forms it is again good practice to have the relevant legislation to hand so as to be sure that no essential requirements are omitted.

All forms may be signed either by the party personally or by his duly appointed agent. It should not, however, be assumed that the notice can be served upon the other party's agent unless there is clear evidence of that agent being duly authorised to accept such service.

Any notice signed by an agent should state the fact of the agency and clearly and correctly identify the principal on whose behalf the notice is given.

Form 1: Request to enter into written tenancy agreement

AGRICULTURAL HOLDINGS ACT 1986

To (landlord or tenant) of (address)

Holding known as:

I (landlord or tenant) of (address) request you in accordance with the Agricultural Holdings Act 1986 Section 6(1) to enter into a written agreement embodying all the terms of the tenancy and containing provision for all the matters specified in Schedule 1 to that Act.

(signature of landlord or tenant)

dated ....

Form 2: Request to supplement existing written agreement

AGRICULTURAL HOLDINGS ACT 1986

To (landlord or tenant) of (address)

Holding known as:

I (landlord or tenant) of (address) request you in accordance with Section 6(1) of the Agricultural Holdings Act 1986 to enter into an agreement supplemental to the tenancy agreement made the   day of   relating to the above holding and which contains no provision for matters specified in the Agricultural Holdings Act 1986 Schedule 1 and set out below to make provision for such matters (list of relevant matters).

(signature of landlord or tenant)

dated ....

Form 3: Request to vary terms of existing agreement to comply with maintenance repair and insurance of fixed equipment regulations

AGRICULTURAL HOLDINGS ACT 1986

To (landlord or tenant) of (address)

Holding known as:

I (landlord or tenant) of (address) request you to vary the tenancy agreement relating to the above holding dated   so that it complies with the provisions of the Agriculture (Maintenance, Repair and Insurance of Fixed Equipment) Regulations 1973/1473.

(signature of landlord or tenant)

dated ....

Form 4: Reference to arbitration on failure to enter into written agreement

AGRICULTURAL HOLDINGS ACT 1986

To (landlord or tenant) of (address)

Holding known as:

I (tenant or landlord) of (address) give you notice under Section 6 of the

Agricultural Holdings Act 1986 that following my request to you dated the
day of   to enter into written agreement embodying all the
terms of the tenancy between us in accordance with Schedule 1 of that Act no
agreement has been concluded and I require that the terms of the tenancy shall
be referred to arbitration under that Act.

(signature of landlord or tenant)

dated ....

Form 5: Reference to arbitration on failure to agree variation of existing agreement in compliance with maintenance repair and insurance of fixed equipment prescribed regulations

AGRICULTURAL HOLDINGS ACT 1986

To (landlord or tenant) of (address)

Holding known as:

I (landlord or tenant) of (address) hereby give you notice under the Agricultural
Holdings Act 1986 Sections 8(1) and 8(2) that I refer to arbitration under that Act
the terms of the tenancy between us relating to the above holding and dated the
day of   with respect to the maintenance repair and insurance
of fixed equipment no agreement having been reached following my request to
you dated the   day of   to so vary the said tenancy agreement
so as to comply with the regulations prescribed by Section 7 of the said Act
relating to Maintenance Repair and Insurance of Fixed Equipment.

(signature of landlord or tenant)

dated ....

Form 6: Requirement by tenant for arbitration of claim against landlord on transfer of liability for maintenance or repair of fixed equipment

AGRICULTURAL HOLDINGS ACT 1986

To (landlord) of (address)

Holding known as:

Pursuant to the transfer of liability for the maintenance repair and insurance of
the items of fixed equipment mentioned in the schedule below being made by
award of (arbitrator) the   day of   with effect from the

day of   (tenant) of (address) pursuant to Section 8 of the Agricultural Holdings Act 1986, I hereby require that my claim in respect of your previous failure to discharge such liability is referred to and determined by arbitration under that Act.

SCHEDULE

(items in respect of which liability is transferred)

(signature of tenant)

dated ....

Note: Time limit for reference to arbitration is one month from the day of the transfer of liability.

Form 7: Request by tenant for provision repair or alteration of fixed equipment

AGRICULTURAL HOLDINGS ACT 1986

To landlord of (address)

Holding known as:

Pursuant to the Provisions of the Agricultural Holdings Act 1986 s.11 I (tenant) of (address) HEREBY REQUEST you to carry out the provision repair or alteration of fixed equipment as set out in the schedule hereunder.

SCHEDULE

(details of work required)

(signature of tenant)

dated ....

Form 8: Notice by landlord requesting and specifying repairs to be effected

AGRICULTURAL HOLDINGS ACT 1986

Agriculture (Maintenance, Repair and Insurance of Fixed Equipment) Regulations 1973/1473

To tenant of (address)

Holding known as:

TAKE NOTICE that I (landlord) of (address) HEREBY REQUEST you pursuant to the above regulations to execute the repairs for which you are liable as specified in those regulations and set out in the schedule below and FURTHER TAKE NOTICE that I hereby call upon you to execute such repairs and if you shall fail to carry out such repairs or any of them within a period of one month from the date of service of this notice I shall exercise my right under the above regulations to enter and execute such repairs and recover the reasonable costs thereof from you immediately.

SCHEDULE

(items to be repaired)   (repair required)

Signed ....   Dated ....
     (landlord)

Form 9: Counter-notice by tenant requiring arbitration of question of liability to execute repairs

AGRICULTURAL HOLDINGS ACT 1986

Agriculture (Maintenance, Repair and Insurance of Fixed Equipment) Regulations 1973/1473

To landlord of (address)

Holding known as:

I have received from you notice dated the   day of   specifying repairs or replacements and calling on me to execute certain repairs and replacements within one month.

TAKE NOTICE that I (tenant) of (address) wish to contest my liability to execute such of those items of repair or replacement as are set out in the schedule upon the grounds therein set out and stated and TAKE NOTICE FURTHER that I wish and require the question of my liability to execute such items of repair or replacement to be determined by arbitration under the above Act.

SCHEDULE

(items of repair or replacement in   (grounds for denial of liability)
respect of which liability is denied)

Signed ....   Dated ....
     (tenant)

Note: This counter-notice must be served within one month of receipt by the tenant of the landlord's notice.

Form 10: Notice by tenant to landlord of intention to remove fixtures or buildings

AGRICULTURAL HOLDINGS ACT 1986

To (landlord) of (address)

Holding known as:

I (tenant) of (address) give you notice under the Agricultural Holdings Act 1986 Section 10 that I intend to exercise my rights under that Section to remove the [fixture[s]] [and] [building[s]] specified in the schedule below.

SCHEDULE

(fixtures and/or buildings specified which tenant intends to remove)

Signed ....
      (tenant)

Dated ....

Note: See S.10.3(b) Agricultural Holdings Act 1986 as to time limit.

Form 11: Counter-notice by landlord electing to purchase fixtures and buildings comprised in tenant's notice

AGRICULTURAL HOLDINGS ACT 1986

To (tenant) of (address)

Holding known as:

With reference to your notice to me dated the   day of   under the Agricultural Holdings Act 1986 Section 10 of your intention to remove the [fixture[s]] [and] [building[s]] specified in your notice, I (landlord) of (address) give you counter-notice under Section 10(4) of that Act that I elect to purchase at the fair value to an incoming tenant the [fixture[s]] [and] [building[s]] specified in your notice and described in the schedule below.

SCHEDULE

(fixtures and/of buildings specified in tenant's notice which landlord intents to purchase)

Signed ....
      (landlord)

Dated ....

Note: See S.10(4) Agricultural Holdings Act 1986 as to time limit.

Form 12: Demand for arbitration as to variation of terms of tenancy relating to permanent pasture

AGRICULTURAL HOLDINGS ACT 1986

To (landlord or tenant) of (address)

Holding known as:

Under the contract for tenancy in respect of the above holding between us made the   day of   provision is made for the maintenance of [specified land] as permanent pasture.

NOW I (landlord or tenant) of (address) give you notice under the Agricultural Holdings Act 1986 Section 14(2) that I demand a reference to arbitration under that Act of the question whether it is expedient in order to secure the full and efficient farming of the above holding that the above mentioned area of land required to be maintained as permanent pasture should be reduced.

Signed ....
             (landlord or tenant)

Dated ....

Form 13: Agreement that specified fixed equipment is obsolete or redundant

AGRICULTURAL HOLDINGS ACT 1986

Agriculture (Maintenance, Repairs and Insurance of Fixed Equipment) Regulations 1973/1473

Holding known as:

WE (landlord) of (address) and (tenant) of (address) landlord and tenant respectively of the above holding agree that the item[s] of fixed equipment specified in the schedule below [is or are] [obsolete or redundant] and that neither of us shall be liable to maintain repair or insure [it or them].

SCHEDULE

(fixed equipment considered to be obsolete or redundant)

(signature of landlord and tenant)

dated ....

Form 14: Demand by landlord or tenant for arbitration of rent payable

AGRICULTURAL HOLDINGS ACT 1986

To (landlord or tenant) of (address)

Holding known as:

TAKE NOTICE that pursuant to the Agricultural Holdings Act 1986 Section 12 I (landlord or tenant) of (address) demand that the rent to be payable in respect of the above holding as from the next termination date as defined in the Act shall be referred to arbitration. This notice is given without prejudice to any other notice or notices act or acts given or done or to be given or done in connection with the holding by me or on behalf of me or any other interested party.

Signed ....
          (landlord or tenant)

Dated ....

Form 15: Appointment of arbitrator by agreement for purpose of determining rent

AGRICULTURAL HOLDINGS ACT 1986

Holding known as:

I (landlord's name and address) landlord of the above holding and I (tenant's name and address) tenant of the above holding HEREBY APPOINT of   as sole arbitrator under the Agricultural Holdings Act 1986 to determine in accordance with the provisions of the said Act the rent to be paid for the above holding as from the next ensuing date at which the tenancy could have been determined by notice to quit duly given.

AS WITNESS our hands this   day of

Signed ....
          (Landlord)

          ....
          (Tenant)

Note: Form of application for appointment of arbitrator as to variation of rent where no appointment has been agreed is obtainable from Royal Institution of Chartered Surveyors – to whom the application must be made within the time limits prescribed.

Form 16: Memorandum for endorsement on tenancy agreement to provide for increase in rent when agreed between parties

MEMORANDUM

Holding known as:

In consideration of (landlord) undertaking not to refer to arbitration the question of rent payable for the above holding (tenant) hereby agrees:

(a) The rent payable in respect of the above holding shall as from the day of   be £   (pounds) which shall be payable in the same way as the existing rent of the said holding.

(b) In consideration of the said agreement all the terms and conditions of the within written tenancy agreement varied as above shall remain in full force and effect and the proviso for re-entry contained in the within written tenancy agreement shall be exercisable in respect of the above-mentioned rent or any part of it.

AS WITNESS our hands this   day of

Signed ....
     (Landlord)

     ....
     (Tenant)

Form 17: Notice requiring increase in rent following carrying out of improvements

AGRICULTURAL HOLDINGS ACT 1986

To (tenant) of (address)

Holding known as:

TAKE NOTICE that I (landlord) of (address) require under the Agricultural Holdings Act 1986 Section 13 that the rent of the above holding shall be increased from the   day of   being the date of completion of the improvement[s] specified in the schedule below by an amount equal to the increase in the rental value of the above holding attributable to the carrying out of the improvement[s] namely the sum of £   (pounds) per year.

SCHEDULE

(short description of improvement(s) and date when each was completed)

Signed ....
     (landlord)

Form 18: Memorandum for endorsement on tenancy agreement of increase in rent in respect of improvements under the Agricultural Holdings Act 1986 Section 13 when agreed between parties

MEMORANDUM

Holding known as:

In consideration of [landlord name] having carried out in agreement with [tenant name] on the above holding the improvement[s] specified in the schedule below it has been agreed between them that:

1. The rent payable in respect of the above holding shall with effect from the   day of   be increased to £   (pounds) per year.
2. This increase of rent shall operate by virtue of the Agricultural Holdings Act 1986 Section 13.
3. The proviso for re-entry contained in the within-written tenancy agreement shall be exercisable in respect of non-payment of the increased rent or any part of it.
4. All the terms and conditions of the within-written tenancy agreement varied as above shall remain in full force and effect.

AS WITNESS our hands the   day of

SCHEDULE

(improvement(s) carried out by landlord)

Signed ....
        (landlord)

Signed ....
        (tenant)

Form 19: Notice to quit given by landlord no reason stated

To (tenant) of

Holding known as:

I (landlord) of   HEREBY GIVE YOU NOTICE to quit and deliver up possession of the holding and premises above described which you hold of me at the expiration of the year of the tenancy which shall expire after the end of twelve months from the date of the service of this notice.

Signed ....
        (landlord)

Dated ....

Form 20: Notice to quit by tenant

AGRICULTURAL HOLDINGS ACT 1986

To (landlord) of (address)

Holding known as:

I (name of tenant) of (address) HEREBY GIVE notice of my intention to quit and deliver up possession of the above named holding and premises which I hold as tenant from you on the expiration of the year of the tenancy which shall expire next after the end of twelve months from the date of service of this notice.

Signed ....
      (tenant)

Dated ....

Form 21: Notice to quit by landlord of part of holding pursuant to provision in tenancy agreement

AGRICULTURAL HOLDINGS ACT 1986

To (tenant) of (address)

Holding known as:

I (landlord) of (address) requiring the premises known as (description) which you hold of me as tenant being part of the above holding for the purpose of the non-agricultural use of   pursuant to Clause   of our contract of tenancy relating to the said holding hereby give you notice to quit and deliver up possession of the premises described above forming part of the above named holding on the   day of

Signed ....
      (Landlord)

Dated ....

Note: See Agricultural Holdings Act 1986 25 (2)(b).

Form 22: Notice to quit given by tenant to sub tenant

AGRICULTURAL HOLDINGS ACT 1986

To (sub tenant) of (address)

Holding known as:

I (tenant) of (address) hereby give you notice to quit and deliver up possession of the holding above described which you hold of me as tenant on the   day of   and I further give you notice that I have been given notice to quit the above holding and premises by my superior landlord from whom I hold as tenant requiring me to give up possession of the above-mentioned holding.

Signed ....
            (Tenant)

Dated ....

Note: See Agricultural Holdings Act 1986 S.25 (2)(c).

Form 23

AGRICULTURAL HOLDINGS ACT 1986
SCHEDULE 3

Notice to Quit (Whole) in Case A, B, C, E, F or G

To: (tenant)

of (address)

Holding known as:

I,   (landlord)

of   (address)

hereby give you notice to quit and deliver up possession of the holding situated at   in the County of   and known as   which you hold of me as tenant, on the   day of   19   . And I have to state that (1)

(1) Set out, in accordance with any of the Cases A, B, C, E, F or G in Schedule 3 to the Agricultural Holdings Act 1986, the circumstance which renders the consent of the Agricultural Land Tribunal unnecessary.

AS WITNESS my hand this   day of   19

(Signed) (landlord)

Form 24: Notice to quit given to personal representatives of a deceased tenant

AGRICULTURAL HOLDINGS ACT 1986

To (personal representatives) of (address)

Holding known as:

I (landlord) of (address) hereby give you notice to quit and deliver up possession of the holding and premises above described which were held of me by the late (tenant) as tenant until his death on the   day of   and are now held by you as personal representatives of the deceased tenant at the expiration of the year of the tenancy which shall expire next after the end of twelve months from the date of service of this notice.

This notice is hereby given pursuant to the provisions of the Agricultural Holdings Act 1986 Schedule 3 Part 1 Case G following and by reason of the death of the person who immediately before his death was the sole tenant under the contract of tenancy relating to the holding and is given within the period specified in Case G of Schedule 3 Part 1 Agricultural Holdings Act 1986.

Signed ....
          (Landlord)

Dated ....

Form 25: Counter-notice by tenant

AGRICULTURAL HOLDINGS ACT 1986
Section 26 (1)

To (landlord) of (address)

Holding known as:

Pursuant to the Agricultural Holdings Act 1986 I (tenant) of (address) give you notice that I require that Section 26 (1) of the Agricultural Holdings Act 1986 shall apply to your notice to quit in respect of the above holding served on me and dated the   day of

No admission is hereby made as to the validity of your notice to quit and this notice is given without prejudice to any matters relating to that notice.

Signed ....
          (Tenant)

Dated ....

Note: This must be served not later than one month from the giving of the Landlord's notice Agricultural Holdings Act 1986 S.26 (1) (b).

This is not the correct form if the Landlord's notice was given under the cases set out in Schedule 3 Part I.

Form 26: Counter-notice by tenant following notice to quit given under Agricultural Holdings Act 1986 Schedule 3 Part 1 Case D (failure to comply with a notice to do work)

To (landlord) of (address)

Holding known as:

I (tenant) of (address) hereby give you notice pursuant to the Agricultural Holdings Act 1986 Section 28 that I require that Section 28 (2) of the Agricultural Holdings Act 1986 shall apply to the notice to quit the above holding served on me and dated the   day of   and I hereby give you this notice without any admission on my part as to the validity of your notice to quit and this notice is given without prejudice to any points which may arise in relation to

Signed ....
        (Tenant)

Dated ....

Note: This counter notice is to be served not later than one month from the giving of the notice to quit unless within such period the tenant serves on the landlord an effective notice requiring the validity of the reason stated in the landlord's notice to be determined by arbitration under the Agricultural Holdings Act 1986. In this case the counter notice has to be served not later than one month from the date on which the arbitrators award is delivered to the tenant.

Form 27: Notice by tenant requiring arbitration (Cases A, B, D or E)

AGRICULTURAL HOLDINGS ACT 1986

To (landlord) of (address)

Holding known as:

I (tenant) of (address) hereby give you notice that I wish to contest certain matters arising out of the reasons stated in the notice to quit the above holding dated the   day of   served on me by you and that I require all questions so arising to be determined by arbitration under the Agricultural

Holdings Act 1986 and I give this notice without any admission as to the validity of the said notice and without prejudice to any matters arising in relation thereto.

Signed ....

      (Tenant)

Dated ....

Form 28: Retirement notice

AGRICULTURAL HOLDINGS ACT 1986
Section 49

To (landlord) of (address)

Holding known as:

I hereby give notice that I (tenant) of (address) being the tenant of the above holding hereby nominate (successor) of (address) to succeed me to the tenancy of this holding on the next day on which the said tenancy could have been determined by notice to quit given on the date of this notice and which falls not less than one year and not more than two years after the date of this notice under the provisions of the Agricultural Holdings Act 1986 (Section 49 (1)(b).

Signed ....

      (Tenant)

Dated ....

Form 29: Notice by tenant to claim compensation for disturbance

AGRICULTURAL HOLDINGS ACT 1986

To (landlord) of (address)

Holding known as:

I (tenant) of (address) give you notice that on quitting the above holding pursuant to your notice to quit served on me and dated the   day of   I intend to claim under Section 60 of the Agricultural Holdings Act 1986 a greater amount than one year's rent of the above holding as compensation for disturbance.

Pursuant to Section 60 (6)(b) of the Agricultural Holdings Act 1986 reasonable opportunity will be given to you of making a valuation of my household goods implements of husbandry fixtures farm produce or farm stock on or used in connection with the holding.

Signed ....
          (Tenant)

Dated ....

Note: This notice must be given not less than one month before the termination of the tenancy. See also Agricultural Holdings Act 1986 S.83 (2) & (3).

Form 30: Notice by landlord or tenant of intention to claim – miscellaneous

AGRICULTURAL HOLDINGS ACT 1986

To (landlord or tenant) of (address)

Holding known as:

I (tenant or landlord) of (address) hereby give notice pursuant to Agricultural Holdings Act 1986 Section 83 (2) of my intention to make against you claims arising out of the termination of the tenancy of the above holding as specified in the schedule below.

SCHEDULE

Brief Specification of Claims

Signed ....
          (Landlord or Tenant)

Dated ....

Note: To be served on other party within two months following Termination.
    This precedent may be used in connection with a milk quota compensation claim – see Agriculture Act 1986 Schedule I para 11 (1).

Form 31: Demand for arbitration of standard milk quota or tenants fraction

AGRICULTURE ACT 1986 Sch 1 para 10

AGRICULTURAL HOLDINGS ACT 1986 S.84

To (Landlord or tenant) of (address)

Holding known as:

I (tenant or landlord) of (address) hereby give notice to you (landlord or tenant) of my demand that the question of [the Standard Quota for the above Holding] or [the Tenants Fraction] for the above holding shall be referred to arbitration pursuant to Section 84 of the Agricultural Holdings Act 1986.

Signed ....
          (Landlord or Tenant)

Dated ....

Note: The Agriculture Act prescribes that the question of Standard Quota *OR* Tenants Fraction may be determined by Arbitration. Whilst it is hard to see any logic as to why these should be in the alternative it may be safer, if both matters are to be arbitrated, to serve separate notices for each matter and then amalgamate the arbitrations by agreement.

Form 32: Application by tenant for consent to long term improvements

AGRICULTURAL HOLDINGS ACT 1986

To (landlord) of (address)

Holding known as:

I (tenant) of (address) hereby give notice of my wish to carry out on the above holding the improvements detailed below. Being improvements specified in the Agricultural Holdings Act 1986 Schedule 7 and pursuant to Section 67 of the said Act I request you to give your written consent to the carrying out of these improvements unconditionally or on such terms as to compensation or otherwise as may be agreed in writing between us.

Signed ....
          (Tenant)

Dated ....

Form 33: Consent by landlord to long term improvements

AGRICULTURAL HOLDINGS ACT 1986

To (tenant) of (address)

Holding known as:

Pursuant to the Agricultural Holdings Act 1986 Section 67 (1) I (landlord) of (address) hereby consent to the carrying out by you on the above holding of the improvements specified in the schedule below being improvements in respect of

which you requested my written consent by notice dated the   day of
. The terms relating to such consent are specified below.

Details of Works   Details of terms

Signed ....
      (Landlord)

Dated ....

Form 34: Notice by tenant of intention to claim compensation for 'high farming'

AGRICULTURAL HOLDINGS ACT 1986

To (landlord) of (address)

Holding known as:

I (tenant) of (address) give you notice that I intend on quitting the above holding on the termination of my tenancy to claim compensation under the Agricultural Holdings Act 1986 Section 70 (1) for the continuous adoption of a special system of farming as mentioned in Section 70 (1) of that Act.

Signed ....
      (Tenant)

Dated ....

Note: This notice must be given not later than one month before the termination of the tenancy. See also S.70 (2)(b).

Form 35: Notice by landlord of intention to claim compensation for general deterioration of the holding

AGRICULTURAL HOLDINGS ACT 1986

To (tenant) of (address)

Holding known as:

I (landlord) of (address) hereby give you notice that, in respect of the holding above described which you hold of me on a tenancy which will determine on the   day of   19   , I intend to claim compensation under section

72 of the Agricultural Holdings Act 1986 (that is to say), compensation for general deterioration of the holding caused by the non-fulfilment of your responsibilities to farm in accordance with the rules of good husbandry.

Signed ....
           (Landlord)

Dated ....

Note: This must be given no later than one month before the termination of the tenancy.

Agricultural land tribunals

Area		Address
Counties	*Districts*	
Northern		
Cumbria	Richmondshire	Government
Northumberland	Hambleton	Buildings,
Tyne and Wear	Ryedale	Kenton Bar,
Durham	Scarborough	Newcastle-on-Tyne,
Cleveland	(*all in North Yorkshire*)	NE1 2YA
Yorkshire and Lancashire		
Lancashire	Craven	Block 2,
Merseyside	Harrogate	Government
Greater Manchester	York	Buildings,
West Yorkshire	Selby	Lawnswood,
South Yorkshire	(*all in North*	Leeds,
Humberside	*Yorkshire*)	LS16 5PY
East Midland		
Derbyshire		Block 2,
Nottinghamshire		Government
Leicestershire		Buildings,
Northamptonshire		Chalfont Drive,
Lincolnshire		Nottingham
		NG8 3RL
West Midland		
Cheshire		Woodthorne,
Staffordshire		Wolverhampton,
Salop		Staffs,
West Midlands		WV6 8TQ
Warwickshire		
Hereford and Worcester		

South Western
  Cornwall   Quantock House,
  Devon   Paul Street,
  Somerset   Taunton,
  Avon   Somerset
  Gloucestershire   TA1 3NX
  Wiltshire
  Dorset
  Isle of Scilly

South Eastern
  Oxfordshire   London boroughs   Block A,
  Buckinghamshire   south of the   Government Offices,
  Berkshire   river Thames   Coley Park,
  Surrey   including   Reading,
  Kent   Richmond-upon-   RG1 6DT
  East Sussex   Thames
  West Sussex
  Hampshire
  Isle of Wight

Eastern
  Bedfordshire   London boroughs   Block C,
  Cambridgeshire   north of the   Government
  Norfolk   river Thames   Buildings,
  Suffolk   except   Brooklands Avenue,
  Essex   Richmond-upon-   Cambridge,
  Hertfordshire   Thames   CB2 2DR

Welsh
  Dyfed   Plas Crug,
  Gwynedd   Aberystwyth,
  Clwyd   Dyfed,
  Powys   SY23 1NG
  Gwent
  South Glamorgan
  Mid Glamorgan
  West Glamorgan

The exception of Boston and South Holland was excluded by SI 1976 No.
208.

Tied Cottages Statutes

Regaining possession: Rent (Agriculture) Act 1976, Schedule 4 Part 1

Case I

Alternative accommodation not provided or arranged by housing authority.

1. The court is satisfied that suitable alternative accommodation is available for the tenant, or will be available for him when the order for possession takes effect.
2. (1) Accommodation shall be deemed suitable in this Case if it consists of –

   (a) premises which are to be let as a separate dwelling such that they will then be let on a protected tenancy within the meaning of [the Rent Act 1977], or
   (b) premises which are to be let as a separate dwelling on terms which will, in the opinion of the court, afford to the tenant security of tenure reasonably equivalent to the security afforded by [Part VII of the Rent Act 1977] in the case of a protected tenancy,

   and, in the opinion of the court, the accommodation fulfils the conditions in paragraph 3 below.
   [(2) For the purposes of sub-paragraph (a)(b) the terms of a tenancy shall not be treated as affording the required security by reason only of the fact that the tenancy is an assured tenancy within the meaning of section 56 of the Housing Act 1980.]
3. (1) The accommodation must be reasonably suitable to the needs of the tenant and his family as regards proximity to place of work and either –

   (a) similar as regards rental and extent to the accommodation afforded by dwelling-houses provided in the neighbourhood by the housing authority concerned for persons whose needs as regards extent are similar to those of the tenant and his family, or
   (b) reasonably suitable to the means of the tenant, and to the needs of the tenant and his family as regards extent and character.

   (2) For the purposes of sub-paragraph (1)(a) above, a certificate of the housing authority concerned stating –

    (a) the extent of the accommodation afforded by dwelling-houses provided by the authority to meet the needs of tenants with families of such number as may be specified in the certificate, and

    (b) the amount of the rent charged by the housing authority concerned for dwelling-houses affording accommodation of that extent,

shall be conclusive evidence of the facts so stated.

  (3) If any furniture was provided by the landlord for use under the tenancy, furniture must be provided for use in the alternative accommodation which is either similar, or is reasonably suitable to the needs of the tenant and his family.

4. Accommodation shall not be deemed to be suitable to the needs of the tenant and his family if the result of their occupation of the accommodation would be that it would be an overcrowded dwelling-house for the purposes of [Part X of the Housing Act 1985].

5. Any document purporting to be a certificate of the housing authority concerned issued for the purposes of this Case and to be signed by the proper officer of the authority shall be received in evidence and, unless the contrary is shown, shall be deemed to be such a certificate without further proof.

6. In this Case no account shall be taken of accommodation as respects which an offer has been made, or notice has been given, as mentioned in paragraph 1 of Case II below.

Case II

Alternative accommodation provided or arranged by housing authority.

1. The housing authority concerned have made an offer in writing to the tenant of alternative accommodation which appears to them to be suitable, specifying the date when the accommodation will be available and the date (not being less than 14 days from the date of offer) by which the offer must be accepted.

or

The housing authority concerned have given notice in writing to the tenant that they have received from a person specified in the notice an offer in writing to rehouse the tenant in alternative accommodation which appears to the housing authority concerned to be suitable, and the notice specifies both the date when the accommodation will be available and the date (not being less than 14 days from the date when the notice was given to the tenant) by which the offer must be accepted.

2. The landlord shows that the tenant accepted the offer (by the housing authority or other person) within the time duly specified in the offer.

or

The landlord shows that the tenant did not so accept the offer, and the tenant does not satisfy the court that he acted reasonably in failing to accept the offer.

3. (1) The accommodation offered must in the opinion of the court fulfil the conditions in this paragraph.

    (2) The accommodation must be reasonably suitable to the needs of the tenant and his family as regards proximity to place of work.

(3) The accommodation must be reasonably suitable to the means of the tenant, and to the needs of the tenant and his family as regards extent.
4. If the accommodation is available for a limited period only, the housing authority's offer or notice under paragraph 1 above must contain an assurance that other accommodation –

    (a) the availability of which is not so limited,
    (b) which appears to them to be suitable, and
    (c) which fulfils the conditions in paragraph 3 above, will be offered to the tenant as soon as practicable.

Case III

Rent lawfully due from the tenant has not been paid, *or*
any other lawful obligation of the tenancy, whether or not it is an obligation created by this Act, has been broken or not performed.

Case IV

The tenant, or any person residing or lodging with him or subtenant of his, has been guilty of conduct which is a nuisance or annoyance to adjoining occupiers, or has been convicted of using the dwelling-house, or allowing the dwelling-house to be used, for immoral or illegal purposes.

Case V

1. The condition of the dwelling-house has, in the opinion of the court, deteriorated owing to acts of waste by, or the neglect or default of, the tenant or any person residing or lodging with him, or any sub-tenant of his.
2. If the person at fault is not the tenant, the court must be satisfied that the tenant has not, before the making of the order for possession, taken such steps as he ought reasonably to have taken for the removal of the person at fault.

Case VI

1. The condition of any furniture provided by the landlord for use under the tenancy has, in the opinion of the court, deteriorated owing to ill-treatment by the tenant or any person residing or lodging with him, or any sub-tenant of his.
2. If the person at fault is not the tenant, the court must be satisfied that the tenant has not, before the making of the order for possession, taken such steps as he ought reasonably to have taken for the removal of the person at fault.

Case VII

1. The tenant has given notice to quit and in consequence of that notice the

landlord has contracted to sell or let the dwelling-house, or has taken any other steps as a result of which he would, in the opinion of the court, be seriously prejudiced if he could not obtain possession.

2. This Case does not apply where the tenant has given notice to terminate his employment and that notice has operated to terminate the tenancy.

Case VIII

1. The tenant has, without the consent of the landlord, assigned, sub-let or parted with possession of the dwelling-house, or any part of it.
2. This case does not apply if the assignment, sub-letting or parting with possession was effected before the operative date.

Case IX

1. The dwelling-house is reasonably required by the landlord for occupation as a residence for –

    (a) himself, or
    (b) any son or daughter of his over 18 years of age, or
    (c) his father or mother, or the father or mother of his wife, or husband, or
    (d) his grandfather or grandmother, or the grandfather or grandmother of his wife, or husband,

   and the landlord did not become landlord by purchasing the dwelling-house, or any interest in it, after 12th April 1976.
2. The court, having regard to all the circumstances of the case, including the question whether other accommodation is available for the landlord or tenant, is satisfied that no greater hardship would be caused by granting the order than by refusing to grant it.

Case X

1. Any part of the dwelling-house is sublet.
2. The court is satisfied that the rent charged by the tenant is or was in excess of the maximum rent recoverable for that part, having regard to the provisions of [... part III or Part V of the Rent Act 1977] or Part II of this Act, as the case may require.
3. Paragraph 2 does not apply to a rental period beginning before the operative date.

Phasing of rent increases: Rent (Agriculture) Act 1976, Schedule 6

Interpretation
1. (1) In this Schedule –

'noted amount' means an amount noted under paragraph 2(1) below:
'period of delay' [means –

(a) if the registered rent has been confirmed by a rent assessment committee, a period beginning with the date from which the registration of the rent took effect and ending one year after the date on which the committee took their decision; and

(b) in any other case, a period of one year beginning with the date from which the registration took effect.]

'permitted increase' means the amount by which the rent for any rental period may be increased;

'previous rent limit' means, subject to sub-paragraph (2) below, the amount which [immediately before the relevant date] was recoverable by way of rent or would have been so recoverable upon service of a notice or notices of increase under section 14 of this Act;

['relevant date' means, in relation to a registered rent –

[(a) if the rent was determined by the rent officer (and whether or not it was confirmed by a rent assessment committee), the date on which the rent was registered by the rent officer; and

(b) if the rent was determined by a rent assessment committee, the date on which the rent officer registered the rent determined by him or, as the case may be, noted in the register his confirmation of the rent for the time being registered];

'service element' means any amount calculated under paragraph 2 below;

'services' means services provided by the landlord or a superior landlord; . . .

(2), (3) . . .

Service element

2. (1) Where –

(a) the registered rent includes a payment in respect of services, and

(b) the rent is not registered as a variable rent in accordance with [section 71 (4) of the Rent Act 1977] as applied by section 13 of this Act, but

(c) not less than 5 per cent of the amount of the registered rent is in the opinion of the rent officer or rent assessment committee fairly attributable to the services,

the amount so attributable shall be noted in the register.

(2) In the cases mentioned in the first column of the Table below, the amount of the service element shall be calculated as specified in the second column.

Table: Calculation of service element

Case	Service element
Case A. A specified amount or proportion was in the previous rent limit attributable to the provision of services, and came to less than the noted amount.	The service element is the difference between the amount or proportion and the noted amount.
Case B. No amount or proportion attributable to the provision of services is specified, but an amount less than the noted amount appears to the rent officer or rent assessment committee to have been attributable to such provision.	The service element is the difference between – (a) an amount bearing to the previous rent limit the same proportion as the noted amount bears to the registered rent, and (b) the noted amount.
Case C. No amount appears to the rent officer or rent assessment committee to have been attributable in the previous rent limit to the provision of services.	The service element is the noted amount.

(3) The amount of the service element shall be recorded in the register, and in Case C above may be recorded by adding to the note under sub-paragraph (1) above a statement that the noted amount is the service element.

General formulae for calculating increases in rent

[3. (1) Subject to sub-paragraph (2) below, the permitted increase for a period falling within the period of delay is an increase to an amount calculated by applying the formula –

$$\tfrac{1}{2}\,(P + S + R)$$

where –

P is the previous rent limit,
S is the service element, and
R is the registered rent.
(2) The maximum permitted increase by virtue of this Schedule is an increase to the registered rent.]

Subsequent registrations

[4. Where the registration of a rent takes effect in a period of delay which began by reference to an earlier registration, then –

   (a) from the date on which the later registration takes effect the limitation under that period of delay shall cease to apply; and

   (b) a fresh period of delay shall begin by reference to the later registration.]

General

5. The amount of any service element or of any amount sought to be noted in the register in pursuance of this Schedule shall be included among the matters with respect to which representations may be made or consultations are to be held or notices given under Part I of [Schedule 11 to the Rent Act 1977] as applied by section 13 of this Act.

6. In ascertaining for the purposes of this Schedule whether there is any difference between amounts, or what that difference is, such adjustments shall be made as may be necessary to take account of periods of different lengths; and for that purpose a month shall be treated as one-twelfth and a week as one-fifty-second of a year.

Table of Cases

Adams *v.* Harris (1982) Wales Area ALT (unrep.) 10.15

Addis *v.* Burrows [1948] 1 KB 444, [1948] 1 All ER 177, [1948] LJR 1033, 64
TLR 169, 92 SJ 124, CA 6.08

Ahearn *v.* Bellman (1879) 4 Ex D 201, 48 LJQB 681, 40 LT 771, 43 JP 621,
27 WR 928, CA 6.05

Allam & Co. Ltd *v.* Europa Poster Services [1968] 1 WLR 638 [1968] 1 All
ER 826; 112 SJ 86 .... 6.08

Ashby *v.* Holliday (1983) Yorks and Lancs ALT (unrep.) 10.04

Auworth *v.* Johnson (1832) 5 C & P 239 .... 4.03

Bahamas International Trust Co. Ltd *v.* Threadgold [1974] 3 All ER 881,
[1974] 1 WLR 1514, 118 SJ 832, HL 2.08, 3.09

Bailey *v.* Purser [1967] 2 QB 500, [1967] 2 WLR 1500, 111 SJ 353, sub nom
Bailey *v.* Purser [1967] 2 All ER 189, 202 Estates Gazette 23, CA 7.14

Barker *v.* Lampard (1986) Eastern Area ALT (unrep.) 7.16

Bathurst (Earl) *v.* Fine [1974] 2 All ER 1160, [1974] 1 WLR 905, 118, SJ 464,
28 P & CR 268, 231 Estates Gazette 1031, CA 9.06

Bebington's Tenancy, Re, Bebington *v.* Wildman [1921] 1 Ch 559, 90 LJ Ch
269, 124 LT 661, 37 TLR 409 65 SJ 343 .... 6.13

Bedfordshire County Council *v.* Clarke (1974) 230 Estates Gazette
1587 .... 3.03, 3.04

Beevers *v.* Mason (1978) 37 P & CR 452; (1978) 122 SJ 610; (1978) 248 EG
781, CA 8.10

Belmont Farm Ltd *v.* Minister of Housing and Local Government (1962) 106
SJ 469, 60 LGR 319, 13 P & CR 417, DC 1.03

Bernays *v.* Prosser [1963] 2 QB 592, [1963] 2 All ER 321, [1963] 2 WLR
1255, 107 SJ 271, CA 2.08, 3.03

Berridge *v.* Fitzroy and ors (1980) West Midland Area ALT (unrep.) 10.04

Bickerdike *v.* Lucy [1920] 1 KB 707 .... 1.03, 12.24

Biss, Re, Biss *v.* Biss [1903] 2 Ch 40, [1900–3] All ER 406, 72 LJ Ch 473, 88
LT 403, 51 WR 504, 47 SJ 383, CA 7.04

Blackmore *v.* Butler [1954] 2 QB 171, [1954] 2 All ER 403, [1954] 3 WLR 62,
98 SJ 405, 52 LGR 345, CA 1.02, *1.04*, 1.10, *2.02*

Blewett *v.* Blewett [1936] 2 All ER 188, CA 9.06

Broadwith *v.* Parkinson Trustees (1984) Yorks & Lancs Area ALT (unrep.)
.... 10.15

Brooks *v.* Brown (1985) (unrep.) CA 3.10, *10.10*

Brooks *v.* Magdalen College (1982) South Eastern Area ALT (unrep.)   10.14

Budge *v.* Hicks [1951] 2 KB 335, [1951] 2 All ER 245, [1951] 2 TLR 349, 95
SJ 501, CA 6.01, 6.05, 8.03, 8.12

Burden *v.* Hannaford [1956] 1 QB 142, [1955] 3 All ER 401, [1955] 3 WLR
606, 99 SJ 780, CA 4.04

Bury *v.* Thompson [1895] 1 QB 696, 64, LJQB 500, 72 LT 187, 59 JP 228, 43
WR 338, 11 TLR 267, 39 SJ 314, CA *6.05*

Busk *v.* Hallett (1969) (unrep.) 8.10

Calabar Properties Ltd *v.* Seagull Autos Ltd [1969] 1 Ch 451; [1968] 2 WLR
361; 112 SJ 49; [1968] 1 All ER 1 .... 9.04

Carr *v.* Berrisford (1982) Western Area ALT (unrep.) 10.16

Carradine Properties Ltd *v.* Aslam [1976] 1 WLR 442; (1975) 120 SJ 166;
[1976] 1 All ER 573; (1975) 32 P & CR 12 .... 6.11

Centaploy Ltd *v.* Matlodge Ltd [1974] Ch 1; [1973] 2 WLR 832; 117 SJ 394;
[1973] 2 All ER 720; 25 P & CR 317 .... 6.02

Chaloner *v.* Bower (1983) 269 EG 725 CA 3.05, 7.04

Cheshire *v.* Elwes and the Colebourne Estate Co. (1979) South Western Area
ALT (unrep.) 10.22

Clegg *v.* Fraser (1982) 264 Estates Gazette 144 .... 8.11

Coates *v.* Diment [1951] 1 All ER 890 .... 6.10, 12.03, 12.08

Collier *v.* Hollinshead (1984) 272 Estates Gazette 941 .... 2.08

Collins *v.* Spierway (1967) 204 EG 801 .... 7.18

Cooke *v.* Bateman (1983) East Midlands Area ALT (unrep.) 10.06

Cooke *v.* Talbot (1977) 243 Estates Gazette 831 .... *7.14*, 7.16, *7.17*

Cowan *v.* Wrayford [1953] 2 All ER 1138, [1953] 1 WLR 1340, 97 SJ 780, 51
LGR 659, CA 6.05, 8.03, 8.04

Cushing's Will Trusts: Cushing *v.* Bailey (unrep.) 24 Jan 1984 CA   *6.02*, 6.15

Dagg *v.* Lovett (1980) 254 Estates Gazette 993; revsd, 256 Estates Gazette
491, CA 10.05, *10.06*

Dagger *v.* Shepherd [1946] KB 215, [1946] 1 All ER 133, 115 LJKB 113, 175
LT 339, 62 TLR 143, 90 SJ 151, CA 6.08

Darby *v.* Williams (1974) 232 Estates Gazette 579, CA 2.02

Datnow & Os *v.* Jones (1985) 275 EG 145 .... 6.15

Davies *v.* Price [1958] 1 All ER 671, [1958] 1 WLR 434, 102 SJ 290, CA
.... 7.10

Deith *v.* Brown (1956) 167 Estates Gazette 513 .... 1.05

Dickinson *v.* Boucher (1983) 269 Estates Gazette 1159, CA 6.11, 8.10

Di Palma *v.* Victoria Square Property Co. Ltd [1985] 2 All ER 998, [1985] 3
WLR 207, 129 SJ 364 CA 9.05

Disraeli Agreement, Re Agricultural Holdings Act 1923, Cleasby *v.* Park
Estate (Hughenden) Ltd [1939] Ch 382, [1938] 4 All ER 658, 108 LJ Ch
100, 160 LY 156, 55 TLR 204, 82 SJ 1031 .... 6.10, 6.17

Doed Aslin *v.* Summerset (1830) 1 B & Ad 135, 8 LJKB 369 .... *6.16*

Dow Agrochemicals Ltd *v.* E. A. Lane (North Lynn) Ltd (1965) 192 Estates
Gazette 737, 115 LJ 76 .... 1.03

Draper *v.* Tiffin (1970) Southern Area ALT (unrep.) 10.15
Duppa *v.* Mayo (1669), n. 1 Wms. Saund (1871) 434 .... 9.05
Dyson Holdings Ltd *v.* Fox [1976] QB 503, [1975] 3 All ER 1030, [1975] 3
    WLR 744, 119 SJ 744, 31 P & CR 229, 239 Estates Gazette 39, CA 8.07

Edell *v.* Dulieu [1942] AC 38, 93, LJKB 286, 130 LT 390, 40 TLR 84, 68 SJ
    183, HL 5.05
Egerton *v.* Jones [1939] 2 KB 720 .... 9.06
Egerton *v.* Rutter [1951] 1 KB 472, [1951] 1 TLR 58 .... 6.15
Elsden *v.* Pick [1980] 3 All ER 235, [1980] 1 WLR 898, 124 SJ 312, 40 P &
    CR 550, 254 Estates Gazette 503, CA *6.09*
English Exporters (London) Ltd *v.* Eldonwall Ltd [1973] Ch 415, [1973] 1 All
    ER 726, [1973] 2 WLR 435, 117 SJ 224, 25 P & CR 379, [1972] RVR 612,
    225 Estates Gazette 433 .... 5.07
Epps *v.* Ledger (1972) 225 Estates Gazette 1373 .... 2.08
Epsom and Ewell Borough Council *v.* C Bell (Tadworth) Ltd [1983] 2 All ER
    59, [1983] 1 WLR 379, 127 SJ 121, 81 LGR 613, 46 P & CR 143, 266
    Estates Gazette 808 .... *3.03*
Esso Petroleum Co. Ltd *v.* Secretary of State for the Environment (unrep.)
    .... 2.03
Evans *v.* Jones [1955] 2 QB 58, [1955] 2 All ER 118, [1955] 2 WLR 936, 99
    SJ 305, 53 LGR 377, CA 12.30
Evans *v.* Roper [1960] 2 All ER 507, [1960] 1 WLR 814, 124 JP 371, 104 SJ
    604, DC 7.11, 7.17, 7.19
Evans *v.* Rudge Trustees (1977) West Midlands Area ALT (unrep.) 10.05
Ewart *v.* Fryer [1901] 1 Ch 499 .... 9.06

Fairclough (T M) & Sons Ltd *v.* Berliner [1931] 1 Ch 60, [1930] All ER 170,
    100 LJ Ch 29, 144 LT 175, 47 TLR 4, 74 SJ 703, 755 .... 9.06
Farimani *v.* Gates (1984) 128 SJ 615, 271 Estates Gazette 887, CA 8.11
Featherstone *v.* Staples [1986] 2 All ER 461 CA .. 3.10, 3.12, 6.17, *7.04*, *7.05*
Finbow *v.* Air Ministry [1963] 2 All ER 647, [1963] 1 WLR 697, 107 SJ 535
    .... 3.03
Flint *v.* Fox (1956) 106, LJ 828 .... 8.10
Foster *v.* Robinson [1951] 1 KB 149, [1950] 2 All ER 342, 66 (pt 2) TLR 120,
    94 SJ 474, CA 9.03
Frankland *v.* Capstick [1959] 1 All ER 209, [1959] 1 WLR 205, 103 SJ 155,
    CA 6.11
Franklin *v.* Duncombe (1986) South Eastern Area ALT (unrep.) 10.15
French *v.* Elliott [1959] 3 All ER 866, [1960] 1 WLR 40, 104 SJ 52 .... 8.10
Furniss *v.* Dawson [1984] AC 474, [1984] 1 All ER 530, [1984] 2 WLR 226,
    128 SJ 132, [1984] STC 153, HL 7.05

Gardner *v.* Ingram (1889) 61 LT 729, [1886–90] All ER 258, 54 JP 311, 6
    TLR 75, DC *6.05*
Gemax Securities Ltd *v.* Spiegal (1978) P & CR 304 .... 6.11
Giacomo Costa Fu Andrea *v.* British Italian Trading Co Ltd (1961) 105 SJ
    1068, [1961] 2 Lloyd's Rep 392; on appeal [1963] 1 QB 201, [1962] 2 All

ER 53, [1962] 3 WLR 512, 106 SJ 219, [1962] 1 Lloyd's Rep 151, CA
.... 13.06
Gladstone *v.* Bower [1960] 2 QB 384, [1960] 3 All ER 353, [1960] 3 WLR
575, 104 SJ 763, 58 LGR 313, CA 2.03, 3.07, 9.02, 10.01, 10.10
Godfrey *v.* Waite (1951) 157 Estates Gazette 582, CA 1.02, 1.04
Goldsack *v.* Shore [1950] 1 KB 708, [1950] 1 All ER 276, 66 (pt 1) TLR
636, 94 SJ, 192, CA *2.08*, 3.08
Good's Lease, Re, Good *v.* Trustee of the Property of W, a Bankrupt and W
[1954] 1 WLR 309; 98 SJ 111; [1954] 1 All ER 275 .... 9.06
Graves *v.* Weld (1833) 5 B & Ad 105, 2 Nev & MKB 725 2 LJKB 176 ... 6.19
Gray *v.* Bonsall [1904] 1 KB 601 .... 9.06
Great Western Railway *v.* Smith (1876) 2 Ch D 235 .... 9.05
Greenwich London Borough Council *v.* McGrady (1983) 81 LGR 288, 46 P
& CR 223, 267 Estates Gazette 515, CA 6.16

Hall and Hall *v.* Shadingfield Pty (1982) Eastern Area ALT (unrep.) 10.15
Halliday *v.* Semple 1960 SLT (Sn.Ct) 11, 1959 SJ 352 .... 13.08
Hallinan (Lady) *v.* Jones (1984) 272 Estates Gazette 1081 .... 6.15
Hammon *v.* Fairbrother [1956] 2 All ER 108, [1956] 1 WLR 490, 100 SJ 322,
54 LGR 271 .... 8.04
Hankey *v.* Clavering [1942] 2 KB 326 .... 6.11
Harding *v.* Marshall (1983) 267 Estates Gazette 161, CA 8.04
Harmond Properties Ltd *v.* Gajdzis [1968] 3 All ER 263, [1968] 1 WLR 1858,
112, SJ 762, 19 P & CR 718, CA 6.15
Harris *v.* Black (1983) 46 P & CR 366 .... *7.04*
Harrison-Broadley *v.* Smith [1964] 1 All ER 867, [1964] 1 WLR 456, 108 SJ
136, CA *2.08*, 3.09, 3.10, 10.10
Harte *v.* Frampton [1948] 1 KB 73, [1947] 2 All ER 604, [1948] LJR 1125,
63 TLR 554, 91 SJ 625, CA 7.14
Hayward *v.* Marshall (1983) Yorks and Lancs ALT (unrep.) 10.05
Heal *v.* Sidcot School (1978) South West Area ALT (unrep.) 10.05
Hereford and Worcester CC *v.* Newman [1975] 2 All ER 675 .... 8.11
Hewitt *v.* Gardner (1983) West Midland Area ALT (unrep.) 10.15
Hickson & Welch Ltd *v.* Cann (1977) 40 P & CR 218n, CA 1.07, *1.08*
Hollings *v.* Swindle (1950) 155 Estates Gazette 269 .... 4.02
Home Office *v.* J.H. Williams (1982) West Midlands Area ALT (unrep.)
.... 7.12
Hooper *v.* Hooper (1982) South Western Area ALT (unrep.) 10.05
Horsey Estate Ltd *v.* Steiger [1899] 2 QB 79, [1895–9] All ER Rep 515, 68
LJQB 743, 80 LT 887, 47 WR 644, 15 TLR 367, CA 9.06
Howkins *v.* Jardine [1951] 1 KB 614, [1951] 1 All ER 320, [1951] 1 TLR 135,
95 SJ 75, CA *1.05*, 1.07, 1.10
Howson *v.* Buxton (1928) 97 LJKB 749, [1928] All ER Rep 434, 139 LT 504,
CA 7.05

Iredell *v.* Brocklehurst (1950) 155 Estates Gazette 268, CA *1.06*

Jackson *v.* Hall [1979] 1 All ER 449, [1979] 2 WLR 505, 123 SJ 64, 30 P &

CR 293, CA; revsd. [1980] AC 854, [1980] 2 WLR 118, 124 SJ 62, 39 P & CR 436, 253 Estates Gazette 145, HL 10.15

James *v.* Lock (1977) 246 Estates Gazette 395, CA 2.08, 3.05

Jelly *v.* Buckman [1974] QB 488, [1973] 3 All ER 853, [1973] 3 WLR 585, 26 P & CR 215, 117 SJ 728, 228 Estates Gazette 1512, CA 6.13

Johnson *v.* Moreton [1980] AC 37, [1978] 3 All ER 37, [1978] 3 WLR 538, 122 SJ 697, 37 P & CR 243, 241 Estates Gazette 759, HL   3.12, *7.05*, 8.12

Jones *v.* Barnett [1984] 3 All ER 129, [1984] 3 WLR 333, 128 SJ 517 ...... 9.05

Jones *v.* Burgoyne (1963) 188 Estates Gazette 497 .... 7.14, 7.17

Jones *v.* Evans [1923] 1 KB 12, 92 LJKB 35, 128 LT 228, CA 13.05

Jones *v.* Gates [1954] 1 All ER 158, [1954] 1 WLR 222, 98 SJ 61, 52 LGR 57, CA 8.08

Jones *v.* Lewis (1973) 117 SJ 373, 25 P & CR 375, 226 Estates Gazette 805, CA 6.16, 8.10

Jones *v.* Pembrokeshire County Council [1967] 1 QB 181 [1966] 1 All ER 1027, [1966] 2 WLR 938, 110 SJ 172, 64 LGR 179, 197 Estates Gazette 1167 .... 13.08

Jones *v.* Phipps (1868) LR 3 QB 567, 9 B & S 761, 37 LJQB 198, 18 LT 813, 33 JP 229, 16 WR 1044 .... 6.15

Jones *v.* Wynn (1986) Wales Area ALT (unrep.) 7.16

Keen *v.* Holland [1984] 1 All ER 75, [1984] 1 WLR 251, 127 SJ 764, 47 P & CR 639 Estates Gazette 1043, CA 3.12

Kempe *v.* Dillon Trenchard (1951) 101 LJ 417 Cty Ct 1.06

Kent *v.* Coniff [1953] 1 QB 361, [1953] 1 All ER 155, [1953] 2 WLR 41, 97 SJ 46, 51 LGR 77, 160 Estates Gazette 582, CA 12.31

Kestell *v.* Langmaid [1950] 1 KB 233, [1949] 2 All ER 749, 65 TLR 699, 93 SJ 726, CA 12.03

King, Re, Robinson *v.* Gray [1963] Ch 459, [1963] 1 All ER 781, [1963] 2 WLR 629, 107 SJ 134, [1963] RVR 245, CA 12.33

Kinson *v.* Swinnerton (1961) 179 Estates Gazette 691 .... 7.14

Lampard *v.* Barker (1984) 272 Estates Gazette 783, CA 3.09

Land and Premises at Liss, Hants, Re [1971] Ch 986 Ch D 2.03

Leek and Moorlands Building Society *v.* Clark [1952] 2 QB 788, [1952] 2 All ER 492, [1952] 2 TLR 401, 96 SJ 561, CA 6.16, 9.03

Lewis *v.* Moss (1961) 181 Estates Gazette 685 .... 7.10

Littlewood *v.* Rolfe [1981] 2 All ER 51, 43 P & CR 262, 258 Estates Gazette 168 .... *10.05*, 10.06

Lloyd's Bank Ltd *v.* Jones [1955] 2 QB 298, [1955] 3 WLR 5, 99 SJ 398, 53 LGR 433, sub. nom. Re Lower Onibury Farm, Onibury, Shropshire, Lloyds Bank Ltd *v.* Jones [1955] 2 All ER 409, CA 8.11

Lloyd *v.* Sadler [1978] QB 774, [1978] 2 All ER 529, [1978] 2 WLR 721, 122 SJ 111, 35 P & CR 78, 245 Estates Gazette 479, CA 7.05

Loewenthal *v.* Venhoute [1947] KB 342 .... 6.12

Look *v.* Davies [1952] EGD 17 .... 1.02

Lory *v.* London Borough of Brent [1971] 1 All ER 1042, [1971] 1 WLR 823, 115 SJ 425, 69 LGR 317, 22 P & CR 393 .... 3.05

Lower *v.* Sorrell [1963] 1 QB 959, [1962] 3 All ER 1074, [1963] 2 WLR 1, CA *6.02*, 6.15

Lowther *v.* Clifford [1927] 1 KB 130, [1926] All ER Rep 290, 95 LJKB 576, 135 LT 200, 90 JP 113, 42 TLR 432, 70 SJ 544, 24 LGR 231, CA 1.03

Mackenzie *v.* Laird 1959 SC 266, 1959 SLT 268 .... *3.05*

McClinton *v.* McFall (1974) 232 Estates Gazette 707, CA 1.03, *1.05*

Mason *v.* Bibby (1864) 2 H & C 881 .... 6.15

May *v.* Borup [1915] 1 KB 830, 84 LJKB 823, 113 LT 694, DC 6.08

Mellor *v.* Watkins (1874) LR 9 QB 400, 23 WR 55 .... 6.17

Midgley *v.* Stott (1977) 244 Estates Gazette 883 .... 3.05

Mills *v.* Edwards [1971] 1 QB 379, [1971] 1 All ER 922, [1971] 2 WLR 418, 114 SJ 973, 22 P & CR 171, CA *6.05*, 8.03

Ministry of Agriculture, Fisheries and Food *v.* Jenkins [1963] 2 QB 317, [1963] 2 All ER 147, [1963] 2 WLR 906, 107 SJ 234, CA 7.15, 8.08

Mitton *v.* Farrow (1980) 255 Estates Gazette 449, CA *2.08*

Monson (Lord) *v.* Bound [1954] 3 All ER 228, [1954] 1 WLR 1321, 98 SJ 751, 52 LGR 511 .... *1.05*

Moses *v.* Hurst (1983) 269 Estates Gazette 853 .... 10.05

Moss *v.* National Coal Board (1982) 264 Estates Gazette 52 .... 13.12

Mountford *v.* Hodkinson [1956] 2 All ER 17, [1956] 1 WLR 422, 100 SJ 301, 167 Estates Gazette 293, CA *7.02*, 7.03

National Coal Board *v.* Naylor [1972] 1 All ER 1153, [1972] 1 WLR 908, 116 SJ 507, 70 LGR 403, 23 P & CR 129, DC 7.11

Newborough (Lord) *v.* Jones [1975] Ch 90, [1974] 3 All ER 17, [1974] 3 WLR 52, 118 SJ 479, 28 P & CR 215, CA 6.15

Newman *v.* Keedwell (1977) 35 P & CR 393, 244 Estates Gazette 469 .... 7.05

Normanton (Earl of) *v.* Giles [1980] 1 All ER 106, [1980] 1 WLR 28, 124 SJ 47, 39 P & CR 478, HL 1.03, 14.05

North West Water Authority *v.* Taylor and ors. (1986) Yorks and Lancs. Area ALT (unrep.) 7.12

Oak Property Co. Ltd *v.* Chapman [1947] KB 886; 63 TLR 338; [1947] 2 All ER 1, CA 9.07

O'Conor and Whitlaw's Arbitration, Re (1919) 88 LJKB 1242, CA 13.06

Official Solicitor to the Supreme Court *v.* Thomas (1986) 279 EG 407 C.A. *6.11*, 8.03, 8.10

Paddock Investments Ltd *v.* Lory (1975) 236 EG 803 CA 6.10, 8.08

Parrish *v.* Kinsey (1983) 268 Estates Gazette 1113, CA   7.13, 7.03, 9.05, 8.06

Peach *v.* Partridge (1953) (unrep.) 8.11

Persey *v.* Bazley (1983) 127 Sol Jo 579, 47 P & CR 37, 267 Estates Gazette 519, CA 6.13

Personal Representatives of Gibbs deceased, Russell *v.* Fellows (1986) (unrep.) CA 2.08, 3.08

Phipps (P) & Co. (Northampton and Towcester Breweries) Ltd *v.* Rogers [1924] 2 KB 45, affd. [1925] 1 KB 14, [1924] All ER Rep 208, 93 LJKB

1009, 132 LT 240, 89 JP 1, 40 TLR 849, 69 SJ 841, CA *6.08*

Pickard *v.* Bishop (1975) 119 SJ 407, 31 P & CR 108, CA 6.11, 8.10

Plews and Middleton, Re, (1845) 6 QB 845, 14 LJQB 139, 115 ER 319   13.08

Plymouth Corporation *v.* Harvey [1971] 1 All ER 623, [1971] 1 WLR 549,
115 SJ 13, 69 LGR 310, 22 P & CR 475 .... 9.06

Ponsford-Raymond *v.* Bahamas International Trust Co. Ltd (1984) West
Midland Area ALT (unrep.) 10.15

Powley *v.* Walker (1793) 5 Term Rep 373 .... 4.03

Price *v.* Romilly [1960] 3 All ER 429, [1960] 1 WLR 1360, 140 SJ 1060   8.10,
8.11

R. *v.* ADHAC for Beds, Cambs and Northants 1986 The Indepedent 24
November 1986 .... 14.18

R. *v.* Agricultural Land Tribunal for South Eastern Area, ex parte Bracey
[1960] 2 All ER 518, [1960] 1 WLR 911, 104 SJ 643, DC 7.18, 13.14

R. *v.* Agricultural Land Tribunal for the South Eastern Area ex parte Parslow
(1979) 251 EG 667 .... 7.14

R. *v.* Agricultural Land Tribunal for Wales and Monmouth Area, ex parte
Davies [1953] 1 All ER 1182, [1953] 1 WLR 722, 97 SJ 335, 51 LGR 368,
DC 7.18, 7.19, 13.14

R. *v.* Hussey (1924) 18 Cr App R 160 .... 9.04

Rajbenback *v.* Mamon [1955] 1 QB 283, [1955] 1 All ER 12 [1955] 2 WLR
21, 99 SJ 29 .... 7.18

Reid *v.* Dawson [1955] 1 QB 214, [1954] 3 All ER 498, [1954] 3 WLR 810. 98
SJ 818, 53 LGR 24, CA 3.05

Riggs, Re, [1901] 2 KB 16 .... 9.06

Rugby Joint Water Board *v.* Foottit [1973] AC 202, [1972] 1 All ER 1057,
[1972] 2 WLR 757, 136 JP 317, 116 SJ 240, 70 LGR 339, 24 P & CR 256,
222 Estates Gazette 815, HL 8.08

Russell *v.* Booker (1982) 263 EG 513, (1982) 5 HLR 10, CA   *1.07*, 1.08, 1.10

Rutherford *v.* Maurer [1962] 1 QB 16, [1961] 2 All ER 775, [1961] 3 WLR
5, 105 SJ 404, 179 Estates Gazette 53, CA *1.08*

Rye *v.* Rye [1962] AC 496, [1962] 1 All ER 146, [1962] 2 WLR 361, 106 SJ
94, HL 3.10

Scala House and District Property Co. Ltd *v.* Forbes [1974] QB 575, [1973] 3
All ER 308, [1973] 3 WLR 14, 117 SJ 467, 227 Estates Gazette 1161, CA
.... 8.11

Scene Estate Ltd *v.* Amos [1957] 2 QB 205, [1957] 2 All ER 325, [1957] 2
WLR 1017, 101 SJ 445, 56 LGR 14, CA 3.05

Sclater *v.* Horton [1954] 2 QB 1, [1954] 1 All ER 712, [1954] 2 WLR 566, 98
SJ 213, 52 LGR 217, CA 5.06, 5.07

Scott *v.* Durham County Council (1979) Northern Area ALT (unrep.)   10.05

Secretary of State for Social Services *v.* Beavington (1981) 262 Estates
Gazette 551 .... 3.09

Segal Securities Ltd *v.* Thoseby [1963] 1 QB 887; [1963] 2 WLR 403; 106 SJ
1053; [1963] 1 All ER 500 .... 8.11, 9.07

Shepherd *v.* Lomas [1963] 2 All ER 902, [1963] 1 WLR 962, 107 SJ 435, CA
.... 8.11

Shiloh Spinners Ltd *v.* Harding [1973] AC 691 .... 9.04
Short Bros (Plant) *v.* Edwards (1978) 249 Estates Gazette 539 .... 3.05
Sidebottom *v.* Holland [1895] 1 QB 378 CA 6.06, 6.07
Skelton *v.* Cholmley Trustees (1984) East Midlands Area ALT (unrep.)
.... 10.16
Smith *v.* Chambers (1982) South Eastern Area ALT (unrep.) 10.15
Smith *v.* Hughes (1871) LR 6 QB 597, [1861-73] All ER Rep 632, 40 LJQB
221, 25 LT 329, 19 WR 1059, DC *3.05*
South West Water Authority *v.* Palmer (1983) 268 Estates Gazette 357, 443,
CA 3.05
Stevens *v.* Sedgeman [1951] 2 KB 434, [1951] 2 All ER 33, [1951] 2 TLR 16,
95 SJ 367, 49 LGR 524, CA 1.02, 1.10
Stiles *v.* Farrow (1977) 241 Estates Gazette 623 .... 13.03
Stoneman *v.* Brown [1973] 2 All ER 225, [1973] 1 WLR 459, 117 SJ 109, 25
P & CR 297, CA 8.10
Street *v.* Mountford [1985] AC 809, [1985] 2 All ER 289; [1985] 2 WLR 877
.... 3.12, 7.05, 14.06
Sumnall *v.* Stott (1984) 271 Estates Gazette 628, CA 8.11
Sykes *v.* Land (1984) 271 Estates Gazette 1264, CA 7.04, *7.05*, 3.10

Thatcher *v.* C.H. Pearce (Contractors) Ltd [1968] 1 WLR 748; (1967) 112 SJ
379; 19 P & CR 682 .... 9.05
Thomas *v.* Fryer [1970] 1 WLR 845; [1970] 2 All ER 1; (1970) 21 P & CR
398; 7.14
Thomas *v.* National Farmers Union Mutual Insurance Society Ltd [1961] 1
All ER 363, [1961] 1 WLR 386, 105 SJ 233, [1960] 2 Lloyd's Rep 444
.... 4.05
Timmins *v.* Rowlinson (1765) 3 Burn 1603 .... 6.04
Trinity College *v.* Caines (1984) 272 Estates Gazette 1287 .... *10.05*
Trustees of James Raine (Senior) *v.* Raine (1985) 275 Estates Gazette 374
.... 10.06, 10.15
Tucker *v.* Linger (1882) 21 Ch D 18, 51 LJ Ch 713, 46 LT 198, 30 WR 425,
CA. affd. (1883) 8 App Cas 508, 52 LJ Ch 941, 49 LT 373, 32 WR 40, 48
JP 4 HL 4.03
Tunstall *v.* Cresswell (1982) Eastern Area ALT (unrep.) 10.05
Turner *v.* Greenwell and Shreiber (1983) Eastern Area ALT (unrep.) ... 10.15

University of Reading *v.* Johnson-Houghton (1986) 276 Estates Gazette 1353
CA 1.03
Urwick *v.* Taylor [1969] EGD 1106 .... 8.10

Varley *v.* Marquess of Northampton (1984) East Midland Area ALT (unrep.)
.... 10.04
Verrall *v.* Farnes [1966] 2 All ER 808, [1966] 1 WLR 1254, 110 SJ 406   2.08

Walsh *v.* Griffith-Jones [1978] 2 All ER 1002 .... 7.05
Walters *v.* Roberts (1980) 41 P & CR 210, 258 Estates Gazette 965 .... *2.08*
Ward *v.* Scott [1950] WN 76; 66 TLR 340; (1950) 945 SJ 97 .... 7.02

Watters *v.* Hunter [1927] SC 310 .... *1.03*, 12.24

Watts *v.* Yeend [1987] 1 All ER 744 .... 3.05

Wetherall *v.* Smith [1980] 2 All ER 530, [1980] 1 WLR 1290, 124 SJ 543, 40
  P & CR 205, 256 Estates Gazette 163, CA 1.03, *1.07*

Williams *v.* Lady Douglas (1980) Wales Area ALT (unrep.) 10.04

Williamson *v.* Thompson [1980] AC 854, [1980] 1 All ER 177, 124 SJ 63, 39
  P & CR 436, 253 Estates Gazette 145, HL 10.13

Wilson *v.* Earl Spencer's Settlement Trustees (1985) 274 EG 1254, 1255
  .... 10.06

Wilts County Council *v.* Habershon (1952) 159 Estates Gazette 157 .... 7.12

Wood *v.* Durose (1958) 108 LJ 730, 172 Estates Gazette 295, CA 13.08

Wyatt *v.* King (1951) 157 Estates Gazette 124, CA 2.08

Yardley *v.* Evans (1980) East Midlands Area ALT (unrep.) 10.15

Table of Statutes

References are to section numbers

Administration of Justice Act 1985
  s.55 .... 9.05
Agriculture Act 1947
  s.21 .... 13.02
  s.109(1) 1.09
Agriculture Act 1967
  s.26(1) 8.15
Agriculture Act 1986 .... 12.01
  s.13 .... 12.02, 12.28
  s.15 .... 5.07
  Schedule 1 .... 12.01
Agriculture (Miscellaneous Provisions) Act 1976 .... 1.07
Agriculture (Safety, Health and Welfare Provisions) Act 1956 ...... 5.09
A.H.A. 1986
  s.1(1) 1.02, 1.05, 1.10, 2.01, 3.02, 3.12
  s.1(2) 1.04, 1.05, 1.07
  s.1(3) 1.06, 1.07
  s.1(5) 2.01, 2.03, 2.07
  s.2   2.03, 2.05, 2.07, 2.08, 3.03, 3.04, 3.05, 3.06, 3.07, 3.09, 5.05, 9.02,
            .... 10.10, 13.02, 13.16
                                                                        Appendix I
  s.3 .... 2.03, 2.04, 2.06, 3.07, 5.05, 7.05, 10.01
  s.5 .... 2.04, 2.05, 3.04, 4.05, 9.02, 10.10
                                                                        Appendix I
  s.6 .... 4.01, 4.02, 5.08, 9.04, 13.02
  s.7 .... 4.01, 4.04
  s.8 .... 4.01, 4.04, 5.08, 13.02
  s.9 .... 4.01, 4.04
  s.10 .... 4.02, 4.04, 12.26, 13.02
  s.11 .... 4.03, 4.04, 13.02
  s.12 .... 5.03, 5.04, 5.05, 5.06, 13.02
  s.13 .... 5.09, 13.02
  s.14 .... 4.05, 13.02

s.15 .... 4.05, 12.32, 13.16
s.16 .... 5.10, 5.11
s.17 .... 5.10, 5.13
s.18 .... 5.10, 5.12, 9.05
s.19 .... 5.10, 5.14
s.20 .... 4.07, 13.02
s.21 .... 6.19
s.22 .... 4.07, 12.20
s.23 .... 4.07, 13.02
s.24 .... 4.06
s.25 .... 5.05, 6.02, 6.07, 6.09, 6.10, 6.17, 8.08, 8.09, 8.13, 12.06
s.26 .... 6.17, 7.02, 7.03, 7.04, 7.06, 8.04, 8.11, 11.07, 12.05, 13.02
                                                                                                             Appendix I
s.27   6.05, 6.17, 7.01, 7.07, 7.09, 7.17, 7.20, 8.01, 8.11, 10.06, 10.19, 12.05,
            .... 13.02
                                                                                                             Appendix I
s.28 .... 8.11
s.31 .... 6.13, 8.08, 12.21
s.32 .... 6.13, 12.03
s.33 .... 5.08, 6.13
s.34 .... 10.01, 11.04
s.35 .... 10.03, 10.04, 10.23, 11.02, 11.03
s.36 .... 10.01, 10.02, 10.05, 10.06, 10.07, 10.23
s.37 .... 10.01, 10.23, 11.02, 11.06, 12.28
s.38 .... 10.01, 11.06, 11.07
s.39 .... 8.14, 10.02, 10.06, 10.14, 10.17, 10.20, 12.28
s.40 .... 10.17
s.41 .... 10.03, 10.06, 10.14
s.42 .... 10.18
s.43 .... 8.14, 12.21
s.44 .... 8.14, 10.06, 10.19, 10.20
s.45 .... 10.21, 10.22, 12.28
s.46 .... 10.21
s.47 .... 10.21
s.48 .... 10.21
s.49 .... 11.04, 11.06
s.50 .... 11.05, 11.07
s.51 .... 11.06, 11.07, 11.09
s.52 .... 11.07
s.53 .... 10.01, 11.06, 11.08, 11.10, 11.12, 12.28
s.54 .... 11.07
s.55 .... 11.11
s.56 .... 11.13
s.57 .... 11.03, 11.07, 11.09, 11.10
s.60 .... 9.03, 9.08, 12.03, 12.04
s.62 .... 12.06
s.63 .... 12.07, 12.08
s.64 .... 12.09

s.66 .... 12.09, 12.14, 12.16
s.67 .... 5.09, 12.09, 12.13, 13.02
s.68 .... 12.12, 12.13
s.69 .... 12.17, 12.19
s.70 .... 4.07, 12.20, 12.30
s.71 .... 12.29, 12.30, 12.31
s.72 .... 12.29, 12.30, 12.31
s.73 .... 12.31
s.74 .... 12.21, 12.33
s.75 .... 12.21
s.76 .... 12.22
s.78 .... 12.01, 12.09, 12.32
s.79 .... 12.24, 12.26
s.80 .... 12.24, 12.27, 13.02
s.81 .... 12.25
s.82 .... 4.05
s.83 .... 12.35
s.84 .... 13.02
s.85 .... 12.35, 13.07
s.88 .... 12.10
s.89 .... 12.11
s.93 .... 6.15, 8.14
s.95 .... 4.04, 12.18
s.96 .... 1.03, 4.04, 8.13, 9.03, 9.08, 12.09
s.97 .... 13.16
Schedule 1 .... 4.01, 4.02, 4.03, 4.04, 9.04
Schedule 2 .... 5.03, 5.07, 5.08
Schedule 3 .... 6.04, 6.05, 6.11, 8.02, 9.04, 11.07, 12.05, 13.02
Pt I
Case A .... 8.07   Case B 8.08
Case C .... 8.09   Case D(a) 8.10
Case E .... 8.12   Case F 8.13
Case G .... 8.14, 10.19   Case H 8.15
Part II
Paras   1–7: 8.07, 8: 8.08, 9: 8.07 10: 8.10, 8.11, 11: 8.12, 12: 8.14
Schedule 4 .... 6.14
Schedule 5 .... 6.18
Schedule 6 .... 3.07, 10.05, 10.07, 10.09, 10.10, 10.11, 10.13, 11.12
Schedule 7 .... 12.09, 12.11, 12.12, 12.20
Schedule 8 .... 12.14, 12.16, 12.20, 12.25
Schedule 9 .... 12.01, 12.15, 12.20, 12.25
Schedule 10 .... 12.25
Schedule 11 .... 4.02, 5.06, 8.05, 13.02, 13.04, 13.06, 13.08
Schedule 12 .... 2.04, 3.03, 3.05, 4.04, 6.10, 12.01, 12.14, 12.16, 12.23
Allotments Act 1925 .... 1.10

Common Law Procedure Act 1952
  ss.210–212 .... 9.05

356   *Farm Tenancies*

County Courts Act 1984
   s.138, 137, 139 .... 9.05, 13.06
Criminal Law Act 1977 .... 9.04

Hill Farming Act 1946
   s.21 .... 13.02

Interpretation Act 1978
   s.7 .... 6.15

Land Drainage Act 1961
   s.40 .... 13.02
Landlord and Tenant Act 1927
   s.18(1) 12.32
Landlord and Tenant Act 1954 .... 1.10, 2.03, 7.04, 14.02, 14.17
Landlord and Tenant Act 1985
   s.11 .... 14.14, 14.15
Law of Property (Amendment) Act 1921
   s.1 .... 9.06
Law of Property Act 1925 .... 12.11
   s.52 .... 9.03
   s.54 .... 9.03
   s.139 .... 6.17, 9.03
   s.140 .... 6.13
   s.141 .... 12.34
   s.146 .... 6.17, 9.06
   s.149(6) 2.03, 2.04, 8.13
   s.205 .... 2.03

Partnership Act 1890 .... 3.10, 7.5

Rent Act 1965
   s.33 .... 14.01
Rent Act 1977 .... 1.10, 3.13, 14.02
   s.1 .... 14.05
   s.10 .... 1.10
   ss.13–16 .... 14.05
   s.70(2) 5.07
   s.137(3) 1.10
   Schedule 8 .... 14.17
   Schedule 15 .... 14.17
Rent (Agriculture) Act 1976 .... 1.10, 3.02
   s.1 .... 14.04
   s.2 .... 14.04, 14.06, 14.07, 14.08
   s.3 .... 14.09
   s.4 .... 14.11, 14.12
   s.6 .... 14.10
   s.9 .... 14.17

s.10 .... 14.13, 14.15
s.11 .... 14.15
s.12 .... 14.15
s.14 .... 14.15
s.16 .... 14.11
s.20 .... 14.10
s.23 .... 14.05, 14.10
s.24 .... 14.17
s.28 .... 14.18
Schedule 2 .... 14.05
Schedule 3 .... 14.05, 14.05, 14.06
Schedule 4 .... 14.16
Schedule 5 .... 14.13, 14.14
Schedule 6 .... 14.15
Schedule 8 .... 1.10
Reserve and Auxiliary Forces (Protection of Civil Interests)
    Act 1957 .... 6.18

Settled Land Act 1925 .... 12.11

Tribunals and Inquiries Act 1971 .... 13.07, 13.08

Universities and College Estates Act 1925 .... 12.11

Wildlife and Countryside Act 1981 .... 8.09

Index

All numbers refer to paragraphs of the text, except for those preceded by 'p' which indicates a page reference.

Readers are also referred to the detailed list of contents, arranged by Chapters, printed at pages vi–ix.

abandonment of use, 1.07
ADHAC, 14.01, 14.18
agricultural holding
  definition, Chs 1, 2, 3
  stat. definition, p. 1
Agricultural Land Tribunal, 13.09–13.15
  challenging decision, 13.14
  costs award, 13.15
  jurisdiction, 13.09–13.15
  list of, App. II
  time limits, 13.12
agricultural tenancy see Tenancy
agricultural unit, 10.05
'Agriculture'
  by context, 1.04
  defined for AHA, 1.03
  permitted use, 1.06
  predominant use, 1.05
  R(A)A, 14.04(a)
allotment
  Allotments Act 1927, 1.10
  as agricultural holding, 1.02
  repossession for, 7.12
arbitrator
  appointment, 13.04
  incontestable notices, 8.05
  jurisdiction, 13.02–13.08
  legal advisor, 13.06
  notice to do work, 8.11
  quasi judicial function, 13.06
  rent review, 5.03–5.09
  stating case for Court, 13.08
  tenancies, 4.01
  tenancies on succession, 4.01, 10.21
  Welsh speaking, 13.04
arbitration, 13.03–13.08
  and incontestable notices to quit, 8.05, 8.07–8.15
  and rent, 5.03–5.09
avoidance of statutory schemes
  exempted arrangements, Ch. 3
  partnerships, 7.05(iii)

restricting counter-notices, 7.05(i)(ii)
sham subtenancies, 6.17(v)
sham transaction, 7.05(iii)

bad husbandry, certificate of, 8.09
bankrupcy/insolvency
  notice to quit, 8.13
building
  as agricultural holding, 1.02
business tenancy, 1.10

certificate of bad husbandry
  incontestible notice, 8.09
change of use, 1.07
C.L.A./N.F.U. 'package', p. 51, p. 187, 5.01
commercial unit test
  defined, 10.08
  occupation, 10.09–10.10
  succession, in, 10.07
compensation, Ch. 12
  disturbance, 12.03–12.06
  effect of forfeiture, 9.08
  high farming, 12.20
  hill farming, 12.13
landlord's claims
  damages during tenancy, 12.32
  general deterioration, 12.31
  specific deterioration, 12.30
  transfer of interest, 12.35
  long term improvements, 12.09–12.11
  market gardens, 12.23–12.27
  'old' improvements, 12.15
  short term improvements, 12.14
  subtenants, 12.07
  tenant right, 12.16
  tenant's claims, on quitting, 12.02–12
contract of tenancy, Ch. 4
  defined, 2.01, 2.03
  extrinsic evidence for, 1.04
  single contract, 2.02
  succession, on, 10.21, 11.13

written form, 4.02
contracting out, 2.06, 3.13, 7.05
  see also avoidance
contractor/manager agreements, 3.11
co-owners
  'captiva', 7.05
  counter notices, 7.04
  death of, 11.10
  eligible to succeed, 10.13
  notice to quit to, from, 6.16
  retirement notice, 11.04
  succession by, 10.17
  succession to, 10.04
  surrender by, 9.03
counter-notice, p. 90, Ch. 7
  application, 7.07
  approved purposes, 7.09–7.16, S.27(3)
  co-owners, 7.04
  contracting out, 7.05
  'fair and reasonable landlord', 7.17
  form, 7.02
  time limits, 7.03
  tribunal consent, 7.06–7.21
  under Case D(b), 8.11
county court, 13.08, 14.01
custom, 4.01, 12.01

distress for rent, 5.10–5.14
  amount, 5.13
  disputes, 5.14
  property available, 5.12
  remedy available, 5.11
dwelling house
  as agricultural holding, 1.04
  under Rent Act 1977, 1.10

'Evesham Custom', 12.27
extrinsic evidence, 1.04

'family', meaning of, 8.07
fixed equipment, 4.04
fixtures, 4.04, 12.26
forfeiture of lease
  compared with Case D(a), p. 181
    (Chart)
  compared with Cases D(b) and E,
    p. 184 (Chart)
  compensation, 9.08
  effect on subtenant, 6.17(iii)
  forfeiture clauses, 9.04–9.06
  incontestable notices as, 6.11
  relief against, 9.04(c) (e) (g)

game, damage by, 4.07(i)
Gladstone v. *Bower* grants, 3.07, 9.02(i),
    10.01(ii)(b)
good agricultural practice, 4.03
good estate management, 4.03, 7.11
good husbandry, rules of, 4.03, 4.05, 7.10,
    8.09
grazing
  as 'agriculture', 1.03, 1.05
  grazing and mowing agreements, 3.05
  limited interest, 2.08
'greater hardship', 7.14

high farming
  compensation for, 12.20
  contract for, 4.05
  forfeiture and, 9.08
hill farming
  compensation, 12.13
horses
  under A(H)A, 1.03
horticulture, 1.03

'incontestable' notices to quit, Ch. 8
  Cases A–H, 8.07–8.15
  challenges to, 8.04
  construction of, 8.03
  forfeiture as, 6.11, 8.03
  form of, 6.05
  grounds, 8.02

'insecure' tenancies, Ch. 3

joint tenants *see* co-owners
joint ventures *see* sharefarming
'land'
  meaning of, 1.02
licences
  gratuitous, 3.08
  insecure, S.2, 2.08
  'licensee only', 10.10
  licensee/purchaser, 2.08(i)
  non-exclusive, 3.09
  'transformed' by S.2, 2.08(iii)
livestock
  meaning in A(H)A, 1.03
  meaning in R(A)A, 14.04(a)

market gardens, 1.03, 12.23–12.27
milk quotas, 4.05, 5.01
  compensation for, 12.28, App. I
  rent review, in, 5.07(g)

Minister's approval (insecure grants)
S2, 2.03, 3.03
S5, 2.05
SS2 ad 5 compared, 3.04
S2 effect, 3.03
S2 no appeal, 3.03
S2 subject matter, 3.03
S2 timing, 3.03
Ministry guidelines, 3.04
Minister's designation, 1.09
'model clauses', 4.04(iii)

notice to quit, Ch. 6
compensation, after, Ch. 12
expiry of, 6.06
form of, 6.04–6.05
mistakes in, 6.11
not a surrender, 6.03
notice to quit part, 6.13
period of notice, 6.07, 6.08
'running notice', 6.08
short notice, 6.10
succession and, 10.01, 10.19, 10.20,
11.07
waiver of period, 6.09
who can give, 6.02
notice to quit part, 6.13
compensation after, 12.08
enlargement of, 6.13

partnerships (-farming), 3.10, 7.05(ii),
7.05(iii), 10.06, 10.10
penal rents, 4.05, 4.06
permanent pasture, 4.05
permit workers, 14.04(c)
predominant use text, 1.05
President of Royal Institute of Chartered
Surveyors
address, 13.04
appointing arbitrations, 5.06, 5.07
fee payable to, 13.04
functions, 13.04
grant of extensions, 13.07
nominating to ALT, 13.10
principal source of livelihood test, 10.05,
10.06

quotas *see* milk quotas

record of condition, 4.07(i), 12.20
rent, Ch. 5
arrears

Case D(a) notice, 8.10
distress for, 5.10–5.15
payment by cheque, 8.03B, 8.10
review
by agreement, 5.02
by arbitration, 5.03–5.09
formula for, 5.07
frequency of, 5.08
landlord's improvements, for, 5.09
tied cottages: low/no rent
low/no rent, 14.05
during statutory tenancy, 14.15,
App. III
restrictive covenants, 1.06

security of tenure, Chs. 6–9
see also avoidance of statutory schemes,
contracting out, partnerships
service of notices, 6.15, 6.16, 7.04
share farming, 3.12
small holdings
Case A notices, 10.01
repossession for, 7.12
retirement from, 8.07, 11.03
subtenant
compensation for disturbance, 12.07
forfeiture, effect of on, 9.05(f)
notice to quit, 6.17
relief against forfeiture, 9.06
Schedule 7 improvements, 12.12
surrender of head tenancy, 9.03
tied cottages, 14.17
succession on death, Ch. 10
applicants, 10.03–10.14
'commercial unit' test, 10.09–10.13
concurrent leases, 10.22
'connected person' arrangements, 10.11
'eligible person', 10.03–05
interests disregarded, 10.10
joint occupiers, 10.13
multiple applicants, 10.17
multiple holdings, 10.18
new tenancy grant, 10.21
suitability test, 10.15
time limits, 10.02, 10.06
Tribunal's duty, 10.16
when available, 10.01
succession on retirement, Ch. 11
agreed retirement, 11.02
death of retiring tenant, 11.10
effect of Tribunal's direction, 11.11
eligibility, 11.05

excluded situations, 11.06
landlord not agreeing, 11.03–11.06
retirement notice, 11.04
tenant's initiative, 11.03
surrender of tenancy, 9.03
not notice to quit, 6.03
subtenants, effect on, 6.17(iv)
surrender and regrant, 10.01
surviving close relative, 10.04
sweeteners, 7.18

tenancy
agricultural tenancy defined, Ch. 2
contract of, *see* 'contract of tenancy'
fixed term tenancy, 2.03
fixed term tenancy extended, 2.04

'from year to year', 2.07
licences, converted into, 2.08
new tenancy on succession, 10.21,
11.13
termination of, Chs. 6–9
tied cottages, Ch. 14
tenants in common *see* co-owners
tied cottage, 1.10, Ch. 14
'trade or business', 1.08

widows
and succession rights, Ch. 10 gerlly
eligibility, 10.05, 10.06
suitability, 10.15
woodlands, 1.03